HOCKEY GUIDE

1984-85 EDITION

Editor/Hockey Guide
LARRY WIGGE

Compiled by
FRANK POLNASZEK

Contributing Editors/Hockey Guide
JOHN HADLEY
BARRY SIEGEL
DAVE SLOAN

President-Chief Executive Officer
RICHARD WATERS

Editor
DICK KAEGEL

Director of Books and Periodicals
RON SMITH

Published by

The Sporting News
1212 North Lindbergh Boulevard
P.O. Box 56 — St. Louis, MO 63166

Copyright © 1984
The Sporting News Publishing Company
a Times Mirror company

IMPORTANT NOTICE

The Hockey Guide is protected by copyright. All information, in the form presented here, except playing statistics, was compiled by the publishers and proof is available.

Information from the Hockey Guide must not be used elsewhere without special written permission, and then only with full credit to the Hockey Guide, published by THE SPORTING NEWS, St. Louis, Missouri.

ISBN 0-89204-167-6   ISSN 0278-4955

TABLE OF CONTENTS

1983-84 NHL Season in Review 3-11
NHL Office Directory 12
NHL Divisional Alignment 13
NHL Team Directories and Rosters 14-55
THE SPORTING NEWS 1983-84 NHL All-Star Team 56
National Hockey League Summary and Statistics, 1983-84 59-88
NHL Miscellaneous Achievements in 1983-84 89-99
NHL Departmental Leaders 100-101
Stanley Cup Playoffs, 1984 102-109
Year-by-Year NHL Standings 110-119
Stanley Cup Winners 120
Stanley Cup Records 121
NHL Awards and Leaders 122-127
NHL Entry Draft 128-132
All-Time Individual Records (National Hockey League, World Hockey
    Association, Central Hockey League, American Hockey League,
    International Hockey League) 133-135
American Hockey League 136
Central Hockey League 152
International Hockey League 159
Atlantic Coast Hockey League 166
Memorial Cup Winners 171
Ontario Hockey League 172
Western Hockey League 185
Quebec Hockey League 196
American College Hockey 204
National Hockey League Schedule for 1984-85 227

ON THE COVER: Wayne Gretzky and his Edmonton Oiler teammates got a measure of revenge against the New York Islanders in the Stanley Cup playoffs, snapping the Isles' Cup-winning streak at four while winning the Edmonton franchise's first Cup in its fifth year in the NHL.
—Photo by Bruce Bennett

Oilers End Islanders Reign With High-Octane Offense

By PAT CALABRIA

Coach Glen Sather and his Edmonton Oilers sat quietly in their locker room after sweeping past the Minnesota North Stars in the Campbell Conference final series. To a man, the Oilers expressed hope that the New York Islanders would beat the Montreal Canadiens in the Wales Conference finals. They wanted a chance to play the four-time defending Stanley Cup champion Islanders one more time.

The Edmonton players were in no mood to celebrate their victory over the North Stars. There was still a lot of work to be done. Those long summer months spent thinking about how they lost in four straight games to the Islanders in the Cup finals one year earlier were fresh in their minds.

"All of a sudden, after the game, the clincher against the North Stars, the whole room went hush," said Edmonton's star center Wayne Gretzky. "Our attitude was, 'we haven't won anything yet.'

"We sat down in the room and about all we could tell ourselves was, 'OK, we've done well up to now. But we haven't won anything. All we've done is get to the place we're supposed to be.' We had to think all summer and throughout the season of getting back to the Stanley Cup finals. We waited a long time to get back to the finals with the series tied 0-0."

Teammate Paul Coffey put it a little more succinctly. "You don't play to win the Campbell Conference championship. It's the Cup that counts," he said. "Forty years from now, nobody will worry about who won the Campbell Conference."

When the torch was passed from New York to Edmonton in the dramatic and conclusive fifth game of the Stanley Cup finals in 1984, the Oilers had indisputably emerged as a worthy successor to one of hockey's mightiest dynasties.

The team that had been spawned in the now-defunct World Hockey Association in 1972-73 and admitted with three other survivors to the NHL in 1979 was able to prove that an electric offense could provide title power. That theory had been laughingly dismissed by the NHL establishment only a year before when the Islanders used a sound defense and hard checking to defeat the high-scoring Oilers in a shocking four-game sweep.

But not only did the Oilers end the Islanders' four-year reign as champions and prevent them from equaling the record of five consecutive Stanley Cups set by the Montreal Canadiens from 1956-60, they also did it with flair. Edmonton became the first team in modern times to win a Cup in only its fifth season in the league.

"If we knew how much fun winning would be," said Mark Messier, the playoff MVP, "we would have done it a lot sooner."

The Oilers, in fact, had long been considered the heir-apparent to the solid, dependable Islanders. Edmonton had finished the regular season with a 57-18-5 record, recording the most victories by an NHL team in eight years and totaling a league-leading 119 points. The Islanders, with a 50-26-4 record and 104 points, were second. The Oilers also had that swift, bold offense that accounted for a record 446 goals and demolished defenses and the psyches of goaltenders from Boston to Los Angeles.

With Gretzky's 87 goals and 113 assists again setting a fast pace, Edmonton burned out more than its share of red goal lamps. Five of the league's top 13 point-getters were members of the Oilers—including Coffey, who was second behind Gretzky with 126 points, the third-highest total ever by a defenseman. In addition, Coffey became only the second defenseman (Bobby Orr was the other) to score 40 goals in a season. Clearly, Edmonton was special.

"I don't feel badly about turning the Cup over to them," Islanders captain Denis Potvin said. "They're truly a worthy champion. This is one great, great team passing the Cup along to a team that is great."

While the Oilers' convincing victory sent the city of Edmonton into delirium, the biggest impact may have been felt by the rest of the league. High-scoring offenses have suddenly become vogue and more franchises are drafting speedy skaters, much to the dismay of the goalies who are being showered by more pucks than ever before.

Thirteen teams scored at least 300 goals in 1983-84, including all five members of Edmonton's Smythe Division. An astonishing eight players scored at least 50 goals, including the Islanders' Mike Bossy,

Edmonton left wing Mark Messier captured the Conn Smythe Trophy as the Oilers won their first Stanley Cup.

who reached that milestone for a record seventh straight time. Not surprisingly, the Oilers set a record by assembling three 50-goal scorers on one club—Gretzky (87), Glenn Anderson (54) and Jari Kurri (52). Gretzky, of course, led the league in nearly every offensive category, which is why he was named The Sporting News Player of the Year for the fourth straight season and the winner of the NHL's Hart Trophy as MVP a record fifth time.

No. 99 earned the accolades by scoring a point in Edmonton's first 51 games, breaking his own record of 30 games (set in 1982-83), and was held scoreless only three times all season. He topped the circuit with 12 shorthanded goals and his plus-minus figure of plus-76 also led the league. To cap another outstanding season, Gretzky was the leading playoff scorer with 13 goals and 22 assists. More than anyone, Gretzky exemplified the rush to develop sharp-shooting forwards who can skate at a breakneck pace.

"We can't board up the net," complained Winnipeg goalie Doug Soetaert after giving up a goal to Gretzky late in 1983-84, "so maybe we'll have to get him with a bazooka or something when he's crossing the blue line."

With the game undergoing that kind of change, it was appropriate that Montreal's Guy Lafleur should become the 10th player in history to score 500 goals. He accomplished the feat in 896 games, making Bobby Hull, Marcel Dionne and Maurice Richard the only hockey players to reach that plateau quicker. Yet, despite the influence of Gretzky and his teammates, powerful offenses were not the answer for every club.

There remained several teams that used a defensive strategy, preferring the Islanders' formula of rugged checking and spectacular goaltending.

The Washington Capitals parlayed a stifling defense and the steady play of goalies Al Jensen and Pat Riggin into a second-place finish in the Patrick Division behind the Islanders. The Caps permitted only 226 goals in recording the best record (48-27-5) in the history of the Washington franchise. Buffalo came within one point of toppling Boston from the top of the Adams Division behind the play of rookie goalie Tom Barrasso. And Montreal, after

Montreal goalie Steve Penney (above) was spectacular in the playoffs as the Canadiens reached the Wales Conference finals while Buffalo's Tom Barrasso (left) won the Calder Trophy with a 2.84 goals-against average.

New Jersey fans reminded Wayne Gretzky about his "Mickey Mouse" comments when he returned for a game at the Meadowlands Arena two months later.

finishing in fourth place in the regular season, used an inspired defense and sensational rookie Steve Penney in the nets to become the Cinderella story of the playoffs.

The spotlight also shined on other teams. Detroit, with the help of rookie center Steve Yzerman, made the playoffs for the first time in six years. St. Louis, which nearly folded a year before, finished a surprising second to Minnesota in the Norris Division. And the New York Rangers, after managing only a fourth-place finish in the tough Patrick Division, extended the Islanders into a heart-fluttering fifth-game overtime before losing in the first round of the playoffs.

If the Oilers were the biggest winner, then the biggest losers had to be the Pittsburgh Penguins and the New Jersey Devils. The Penguins had the worst record in the NHL at 16-58-6, entitling them to the first overall pick in the June entry draft. Pittsburgh cashed that reward in for junior scoring star Mario Lemieux, who quickly signed a long-term contract guaranteeing him a six-figure income.

The Devils, however, would have to go a long way toward reversing the embarrassment of a dismal season. They began the season with a 2-18 record, the worst start since the old Philadelphia Quakers went 1-19-1 in 1930. It was so bad that when the Oilers bombed New Jersey, 13-4, in one of the most lopsided scores of the season, the result brought attention not only to the Devils, but to Gretzky and the Oilers as well.

It was after that game that a tired Gretzky uttered a critique of the Devils' management he later would regret. Said Gretzky: "It's not funny, it's disappointing. These guys better get their act together ... (they're) ruining hockey. They are putting a Mickey Mouse operation on the ice."

Stung not only by the criticism but by their sinking fortunes, the Devils fired Coach and General Manager Bill MacMillan. A backlash of opinion against Gretzky surfaced and he moved to soothe the New Jersey fans by dispatching a telegram of apology to Chairman John McMullen.

But a reprise was yet to come. When the Oilers visited the Meadowlands Arena to play the Devils a month later, many fans in the sellout crowd were wearing Mickey Mouse ears. One spectator held a banner that said, "Gretzky is Goofy." And when the Devils scored two third-period goals in what would become a 5-4 loss, the crowd spelled out for Gretzky the name of that cartoon hero of generations: "M-I-C-K-E-Y M-O-U-S-E."

Three other occurrences had more serious repercussions.

The most serious involved Boston winger Craig MacTavish, who was sentenced to a year in prison for vehicular manslaughter, drunken driving and driving without a license after his car crashed into another vehicle in Peabody, Mass., on January 25. The woman driving the other car died.

Another incident hit the newspapers before training camp was even over. Montreal defenseman Ric Nattress was told he would be out for the season. The news came from NHL President John Ziegler. Nattress was suspended after being convicted for possession of three grams of marijuana and fined $150. Nattress was puzzled because his arrest had come in 1982, before he was ever a member of the league. Ziegler did, however, commute the sentence to a 30-game suspension and Nattress rejoined his team in December.

If the league was determined to make an example out of players involved with drugs, it also was interested in protecting its referees and officials after an ugly incident between Chicago's Tom Lysiak and linesman Ron Foyt.

The Black Hawks were playing the Hartford Whalers in a game October 30 when Lysiak lined up for a faceoff. Foyt dropped the puck and it appeared that Lysiak dropped Foyt, tripping him to the ice. Lysiak later claimed he was trying to dig the puck out from under Foyt's skates, but Lysiak was suspended immediately for 20 games—one-fourth of the regular season. When Lysiak appealed, the suspension was upheld by the board of governors. Except for lifetime suspensions for gambling, drug involvement and assaulting referees, Lysiak's sentence was the longest in the league's history.

Surely, the Black Hawks missed him. In a surprising turnabout, Chicago, a division winner in 1982-83, plunged to fourth place in the Norris Division standings. And it had company. Montreal finished in fourth place and under .500 for the first time since 1950-51.

Indeed, the old guard of the NHL seemed to be giving away to younger and fresher teams. Of the six original NHL franchises, only Boston finished in first place and none of the others was higher than third. By far, the most competitive race was in the Patrick Division, where 11 points separated the first-place Islanders and the fourth-place Rangers. That standing paired them in the first round of the playoffs in a meeting that proved memorable and exciting.

The entire playoffs, in fact, were memorable.

The Adams Division championship was decided in a series between Quebec and Montreal, the third and fourth-place finishers during the regular season. Even powerful Edmonton was not immune. The Oilers were extended to a decisive seventh game in the Smythe Division finals by upstart Calgary. That would be the Oilers' toughest fight en route to their Stanley Cup battle against the Islanders and first NHL championship.

Not only did the Islanders and the Oilers approach the game differently, but they nursed a brewing rivalry. It didn't ease tensions when the Islanders met the Rangers in the first round of the playoffs and several Oilers predicted the Rangers would win. The Islanders, on the other hand, crowed about their outstanding record against the Oilers. Entering the finals, they had beaten Edmonton 10 straight times, a domination that clearly had become a sore point among the Oilers.

"That's all anyone seems to talk about," said Oilers defenseman Kevin Lowe on the eve of the series. "We think about it, too,"

It didn't take long, however, for the Oilers to quiet the skeptics. Behind the superb goaltending of Grant Fuhr, who had been relegated to the minors one season earlier, the Oilers opened the series with a stunning 1-0 victory at Nassau Coliseum, breaking the Islanders' spell and helping improve their own mounting confidence. Ironically, the shutout came one year to the day that the Islanders had started their sweep of Edmonton. That was soon forgotten.

Never before had the Oilers shut out an opponent in the playoffs. It was, however, the third time the Islanders had been blanked in these playoffs as their offense continued to lag, a problem that would come back to haunt them. The Oilers, in fact, had not even held a lead over the Islanders since the finals in 1983, and that lasted all of six minutes. All along, the Islanders had staked their hopes on goalie Billy Smith, who finally met his match.

"The best two players on the ice," said Bill Torrey, Islanders' general manager, "were the goalies."

Torrey was correct. But what surprised the Islanders even more was the Oilers' ability to check hard and dig the puck out of the corners. The Islanders always had done that better than anyone else. Instead, Kevin McClelland, acquired in a midseason trade from Pittsburgh, led the fight along the boards and scored an early third-period goal that stood as the margin of victory.

"It was the best I've ever seen this team

Grant Fuhr was dazzling in the Edmonton goal crease in the Stanley Cup finals, shutting out the Islanders in Game 1 and keeping New York off the scoreboard early in Game 3.

play," Gretzky said. "And I mean ever."

It gave the Oilers the feeling that they really could beat the Islanders, a belief they badly needed. Not even the Islanders' easy 6-1 victory in Game 2 could burst Edmonton's bubble. Clark Gillies scored three goals and the Islanders defense held Gretzky without a point. The Islanders also held the powerful Edmonton shooters to just 23 shots on goal and scored three power-play goals. It was a consummate effort that could not be repeated.

For whatever reason, the Islanders no longer seemed to have the punch and enthusiasm that had marked the other years of their reign. For one thing, they had endured a wearying road to the final round. For another, they were badly bruised, missing a key player like Bob Bourne while others such as Dave Langevin and Ken Morrow were hobbled by injuries. Against a lesser team, the Islanders might have been able to steal the show one more time. But the Oilers were too good, too fast and playing too confidently. There was never more evidence of that than in the pivotal third game.

First, Fuhr weathered a furious Islanders assault in the opening minutes when the Oilers seemed to be hanging on for dear life. But the Islanders couldn't deliver the knockout punch and the Oilers, with the second period coming to a close, scored what may well have been the two most crucial goals of the series. They came just 17 seconds apart and sparked the Oilers to a rousing 7-2 victory. Edmonton scored more goals in one game than they did in the entire 1983 finals.

Messier had tied the score at 2-2 on a dazzling one-man rush and the period was coming to a close when Gretzky poked the puck away from Potvin behind the Islanders net. The play resulted in a goal by Anderson with just 48 seconds left. A goal by Coffey 17 seconds later stunned the Islanders and Edmonton went on to dominate the game. Gretzky managed two assists for his first points of the series. The year before, Gretzky had been held to four points, all assists, when his team was swept.

Gretzky, finally in the scoring column, added two goals in an identical 7-2 victory in Game 4. He struck the decisive blow just 1:53 into the contest, when the Islanders sorely needed to score early and snap Edmonton's momentum.

"No question, it was the biggest relief I've felt in my life after not scoring against them for so long," said Gretzky, referring to his first playoff goal in eight final games against the Islanders. "I think subconsciously my teammates were questioning me. They had to be wondering, 'When is he going to get one?'"

Once in the lead, the Oilers kept on the pressure. Just 68 seconds later, Willy Lindstrom scored. Quickly, the Islanders' poise evaporated under a hail of shots. Messier, the biggest offensive catalyst for Edmonton in the series, scored for a 3-1 lead. Later, Smith was driven to the bench under a chorus of boos from the sellout crowd in the Northlands Coliseum as the Islanders continued to look harmless, even when they had the puck. They failed to score despite a power-play advantage of four minutes and 31 seconds.

The city of Edmonton poised itself for a raucous celebration with its team just one victory away from the elusive Cup.

The Oilers had been given a reasonable chance to win the previous year. And in 1982, they won the Smythe Division and were waiting to be crowned champions when they were upset by lowly Los Angeles in the first round of the playoffs. Now, with Game 5 in Edmonton, the Oilers were determined not to let the opportunity slip away again. They began to think what winning the title would be like. "It would be like Christmas," Lowe said.

Christmas came early in Edmonton. After Dave Lumley had slid the puck 200 feet into an empty net to cap the Oilers 5-2 victory, Gretzky cradled the Cup in his arms while a shower of confetti fell around him. It was Gretzky who had ignited the clinching victory, scoring two breakaway goals in the first period. Smith again was replaced after the first period by Rollie Melanson. Ken Linseman greeted Melanson just 38 seconds into the second period with a goal for a 3-0 lead. The crowd impatiently stamped its feet and waved orange scarfs. The lead would grow to 4-0 before the Islanders made one last gasp.

Pat LaFontaine, the heralded junior who had joined the Islanders after the Winter Olympics, nearly got the Islanders back into the game singlehandedly. He scored two goals in the first 35 seconds of the third period and the Islanders began storming goalie Andy Moog, a surprise replacement for the injured Fuhr. But Moog held on and preserved the lead before

Islanders Coach Al Arbour, who saw his dream of a record-tying five straight Cups ended by Edmonton, will be back behind the New York bench in 1984-85.

Lumley clinched the victory with the open net yawning at him from the other end of the ice. The dynasty was over.

"We carved a spot in history," said a red-eyed Gillies. "It was a tremendous accomplishment."

Indeed, it was.

The Oilers were generous in their praise of the team they had just dethroned. They were even more generous in praise of themselves.

Said Gretzky: "I've won a lot of individual awards, but nothing compares to this. I remember when I was young I saw pictures of Jean Beliveau holding up the Cup and I thought about that when I picked it up."

A changing of the guard took place off the ice as well as on.

The Philadelphia Flyers, swept out of the playoffs in the first round by Washington, dismissed General Manager and Coach Bob McCammon. Bobby Clarke, who announced his retirement as a player after one of the most productive careers in NHL history, took his place. The Devils named Doug Carpenter, a highly successful junior coach, to move behind the bench in New Jersey, replacing Tom McVie, and Dan Maloney succeeded Mike Nykoluk in Toronto. Bob Berry, fired by Montreal in midseason, became coach of the Penguins. Pat Quinn took over in Los Angeles, where he replaced Roger Neilson, who had earlier stepped in for Don Perry.

Neilson had started the season behind the Vancouver bench, but was replaced by Canucks' G.M. Harry Neale, who in turn handed the reins to junior coach Bill LaForge for the 1984-85 season. Jacques Lemaire replaced Berry in Montreal and led the Canadiens to their surprising playoff performance. Finally, Barry Long stood in at Winnipeg following Tom Watt and John Ferguson.

Rogie Vachon, an assistant coach under Perry at the start of the season, made the most steps up the ladder, taking over for Perry for a few games before being named the Kings' general manager in February, replacing George Maguire.

After the season, Arbour said he was considering retirement as coach of the Islanders. More than six weeks of speculation followed before Arbour decided he would return for a 12th season behind the Islanders bench. Arbour's 109 playoff victories moved him just two behind all-time leader Scotty Bowman of the Buffalo Sabres.

Not surprisingly, the Oilers and Islanders dominated the postseason awards. Bossy won the Lady Byng Trophy for the second straight year. Washington's Doug Jarvis won the Frank Selke Trophy and teammate Rod Langway repeated as winner of the Norris Trophy as best defenseman. Barrasso won the Calder Trophy for Rookie of the Year. Gretzky won the Hart and Ross awards and Washington's Bryan Murray was named Coach of the Year.

Two Oilers and three Islanders were named to The Sporting News' all-star teams. Gretzky was named to the first team along with Boston right wing Rick Middleton, Quebec left wing Michel Goulet, defensemen Langway and Ray Bourque of Boston and goalie Pat Riggin. Islanders Bossy, Trottier and Potvin were named to the second team with Detroit left wing John Ogrodnick, Barrasso and Coffey.

Washington G.M. David Poile was named TSN's Executive of the Year for the second consecutive season while Washington's Murray was selected Coach of the Year. In addition to Gretzky as the Player of the Year, the other major award went to Detroit's Steve Yzerman, who was chosen Rookie of the Year.

The biggest single change of the 1983-84 season was the addition of the five-minute overtime period. NHL teams had not played overtime since 1942, when the league dropped the extra period because of tight wartime train schedules. The sudden-death format was instituted to try to cut down the number of needless tie games. If the first season was any indication, the overtime was a success because 54 of the 140 ties were broken in sudden death.

Another experiment was the use of movable goalposts in Toronto. They were designed to prevent serious injuries when players collide into the netting. That trial proved so successful that the league's board of governors voted to make it a permanent part of the equipment used at each NHL arena in 1984-85.

On the ice, the young Buffalo Sabres set a record with 10 straight road victories, breaking the old league mark of eight held by several clubs. The Sabres also became the first division rival to sweep the Montreal Canadiens since 1940, compiling an 8-0 record against the Habs.

The Washington Capitals had the league's longest streak, going 14 games without a loss from January 15 to February 19. The Hartford Whalers, a perennial loser, showed a facelift under the direction of Emile Francis. The Whalers, in fact, set a club record for victories, and, were it not for a dismal 0-7-1 record against divisional rival Montreal, might have supplanted the Canadiens for the final playoff berth in the Adams Division.

The league was replete with record-setters in '83-84, all the way from Gretzky to Toronto's Greg Terrion. Terrion, who had only 15 goals the entire season, tied a league record with a pair of penalty-shot goals (Pat Egan of the New York Americans had two in 1941-42). Ironically, both of Terrion's penalty-shot goals came against Chicago. He scored one against Tony Esposito and the other against Murray Bannerman. There were 18 penalty shots taken, eight of them finding the net.

Buffalo's Phil Housley, who turned 20 in March, became the youngest defenseman in league history to score 20 goals in a season, breaking Bobby Orr's mark of 22. Housley finished with 31 goals.

Joe Mullen of the St. Louis Blues scored 41 goals, breaking the old mark for a U.S.-born player of 38 set by Minnesota's Neal Broten in 1981-82. Detroit defenseman Reed Larson became the highest-scoring

Washington Coach Bryan Murray directed his defense-minded team to a 48-27-5 record, fifth-best in the league, and was named NHL Coach of the Year.

American when he surpassed the mark of 357 points by 10-year veteran Tommy Williams, who played for several teams in the 1960s and '70s. Larson also became the first defenseman to score 20 or more goals in five straight seasons.

Detroit's Brad Park moved ahead of Orr's record for most assists by a defenseman (645) and Potvin of the Islanders became the first defenseman to score 20 goals in eight different seasons.

Records were not confined to forwards and defensemen, however. Edmonton goalie Fuhr smashed a record with 14 assists, six more than the previous mark for goaltenders established by Washington's Mike Palmateer in 1980-81. And Quebec's Mario Gosselin, who starred for the Canadian Olympic Team, shut out the St. Louis Blues, 4-0, in his debut, the first netminder to break into the majors with a shutout since Mario Lessard did it for Los Angeles in October of 1978.

Another goaltending performance of note was turned in by Toronto rookie Alan Bester. Though he lost to the Hartford Whalers, 5-3, on March 15, he made them earn their victory. The Whalers outshot the Maple Leafs, 65-22, peppering Bester with 32 shots in the second period. Bester and the Leafs were leading, 2-1, entering the third period.

For the first time in history, four brothers played on the ice in a game at the same time when Brent and Duane Sutter of the Islanders and Ron and Rich Sutter of the Philadelphia Flyers met on October 30. The feat was made possible when Pittsburgh traded Rich to Philadelphia eight days earlier.

Rich Sutter was just one of many key players traded during the season. The biggest names dealt in '83-84 were Minnesota's Bobby Smith, who was traded to Montreal for Mark Napier and Keith Acton, former Norris Trophy winner Randy Carlyle, who was sent from Pittsburgh to Winnipeg for defenseman Moe Mantha and a first-round draft choice, and Paul Holmgren, who was dealt by Philadelphia to Minnesota for U.S. Olympian Paul Guay. St. Louis traded Perry Turnbull to Montreal for Doug Wickenheiser, Gilbert Delorme and Greg Paslawski in one of the largest deals of the season. Veteran center Pete McNab was shipped from Boston to Vancouver for winger Jim Nill.

"In and out," McNab said upon leaving the Boston locker room for the last time. "It's funny. You pour so much into a job for eight years, and you walk out with a dozen sticks and two pair of skates."

National Hockey League

Organized November 22, 1917

NHL Offices

John A. Ziegler, Jr.

Sun Life Building
1155 Metcalfe Street, Suite 960
Montreal, Que., Canada H3B 2W2
Phone—(514) 871-9220
TWX—(610) 421-4260

Central Scouting & Officiating
Suite 200, 1 Greensboro Drive
Rexdale, Ont. M9W 1C8
Phone—(416) 245-2926
TWX—(610) 492-2703

34th Floor
500 Fifth Avenue
New York, NY 10110
Phone—(212) 398-1100
TWX—(710) 581-2736

Chairman of the Board	WILLIAM W. WIRTZ
President	JOHN A. ZIEGLER, JR.
Vice-Chairman	FRANK A. GRIFFITHS

Secretary	ROBERT O. SWADOS
Executive Vice-President	BRIAN F. O'NEILL
Vice-President and General Counsel	GILBERT STEIN
Vice-President, Finance	KENNETH G. SAWYER
Vice-President, Officiating	IAN "SCOTTY" MORRISON
Vice-President, Broadcasting	JOEL NIXON
Vice-President, Marketing-Public Relations	STEVE RYAN
Director of Communications	John Halligan
Director of Marketing	Glen Dickout
Director of Central Registry	Garry Lovegrove
Director of Central Scouting	Jim Gregory
Director of Information (Prince of Wales Conference)	Dan Leary (New York)
Director of Information (Clarence Campbell Conference)	Mike Griffin (Montreal)
Assistant Director of Officiating	John McCauley
Supervisors of Officials	Frank Udvari, William "Dutch" Van Deelen, Matt Pavelich, Lou Maschio
Director of Administration	Phil Scheuer
Director of Security	Frank Torpey
Assistant Director of Security	Al Wiseman

National Hockey League
1984-85

Campbell Conference
Smythe Division
Calgary Flames
Edmonton Oilers
Los Angeles Kings
Vancouver Canucks
Winnipeg Jets

Norris Division
Chicago Black Hawks
Detroit Red Wings
Minnesota North Stars
St. Louis Blues
Toronto Maple Leafs

Prince Of Wales Conference
Patrick Division
New Jersey Devils
New York Islanders
New York Rangers
Philadelphia Flyers
Pittsburgh Penguins
Washington Capitals

Adams Division
Boston Bruins
Buffalo Sabres
Hartford Whalers
Montreal Canadiens
Quebec Nordiques

Board of Governors

Paul A. Mooney .... Boston	John O. Pickett, Jr. .... N. Y. Islanders
Seymour H. Knox, III .... Buffalo	John H. Krumpe .... N. Y. Rangers
Cliff Fletcher .... Calgary	Jay Snider .... Philadelphia
William W. Wirtz .... Chicago	Paul Martha .... Pittsburgh
Michael Ilitch .... Detroit	Marcel Aubut .... Quebec
Peter Pocklington .... Edmonton	Harry Ornest .... St. Louis
Howard Baldwin .... Hartford	Harold E. Ballard .... Toronto
Dr. Jerry Buss .... Los Angeles	Frank A. Griffiths .... Vancouver
Gordon Gund .... Minnesota	Abe Pollin .... Washington
Ronald Corey .... Montreal	Barry Shenkarow .... Winnipeg
John J. McMullen .... New Jersey	

Boston Bruins
Adams Division

President and Governor	Paul A. Mooney
General Manager and Alternate Governor	Harry Sinden
Assistant General Manager	Tom Johnson
Coach	Gerry Cheevers
Assistant Coaches	Gary Doak, Jean Ratelle
Director of Public Relations	Nate Greenberg
Coordinator of Minor League Player Personnel/Scouting	Bob Tindall
Director of Player Evaluation	Bart Bradley
Scouting Staff	Jim Morrison, Andre Lachapelle, Joe Lyons, Don Saatzer, Lars Waldner
Controller	John J. Dionne
Trainer-Physical Therapist	Jim Kausek
Trainers	Dan Canney and John Forristall
Sales and Marketing	Steve Nazro
Home Ice	Boston Garden
Address	150 Causeway Street, Boston, Mass. 02114
Capacity for hockey	14,451
Club colors	Gold, Black and White
Phone	(617) 227-3206

Paul Mooney

Harry Sinden

Tom Johnson

Gerry Cheevers

Boston Bruins 1984-85 Roster

FORWARDS

Name	Hgt.	Wgt.	Place of Birth	Date	1983-84 Club	G.	A.	Pts.
Byers, Lyndon	6:01	190	Nipawin, Sask.	2-29-64	Regina-Boston	34	61	95
Courtnall, Geoff	6:00	165	Victoria, B.C.	8-18-62	Hershey-Boston	14	12	26
Crowder, Bruce	6:00	195	Essex, Ont.	3-25-57	Boston	6	14	20
Crowder, Keith	6:00	195	Windsor, Ont.	1-6-59	Boston	24	28	52
Donnelly, Dave	5:11	185	Edmonton, Alta.	2-2-62	Can. Olympic-Boston	21	18	39
Dufour, Luc	5:11	180	Chicoutimi, Que.	2-13-63	Hershey-Boston	15	23	38
Fergus, Tom	6:00	200	Chicago, Ill.	6-16-62	Boston	25	36	61
Gillis, Mike	6:01	195	Sudbury, Ont.	12-1-58	Hershey-Boston	14	32	46
Johnston, Greg	6:01	190	Barrie, Ont.	1-14-65	Toronto Jrs.-Boston	40	36	76
Kasper, Steve	5:08	175	Montreal, Que.	9-28-61	Boston	3	11	14
Kostynski, Doug	6:01	170	Castlegar, B.C.	2-23-63	Hershey-Boston	16	28	44
Laforest, Bob	5:10	195	Sault Ste. Marie, Ont.	5-19-63	New Haven-Hershey-L.A.	14	23	37
Linseman, Ken	5:11	175	Kingston, Ont.	8-11-58	Edmonton	18	49	67
Markwart, Nevin	5:10	175	Toronto, Ont.	12-9-64	Boston	14	16	30
McLellan, Scott	6:01	175	Toronto, Ont.	2-10-63	Hershey	9	12	21
Middleton, Rick	5:11	175	Toronto, Ont.	12-4-53	Boston	47	58	105
Morrison, Doug	5:11	185	Vancouver, B.C.	2-1-60	Hershey	38	40	78
Nill, Jim	6:00	185	Hanna, Alta.	4-11-58	Vancouver-Boston	12	8	20
O'Reilly, Terry	6:01	200	Niagara, Falls, Ont.	6-7-51	Boston	12	18	30
Palmer, Brad	6:00	185	Duncan, B.C.	9-14-61	Hershey	25	32	57
Pasin, Dave	6:01	190	Edmonton, Alta.	7-8-66	Prince Albert	68	54	122
Pederson, Barry	5:11	185	Big River, Sask.	3-13-61	Boston	38	77	116
Podloski, Ray	6:02	210	Edmonton, Alta.	1-5-66	Portland	46	50	96
Reid, Dave	6:00	205	Toronto, Ont.	5-15-64	Peterboro-Boston	34	64	98
Silk, Dave	5:11	190	Scituate, Mass.	1-1-58	Hershey-Boston	24	27	51

DEFENSEMEN

Name	Hgt.	Wgt.	Place of Birth	Date	1983-84 Club	G.	A.	Pts.
Blum, John	6:03	205	Detroit, Mich.	10-8-59	Moncton-Edmonton-Boston	4	24	28
Bourque, Ray	5:11	205	Montreal, Que.	12-28-60	Boston	31	65	96
Curran, Brian	6:04	220	Toronto, Ont.	11-5-63	Hershey-Boston	1	3	4
Hillier, Randy	6:00	185	Toronto, Ont.	3-30-60	Boston	3	12	15
Kluzak, Gord	6:04	210	Climax, Sask.	3-4-64	Boston	10	27	37
Meulenbroeks, John	6:00	180	Kingston, Ont.	4-3-64	Brantford	7	25	32
Milbury, Mike	6:01	205	Brighton, Mass.	1-17-52	Boston	2	17	19
O'Connell, Mike	5:09	185	Chicago, Ill.	11-25-55	Boston	18	42	60
Thelin, Mats	5:10	185	Stockholm, Sweden	3-30-61	AIK (Sweden)	4	1	5

GOALTENDERS

Name	Hgt.	Wgt.	Place of Birth	Date	1983-84 Club	Mins.	GA.	SO.
Daskalakis, Cleon	5:09	175	Boston, Mass.	9-29-62	Boston University	1972	96	0
Keans, Doug	5:07	170	Pembroke, Ont.	1-7-58	Boston	1779	92	2
LaRochelle, Alain	5:09	185	Pontiez, Sask.	10-27-64	Saskatoon	3003	244	0
Peeters, Pete	6:00	185	Edmonton, Alta.	8-1-57	Boston	2868	151	0

Buffalo Sabres
Adams Division

Chairman of the Board	Seymour H. Knox III
President	Northrup R. Knox
Vice-Chairman of the Board	David G. Forman
Vice-President and Counsel	Robert O. Swados
Administrative Vice-President	Mitchell Owen
Vice-President, Finance	Robert W. Pickel
Secretary	James E. Rolls
Treasurer	Joseph T. J. Stewart
Director of Hockey Operations, G.M. and Coach	Scotty Bowman
Assistant General Manager	Gerry Meehan
Associate Coach	Jimmy Roberts
Director of Communications	Paul Wieland
Director of Public Relations	Gerry Helper
Director of Marketing	Robert E. Chambers, Jr.
Head Trainer	Frank Christie
Assistant Trainer	Bob Simonick
Home Ice	Memorial Auditorium
Address	Memorial Auditorium, Buffalo, N.Y. 14202
Capacity for hockey	16,433 (including standees)
Club Colors	Blue, White and Gold
Phone	(716) 856-7300

Seymour Knox

Northrup Knox

Scotty Bowman

Buffalo Sabres 1984-85 Roster

FORWARDS	Hgt.	Wgt.	Place of Birth	Date	1983-84 Club	G.	A.	Pts.
Andersson, Bo Mikael	5:09	183	Malmo, Sweden	5-10-66	Vastra Frolunda	0	2	2
Andreychuk, Dave	6:03	200	Hamilton, Ont.	9-29-63	Buffalo	38	42	80
Cloutier, Real	5:10	185	St. Emile, Que.	7-30-56	Buffalo	24	36	60
Creighton, Adam	6:05	205	Burlington, Ont.	6-2-65	Buffalo-Ottawa	44	51	95
Cunneyworth, Randy	6:00	180	Etobicoke, Ont.	5-10-61	Rochester	18	17	35
Cyr, Paul	5:10	185	Port Alberni, B.C.	10-31-63	Buffalo	16	27	43
Davis, Malcolm	5:11	180	Lockeport, N.S.	10-10-56	Buffalo-Rochester	57	49	106
Foligno, Mike	6:02	195	Sudbury, Ont.	1-29-59	Buffalo	32	31	63
Hajdu, Richard	6:00	170	Victoria, B.C.	4-10-65	Victoria	17	10	27
Hamel, Gilles	6:00	185	Asbestos, Que.	3-18-60	Buffalo	21	23	44
Harper, Warren	6:00	175	Prince Albert, Sask.	5-10-63	Rochester	25	28	53
Lacombe, Normand	5:11	205	Pierrefonds, Que.	10-18-64	Rochester	10	16	26
Langevin, Chris	6:00	190	Montreal, Que.	11-27-59	Buffalo-Rochester	12	14	26
McKenna, Sean	6:00	185	Asbestos, Que.	3-7-62	Buffalo	20	10	30
McKinnon, Brian	5:11	185	Toronto, Ont.	10-4-64	Ottawa	31	27	58
Moller, Mike	6:00	190	Calgary, Alta.	6-16-61	Buffalo	5	11	16
Norman, Rob	5:11	170	Kingston, Ont.	1-19-64	Cornwall	43	37	80
Patrick, Steve	6:04	205	Winnipeg, Man.	2-4-61	Buffalo-Rochester	9	18	27
Perreault, Gilbert	6:00	200	Victoriaville, Que.	11-13-50	Buffalo	31	59	90
Peterson, Brent	6:00	190	Calgary, Alta.	2-15-58	Buffalo	9	12	21
Ramsay, Craig	5:10	175	Weston, Ont.	3-17-51	Buffalo	9	17	26
Robertson, Geordie	6:00	165	Victoria, B.C.	8-1-59	Rochester	37	54	91
Ruff, Lindy	6:02	190	Warburg, Alta.	2-17-60	Buffalo	14	31	45
Seiling, Ric	6:01	180	Elmira, Ont.	12-15-57	Buffalo	13	22	35
Tucker, John	6:00	185	Windsor, Ont.	9-29-64	Buffalo-Kitchener	52	64	116
Verret, Claude	5:09	165	Lachine, Que.	4-20-63	Buffalo-Rochester	41	56	97
DEFENSEMEN								
Chisholm, Colin	6:02	190	Edmonton, Alta.	2-25-63	University of Alberta	1	16	17
Dykstra, Steve	6:02	190	Edmonton, Alta.	2-3-62	Rochester	3	19	22
Fenyves, Dave	5:11	190	Dunnville, Ont.	4-29-60	Buffalo-Rochester	3	20	23
Fischer, Ron	6:02	195	Merritt, B.C.	4-12-59	Rochester	10	32	42
Hajt, Bill	6:03	205	Radisson, Sask.	11-18-51	Buffalo	3	24	27
Housley, Phil	5:10	180	St. Paul, Minn.	3-9-64	Buffalo	31	46	77
Jutila, Timo	5:07	175	Finland	12-24-63	Finland	..	..	..
Naud, Daniel	5:10	190	Trois Rivieres, Que.	2-20-62	Rochester	15	44	59
Playfair, Larry	6:04	215	Ft. St. James, B.C.	6-23-58	Buffalo	5	11	16
Ramsey, Mike	6:03	190	Minneapolis, Minn.	12-3-60	Buffalo	9	22	31
Renaud, Mark	6:00	185	Windsor, Ont.	2-21-59	Buffalo-Rochester	10	36	46
Rueter, Dirk	5:11	195	Toronto, Ont.	4-18-62	Rochester	0	16	16
Sebek, Venci	5:11	195	New York, N.Y.	5-25-63	Rochester	2	5	7
Stambert, Orwar	5:11	198	Stockholm, Sweden	9-30-60	Djurgardens, Sweden	4	15	19
Virta, Hannu	6:00	180	Turku, Finland	3-22-63	Buffalo	6	30	36
Wiemer, Jim	6:04	200	Sudbury, Ont.	1-9-61	Buffalo-Rochester	9	26	35

GOALTENDERS	Hgt.	Wgt.	Place of Birth	Date	1983-84 Club	Mins.	GA.	SO.
Barrasso, Tom	6:03	195	Boston, Mass.	3-31-65	Buffalo	2475	117	2
Cloutier, Jacques	5:07	155	Noranda, Que.	1-3-60	Rochester	2842	172	1
Craig, Mike	6:00	165	Calgary, Alta.	11-1-62	Billings	..	..	..
McNamara, Bob	5:10	160	Toronto, Ont.	8-6-61	Rochester	171	15	0
Myre, Phil	6:01	185	Ste. A. Bellevue, Que.	11-1-48	Rochester	1802	104	3
Sauve, Bob	5:08	165	Ste. Genevieve, Que.	6-17-55	Buffalo	2375	138	0

Calgary Flames
Smythe Division

Owners	Norman Green, Harley Hotchkiss, Ralph Scurfield, B. J. Seaman, D. K. Seaman, Norman Kwong
President, General Manager and Governor	Cliff Fletcher
Assistant to the President	Al Coates
Assistant General Manager	Al MacNeil
General Counsel	Doug Mitchell
Coach	Bob Johnson
Assistant Coach	Bob Murdoch
V.P., Marketing and Broadcasting	Leo Ornest
Director of Public Relations	Rick Skaggs
Assistant Public Relations Director	Jane Kennelly
Chief Scout	Gerry Blair
Coordinator of Scouting	Ian McKenzie
U.S. and College Scout	Jack Ferreira
Scouting Staff	Bill White, Aldo Giampaolo, Pentti Lindegren, Larry McNab, Lars Normann, Ben Hayes
Controller	Lynne Tosh
Trainer	Jim Murray
Equipment Manager	Bobby Stewart
Home Ice	The Olympic Saddledome
Address	P.O. Box 1540, Station M, Calgary, Alta. T2P 3B9
Seating Capacity	16,520
Club colors	White, Red and Gold
Phone	(403) 261-0475

Cliff Fletcher

Al MacNeil

Bob Johnson

Bob Murdoch

Calgary Flames 1984-85 Roster

FORWARDS

Name	Hgt.	Wgt.	Place of Birth	Date	1983-84 Club	G.	A.	Pts.
Beers, Eddy	6:02	198	Merritt, B.C.	10-12-59	Calgary	36	39	75
Bekkers, John	6:02	196	Halifax, N.S.	5-18-65	Regina-Portland	29	15	44
Bolduc, Dan	5:09	190	Waterville, Me.	4-6-53	Colorado-Calgary	37	18	55
Bozek, Steve	5:11	180	Kelowna, B.C.	11-26-60	Calgary	10	10	20
Bradley, Brian	5:09	163	Kitchener, Ont.	1-21-65	London	40	60	100
Cavallini, Gino	6:02	215	Toronto, Ont.	11-24-62	Bowling Green Univ.	25	23	48
Clayton, Mike	6:00	190	Jamaica	6-20-63	Colorado	20	16	36
Courteau, Yves	5:10	188	Cote des Neiges, Que.	4-25-64	Laval	45	75	120
Eakin, Bruce	5:11	195	Winnipeg, Man.	9-28-62	Colorado-Calgary	35	70	105
Eaves, Mike	5:10	178	Denver, Colo.	6-10-56	Calgary	14	36	50
Hampson, Gord	6:03	220	Vancouver, B.C.	2-13-59	Colorado	19	25	44
Hindmarch, Dave	6:00	180	Vancouver, B.C.	10-15-58	Calgary	6	5	11
Hislop, Jamie	5:10	180	Sarnia, Ont.	1-20-54	Calgary	1	8	9
Hooey, Todd	6:01	185	Oshawa, Ont.	6-23-63	Colorado	19	21	40
Hunter, Tim	6:02	202	Calgary, Alta.	9-10-59	Calgary	4	4	8
Jackson, Jim	5:10	181	Oshawa, Ont.	2-1-60	Calgary-Colorado	11	41	52
Kane, Dan	5:11	170	Clinton, N.Y.	6-12-62	Bowling Green Univ.	24	48	72
Kromm, Richard	5:11	180	Trail, B.C.	3-29-64	Portland-Calgary	21	16	37
Lamb, Mark	5:09	160	Swift Current, Sask.	8-3-64	Medicine Hat	59	77	136
Loob, Hakan	5:09	178	Karlstad, Sweden	7-3-60	Calgary	30	25	55
McDonald, Lanny	6:00	194	Hanna, Alta.	2-16-53	Calgary	33	33	66
Nilsson, Kent	6:01	195	Nynashamn, Sweden	8-31-56	Calgary	31	49	80
Patterson, Colin	6:02	195	Rexdale, Ont.	5-11-60	Colorado-Calgary	15	17	32
Pearson, Ted	5:10	174	Edina, Minn.	1-9-62	U. of Wisconsin	13	20	33
Peplinski, Jim	6:03	209	Renfrew, Ont.	10-24-60	Calgary	11	22	33
Quinn, Dan	5:10	176	Ottawa, Ont.	6-1-65	Belleville-Calgary	42	69	111
Rioux, Pierre	5:09	151	Quebec City, Que.	2-1-62	Colorado	37	46	83
Risebrough, Doug	5:11	185	Kitchener, Ont.	1-29-54	Calgary	23	28	51
Roberts, Gary	6:01	189	North York, Ont.	5-23-66	Ottawa	27	30	57
Simioni, Mario	6:01	204	Toronto, Ont.	4-1-63	Colorado	16	21	37
Tambellini, Steve	6:00	184	Trail, B.C.	5-14-58	Calgary	15	10	25
White, George	6:00	175	Arlington, Mass.	2-17-61	Colorado-Peoria	7	12	19
Wilson, Carey	6:02	205	Winnipeg, Man.	5-19-62	Can. Olympic-Calgary	21	29	50

DEFENSEMEN

Name	Hgt.	Wgt.	Place of Birth	Date	1983-84 Club	G.	A.	Pts.
Baxter, Paul	5:11	194	Winnipeg, Man.	10-25-55	Calgary	7	20	27
Bourgeois, Charles	6:04	217	Moncton, N.B.	11-11-59	Colorado-Calgary	13	35	48
Degray, Dale	6:00	202	Oshawa, Ont.	9-3-63	Colorado	16	14	30
Eloranta, Kari	6:02	197	Lahti, Finland	2-29-56	Calgary	5	34	39
Guy, Kevan	6:02	193	Edmonton, Alta.	7-16-65	Medicine Hat	15	42	57
Hanson, Keith	6:05	215	Ada, Minn.	4-26-57	Colorado-Calgary	5	23	28
Kiriakou, Lou	6:00	195	Toronto, Ont.	4-2-64	Toronto Jrs.	10	35	45
Kivell, Rob	6:01	202	North Bay, Ont.	1-14-65	Victoria	16	33	49
Konroyd, Steve	6:01	196	Scarborough, Ont.	2-10-61	Calgary	1	13	14
MacInnis, Allan	6:02	196	Inverness, N.S.	7-11-63	Colorado-Calgary	16	48	64
Macoun, Jamie	6:02	197	Newmarket, Ont.	8-17-61	Calgary	9	23	32
Reinhart, Paul	5:11	205	Kitchener, Ont.	1-8-60	Calgary	6	15	21
Sheehy, Neil	6:02	215	Fort Francis, Ont.	2-9-60	Colorado-Calgary	6	18	24
Stiles, Tony	5:11	208	Carstairs, Alta.	8-12-59	Colorado-Calgary	5	25	30
Turnbull, Randy	6:00	179	Red Deer, Alta.	2-7-62	New Haven-Peoria	3	18	21
Volcan, Mickey	6:00	181	Edmonton, Alta.	3-3-62	Colorado-Calgary	9	13	22

GOALTENDERS

Name	Hgt.	Wgt.	Place of Birth	Date	1983-84 Club	Mins.	GA.	SO.
D'Amour, Marc	5:10	165	Sudbury, Ont.	4-29-61	Colorado	1917	131	0
Edwards, Don	5:09	164	Hamilton, Ont.	9-28-55	Calgary	2303	157	0
Hogg, Jeff	5:11	170	Guelph, Ont.	1-28-65	Kingston	1096	105	0
Lemelin, Rejean	5:11	170	Quebec City, Que.	11-19-54	Calgary	2568	150	0
Meszaros, Dave	5:09	179	Toronto, Ont.	2-16-64	Toronto Jrs.	3106	232	1
Vernon, Mike	5:09	155	Calgary, Alta.	2-24-63	Colorado-Calgary	2659	152	1

Chicago Black Hawks
Norris Division

President	William W. Wirtz
Vice-President	Arthur M. Wirtz, Jr.
Vice-President and Assistant to the President	Thomas N. Ivan
General Manager	Bob Pulford
Assistant G.M. and Director of Player Personnel	Jack Davison
Coach	Orval Tessier
Assistant Coach	Roger Neilson
Scouts	Jimmy Walker, Don Smith, Dave Lucas, Michel Dumas, Jim Pappin, Jan Spieczny
Public Relations	Jim DeMaria
Trainers	Charles "Skip" Thayer and Lou Varga
Home Ice	Chicago Stadium
Address	1800 W. Madison Street, Chicago, Illinois 60612
Capacity for hockey	17,263
Club colors	Red, Black and White
Phone	(312) 733-5300

William W. Wirtz

Bob Pulford

Jack Davison

Orval Tessier

Chicago Black Hawks 1984-85 Roster

FORWARDS

Name	Hgt.	Wgt.	Place of Birth	Date	83-84 Club	G.	A.	Pts.
Birnie, Scot	6:01	190	Kingston, Ont.	5- 1-65	North Bay	10	24	34
Brown, Bill	6:01	170	Dayton, O.	10- 9-66	Simley H.S. (Minn.)	36	29	65
Camazzola, Jim	5:11	190	Vancouver, B.C.	1- 5-64	Kamloops-Chicago	27	25	52
Eriksson, Tom	5:11	183	Umea, Sweden	5- 3-66	Modo Aik	..	..	..
Fraser, Curt	6:00	200	Cincinnati, O.	1-12-58	Chicago	5	12	17
Frawley, Dan	6:00	170	Sturgeon Falls, Ont.	6- 2-62	Springfield-Chicago	22	34	56
Frere, Marcel	6:00	180	Trochu, Alta.	1-16-62	Springfield-Peoria	5	10	15
Gardner, Bill	5:10	177	Toronto, Ont.	3-19-60	Chicago	27	21	48
Greenough, Glenn	5:11	198	Sudbury, Ont.	7-20-66	Sudbury	26	43	69
Larmer, Jeff	5:10	179	Peterborough, Ont.	10-10-62	New Jersey-Chicago	15	26	41
Larmer, Steve	5:10	189	Peterborough, Ont.	6-16-61	Chicago	35	40	75
La Varre, Mark	5:11	170	Evanston, Ill.	2-21-65	North Bay	19	22	41
Ludzik, Steve	5:11	186	Toronto, Ont.	4- 3-62	Chicago	9	20	29
Lysiak, Tom	6:01	204	High Prairie, Alta.	4-22-53	Chicago	17	30	47
MacMillan, Bob	5:11	185	Charlottetown, P.E.I.	9- 3-52	New Jersey	17	23	40
McMurchy, Tom	5:10	170	New Westminster, B.C.	12- 2-63	Springfield-Chicago	19	15	34
Murray, Troy	6:01	195	Calgary, Alta.	7-31-62	Chicago	15	15	30
Noonan, Brian	6:01	180	Boston, Mass.	5-29-65	Arch. Wms. H.S.	14	23	37
Olczyk, Ed	6:01	195	Chicago, Ill.	8-16-66	Team USA	21	47	68
Ollson, John	5:09	170	Nepean, Ont.	7-31-63	Springfield	29	43	72
Paterson, Rick	5:09	187	Kingston, Ont.	2-10-58	Chicago	7	6	13
Patterson, Phil	5:09	178	Kemtville, Que.	7-18-64	Ottawa	22	17	39
Pelensky, Perry	6:01	190	Edmonton, Alta.	3-20-62	Springfield-Chicago	22	16	38
Pepin, Steve	5:10	173	Sherbrooke, Que.	3-21-65	Drummondville	54	58	112
Persson, Joakim	5:08	163	Gavle, Sweden	5-15-66	Gavle-Div. I	..	..	..
Presley, Wayne	5:11	172	Detroit, Mich.	3-23-65	Kitchener	63	76	139
Robidoux, Florent	6:02	198	Cypress River, Man.	5- 5-60	Springfield-Chicago	26	22	48
Robinson, Kevin	5:11	170	Toronto, Ont.	1-24-64	Toronto Juniors	40	45	85
Savard, Denis	5:10	167	Pt. Gatineau, Que.	2- 4-61	Chicago	37	57	94
Sceviour, Darin	5:10	185	Lacombe, Alta.	11-30-65	Lethbridge	37	28	65
Secord, Al	6:01	212	Sudbury, Ont.	3- 3-58	Chicago	4	4	8
Shaw, Brian	6:00	180	Edmonton, Alta.	5-20-62	Springfield-Peoria	29	28	57
Smith, Jeff	6:00	200	Brampton, Ont.	7-31-63	Springfield	6	13	19
Stapleton, Mike	5:10	163	Sarnia, Ont.	5- 5-66	Cornwall	24	45	69
Sutter, Darryl	5:11	176	Viking, Alta.	8-19-58	Chicago	20	20	40
Watson, William	6:00	180	Pine Falls, Man.	3-30-64	U. Minn.-Duluth	35	51	86
Yaremchuk, Ken	5:11	187	Edmonton, Alta.	1- 1-64	Chicago	6	7	13

DEFENSEMEN

Name	Hgt.	Wgt.	Place of Birth	Date	83-84 Club	G.	A.	Pts.
Anholt, Darrell	6:01	230	Hardisty, Alta.	11-23-62	Springfield-Chicago	13	21	34
Badeau, Rene	6:00	190	Trois-Rivieres, Que.	1-31-64	Laval	13	40	53
Beck, Brad	5:11	185	Vancouver, B.C.	2-10-64	Michigan St.	2	7	9
Bergevin, Marc	5:11	178	Montreal, Que.	8-11-65	Chicoutimi-Springfield	10	36	46
Blyth, Steve	6:03	200	Calgary, Alta.	7-16-60	Springfield	4	20	24
Boyd, Randy	5:11	192	Coniston, Ont.	1-23-62	Balt.-Pitts.-Chi.-Sprg.	8	29	37
Brown, Keith	6:01	191	Cornerbrook, Nfld.	5- 6-60	Chicago	10	35	35
Cassidy, Bruce	5:11	176	Ottawa, Ont.	5-20-65	Ottawa-Chicago	27	68	95
DiFiori, Ralph	6:01	181	Montreal, Que.	4-20-66	Shawinigan	6	22	28
DuPont, Jerome	6:03	201	Ottawa, Ont.	2-21-62	Chicago-Springfield	4	5	9
Feamster, Dave	5:11	178	Detroit, Mich.	9-10-58	Chicago	6	7	13
Hatcher, Mark	6:07	232	Detroit, Mich.	9-15-64	North Bay	1	12	13
Howard, Tarek	6:01	185	Tucson, Ariz.	2- 6-65	U. of North Dakota	0	1	1
James, Mike	6:02	168	Toronto, Ont.	1-31-64	Ottawa	7	13	20
Murray, Bob	5:10	186	Kingston, Ont.	11-26-54	Chicago	11	37	48
Ness, Jay	5:11	180	Roseau, Minn.	10-17-63	U. of N. Dakota		Injured	
O'Callahan, Jack	6:01	189	Charleston, Mass.	7-24-57	Chicago	4	13	17
Paynter, Kent	6:00	186	Summerside, P.E.I.	4-27-65	Kitchener	9	27	36
Williams, Dan	6:02	180	Oak Park, Ill.	4-15-66	Chicago Jets	28	38	66
Wilson, Behn	6:03	210	Toronto, Ont.	12-19-58	Chicago	10	22	32
Wilson, Doug	6:01	187	Ottawa, Ont.	7- 5-57	Chicago	13	45	58
Yawney, Trent	6:03	183	Hudson Bay, Sask.	9-29-65	Saskatoon	13	46	59

GOALTENDERS

Name	Hgt.	Wgt.	Place of Birth	Date	83-84 Club	Mins.	GA.	SO.
Bannerman, Murray	5:11	185	St. Francis, Ont.	4-27-57	Chicago	3335	188	2
Clifford, Chris	5:09	139	Kingston, Ont.	5-26-66	Kingston	2808	229	2
Lehkonen, Timo	5:11	165	Helsinki, Finland	1- 8-60	Jokerit	..	..	..
Ralph, Jim	5:11	167	Sault Ste. Marie, Ont.	5-13-62	Springfield-Baltimore	1934	129	0
Skorodenski, Warren	6:01	180	Winnipeg, Man.	3-22-60	Sherbrooke-Springfield	1805	154	0

Detroit Red Wings
Norris Division

President and Owner	Michael Ilitch
Executive Vice-President	James Lites
Secretary/Treasurer	Marian Ilitch
General Counsel	Denise Ilitch-Lites
General Manager and Director of Scouting	James Devellano
Assistant General Manager/Head Coach	Nick Polano
Assistant Coach	Danny Belisle
Goaltending Consultant	Dave Dryden
Director of Public Relations	Bill Jamieson
Director Scouting/United States	Billy Dea
Eastern USA Scout	Jerry Moschella
Director Scouting/Eastern Canada	Alex Davidson
Director Scouting/Western Canada	Wayne Meier
Director of Professional Scouting/Farm System	Neil Smith
Scouts	Frank Michalek, Dave Polano, Bob Daurie, Herb Butz, Percy Kosak, Ron Roman, Carl Wetzel, Mike Daski
Director of Marketing	Rosanne Kozerski-Brown
Director of Advertising Sales/Promotions	Terry Murphy
Athletic Therapist	James Pengelly
Trainer	Bert Godin
Home Ice	Joe Louis Sports Arena
Address	600 Civic Center Drive, Detroit, Mich. 48226
Seating Capacity	19,275
Club colors	Red and White
Phone	(313) 567-3900

Mike Ilitch

Jim Devellano

Nick Polano

Detroit Red Wings 1984-85 Roster

FORWARDS

Name	Hgt.	Wgt.	Place of Birth	Date	1983-84 Club	G.	A.	Pts.
Aubry, Pierre	5:10	170	Cap Mad'leine, Que.	4-15-60	Fredericton-Quebec-Detroit	9	7	16
Boldirev, Ivan	6:00	190	Zranjanin, Yugoslavia	8-15-49	Detroit	35	48	83
Burr, Shawn	6:01	180	Sarnia, Ont.	7-1-66	Kitchener	41	44	85
Cernik, Francisek	5:09	189	Novy Jicin, Czech.	6-3-53	Vitkovice (Czech.)	25	23	48
Craven, Murray	6:01	185	Medicine Hat, Alta.	7-20-64	Medicine Hat-Detroit	38	60	98
Duguay, Ron	6:02	210	Sudbury, Ont.	7-6-57	Detroit	33	47	80
Foster, Dwight	5:11	190	Toronto, Ont.	4-2-57	Detroit	9	12	21
Gage, Jody	6:00	185	Toronto, Ont.	11-29-59	Adirondack-Detroit	40	32	72
Gallant, Gerard	5:10	158	Summerside, P.E.I.	9-2-63	Adirondack	31	33	64
Gare, Danny	5:09	175	Nelson, B.C.	5-14-54	Detroit	13	13	26
Johnstone, Ed	5:09	175	Brandon, Man.	3-2-54	Detroit	12	11	23
Kaiser, Tim	6:00	200	Leamington, Ont.	2-26-66	Guelph	6	8	14
Karlsson, Lars	6:03	176	Karlstad, Sweden	8-18-66	Farjestad	..	..	..
Kisio, Kelly	5:09	170	Wetaskiwin, Alta.	9-18-59	Detroit	23	37	60
Klima, Petr	6:00	190	Chaomutov, Czech.	12-23-64	Czech Army-Czech Jr. Team	26	21	47
Kocur, Joe	6:01	204	Calgary, Alta.	12-21-64	Saskatoon-Adirondack	40	45	85
Lambert, Lane	5:11	178	Melfort, Sask.	11-18-64	Detroit	20	15	35
Loiselle, Claude	5:11	190	Ottawa, Ont.	5-29-63	Adirondack-Detroit	17	22	39
Lundstrom, Mats	5:10	178	Skelleftea, Sweden	4-23-66	Skelleftea-Jr. Nationals	9	5	14
Manno, Bob	6:00	185	Niagara Falls, Ont.	10-31-56	Detroit-Adirondack	14	24	38
Nickolau, Tom	6:02	189	Scarborough, Ont.	4-11-66	Guelph	5	13	18
Nordin, Urban	6:01	181	Ornskioldsvik, Sweden	4-11-66	MoDo-Swd Jr.- Swd Nat'l	..	..	..
Ogrodnick, John	6:00	189	Ottawa, Ont.	6-20-59	Detroit	42	36	78
Paterson, Joe	6:02	204	Toronto, Ont.	6-25-60	Adirondack-Detroit	12	20	32
Polonich, Dennis	5:06	165	Foam Lake, Sask.	12-4-53	Adirondack	14	26	40
Probert, Bob	6:03	208	Windsor, Ont.	6-5-65	Brantford	35	38	73
Shibicky, Bill	5:11	180	Burnaby, B.C.	1-25-64	Michigan State	18	37	55
Skjodt, Charles	6:00	190	Toronto, Ont.	6-10-56	Adirondack	11	27	38
Smith, Brad	6:01	195	Windsor, Ont.	4-13-58	Adirondack-Detroit	17	30	47
Speers, Ted	5:11	175	Cloquet, Minn.	5-28-65	Adirondack	15	25	40
St. Laurent, Andre	5:10	180	Rouyn-Noranda, Que.	2-16-53	Pitts.-Adiron.-Detroit	29	46	75
Stern, Mike	6:04	210	Kitchener, Ont.	6-12-64	Oshawa	38	38	76
Vani, Carmine	6:01	180	Toronto, Ont.	8-7-64	Kitchener-North Bay	29	11	40
Williams, Tiger	5:11	188	Weyburn, Sask.	2-3-54	Vancouver	15	16	31
Woods, Paul	5:10	172	Hespeler, Ont.	4-12-55	Detroit	2	5	7
Yzerman, Steve	5:11	170	Cranbrook, B.C.	5-9-65	Detroit	39	48	87

DEFENSEMEN

Name	Hgt.	Wgt.	Place of Birth	Date	1983-84 Club	G.	A.	Pts.
Barrett, John	6:00	208	Ottawa, Ont.	7-1-58	Detroit	2	8	10
Beukeboom, John	6:02	197	Ajax, Ont.	1-1-61	Montana-Adirondack	8	28	36
Campbell, Colin	5:09	190	London, Ont.	1-28-53	Detroit	3	4	7
Chalupa, Milan	5:10	183	Oudolen, Czech.	7-4-53	Dukla Jihlava (Czech.)	3	11	14
Cloutier, Rejean	6:01	187	Windsor, Que.	2-15-60	Adirondack	9	30	39
Houda, Doug	6:02	195	Blairmore, Alta.	6-3-66	Calgary Jrs.	6	30	36
Huesing, Ted	6:01	185	Detroit, Mich.	3-23-57	Adirondack	7	31	38
Joly, Greg	6:00	190	Rocky Mt. House, Alta.	5-30-54	Adirondack	10	33	43
Korol, David	6:00	175	Winnipeg, Man.	3-1-65	Winnipeg Jrs.-Adirondack	15	52	67
Ladouceur, Randy	6:02	220	Brockville, Ont.	6-30-60	Detroit-Adirondack	6	22	28
Larson, Reed	6:00	195	Minneapolis, Minn.	7-30-56	Detroit	23	39	62
Larsson, Stefan	5:11	160	Goteborg, Sweden	6-14-65	Vasta Frolunda-Swd Nat. Jrs.	5	5	10
Melrose, Barry	6:00	205	Kelvington, Sask.	7-15-56	Detroit-Adirondack	2	2	4
Park, Brad	6:00	200	Toronto, Ont.	7-6-48	Detroit	5	53	58
Rose, Jay	6:00	181	Newton, Mass.	7-6-66	New Prep School (Mass.)	3	26	29
Smith, Greg	6:00	195	Ponoka, Alta.	7-18-55	Detroit	3	20	23
Trader, Larry	6:01	178	Barry's Bay, Ont.	7-7-63	Adirondack	13	28	41
Zombo, Rick	6:01	195	Des Plaines, Ill.	5-8-63	U. of North Dakota	7	24	31

GOALTENDERS

Name	Hgt.	Wgt.	Place of Birth	Date	1983-84 Club	Mins.	GA.	SO.
Hansch, Randy	5:10	165	Edmonton, Alta.	2-8-66	Victoria	1894	144	0
Holland, Ken	5:08	160	Vernon, B.C.	11-10-55	Adirondack-Detroit	2641	207	0
LaForest, Mark	5:10	178	Welland, Ont.	7-10-62	Adirondack-Kalamazoo	1069	77	1
Micalef, Corrado	5:08	172	Montreal, Que.	4-20-61	Detroit-Adirondack	2577	184	0
Mio, Ed	5:10	180	Windsor, Ont.	1-31-54	Detroit-Adirondack	1545	106	1
Pusey, Chris	6:00	180	Brantford, Ont.	6-20-65	Brantford	2858	158	2
Stefan, Greg	5:11	178	Brantford, Ont.	2-11-61	Detroit	2600	152	2

Edmonton Oilers
Smythe Division

Owner/Governor	Peter Pocklington
Alternate Governor	Glen Sather
General Counsels	Gary Frohlich, Bob Kinasewich
President, General Manager and Coach	Glen Sather
Assistant General Manager	Bruce MacGregor
Assistant Coaches	Ted Green, John Muckler
Director of Player Personnel/Chief Scout	Barry Fraser
Scouting Staff	Lorne Davis, Ace Bailey, Bob Freeman, Ed Chadwick
Director of A.H.L. Operations	John Blackwell
Controller	Werner Baum
Executive Secretary	Diana Hrynchuk
Director of Public Relations	Bill Tuele
Assistant Public Relations Director	Elaine Ell
Director of Marketing	Mark Hall
Community Relations and Advertising	Trish Wilson
Trainer	Barrie Stafford
Assistant Trainer	Lyle Kulchisky
Athletic Therapist	Peter Millar
Team Physician	Dr. Gordon Cameron
Home Ice	Northlands Coliseum
Address	Edmonton, Alta. T5B 4M9
Seating Capacity	17,308 (Standing 190)
Club colors	Blue, Orange and White
Phone	(403) 474-8561

Peter Pocklington

Glen Sather

Ted Green

John Muckler

Edmonton Oilers 1984-85 Roster

FORWARDS

Name	Hgt.	Wgt.	Place of Birth	Date	1983-84 Club	G.	A.	Pts.
Anderson, Glenn	5:11	185	Vancouver, B.C.	10- 2-60	Edmonton	54	45	99
Berry, Ken	5:09	170	Vancouver, B.C.	6-21-60	Edmonton-Moncton	20	23	43
Bidner, Todd	6:02	195	Petrolia, Ont.	7- 5-61	Moncton	17	16	33
Brubaker, Jeff	6:02	210	Frederick, Md.	2-24-58	Calgary-Colorado	16	19	35
Clark, Dean	6:01	185	Edmonton, Alta.	1-16-64	Kamloops-Edmonton	28	28	46
Conacher, Pat	5:09	188	Edmonton, Alta.	5- 1-59	Moncton-Edmonton	9	24	33
Cote, Ray	5:11	165	Pincher Creek, Alta.	5-31-61	Edmonton-Moncton	26	36	62
Curtis, Joel	6:01	181	Montreal, Que.	1-13-66	Oshawa	8	12	20
Dachyshyn, Dean	6:01	195	West Bank, B.C.	5- 4-59	Moncton	9	7	16
Derkatch, Dale	5:05	140	Preeceville, Sask.	10-17-64	Regina	72	87	159
Ewen, Todd	6:02	183	Saskatoon, Sask.	3-26-66	New Westminster	11	13	24
Golden, Mike	6:01	190	Boston, Mass.	6-17-65	Stratford Jr. B.	20	38	58
Graves, Steve	5:10	180	Kingston, Ont.	4- 7-64	Sault Ste. Marie-Edmonton	41	48	89
Gretzky, Wayne	6:00	170	Brantford, Ont.	1-26-61	Edmonton	87	118	205
Habscheid, Marc	6:00	180	Swift Current, Sask.	3- 1-63	Edmonton-Moncton	20	37	57
Houck, Paul	6:00	185	Vancouver, B.C.	8-12-63	Univ. of Wisconsin	20	20	40
Hughes, Pat	6:00	190	Calgary, Alta.	3-25-55	Edmonton	27	28	55
Hunter, Dave	6:00	200	Petrolia, Ont.	1- 1-58	Edmonton	22	26	48
Jalo, Risto	5:11	185	Tampere, Finland	7-18-62	Tampere-Ilves	13	32	45
Krensing, Mike	6:01	185	Ely, Minn.	8- 7-61	Milwaukee-Muskegon	49	30	79
Kurri, Jari	6:00	187	Helsinki, Finland	5-18-60	Edmonton	52	61	113
Kyle, Doug	5:11	190	Regina, Sask.	5-15-63	Saskatoon	56	59	115
Lindstrom, Willy	6:01	180	Grunns, Sweden	5- 5-51	Edmonton	22	16	38
Lumley, Dave	5:11	180	Toronto, Ont.	9- 1-54	Edmonton	6	15	21
McClelland, Kevin	6:00	180	Oshawa, Ont.	7- 4-62	Pittsburgh-Baltimore-Edmonton	11	25	36
Messier, Mark	6:01	205	Edmonton, Alta.	1-18-61	Edmonton	37	64	101
Molle, Tim					Moncton	0	0	0
Pouzar, Jaroslav	6:00	200	Cakovec, Czech.	1-23-52	Edmonton	13	19	32
Rowe, Tom	6:00	190	Lynn, Mass.	5-23-56	Moncton	28	16	44
Semenko, Dave	6:03	213	Winnipeg, Man.	7-12-57	Edmonton	6	11	17
Sherven, Gord	6:00	185	Gravelbourg, Sask.	8-21-63	Can. Oly-U of N. Dak.-Edm.	15	18	33
Strueby, Todd	6:01	186	Lannigan, Sask.	6-15-63	Moncton-Edmonton	17	26	43
Summanen, Raimo	5:11	185	Jyvaskyla, Finland	3- 2-62	Tampere-Ilves-Finn. Oly-Edm.	33	30	63
Tikkanen, Esa	5:11	181	Helsinki, Finland	11-25-65	IFK Helsinki, Finland	19	11	30
Wheeldon, Simon	5:11	175	Vancouver, B.C.	8-30-66	Victoria	14	24	38

DEFENSEMEN

Name	Hgt.	Wgt.	Place of Birth	Date	1983-84 Club	G.	A.	Pts.
Beukeboom, Jeff	6:04	210	Ajax, Ont.	3-28-65	Sault Ste. Marie	6	30	36
Bilodeau, Joe	6:01	190	Edmonton, Alta.	10-19-62	Mohawk Valley	4	21	25
Boettger, Dwayne	6:00	190	Brampton, Ont.	2- 6-63	Moncton	1	18	19
Coffey, Paul	6:00	200	Weston, Ont.	6- 1-61	Edmonton	40	86	126
Fogolin, Lee	6:00	200	Chicago, Ill.	2-15-55	Edmonton	5	16	21
Gani, Darren	6:00	181	Perth, Australia	11- 2-65	Belleville	16	40	56
Gregg, Randy	6:04	212	Edmonton, Alta.	2-19-56	Edmonton	13	27	40
Huddy, Charlie	6:00	200	Oshawa, Ont.	6- 2-59	Edmonton	8	34	42
Jackson, Don	6:03	210	Minneapolis, Minn.	9- 2-56	Edmonton	8	12	20
Loveday, Lowell	6:00	200	Simcoe, Ont.	7-30-59	Moncton	7	21	28
Lowe, Kevin	6:01	195	Lachute, Que.	4-15-59	Edmonton	4	42	46
Melnyk, Larry	6:00	180	New Westminster, B.C.	2-21-60	Hershey-Moncton	0	21	21
Miner, John	5:10	180	Moose Jaw, Sask.	8-28-65	Regina	27	42	69
Odelein, Selmar	6:00	195	Quill Lake, Sask.	4-11-66	Regina	9	42	51
Playfair, Jim	6:03	200	Vanderhoof, B.C.	5-22-64	Calary	11	15	26
Smith, Steve	6:02	200	Glasgow, Scotland	4-30-63	Moncton	1	8	9
Viveiros, Emanuel	5:11	160	St. Albert, Alta.	1- 8-66	Prince Albert	15	94	109

GOALTENDERS

Name	Hgt.	Wgt.	Place of Birth	Date	1983-84 Club	Mins.	GA.	SO.
Fuhr, Grant	5:10	185	Spruce Grove, Alta.	9-28-62	Edmonton	2625	171	1
Moog, Andy	5:09	170	Penticton, B.C.	2-18-60	Edmonton	2212	139	1
Reaugh, Daryl	6:04	200	Prince George, B.C.	2-13-65	Kamloops	2748	199	1
Smith, Chris	5:10	180	Ajax, Ont.	2- 6-62	Moncton	2243	130	0
Wood, Ian	5:10	160	Rotheram, England	2-10-64	Portland	2049	207	0
Zanier, Mike	5:11	183	Trail, B.C.	8-22-62	Moncton	1732	96	0

Hartford Whalers
Adams Division

Managing General Partner, Chairman and Governor	Howard L. Baldwin
President, G.M. and Alternate Govenor	Emile Francis
Alternate Governor	Donald G. Conrad
Coach	Jack Evans
Director of Hockey Administration	Bob Crocker
Special Assistant to Managing General Partner	Gordie Howe
Assistant Coach	Claude Larose
Director of Player Personnel	Steve Brklacich
Scouts	John Cunniff, David McNab, Leo Boivin
Trainer	Tommy Woodcock
Equipment Manager	Skip Cunningham
Director of Marketing	William E. Barnes
Assistant to Managing General Partner	Camille Beck
Treasurer	Robert L. Kelly
Controller	Michael J. Amendola
Director of Public Relations	Phil Langar
Assistant Director of Public Relations	Jeanne Dennis
Chief Statistician	Frank Polnaszek
Home Ice	Hartford Civic Center
Address	One Civic Center Plaza, Hartford, Conn. 06103
Seating Capacity	14,800
Club colors	Blue, Green and White
Phone	(203) 728-3366

Howard Baldwin

Emile Francis

Bob Crocker

Jack Evans

Hartford Whalers 1984-85 Roster

FORWARDS

Name	Hgt.	Wgt.	Place of Birth	Date	1983-84 Club	G.	A.	Pts.
Bourbonnais, Dan	5:10	185	Winnipeg, Man.	3-6-62	Hartford-Binghamton	16	48	64
Crawford, Bob	5:11	177	Belleville, Ont.	4-6-59	Hartford	36	25	61
Crombeen, Mike	5:11	192	Sarnia, Ont.	4-16-57	Hartford	1	4	5
Currie, Tony	5:11	165	Sydney Mines, N.S.	11-21-57	Vancouver-Hartford	15	19	34
Dineen, Kevin	5:10	185	Toronto, Ont.	10-28-63	Can. Olympic Team	5	11	16
Fenton, Paul	5:11	180	Springfield, Mass.	12-22-59	Binghamton	41	24	65
Ferraro, Ray	5:10	160	Trail, B.C.	8-23-64	Brandon	108	84	192
Francis, Ron	6:02	195	Sault Ste Marie, Ont.	3-1-63	Hartford	23	60	83
Fridgen, Dan	5:11	175	Arnprior, Ont.	5-18-59	Binghamton	23	27	50
Gilhen, Randy	5:10	190	Zweibrucken, W. Ger.	6-13-63	Binghamton	3	21	24
Hoffman, Mike	5:11	190	Cambridge, Ont.	2-26-63	Binghamton	11	13	24
Jensen, David A.	6:01	180	Needham, Mass.	8-19-65	U.S. Olympic Team	27	59	86
Johnson, Mark	5:09	160	Minneapolis, Minn.	9-22-57	Hartford	35	52	87
Lawless, Paul	5:11	180	Scarboro, Ont.	7-2-64	Hartford-Windsor	31	52	83
Loney, Brent	6:00	170	Cornwall, Ont.	5-25-64	Cornwall	24	38	62
MacDermid, Paul	6:01	200	Chesley, Ont.	4-14-63	Hartford-Binghamton	31	30	61
Malone, Greg	6:00	190	Chatham, N.B.	3-8-56	Hartford	17	37	54
Monleon, Robin	6:01	200	Tyngsboro, Mass.	12-26-61	Boston College	..	..	..
Neufeld, Ray	6:03	210	St. Boniface, Man.	4-15-59	Hartford	27	42	69
Pierce, Randy	5:11	185	Arnprior, Ont.	11-23-57	Hartford-Binghamton	27	27	54
Robertson, Torrie	5:11	185	Victoria, B.C.	8-2-61	Hartford	7	13	20
Stoyanovich, Steve	6:02	205	London, Ont.	5-2-57	Binghamton-Hartford	14	13	27
Tippett, Dave	5:10	175	Moosomin, Sask.	8-25-61	Can. Olympic-Hartford	16	20	36
Turgeon, Sylvain	6:00	190	Noranda, Que.	1-17-65	Hartford	40	32	72
Zuke, Mike	6:00	180	Sault Ste Marie, Ont.	4-16-54	Hartford	6	23	29

DEFENSEMEN

Name	Hgt.	Wgt.	Place of Birth	Date	1983-84 Club	G.	A.	Pts.
Brownschidle, Jack	6:02	195	Buffalo, N.Y.	10-2-55	St. Louis-Hartford	3	9	12
Connolly, Tom	6:00	197	Quincy, Mass.	1-10-62	Boston University	3	17	20
Cote, Sylvain	6:00	170	Quebec City, Que.	1-19-66	Quebec	15	50	65
Cronin, Tom	6:00	195	Melrose, Mass.	9-9-60	Binghamton	2	12	14
Dunn, Richie	6:00	195	Boston, Mass.	5-12-57	Hartford	5	20	25
Fusco, Mark	5:09	175	Burlington, Mass.	3-12-61	U.S. Olympic-Hartford	4	28	32
Howe, Marty	6:01	195	Detroit, Mich.	2-18-54	Hartford	0	11	11
Kleinendorst, Scot	6:03	205	Grand Rapids, Minn.	1-16-60	Tulsa-New York Rangers	4	7	11
Kotsopolous, Chris	6:03	215	Scarborough, Ont.	11-27-58	Hartford	5	13	18
Mokosak, John	5:11	200	Edmonton, Alta.	9-7-63	Binghamton	3	21	24
Paterson, Mark	5:11	180	Ottawa, Ont.	2-22-64	Hartford-Ottawa	10	16	26
Quenneville, Joel	6:00	190	Windsor, Ont.	9-15-58	Hartford	5	8	13
Siltanen, Risto	5:09	180	Manta, Finland	10-31-58	Hartford	15	38	53
Shaw, Brad	5:10	170	Cambridge, Ont.	4-28-64	Ottawa	11	71	82
Sameulson, Ulf	6:01	195	Leksand, Sweden	3-26-64	Leksand, Sweden	5	10	15

GOALTENDERS

Name	Hgt.	Wgt.	Place of Birth	Date	1983-84 Club	Mins.	GA.	SO.
Abrick, Pete	6:01	173	Scarborough, Ont.	7-16-65	North Bay	2556	180	0
Fricker, Paul	6:01	190	Westlock, Alta.	10-20-60	Binghamton	1731	149	0
Millen, Greg	5:09	175	Toronto, Ont.	6-25-57	Hartford	3575	1817	2
Poeschl, Jeff	5:11	160	St. Paul, Minn.	1-29-62	Northern Michigan University	..	..	..
Staniowski, Ed	5:09	170	Moose Jaw, Sask.	7-7-55	Winnipeg-Hartford	1081	82	0
Weicker, Gray	6:03	195	Greenwich, Conn.	10-14-60	Mohawk Valley-Binghamton	2165	183	0

Los Angeles Kings
Smythe Division

Owner	Dr. Jerry Buss
President	George Maguire
Alternate Governors	George Maguire, Ken Doi
General Manager	Rogie Vachon
Coach	Pat Quinn
Assistant Coach	Mike Murphy
Administrative Assistant	John Wolf
Head Scout	Ted O'Connor
Scouting Staff	Ross Tyrell, Alex Smart, Skip Schamehorn, Jim Anderson, Doug Woog, Don Perry, Bob Owen
Director of Public Relations	Larry Rosoff
Trainer	Pete Demers
Assistant Trainer	Mark O'Neill
Home Ice	The Forum
Address	3900 West Manchester Blvd., P. O. Box 10, The Forum, Inglewood, Calif. 90306
Seating Capacity	16,005
Club Colors	Purple and Gold
Phone	(213) 674-6000

Dr. Jerry Buss

George Maguire

Rogie Vachon

Pat Quinn

Los Angeles Kings 1984-85 Roster

FORWARDS

Name	Hgt.	Wgt.	Place of Birth	Date	1983-84 Club	G.	A.	Pts.
Benoit, Guy	5:10	187	St. Hyacinthe, Que.	6-18-65	Drummondville	26	56	82
Blaha, Jan	5:10	175	Czechoslovakia	3- 3-65	Kladno	..	..	..
Brennan, Dan	6:03	215	Dawson Creek, B.C.	10- 1-60	University of North Dakota	28	37	65
Christoff, Steve	6:01	180	Springfield, Ill.	1-23-58	Los Angeles	8	7	15
Crossman, Jeff	6:00	200	Toronto, Ont.	12- 3-64	Western Michigan	9	12	21
Dallman, Marty	5:10	181	Niagara Falls, Ont.	2- 5-63	RPI	30	24	54
Delgan, Shannon	6:02	190	Montreal, Que.	3-19-66	University of Vermont	5	5	10
Dionne, Marcel	5:08	185	Drummondville, Que.	8- 3-51	Los Angeles	39	53	92
Evans, Daryl	5:08	185	Toronto, Ont.	1-12-61	New Haven-Los Angeles	51	36	87
Fishback, Bruce	6:01	185	White Bear Lake, Mich.	1-19-65	U. Minnesota-Duluth	2	2	4
Fox, Jim	5:08	175	Coniston, Ont.	5-18-60	Los Angeles	30	42	72
Gans, Dave	5:11	185	Brantford, Ont.	6- 6-64	Oshawa	56	76	132
Glavine, Tom	6:00	170	Concord, Mass.	3-25-66	Billerica H.S.	47	47	94
Grannis, Dave	6:00	190	St. Paul, Minn.	1-18-66	S. St. Paul H.S.	20	23	43
Hakansson, Anders	6:02	191	Munkfors, Sweden	4-27-56	Los Angeles	15	17	32
Hanley, Tim	6:00	200	Greenfield, Mass.	10-10-64	Deerfield Academy	18	25	43
Hopkins, Dean	6:01	210	Cobourg, Ont.	6- 6-59	New Haven	35	47	82
Johnson, Chad	6:01	175	Roseau, Minn.	12-12-64	University of Chicago-Illinois	7	5	12
Kelly, John Paul	6:01	215	Edmonton, Alta.	11-15-59	Los Angeles	7	14	21
Lofthouse, Mark	6:01	185	New Westminster, B.C.	4-21-57	New Haven	37	64	101
MacLellan, Brian	6:03	212	Guelph, Ont.	10-27-58	New Haven-Los Angeles	25	31	56
Martin, Brian	6:00	180	St. Catharines, Ont.	3-27-66	Belleville	21	41	62
Mokosak, Carl	6:01	200	Ft. Saskatchewan, Alta.	9-22-64	New Haven	18	21	39
Nicholls, Bernie	6:00	185	Haliburton, Ont.	6-24-61	Los Angeles	41	54	95
O'Dwyer, Bill	6:00	190	S. Boston, Mass.	1-25-60	New Haven-Los Angeles	15	42	57
Robitaille, Luc	6:01	188	Montreal, Queb.	2-17-66	Hull	32	53	85
Roy, Darcy	5:11	190	Halleybury, Ont.	5-10-64	Ottawa	21	41	62
Ruskowski, Terry	5:09	180	Prince Albert, Sask.	12-31-54	Los Angeles	7	25	32
Seguin, Steve	6:02	198	Cornwall, Ont.	4-10-64	Peterborough	55	51	106
Shero, Ray	5:10	185	Hartsdale, N.Y.	7-28-62	St. Lawrence	15	27	42
Simmer, Charlie	6:03	210	Terrace Bay, Ont.	3-20-54	Los Angeles	44	48	92
Smith, Doug	5:11	178	Ottawa, Ont.	5-17-63	Los Angeles	16	20	36
Sykes, Phil	5:10	180	Dawson Creek, B.C.	3-18-59	New Haven-Los Angeles	29	37	66
Taylor, Dave	6:00	195	Levack, Ont.	12- 4-55	Los Angeles	20	29	49
Wilks, Brian	5:11	175	North York, Ont.	2-27-66	Kitchener	21	54	75

DEFENSEMEN

Name	Hgt.	Wgt.	Place of Birth	Date	1983-84 Club	G.	A.	Pts.
Anderson, Russ	6:02	200	Des Moines, Iowa	3- 8-59	Los Angeles	5	12	17
Burgess, Tim	5:11	185	Ottawa, Ont.	1-25-65	Windsor	3	6	9
Chartier, Dave	5:11	180	Saskatoon, Sask.	3-16-54	Saskatoon	9	21	30
Engblom, Brian	6:02	200	Winnipeg, Man.	1-27-55	Washington-Los Angeles	2	28	30
English, John	6:02	190	Toronto, Ont.	5-13-66	Sault Ste Marie	6	11	17
Galley, Gary	5:11	190	Ottawa, Ont.	4-16-63	Bowling Green St.	15	52	67
Hammond, Ken	6:01	190	Point Credit, Ont.	8-22-63	RPI	5	11	16
Hardy, Mark	5:11	187	Semaden, Switzerland	2- 1-59	Los Angeles	8	41	49
Heidt, Mike	6:01	196	Calgary, Alta.	11- 4-63	New Haven-Los Angeles	4	20	24
Kennedy, Dean	6:02	200	Redvers, Sask.	1-18-63	New Haven-Los Angeles	2	12	14
Lundmark, Dave	6:00	190	Virginia, Minn.	2-14-65	Kingston	2	9	11
Redmond, Craig	5:10	190	Dawson Creek, B.C.	9-22-65	Team Canada	12	11	23
Sawkins, Peter	6:03	190	Skagen, Denmark	8-29-63	Yale University	2	14	16
Scruton, Howard	6:03	195	Toronto, Ont.	4-10-62	New Haven	1	4	5
Shoebottom, Bruce	6:02	200	Mississauga, Ont.	8-20-63	Peterborough	0	5	5
Tuer, Allan	6:00	195	N. Battleford, Sask.	7-19-63	New Haven	0	20	20
Wells, Jay	6:01	205	Paris, Ont.	5-18-59	Los Angeles	3	18	21

GOALTENDERS

Name	Hgt.	Wgt.	Place of Birth	Date	1983-84 Club	Mins.	GA.	SO.
Blake, Mike	6:01	190	Kitchener, Ont.	6- 6-56	Los Angeles-New Haven	2498	182	0
Eliot, Darren	6:01	175	Milton, Ont.	11-26-61	Team Canada-New Haven	1890	128	0
Franzosa, John	5:07	175	Reading, Mass.	3- 3-63	Brown University	752	54	0
Janecyk, Bob	6:01	180	Chicago, Ill.	5-18-57	Chicago-Springfield	2076	122	0
Kenny, Paul	6:03	195	St. John's, Nfld.	3-30-65	Cornwall	2101	163	1
Laskoski, Gary	6:01	175	Ottawa, Ont.	6- 6-59	Los Angeles-New Haven	1845	152	0
Ross, Dave	6:00	175	Victoria, B.C.	5-29-62	New Haven-Ft. Wayne-Kala.	1201	102	0
Strome, Greg	5:09	160	Muenster, Sask.	7-18-65	University of North Dakota	80	7	0

Minnesota North Stars

Norris Division

Co-Chairmen of the Board	George Gund III and Gordon Gund
President	John Karr
Vice-President	Walter Bush, Jr.
Vice-President, General Manager	Lou Nanne
Vice-President of Finance	George Wettstaedt
Assistant General Manager	John Mariucci
Director of Player Development	Glen Sonmor
Coach	Bill Mahoney
Assistant Coaches	Murray Oliver, J.P. Parise
Chief Scout	Harry Howell
Special Assignment Scout	Dick Bouchard
Director of Hockey Information	Dick Dillman
Scouts	George Agar, Gump Worsley
Trainer	Dick Rose
Assistant Trainer	Larry Ness
Home Ice	Metropolitan Sports Center
Address	7901 Cedar Avenue S., Bloomington, Minn. 55420
Seating Capacity	15,184
Club colors	Green, White, Gold and Black
Phone	(612) 853-9333

George Gund III

Gordon Gund

Lou Nanne

Bill Mahoney

Minnesota North Stars 1984-85 Roster

FORWARDS

Name	Hgt.	Wgt.	Place of Birth	Date	1983-84 Club	G.	A.	Pts.
Acton, Keith	5:08	170	Stouffville, Ont.	4-15-58	Montreal-Minnesota	20	45	65
Ashton, Brent	6:01	210	Saskatoon, Sask.	5-18-60	Minnesota	7	10	17
Bellows, Brian	5:11	195	St. Catharines, Ont.	9-1-64	Minnesota	41	42	83
Biggs, Don	5:08	178	Mississauga, Ont.	4-7-65	Oshawa	31	60	91
Bjugstad, Scott	6:01	175	St. Paul, Minn.	6-2-61	Minnesota-Salt Lake	10	8	18
Broten, Neal	5:09	160	Roseau, Minn.	11-29-59	Minnesota	28	61	89
Ciccarelli, Dino	5:10	180	Sarnia, Ont.	2-8-60	Minnesota	38	33	71
Coulis, Tim	6:00	200	Kenora, Ont.	2-24-58	Minnesota-Salt Lake	25	35	60
Ferguson, George	6:00	195	Trenton, Ont.	8-22-52	Minnesota	6	10	16
Friest, Ron	5:11	185	Windsor, Ont.	11-4-58	Minnesota	..	..	..
Graham, Dirk	5:11	190	Regina, Sask.	7-29-59	Minnesota-Salt Lake	38	58	96
Holmgren, Paul	6:03	210	St. Paul, Minn.	12-2-55	Philadelphia-Minnesota	11	18	29
Lakso, Bob	5:11	180	Aurora, Minn.	4-3-62	U of Minnesota-Duluth	20	18	38
Lawton, Brian	6:00	180	New Brunswick, N.J.	6-29-65	Minnesota	10	21	31
Maruk, Dennis	5:08	165	Toronto, Ont.	11-17-55	Minnesota	17	43	60
McCarthy, Tom	6:02	197	Toronto, Ont.	7-31-60	Minnesota	39	31	70
Napier, Mark	5:10	185	Toronto, Ont.	1-28-57	Montreal-Minnesota	16	30	46
Payne, Steve	6:02	210	Toronto, Ont.	8-16-58	Minnesota	28	31	59
Plett, Willi	6:03	205	Paraguay, S. America	6-7-55	Minnesota	15	23	38
Poner, Jiri	6:02	175	Czechoslovakia		Landshut, West Germany	..	..	..
Solheim, Ken	6:03	210	Hythe, Alta.	3-27-61	Adirondack	..	..	..
Stewart, Bill	6:00	180	The Pas, Man.	7-12-61	Salt Lake	23	27	50
Tait, Terry	6:02	205	Thunder Bay, Ont.	9-10-63	Salt Lake-Toledo	1	7	8

DEFENSEMEN

Name	Hgt.	Wgt.	Place of Birth	Date	1983-84 Club	G.	A.	Pts.
Giles, Curt	5:08	180	The Pas, Man.	11-30-58	Minnesota	6	22	28
Hartsburg, Craig	6:01	200	Stratford, Ont.	6-29-59	Minnesota	7	7	14
Hirsch, Tom	6:04	210	Minneapolis, Minn.	1-27-63	Minnesota	1	3	4
Jensen, David	6:01	190	Minneapolis, Minn.	5-3-61	Salt Lake-Minnesota	0	8	8
Levie, Craig	5:11	190	Calgary, Alta.	8-17-59	Salt Lake-Minnesota	14	33	47
Maly, Miroslav	6:02	190	West Germany	4-10-63	Bayreuth, W. Germany	..	..	..
Mandich, Dan	6:03	205	Brantford, Ont.	6-12-60	Minnesota-Salt Lake	4	9	13
Maxwell, Brad	6:02	195	Brandon, Man.	7-8-57	Minnesota	19	54	73
Pryor, Chris	6:00	200	St. Paul, Minn.	1-23-61	Salt Lake	7	21	28
Richter, Dave	6:05	217	Winnipeg, Man.	4-8-60	Minnesota-Salt Lake	3	7	10
Roberts, Gordie	6:00	193	Detroit, Mich.	10-2-57	Minnesota	8	45	53
Rouse, Bob	6:02	215	Surrey, B.C.	6-18-64	Lethbridge	18	42	60
Snepsts, Harold	6:03	215	Edmonton, Alta.	10-24-54	Vancouver	4	16	20
Velischek, Randy	6:01	200	Montreal, Que.	2-10-62	Salt Lake-Minnesota	9	23	32

GOALTENDERS

Name	Hgt.	Wgt.	Place of Birth	Date	1983-84 Club	Mins.	GA.	SO.
Beaupre, Don	5:08	149	Kitchener, Ont.	9-19-61	Minnesota-Salt Lake	2210	153	0
Casey, Jon	5:10	155	Grand Rapids, Minn.	3-29-62	North Dakota	2180	114	2
Komonosky, Ward	6:01	194	Saskatoon, Sask.	12-3-64	Prince Albert	2521	207	1
Meloche, Gilles	5:09	185	Montreal, Que.	7-12-50	Minnesota	2883	201	2
Molleken, Lorne	6:01	190	Regina, Sask.	6-11-56	Toledo	3345	196	1
Sands, Mike	5:09	146	Sudbury, Ont.	4-6-63	Salt Lake	1145	93	0
Takko, Kari	6:00	178	Pori, Finland	6-23-62	Assat, Finland	...	..	..

Montreal Canadiens
Adams Division

President	Ronald Corey
Managing Director	Serge Savard
Senior Vice-President, Corporate Affairs	Jean Beliveau
Special Ambassador	Maurice Richard
Senior Vice-President, Operations and Special Events	Gerry Grundman
Vice-President, Finance and Administration	Fred Steer
Vice-President, Marketing	Francois-Xavier Seigneur
Coach	Jacques Lemaire
Assistant Coaches	Jacques Laperriere, Jean Perron
Special goaltending coach	Jacques Plante
Director of Player Development	Claude Ruel
Director of Scouting	Andre Boudrias
Chief Scout	Doug Robinson
Director of Special Events	Camil DesRoches
Director of Advertising Sales	Floyd Curry
Director of Public Relations	Claude Mouton
Director of Publicity	Yvon Robert
Club Physician	Dr. D.G. Kinnear
Trainer	Eddy Palchak
Assistant Trainers	Gaetan Lefevre, Sylvain Toupin
Home Ice	Montreal Forum
Address	2313 St. Catherine Street West, Montreal, Que. H3H 1N2
Seating capacity	16,074
Club colors	Red, White and Blue
Phone	(514) 932-2582

Ronald Corey

Serge Savard

Jacques Lemaire

Montreal Canadiens 1984-85 Roster

FORWARDS

Name	Hgt.	Wgt.	Place of Birth	Date	1983-84 Club	G.	A.	Pts.
Baron, Normand	6:00	205	Verdun, Que.	12-15-57	Nova Scotia-Montreal	11	11	22
Carbonneau, Guy	5:11	177	Sept-Iles, Que.	3-18-60	Montreal	24	30	54
Chabot, John	6:02	197	Summerside, P.E.I.	5-18-62	Montreal	18	25	43
Corson, Shayne	6:00	175	Barrie, Ont.	8-13-66	Brantford	25	46	71
DeBlois, Lucien	5:11	200	Joliette, Que.	6-21-57	Winnipeg	34	45	79
Francis, Todd	6:00	217	Kitchener, Ont.	1- 8-65	Brantford	13	33	46
Gainey, Bob	6:01	200	Peterborough, Ont.	12-13-53	Montreal	17	22	39
Heroux, Alain	6:01	180	Terrebonne, Que.	5-20-64	Chicoutimi-Nova Scotia	32	43	75
Hunter, Mark	6:00	203	Petrolia, Ont.	11-12-62	Montreal	6	4	10
Kolioupoulos, Tom	6:01	185	Detroit, Mich.	2-10-64	Verdun	16	15	31
Lafleur, Guy	6:00	185	Thurso, Que.	9-20-51	Montreal	30	40	70
Landon, Larry	6:00	191	Niagara Falls, Ont.	5- 4-58	Nova Scotia-Montreal	26	30	56
Lemieux, Claude	6:00	215	Buckingham, Que.	7-16-65	Verdun-Montreal	42	46	88
Letendre, Daniel	6:01	200	Sorel, Que.	1-21-65	Quebec Jrs.	25	41	66
McPhee, Mike	6:02	205	Sydney, N.S.	2-14-60	Nova Scotia-Montreal	27	35	62
Momesso, Sergio	6:03	202	Montreal, Que.	9- 4-65	Shawinigan-Montreal	42	88	130
Mondou, Pierre	5:10	186	Sorel, Que.	11-27-55	Montreal	15	22	37
Naslund, Mats	5:07	156	Timra, Sweden	10-31-59	Montreal	29	35	64
Nesich, Jim	5:11	161	Dearborn, Michigan	2-22-66	Verdun	22	24	46
Newberry, John	6:00	195	Port Alberni, B.C.	4- 8-62	Nova Scotia-Montreal	25	37	62
Nilan, Chris	6:00	206	Boston, Mass.	2- 9-58	Montreal	16	10	26
Richer, Stephane	6:00	190	Buckingham, Que.	6- 7-66	Granby	39	37	76
Rundqvist, Per Thomas	6:03	194		5- 4-60	Farjestad BK	13	22	35
Shutt, Steve	5:11	185	Toronto, Ont.	7- 1-52	Montreal	14	23	37
Skrudland, Brian	6:00	180	Peace River, Alta.	7-31-63	Nova Scotia	13	12	25
Smith, Bobby	6:04	210	North Sydney, N.S.	2-12-58	Minnesota-Montreal	29	43	72
Teal, Jeffrey	6:03	206	Edina, Minn.	5-30-60	Nova Scotia	8	4	12
Tremblay, Mario	6:00	190	Alma, Que.	9- 2-56	Montreal	14	25	39
Turcotte, Alfie	5:09	180	Gary, Indiana	1- 5-65	Port. Winter Hawks-Mont.	29	48	77
Walter, Ryan	6:00	193	New Westminster, B.C.	4-23-58	Montreal	20	29	49

DEFENSEMEN

Name	Hgt.	Wgt.	Place of Birth	Date	1983-84 Club	G.	A.	Pts.
Annear, Ron	6:02	195	Montague, P.E.I.	4-28-65	San Diego University	..	..	..
Allison, Dave	6:01	200	Fort Frances, Ont.	4-14-59	Nova Scotia-Montreal	2	18	20
Bergeron, Jean-Guy	5:11	196	Montreal, Que.	4-14-65	St. Jean	9	34	43
Carlson, Kent	6:03	210	Concord, N.H.	1-11-62	Montreal	3	7	10
Chelios, Chris	6:01	190	Chicago, Ill.	1-25-62	Montreal	0	2	2
Gauvreau, Jocelyn	5:11	190	Masham, Que.	3- 4-64	Granby-Nova Scotia-Montreal	19	40	59
Green, Rick	6:03	220	Belleville, Ont.	2-20-56	Montreal	0	1	1
Hamel, Jean	5:11	195	Asbestos, Que.	6- 6-52	Montreal	1	12	13
Kordic, John	6:01	188	Edmonton, Alta.	3-22-65	Portland	9	50	59
Kurvers, Tom	6:00	190	Minneapolis, Minn.	10-14-62	U. of Minnesota-Duluth	11	34	45
Ludwig, Craig	6:03	210	Eagle River, Wis.	3-15-61	Montreal	7	18	25
MacTavish, Scott	6:03	200	Fredericton, N.B.	1-25-66	Fredericton High School	..	..	..
Nattress, Ric	6:03	210	Hamilton, Ont.	5-25-62	Montreal	0	12	12
Robinson, Larry	6:03	218	Winchester, Ont.	6- 2-51	Montreal	9	34	43
Root, Bill	6:00	208	Toronto, Ont.	9- 6-59	Montreal	4	13	17
Svoboda, Petr	6:01	174	Most, Czechoslovakia	2-14-66	Czechoslovakia Jr.	15	21	36

GOALTENDERS

Name	Hgt.	Wgt.	Place of Birth	Date	1983-84 Club	Mins.	GA.	SO.
Burrows, Dan	6:02	205	Toronto, Ont.	3-15-63	Flint	238	19	0
Crosby, Troy	6:00	170	Halifax, N.S.	9-11-66	Verdun	1863	125	1
Holden, Mark	5:10	165	Weymouth, Mass.	6-12-57	Nova Scotia-Montreal	2791	157	0
Moffett, Greg	5:11	175	Bath, Me.	4- 1-59	Nova Scotia	493	35	0
Penney, Steve	6:01	190	Ste. Foy, Que.	2- 2-61	Nova Scotia-Montreal	1811	111	0
Roy, Patrick	6:00	164	Quebec, Que.	10- 5-65	Granby	3585	265	0

New Jersey Devils
Patrick Division

Chairman	John J. McMullen
President	Robert J. Butera
Vice President, Hockey Operations and G.M.	Max McNab
Vice President, Finance	Larry Merse
Vice President, Sales and Marketing	Peter Gladstone
Coach	Doug Carpenter
Assistant Coach	Lou Vairo
Director of Player Personnel	Marshall Johnston
Scouts	To be announced
Athletic Trainer	Chris Ipson
Director of Public Relations	Larry Brooks
Assistant Director of Public Relations	David Freed
Executive Offices	Byrne Meadowlands Arena
Home Ice	Byrne Meadowlands Arena
Address	Meadowlands Arena, P.O. Box 504, East Rutherford, N.J. 07073
Seating Capacity	19,023
Club Colors	Red, Green and White
Phone	(201) 935-6050

John McMullen

Robert Butera

Max McNab

Doug Carpenter

New Jersey Devils 1984-85 Roster

FORWARDS

Name	Hgt.	Wgt.	Place of Birth	Date	1983-84 Club	G.	A.	Pts.
Adams, Greg	6:02	185	Nelson, B.C.	8- 1-63	No. Arizona U.	40	50	90
Antonovich, Mike	5:06	155	Calumet, Minn.	10-18-51	New Jersey-Maine	20	18	38
Army, Tim	6:00	175	Providence, R.I.	4-26-63	Providence College	20	26	46
Bridgman, Mel	6:00	190	Trenton, Ont.	4-28-55	New Jersey	19	31	50
Broten, Aaron	5:10	175	Roseau, Minn.	11-14-60	New Jersey	13	23	36
Cameron, Dave	6:00	185	Charlottetown, P.E.I.	7-29-58	New Jersey	9	12	21
Chernomaz, Rich	5:09	175	Selkirk, Man.	9- 1-63	Maine-New Jersey	19	30	49
Dorian, Dan	5:09	175	Astoria, N.Y.	3- 2-63	Western Michigan Univ.	40	44	84
Evtushevski, Greg	5:08	180	St. Paul, Alta.	5- 4-65	Kamloops	27	43	70
Floyd, Larry	5:08	180	Peterborough, Ont.	5- 1-61	Maine-New Jersey	38	52	90
Fulcher, Paul	5:11	185	Sarnia, Ont.	12-26-62	Muskegon	24	37	61
Gagne, Paul	5:10	180	Iroquois Falls, Ont.	2- 6-62	New Jersey	14	18	32
Gilliard, Tony	6:00	195	Strathroy, Ont.	1-21-63	Muskegon	5	16	21
Higgins, Tim	6:01	185	Ottawa, Ont.	2- 7-58	New Jersey-Chicago	19	14	33
Johannson, John	6:01	175	Rochester, Minn.	10-18-61	Univ. of Wisconsin-New Jersey	21	25	46
Lekun, Mike	5:09	190	Sudbury, Ont.	2-26-63	Maine	12	9	21
Lever, Don	5:11	185	South Porcupine, Ont.	11-14-52	New Jersey	14	19	33
Ludvig, Jan	5:10	190	Liberec, Czech.	9-17-61	New Jersey	22	32	54
MacLean, John	6:00	195	Oshawa, Ont.	11-20-64	Oshawa-New Jersey	24	36	60
Marini, Hector	6:01	200	Timmins, Ont.	1-27-57	New Jersey-Maine	9	6	15
Maxwell, Kevin	5:09	165	Edmonton, Alta.	3-30-60	Maine-New Jersey	21	30	51
McAdam, Gary	5:11	175	Smith Falls, Ont.	12-31-55	Maine-Wash.-New Jersey	13	15	28
Meagher, Rick	5:08	175	Belleville, Ont.	11- 4-53	New Jersey-Maine	20	18	38
Merkosky, Glenn	5:10	175	Edmonton, Alta.	4- 8-60	Maine-New Jersey	29	28	57
Morris, Jon	6:00	165	Lowell, Mass.	5- 6-66	Chelmsford H.S. (Mass.)	31	50	81
Muller, Kirk	5:11	186	Kingston, Ont.	2- 8-66	Guelph-Team Canada	35	66	101
Mulvey, Grant	6:04	200	Sudbury, Ont.	9-17-56	Maine-New Jersey	7	10	17
Preston, Rich	5:11	190	Regina, Sask.	5-22-52	Chicago	10	18	28
Shaw, Brent	5:11	180	Vancouver, B.C.	6-24-62	Muskegon-Maine	22	18	40
Sommer, Roy	6:00	180	Oakland, Calif.	4- 5-57	Maine	7	10	17
Stewart, Al	5:11	175	Fort St. John, B.C.	1-31-64	Prince Albert	44	39	83
Sulliman, Doug	5:09	195	Glace Bay, N.S.	8-29-59	Hartford	6	13	19
Trottier, Rocky	5:11	185	Climax, Sask.	4-11-64	Medicine Hat-New Jersey	35	51	86
Tsujiura, Steve	5:05	155	Coaldale, Alta.	2-28-62	Springfield	24	56	80
Vautour, Yvon	6:00	200	St. John, N.B.	9-10-56	New Jersey-Maine	11	16	27
Verbeek, Pat	5:09	190	Sarnia, Ont.	5-24-64	New Jersey	20	27	47
Wilson, Mitch	5:09	190	Calgary, Alta.	2-15-62	Maine	6	8	14
Ysebaert, Paul	6:01	170	Sarnia, Ont.	5-15-66	Petrolia Jr. "B"	35	42	77

DEFENSEMEN

Name	Hgt.	Wgt.	Place of Birth	Date	1983-84 Club	G.	A.	Pts.
Brumwell, Murray	6:01	190	Calgary, Alta.	3-31-60	New Jersey-Maine	11	38	49
Cirella, Joe	6:03	210	Hamilton, Ont.	5- 9-63	New Jersey	11	33	44
Daneyko, Ken	6:00	195	Windsor, Ont.	4-16-64	Kamloops-New Jersey	7	32	39
Davey, Neil	6:02	205	Edmonton, Alta.	12-29-65	Michigan State	1	5	6
Dietrich, Don	6:02	205	DeLoraine, Man.	4- 5-61	Springfield-Chicago	14	26	40
Driver, Bruce	6:00	180	Toronto, Ont.	4-29-62	Team Canada-Maine-N. Jersey	13	24	37
Evans, Shawn	6:03	200	Kingston, Ont.	9- 7-65	Peterborough	21	88	109
Ferguson, Ian	6:02	175	Winnipeg, Man.	6-24-66	Oshawa	2	7	9
Hepple, Alan	5:09	200	Blaydon-on-Tyne, Eng.	8-16-63	Maine-New Jersey	4	23	27
Hiemer, Ullrich	6:01	190	Fussen, West Germany	9-21-62	Koln	23	23	46
Hoffmeyer, Bob	6:00	180	Dodsland, Sask.	7-27-55	New Jersey-Maine	7	13	20
Hordy, Mike	5:10	190	Thunder Bay, Ont.	10-10-56	Maine	11	40	51
Kiene, Chris	6:05	215	S. Windsor, Conn.	3-16-66	Springfield	23	18	41
Kitchen, Mike	5:10	180	Newmarket, Ont.	2- 1-56	New Jersey	1	4	5
Lewis, Dave	6:02	200	Kindersley, Sask.	7- 3-53	New Jersey	2	5	7
Lorimer, Bob	6:01	200	Toronto, Ont.	8-25-53	New Jersey	2	10	12
Mark, Gordon	6:03	205	Edmonton, Alta.	9-10-64	Kamloops	12	30	42
McGrath, Doug	6:00	190	Sheila, N.B.	8- 6-63	Maine-Montana	5	11	16
Octeau, Jay	5:10	180	Providence, R.I.	3-24-65	Boston University	1	5	6
Palmer, Rob	5:11	190	Sarnia, Ont.	9-10-56	New Jersey-Maine	5	15	20
Peluso, Mike	6:04	200	Hibbing, Minn.	11- 8-65	Greenway H.S. (Minn.)	5	15	20
Roth, Mike	6:02	215	St. Paul, Minn.	9- 9-66	Hill-Murray H.S. (Minn.)	5	7	12
Russell, Phil	6:02	200	Edmonton, Alta.	7-21-52	New Jersey	9	22	31
Schurman, M.F.	6:03	205	Summerside, P.E.I.	7-18-57	Maine	5	15	20

GOALTENDERS

Name	Hgt.	Wgt.	Place of Birth	Date	1983-84 Club	Mins.	GA.	SO.
Baker, Steve	6:03	200	Boston, Mass.	6- 6-57	Maine-Binghamton	1089	76	0
Billington, Craig	5:10	150	London, Ont.	9-11-66	Belleville	2335	162	1
Low, Ron	6:01	205	Birtle, Man.	6-21-50	New Jersey	2218	161	0
MacKenzie, Shawn	5:10	175	Bedford, N.S.	8-22-62	Maine	1946	113	0
McLean, Kirk	6:01	173	Willowdale, Ont.	6-26-66	Oshawa	940	67	0
Resch, Glenn	5:09	165	Moose Jaw, Sask.	7-10-48	New Jersey	2641	184	1
Terreri, Chris	5:09	155	Providence, R.I.	11-15-64	Providence College	391	20	0

New York Islanders
Patrick Division

Chairman of the Board/Governor	John O. Pickett, Jr.
President and General Manager	William A. Torrey
Vice-President and General Counsel	James Nagourney
Vice-President, Finance	Joseph H. Dreyer
Alternate Governor	William M. Skehan
Coach	Al Arbour
Assistant Coaches	Brian Kilrea, Butch Goring
Assistant General Manager/Director of Scouting	Gerry Ehman
Scouting Staff	Harry Boyd, Richard Green, Hal Laycoe, Mario Saraceno, Jack Vivian, Stig Nilsson
Publicity Director	Les Wagner
Assistant Publicity Director	Jill Knee
Communications Consultant	Barney Kremenko
Controller	Ralph Sellitti
Trainer	Craig Smith
Assistant Trainer	Jim Pickard
Home Ice	Nassau Veterans Memorial Coliseum
Address	Uniondale, N. Y. 11553
Seating Capacity	15,861
Club colors	Blue, White and Orange
Phone	(516) 794-4100

John Pickett

Bill Torrey

Al Arbour

New York Islanders 1984-85 Roster

FORWARDS

Name	Hgt.	Wgt.	Place of Birth	Date	1983-84 Club	G.	A.	Pts.
Bossy, Mike	6:00	185	Montreal, Que.	1-22-57	N.Y. Islanders	51	'67	118
Bourne, Bob	6:03	202	Netherhill, Sask.	6-21-54	N.Y. Islanders	22	34	56
Carroll, Billy	5:10	180	Toronto, Ont.	1-19-59	N.Y. Islanders	5	2	7
Coulter, Neal	6:02	190	Toronto, Ont.	1- 2-63	Indianapolis	7	10	17
Flatley, Pat	6:02	195	Toronto, Ont.	10- 3-63	N.Y. Islanders	2	7	9
Gilbert, Greg	6:01	194	Mississauga, Ont.	1-22-62	N.Y. Islanders	31	35	66
Gillies, Clark	6:03	210	Moose Jaw, Sask.	4- 7-54	N.Y. Islanders	12	16	28
Goring, Butch	5:09	166	St. Boniface, Man.	10-22-49	N.Y. Islanders	22	24	46
Hallin, Mats	6:02	202	Eskilstuna, Sweden	3-19-58	N.Y. Islanders	2	5	7
Hamway, Mark	6:00	185	Detroit, Mich.	8-'9-61	Indianapolis	22	32	54
Handy, Ron	5:11	175	Toronto, Ont.	1-15-63	Indianapolis	29	46	75
Kallur, Anders	5:10	190	Ludvika, Sweden	7- 6-52	Indianapolis	9	14	23
Kortko, Roger	5:11	175	Hafford, Sask.	2- 1-63	Indianapolis	16	27	43
LaFontaine, Pat	5:10	177	St. Louis, Mo.	2-22-65	N.Y. Islanders	13	6	19
Nystrom, Bob	6:01	200	Stockholm, Sweden	10-10-52	N.Y. Islanders	15	29	44
Simpson, Dave	6:00	190	London, Ont.	3- 3-62	Indianapolis	24	43	67
Sutter, Brent	5:11	175	Viking, Alta.	6-11-62	N.Y. Islanders	34	15	49
Sutter, Duane	6:01	189	Viking, Alta.	3-16-60	N.Y. Islanders	17	23	40
Sylvestre, Jacques	6:00	175	Sherbrooke, Que.	2- 9-63	Indianapolis	22	16	38
Tonelli, John	6:01	197	Hamilton, Ont.	3-23-57	N.Y. Islanders	27	40	67
Trottier, Bryan	5:11	195	Val Marie, Sask.	4-17-56	N.Y. Islanders	40	71	111
Trottier, Monty	5:09	175	Val Marie, Sask.	7-25-61	Indianapolis	18	23	41

DEFENSEMEN

Name	Hgt.	Wgt.	Place of Birth	Date	1983-84 Club	G.	A.	Pts.
Boutilier, Paul	6:00	200	Sidney, N.S.	5- 3-63	Indianapolis-N.Y.Islanders	6	28	34
Dineen, Gord	5:11	185	Toronto, Ont.	9-21-62	Indianapolis-N.Y. Islanders	5	24	29
Dowd, Bill	6:02	195	Hamilton, Ont.	4-17-63	Toledo-Indianapolis	2	12	14
Jonsson, Tomas	5:10	176	Falun, Sweden	4-12-60	N.Y. Islanders	11	36	47
Lane, Gord	6:01	185	Brandon, Man.	3-31-53	N.Y. Islanders	0	3	3
Langevin, Dave	6:02	215	St. Paul, Minn.	5-15-54	N.Y. Islanders	3	16	19
Leiter, Ken	6:01	195	Detroit, Mich.	4-19-61	Indianapolis	10	26	36
Lockridge, Tim	6:01	215	Barrie, Ont.	1-18-59	Indianapolis	2	16	18
Morrow, Ken	6:04	205	Flint, Mich.	10-17-56	N.Y. Islanders	3	11	14
Persson, Stefan	6:01	189	Umea, Sweden	12-22-54	N.Y. Islanders	9	24	33
Potvin, Denis	6:00	202	Ottawa, Ont.	10-29-53	N.Y. Islanders	22	63	85

GOALTENDERS

Name	Hgt.	Wgt.	Place of Birth	Date	1983-84 Club	Mins.	GA.	SO.
Hrudey, Kelly	5:10	182	Edmonton, Alta.	1-13-61	Indianapolis-N.Y. Islanders	905	49	0
Lumbard, Todd	6:00	185	Brandon, Man.	8-31-63	Indianapolis	1491	106	0
Melanson, Roland	5:10	178	Moncton, N.B.	6-28-60	N.Y. Islanders	2019	110	0
Smith, Bill	5:10	185	Perth, Ont.	12-12-50	N.Y. Islanders	2279	130	2

New York Rangers
Patrick Division

President	John H. Krumpe
Vice-President	Richard H. Zahnd
Vice-President, Controller	Mel Lowell
Secretary	Edwin M. Ost Jr.
Treasurer	Stephen Schwartz
Vice-President and General Manager	Craig Patrick
Coach	Herb Brooks
Assistant Coaches	Wayne Thomas, Carol Vadnais
Manager of Team Operations	Joe Bucchino
Public Relations Director	Vince Casey
Assistant Director of Public Relations	Bonnie Murman
Chief Scout	Dan Summers
Scouting Staff	Ray Clearwater, Paul Henry, Chuck Grillo, Lou Jankowski, Richard Rose, Lars-Erik Sjoberg
Trainers	Jerry Maloney, Joe Murphy, Bob Williams, Jeff Berg
Home Ice	Madison Square Garden
Address	4 Pennsylvania Plaza, New York, N. Y. 10001
Seating Capacity	17,500
Club colors	Blue, Red and White
Phone	(212) 563-8000

Craig Patrick

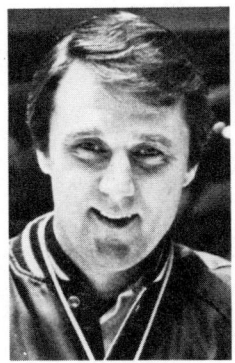

Herb Brooks

New York Rangers 1984-85 Roster

FORWARDS	Hgt.	Wgt.	Place of Birth	Date	1983-84 Club	G.	A.	Pts.
Allison, Mike	6:00	200	Fort Francis, Ont.	3-28-61	N.Y. Rangers	8	12	20
Andonoff, Jim	6:02	200	Grosse Pointe, Mich.	8- 7-65	Belleville	7	24	31
Backman, Mike	5:10	175	Halifax, N.S.	1- 2-55	Tulsa-N.Y. Rangers	12	29	41
Blaisdell, Mike	6:01	200	Moose Jaw, Sask.	1-18-60	Tulsa-N.Y. Rangers	15	14	29
Brooke, Bob	6:02	205	Melrose, Mass.	12-18-60	U.S. Olym. Team/N.Y. Rangers	7	18	25
Connor, Cam	6:02	200	Winnipeg, Man.	8-10-54	Tulsa	18	32	50
DeGrio, Gary	5:11	180	Duluth, Minn.	2-16-60	Tulsa	10	19	29
Erixon, Jan	6:00	190	Skelleftea, Sweden	7- 8-62	N.Y. Rangers	5	25	30
Fotiu, Nick	6:02	210	Staten Island, N.Y.	5-25-52	N.Y. Rangers	7	6	13
Ftorek, Rob	5:10	155	Needham, Mass.	1- 2-52	Tulsa-N.Y. Rangers	14	13	27
Gagner, Dave	5:10	180	Chatham, Ont.	12-11-64	Can. Olympic Team/Brantford	31	33	64
Glynn, Brian	5:10	165	Tonawanda, N.Y.	3-12-64	Univ. of Minn.-Duluth	2	5	7
Heath, Randy	5:08	160	Vancouver, B.C.	11-11-64	Portland	9	12	21
Hedberg, Anders	5:11	175	Ornskoldsvik, Sweden	2-25-51	N.Y. Rangers	32	35	67
Helminen, Raimo	6:00	183	Tampere, Finland	3-11-64	Ilves (Finland)	17	13	30
Kleinendorst, Kurt	6:02	190	Grand Rapids, Minn.	12-31-60	Tulsa	4	9	13
Kontos, Chris	6:01	195	Toronto, Ont.	12-10-63	Tulsa-N.Y. Rangers	5	14	19
Larouche, Pierre	5:11	175	Taschereau, Que.	11-16-55	N.Y. Rangers	48	33	81
McPhee, George	5:09	170	Guelph, Ont.	7- 2-58	Tulsa-N.Y. Rangers	21	29	50
Magnuson, Eric	6:02	210	Belmont, Mass.	9-17-61	Rensselaer Poly. Inst.	7	24	31
Malone, Jim	6:01	190	Chatham, B.C.	2-20-62	Tulsa	16	11	27
Maloney, Don	6:01	190	Lindsay, Ont.	9- 5-58	N.Y. Rangers	24	42	66
Martinson, Steve	6:01	200	Minnetonka, Minn.	6-21-57	Tulsa	3	6	9
Miller, Kelly	5:11	185	Detroit, Mich.	3- 3-63	Michigan State Univ.	28	21	49
Morrison, Mark	5:08	150	Delta, B.C.	3-11-63	Tulsa-N.Y. Rangers	4	4	8
Osborne, Mark	6:02	200	Toronto, Ont.	8-13-61	N.Y. Rangers	23	28	51
Pavelich, Mark	5:08	170	Eveleth, Minn.	2-28-58	N.Y. Rangers	29	53	82
Patey, Larry	6:01	190	Toronto, Ont.	3-19-53	St. Louis-N.Y. Rangers	1	3	4
Rogers, Mike	5:08	175	Calgary, Alta.	10-24-54	N.Y. Rangers	23	38	61
Sandstrom, Peter	6:02	200	Fagersta, Sweden	9- 4-64	Brynas (Sweden)	20	10	30
Sapergia, Brent	5:11	190	Moose Jaw, Sask.	12-16-62		..	..	..
Stoughton, Blaine	5:11	185	Gilbert Plains, Man.	3-13-53	Hartford-N.Y. Rangers	28	16	44
Sundstrom, Peter	6:00	180	Skelleftea, Sweden	12-14-61	N.Y. Rangers	22	22	44
Walker, Gordie	6:00	185	Castlegar, B.C.	8-12-65	Portland	8	11	19
Zanatta, Ivan	5:11	190	Toronto, Ont.	8- 3-60		..	..	..
DEFENSEMEN								
Baran, Doug	6:00	185	Winnipeg, Man.	10-14-62	Tulsa	5	7	12
Beck, Barry	6:03	215	Vancouver, B.C.	6- 3-57	N.Y. Rangers	9	27	36
Carkner, Terry	6:03	201	Smith Falls, Ont.	3- 7-66	Peterborough	4	21	25
Greschner, Ron	6:02	205	Goodsoil, Sask.	12-22-54	N.Y. Rangers	12	44	56
Guentzel, Mike	6:01	190	Grand Rapids, Minn.	8-23-62	University of Minnesota	11	21	32
Huber, Willie	6:05	225	Strasskirchen, Germany	1-15-58	N.Y. Rangers	9	14	23
Laidlaw, Tom	6:02	215	Brampton, Ont.	4-15-58	N.Y. Rangers	3	15	18
Ledyard, Grant	6:02	190	Winnipeg, Man.	11-19-61	Tulsa	9	17	26
Maloney, Dave	6:01	195	Kitchener, Ont.	7-31-56	N.Y. Rangers	7	26	33
Patrick, James	6:02	185	Winnipeg, Man.	6-14-63	N.Y. Rangers	1	7	8
Renaud, Chris	5:11	185	Windsor, Ont.	4-25-60	Tulsa	3	18	21
Richmond Steve	6:01	205	Chicago, Ill.	12-11-59	Tulsa-N.Y. Rangers	3	22	25
Roma, Paul	6:02	200	Jamaica, N.Y.	10-20-54		..	..	..
Ruotsalainen, Reijo	5:08	170	Oulu, Finland	4- 1-60	N.Y. Rangers	20	39	59
Saarinen, Simo	5:10	170	Helsinki, Finland	2-10-63	Helsinki IFK (Finland)	7	7	14
Salo, Vesa	6:03	185	Rauma, Finland	2-17-65	Lukko (Finland)	4	15	19
Walker, Bryan	6:03	203	Red Deer, Alta.	1-21-65	Portland	0	8	8

GOALTENDERS	Hgt.	Wgt.	Place of Birth	Date	1983-84 Club	Mins.	GA.	SO.
Hanlon, Glen	6:00	185	Brandon, Man.	2-20-57	N.Y. Rangers	2837	166	1
Proulx, Mario	5:11	180	Drummondville, Ont.	11-19-61	Providence College	1672	101	1
Scott, Ron	5:08	155	Guelph, Ont.	7-21-60	Tulsa-N.Y. Rangers	2202	138	0
Vanbiesbrouck, John	5:07	165	Detroit, Mich.	9- 4-63	Tulsa-N.Y. Rangers	2333	134	3
Weeks, Steve	5:11	165	Scarborough, Ont.	6-30-58	Tulsa-N.Y. Rangers	1541	169	0
Watts, Jeff	6:03	190	New York, N.Y.	5-19-62	Cornell University	840	39	1

Philadelphia Flyers
Patrick Division

Chairman of the Executive Committee	Edward M. Snider
Chairman of the Board	Joseph C. Scott
President	Jay T. Snider
Executive Vice-President	Keith Allen
Vice-President, Finance and Administration	Donn Patton
General Manager	Bob Clarke
Head Coach	Mike Keenan
Assistant General Manager	Gary Darling
Assistant Coach	Ted Sator
Goaltending Instructor	Bernie Parent
Physical Conditioning and Rehabilitation Coach	Pat Croce
Scouts	Jerry Melnyk, Walt Atanas, Dennis Patterson
Assistant to the President	John Brogan
Public Relations Director	Rodger Gottlieb
Assistant Public Relations Director	Mark Piazza
Ticket Manager	Ceil Baker
Director of Marketing	Jack Betson
Director of Broadcast Sales	Pete Huver
Trainer	Dave Settlemyre
Assistant Trainer	Kurt Mundt
Controller	Bob Baer
Team Physician	Edward Viner, M.D.
Home Ice	The Spectrum
Address	Pattison Place, Philadelphia, Pa. 19148
Seating Capacity	17,191
Club colors	Orange, White and Black
Phone	(215) 465-4500

Ed Snider

Joe Scott

Bob Clarke

Mike Keenan

Philadelphia Flyers 1984-85 Roster

FORWARDS

Name	Hgt.	Wgt.	Place of Birth	Date	1983-84 Club	G.	A.	Pts.
Allison, Ray	5:10	195	Cranbrook, B.C.	3- 4-59	Philadelphia	8	13	21
Barber, Bill	6:00	195	Callander, Ont.	7-11-52	Philadelphia	22	32	54
Bergen, Todd	6:03	190	Prince Albert, Sask.	7-11-63	Prince Albert	57	39	96
Brown, Dave	6:05	205	Saskatoon, Sask.	10-12-62	Springfield-Philadelphia	18	19	37
Dobbin, Brian	5:11	195	Petrolia, Ont.	8-18-66	London	30	40	70
Dzikowski, John	6:03	190	P. La Prairie, Man.	1-28-66	Brandon	12	11	23
Fersovitch, Daryn	5:11	175	Edmonton, Alta.	8- 7-66	St. Albert	26	31	57
Fitzpatrick, Ross	6:00	195	Penticton, B.C.	10- 7-60	Springfield-Philadelphia	37	32	69
Guay, Paul	6:00	185	Providence, R.I.	9- 2-63	Philadelphia	2	6	8
Hachborn, Len	5:10	185	Brantford, Ont.	9- 9-61	Springfield-Philadelphia	29	63	92
Hanson, Dave	6:04	225	Grand Forks, N.D.	7-18-66	Grand Forks, H.S.	28	32	60
Kerr, Tim	6:03	225	Windsor, Ont.	1- 5-60	Philadelphia	54	39	93
McLay, Dave	5:11	175	Chilliwack, B.C.	5-13-66	Kelowna	34	34	68
Mellanby, Scott	6:01	195	Montreal, Que.	6-11-66	Henry Carr Jr. B	37	37	74
Michayluk, Dave	5:10	180	Wakaw, Sask.	5-18-62	Springfield	18	44	62
Mormina, Bob	5:10	165	St. Leonard, Que.	7-20-63	Springfield	14	27	41
Nichols, Rob	5:11	175	Hamilton, Ont.	8- 4-64	North Bay	41	40	81
Poulin, Dave	5:11	180	Timmins, Ont.	12-17-58	Philadelphia	31	45	76
Powers, Bill	6:00	175	Cambridge, Mass.	4-10-66	Matignon H.S.	18	20	38
Propp, Brian	5:09	190	Lanigan, Sask.	2-15-59	Philadelphia	39	53	92
Sinisalo, Ilkka	6:01	190	Valeakoski, Finland	7-10-58	Philadelphia	29	17	46
Sittler, Darryl	6:00	190	Kitchener, Ont.	9-18-50	Philadelphia	27	36	63
Smith, Derrick	6:01	185	Scarboro, Ont.	1-22-65	Peterborough	30	36	66
Sutter, Rich	5:11	170	Viking, Alta.	12- 2-63	Pittsburgh-Philadelphia	16	12	28
Sutter, Ron	5:11	175	Viking, Alta.	12- 2-63	Philadelphia	19	32	51
Tocchet, Rick	5:11	195	Scarborough, Ont.	4- 9-64	Sault St. Marie	44	64	108
Vitale, Luke	5:11	180	Toronto, Ont.	4-17-66	Henry Carr Jr. B	24	48	72
Zezel, Peter	5:09	200	Toronto, Ont.	4-22-65	Toronto Jrs.	47	86	133

DEFENSEMEN

Name	Hgt.	Wgt.	Place of Birth	Date	1983-84 Club	G.	A.	Pts.
Allen, Tom	6:02	180	London, Ont.	5- 3-66	Kitchener	1	7	8
Bakos, Juraj	5:11	180	Bratislava, Czech.	6- 4-60	VSZ Kosice	..	..	..
Campbell, Bill	6:00	185	Montreal, Que.	2-24-64	Verdun	24	66	90
Carrier, Jerome	5:11	160	Beaumont, Que.	6-10-65	Verdun	14	38	52
Chychrun, Jeff	6:04	185	LaSalle, Que.	5- 3-66	Kingston	1	13	14
Cochrane, Glen	6:02	210	Cranbrook, B.C.	1-29-58	Philadelphia	7	16	23
Crossman, Doug	6:02	190	Peterborough, Ont.	6-30-60	Philadelphia	7	28	35
Dvorak, Miroslav	5:10	200	Hluboka Blt'ov, Czech.	10-11-51	Philadelphia	4	27	31
Eriksson, Thomas	6:02	185	Stockholm, Sweden	10-16-59	Philadelphia	11	33	44
Hospodar, Ed	6:02	210	Bowling Green, Ohio	2- 9-59	Hartford	0	9	9
Howe, Mark	5:11	190	Detroit, Mich.	5-28-55	Philadelphia	19	34	53
McCrimmon, Brad	5:11	200	Dodsland, Sask.	3-23-59	Philadelphia	0	24	24
Smith, Steve	5:09	195	Trenton, Ont.	4- 4-63	Springfield	4	25	29
Smyth, Greg	6:03	195	Oakville, Ont.	4-23-66	London	4	21	25
Stanley, Daryl	6:02	200	Winnipeg, Man.	12- 2-62	Springfield-Philadelphia	5	14	19
Stevens, John	6:01	185	Completon, N.B.	5- 4-66	Oshawa	1	10	11
Stothers, Mike	6:04	210	Toronto, Ont.	2-22-62	Maine	2	10	12
Villeneuve, Andre	6:00	190	Alma, Que.	1-19-63	Springfield	1	5	6

GOALTENDERS

Name	Hgt.	Wgt.	Place of Birth	Date	1983-84 Club	Mins.	GA.	SO.
Froese, Bob	5:11	175	St. Catharines, Ont.	6-30-58	Philadelphia	2863	150	2
Hextall, Ron	6:01	175	Winnipeg, Man.	5- 3-64	Brandon	2670	190	0
Hudon, Gil	6:02	190	Zenon Park, Sask.	2-12-62	Springfield	1395	101	0
Jensen, Darren	5:09	165	Creston, B.C.	5-27-60	Fort Wayne	3330	162	4
Lindbergh, Pelle	5:09	165	Stockholm, Sweden	5-24-59	Springfield-Philadelphia	2239	147	1
St. Laurent, Sam	5:10	190	Arvida, Que.	2-26-59	Maine	2158	145	0

Pittsburgh Penguins
Patrick Division

Chairman of the Board and President	Edward J. DeBartolo, Sr.
Vice-President	Marie Denise DeBartolo York
Vice-President	J. Paul Martha
Vice-President and General Counsel	Thomas F. Rossetti
Vice-President and Treasurer	Eddie Johnston
General Manager	Bob Berry
Coach	To be announced
Assistant Coach	Ken Schinkel
Director of Player Personnel and Assistant G.M.	Billy Taylor
Eastern Scout	To be announced
Western Scout	Albert Mandanici
Quebec Scout	Paul Steigerwald
Director of Marketing	Terry Schiffhauer
Director of Media Relations	Steve Thomas
Trainer	John Doolan
Equipment Manager	Civic Arena
Home Ice	Civic Arena, Gate No. 7, Pittsburgh, Pa. 15219
Address	16,033
Seating Capacity	Black, Gold and White
Club Colors	(412) 642-1800
Phone	

Edward DeBartolo

Eddie Johnston

Bob Berry

Pittsburgh Penguins 1984-85 Roster

FORWARDS

Name	Hgt.	Wgt.	Place of Birth	Date	1983-84 Club	G.	A.	Pts.
Belanger, Roger	6:00	182	St. Catharines, Ont.	12- 1-65	Kingston	44	46	90
Boutette, Pat	5:08	175	Windsor, Ont.	3- 1-52	Pittsburgh	14	26	40
Brickley, Andy	6:00	195	Melrose, Mass.	8- 9-61	Balt-Sp'f'ld-Pitt	19	30	49
Bullard, Mike	5:10	185	Ottawa, Ont.	3-10-61	Pittsburgh	51	41	92
Bulley, Ted	6:01	192	Windsor, Ont.	3-25-55	Pittsburgh-Baltimore	19	21	40
Carlson, Steve	6:03	180	Virginia, Minn.	8-26-55	Baltimore	9	30	39
DeFazio, Dean	5:11	185	Ottawa, Ont.	4-16-63	Pittsburgh-Baltimore	18	15	33
Errey, Bob	5:10	183	Montreal, Que.	9-21-64	Pittsburgh	9	13	22
Flockhart, Ron	5:11	185	Smithers, B.C.	10-10-60	Philadelphia-Pittsburgh	27	21	48
Gatzos, Steve	5:11	182	Toronto, Ont.	6-22-61	Pittsburgh-Baltimore	17	22	39
Geale, Robert	5:11	175	Edmonton, Alta.	4-17-62	Pittsburgh-Baltimore	17	23	40
Haidy, Alec	6:01	175	Windsor, Ont.	1- 1-65	Sault Ste. Marie	17	20	37
Hamilton, Jim	6:00	180	Barrie, Ont.	1-18-57	Pittsburgh-Baltimore	36	47	83
Hannan, David	5:10	173	Sudbury, Ont.	11-26-61	Pittsburgh-Baltimore	20	27	47
Hrynewich, Tim	5:11	187	Leamington, Ont.	10- 2-63	Pittsburgh-Baltimore	17	22	39
Javanainen, Arto	6:00	183	Pori, Finland	4- 8-59	Assat Pori (Finland)	37	25	62
Kehoe, Rick	5:11	180	Windsor, Ont.	7-15-51	Pittsburgh	18	27	45
Lamoureux, Mitch	5:06	173	Ottawa, Ont.	8-22-62	Pittsburgh-Baltimore	31	39	70
Lemieux, Mario	6:04	200	Montreal, Que.	10- 5-65	Laval	133	149	282
Loney, Troy	6:03	215	Bow Island, Alta.	9-21-63	Pittsburgh-Baltimore	18	13	31
McSorley, Marty	6:01	189	Hamilton, Ont.	5-18-63	Pittsburgh	2	7	9
O'Regan, Tom	5:10	182	Cambridge, Mass.	12-29-61	Pittsburgh-Baltimore	17	27	44
Rissling, Gary	5:09	175	Saskatoon, Sask.	8- 8-56	Pittsburgh-Baltimore	16	26	42
Roulston, Tom	6:01	185	Winnipeg, Man.	11-20-57	Edmonton-Pittsburgh	16	24	40
Sasser, Grant	5:11	175	Edmonton, Alta.	4-17-62	Pittsburgh-Portland	44	69	113
Schutt, Rod	5:10	185	Bancroft, Ont.	10-13-56	Pittsburgh-Baltimore	16	22	38
Shedden, Doug	6:00	184	Wallaceburg, Ont.	4-26-61	Pittsburgh	22	35	57
Taylor, Mark	5:11	185	Vancouver, B.C.	1-26-58	Philadelphia-Pittsburgh	24	31	55
Teevens, Mark	6:00	180	Ottawa, Ont.	6-17-66	Peterborough	27	37	64
Tookey, Tim	5:11	180	Edmonton, Alta.	8-29-60	Pittsburgh-Baltimore	16	30	46
Young, Warren	6:03	195	Toronto, Ont.	1-11-56	Pittsburgh-Baltimore	26	45	71

DEFENSEMEN

Name	Hgt.	Wgt.	Place of Birth	Date	1983-84 Club	G.	A.	Pts.
Bodger, Doug	6:02	200	Chemainus, B.C.	6-18-66	Kamloops	21	77	98
Bourque, Phil	6:01	190	Chelmsford, Mass.	6- 8-62	Pittsburgh-Baltimore	5	18	23
Buskas, Rod	6:01	197	Wetaskiwin, Alta.	1- 7-61	Pittsburgh-Baltimore	4	16	20
Charlesworth, Todd	6:01	186	Calgary, Alta.	3-22-65	Oshawa-Pittsburgh	11	35	46
Fox, Greg	6:02	190	Port McNeil, B.C.	8-12-53	Chicago-Pittsburgh	2	10	12
Goertz, David	5:11	210	Edmonton, Alta.	3-28-65	Prince Albert	13	47	60
Hotham, Greg	5:11	183	London, Ont.	3- 7-56	Pittsburgh	5	25	30
Lundberg, Brian	5:11	190	Burnaby, B.C.	6- 5-60	Baltimore-Muskegon	4	17	21
Mantha, Moe	6:02	195	Lakewood, Ohio	1-21-61	Sherbrooke-Winnipeg	17	39	56
Maxwell, Bryan	6:02	200	North Bay, Ont.	9- 7-55	Winnipeg-Pittsburgh	3	15	18
McCarthy, Kevin	5:11	195	Winnipeg, Man.	7-14-57	Vancouver-Pittsburgh	6	30	36
Meighan, Ron	6:03	194	Montreal, Que.	5-26-63	Baltimore	4	16	20
Rowe, Mike	6:01	212	Kingston, Ont.	3- 8-65	Toronto Jrs.	9	36	45
Schmidt, Norm	5:11	190	S. Ste. Marie, Ont.	1-24-63	Pittsburgh-Baltimore	10	24	34
Tebbutt, Greg	6:02	215	N. Vancouver, B.C.	5-11-57	Pittsburgh-Baltimore	12	42	54
Thornbury, Tom	5:11	175	Lindsay, Ont.	3-17-63	Pittsburgh-Baltimore	18	54	72
Wolf, Bennett	6:03	205	Kitchener, Ont.	10-23-59	Baltimore	3	13	16

GOALTENDERS

Name	Hgt.	Wgt.	Place of Birth	Date	1983-84 Club	Mins.	GA.	SO.
Dion, Michel	5:10	184	Granby, Que.	2-11-54	Pittsburgh	1553	138	0
Gagnon, Georges	5:09	156	McGregor, Ont.	5-24-59	Kalamazoo	3889	225	1
Herron, Denis	5:11	165	Chambly, Que.	6-18-52	Pittsburgh	2028	138	1
Pietrangelo, Frank	5:11	178	Niagara Falls, Ont.	12-17-64	U. of Minnesota	1141	66	0
Romano, Roberto	5:06	172	Montreal, Que.	10-29-62	Baltimore-Pittsburgh	2779	184	1

Quebec Nordiques
Adams Division

President and Governor	Marcel Aubut
Assistant to President/Administration	Richard Blouin
General Manager	Maurice Filion
Assistant G.M. and Director of Personnel Development	Gilles Leger
Director of Recruiting	Martin Madden
Coach	Michel Bergeron
Associate Coaches	Simon Nolet, Guy Lapointe
Special Counsellor to Hockey Department	Charles Thiffault
Chief Scout	George Armstrong
Scouts	Serge Aubry, Sheldon Ferguson
General Counsel	Jean Pelletier
Director of Finance	Jean Laflamme
Director of Marketing and Communications	Robert Ayotte
Director of Press Relations	To be announced
Supervisor of Public Relations	Marius Fortier
Trainers	Rene Lacasse, Rene Laviguer, Brian Turpin
Home Ice	Quebec Coliseum
Address	2205 Ave. du Colisee, Quebec, Que. G1L 4W7
Seating Capacity	15,434
Club Colors	Blue, White and Red
Phone	(418) 529-8441

Marcel Aubut

Maurice Filion

Gilles Leger

Michel Bergeron

Quebec Nordiques 1984-85 Roster

FORWARDS

Name	Hgt.	Wgt.	Place of Birth	Date	1983-84 Club	G.	A.	Pts.
Berglund, Bo	5:10	175	Sjavelad, Sweden	4- 6-55	Quebec	16	27	43
Chartrain, Andre	5:08	175	Beaconsfield, Que.	3-24-62	Fredericton	0	0	0
Cote, Alain	5:10	203	Matane, Que.	5- 3-57	Quebec	19	24	43
Cote, Andre	6:01	186	Baie-Comeau, Que.	6-19-61	Fredericton-Milwaukee	8	19	27
Dobson, Jim	6:01	185	Winnipeg, Man.	2-29-60	Fredericton	33	44	77
Eagles, Mike	5:10	180	Sussex, N.B.	3- 7-63	Fredericton	13	29	42
Gaulin, Jean-Marc	5:10	182	Balve, Germany	3- 3-62	Quebec-Fredericton	14	28	42
Gillis, Paul	5:11	190	Toronto, Ont.	12-31-63	Quebec-Fredericton	15	17	32
Goulet, Michel	6:01	185	Peribonka, Que.	4-21-60	Quebec	56	65	121
Groulx, Wayne	5:09	176	Welland, Ont.	2- ,2-65	Sault Ste. Marie	59	78	137
Heroux, Yves	5:11	185	Terrebonne, Que.	4-27-65	Chicoutimi	28	25	53
Hough, Mike	6:01	190	Montreal, Que.	2- 6-63	Fredericton	11	16	27
Hunter, Dale	5:09	190	Petrolia, Ont.	7-31-60	Quebec	24	55	79
Kumpel, Mark	6:00	190	Wakefield, Mass.	3- 7-61	U.S. Oly. Fredericton	16	20	36
Mann, Jimmy	6:00	205	Montreal, Que.	4-17-59	Winnipeg-Quebec	1	2	3
McKegney, Tony	6:01	198	Montreal, Que.	2-15-58	Quebec	24	27	51
Paiement, Wilf	6:01	210	Earlton, Ont.	10-16-55	Quebec	39	37	76
Sauve, Jean-Francois	5:06	175	Ste. Genevieve, Que.	1-23-60	Quebec-Fredericton	29	48	77
Savard, Andre	6:01	185	Temiscamingue, Que.	2- 9-53	Quebec	20	24	44
Sleigher, Louis	5:11	200	Nouvelle, Que.	10-23-58	Quebec	15	19	34
Stastny, Anton	6:00	185	Bratislava, Czech.	8- 5-59	Quebec	25	37	62
Stastny, Marian	5:10	192	Bratislava, Czech.	1- 8-53	Quebec	20	32	52
Stastny, Peter	6:01	195	Bratislava, Czech.	9-18-56	Quebec	46	73	119
Tanguay, Christian	5:10	190	Beauport, Que.	8- 4-62	Milwaukee-Fredericton	43	50	93
Wood, Dan	5:11	190	Toronto, Ont.	10-30-62	Can. Oly.-Montana-Springfield	12	19	31
Zemlak, Richard	6:02	190	Wynard, Sask.	3- 3-63	Toledo	8	19	27

DEFENSEMEN

Name	Hgt.	Wgt.	Place of Birth	Date	1983-84 Club	G.	A.	Pts.
Bell, Bruce	5:11	180	Toronto, Ont.	2-15-65	Brantford	7	41	48
Bolduc, Michel	6:02	210	Ange-Gardien, Que.	3-13-61	Fredericton	2	15	17
Donnelly, Gord	6:02	195	Montreal, Que.	4- 5-62	Quebec-Fredericton	2	8	10
Dore, Andre	6:02	200	Montreal, Que.	2-11-58	St. Louis-Quebec	4	28	32
Hagglund, Roger	6:01	191	Bjorkloven, Sweden	7- 2-61	Bjorkloven	..	..	..
Julien, Claude	6:00	195	Blind River, Ont.	4-23-60	Fredericton	7	22	29
Lapointe, Rick	6:02	200	Victoria, B.C.	8- 2-55	Quebec-Fredericton	10	32	42
Marois, Mario	5:11	190	Ancienne-Lorette, Que.	12-15-57	Quebec	13	36	49
Moller, Randy	6:02	205	Red Deer, Alta.	8-23-63	Quebec	4	14	18
Poudrier, Daniel	6:02	185	Thetford Mines, Que.	2-15-64	Drummondville	7	28	35
Price, Pat	6:02	195	Nelson, B.C.	3-24-55	Quebec	3	25	28
Rochefort, Normand	6:01	200	Trois-Rivieres, Que.	1-28-61	Quebec	2	22	24
Shaw, Dave	6:02	187	St. Thomas, Ont.	5-25-64	Quebec-Kitchener	14	34	48
Turmel, Richard	6:03	226	Beauce, Que.	7-29-62	Fredericton-Milwaukee	2	14	16
Van Boxmeer, John	6:00	190	Petrolia, Ont.	11-20-52	Quebec-Fredericton	15	37	52
Weir, Wally	6:02	205	Verdun, Que.	6- 3-54	Quebec-Fredericton	8	20	28
Wesley, Blake	6:01	200	Red Deer, Alta.	7-10-59	Quebec	2	8	10

GOALTENDERS

Name	Hgt.	Wgt.	Place of Birth	Date	1983-84 Club	Mins.	GA.	SO.
Bouchard, Daniel	6:00	190	Val d'Or, Que.	12-12-50	Quebec	3373	180	1
Dufour, Michel	5:06	160	Val d'Or, Que.	8- 3-62	Milwaukee-Fredericton	1621	98	0
Ford, Brian	5:10	170	Edmonton, Alta.	9-22-61	Quebec-Fredericton	2265	118	2
Gosselin, Mario	5:08	160	Thetford-Mines, Que.	6-15-63	Canadian Oly.-Quebec	2155	129	1
Guenette, Luc	5:09	162	St. Jerome, Que.	7-22-64	Quebec Jrs.	2946	284	0
Malarchuk, Clint	5:10	172	Grande, Alta.	5- 1-61	Quebec-Fredericton	1878	120	0
Sevigny, Richard	5:08	178	Montreal, Que.	11-04-57	Montreal	2203	124	1

St. Louis Blues
Norris Division

Board of Directors	Harry Ornest, Ruth Ornest, Michael Ornest, Jack Quinn
Chairman of the Board, President and Governor	Harry Ornest
Vice-Chairwoman and Treasurer	Ruth Ornest
Executive Vice-President	Jack Quinn
Vice-President and Director of Hockey Operations	Ron Caron
Vice-President and Secretary	Mike Ornest
Vice-President, Administration	Cindy Ornest
Director of Scouting	Ted Hampson
Coach	Jacques Demers
Assistant Coach	Barclay Plager
Public Relations Director	Susie Mathieu
Trainer	Norm Mackie
Home Ice	The Arena
Address	5700 Oakland Avenue, St. Louis, Missouri 63110
Seating Capacity	17,600
Club Colors	Blue, Gold, Red and White
Phone	(314) 781-5300

Harry Ornest

Jack Quinn

Ron Caron

Jacques Demers

St. Louis Blues 1984-85 Roster

FORWARDS	Hgt.	Wgt.	Place of Birth	Date	1983-84 Club	G.	A.	Pts.
Anderson, Perry	6:00	195	Barrie, Ont.	10-14-61	St. Louis-Montana	14	8	22
Babych, Wayne	5:11	195	Edmonton, Alta.	5- 6-58	St. Louis	13	29	42
Barr, David	6:01	195	Edmonton, Alta.	11-30-60	Tulsa-St. Louis	28	37	65
Cupolo, Mark	6:00	180	Niagara Falls, Ont.	11-17-65	Guelph	28	13	41
Federko, Bernie	6:00	195	Foam Lake, Sask.	5-12-56	St. Louis	41	66	107
Ganchar, Perry	5:09	180	Saskatoon, Sask.	10-28-63	Montana-St. Louis	23	22	45
Gilmour, Doug	5:11	160	Kingston, Ont.	6-25-63	St. Louis	25	28	53
Hickey, Pat	6:01	190	Brantford, Ont.	5-15-53	St. Louis	9	11	20
Jomphe, Daniel	6:02	200	Is De. Madeleine, Que.	1-19-66	Granby	7	9	16
Mullen, Joe	5:10	182	New York, N.Y.	3-16-62	St. Louis	41	44	85
Paslawski, Greg	5:11	189	Kindersley, Sask.	8-25-61	Montreal-St. Louis	9	10	19
Pettersson, Jorgen	6:02	185	Gothenburg, Sweden	7-11-56	St. Louis	28	34	62
Reeds, Mark	5:10	190	Burlington, Ont.	1-24-60	St. Louis	11	14	25
Ronning, Clifford	5:08	157	Vancouver, B.C.	10- 1-65	New Westminster	69	67	136
Schofield, Dwight	6:03	195	Waltham, Mass.	3-25-56	St. Louis	4	10	14
Sutter, Brian	5:11	180	Viking, Alta.	10- 7-58	St. Louis	32	51	83
Wickenheiser, Doug	6:01	196	Regina, Sask.	3-30-61	Montreal-St. Louis	12	26	38

DEFENSEMEN	Hgt.	Wgt.	Place of Birth	Date	1983-84 Club	G.	A.	Pts.
Benning, Brian	6:00	175	Edmonton, Alta.	6-10-66	Portland	6	41	47
Bothwell, Tim	6:03	190	Vancouver, B.C.	5- 6-55	Montana-St. Louis	2	16	18
Delorme, Gilbert	6:01	203	Boucherville, Que.	11-25-62	Montreal-St. Louis	2	12	14
Dirk, Robert	6:04	207	Regina, Sask.	8-20-66	Regina	2	10	12
Herring, Graham	6:00	160	Montreal, Que.	10-27-65	Longueuil	9	44	53
Johnson, Terry	6:03	210	Calgary, Alta.	11-28-58	St. Louis	2	6	8
Pavese, Jim	6:02	205	New York, N.Y.	5- 8-62	Montana-St. Louis	1	20	21
Pichette, Dave	6:03	190	Grand Falls, Nfld.	2- 4-60	Quebec-St. Louis	2	18	20
Posavad, Mike	5:11	196	Brantford, Ont.	1- 3-64	Peterborough	3	25	28
Ramage, Rob	6:02	210	Byron, Ont.	1-11-59	St. Louis	15	45	60
Ruff, Marty	6:01	195	Warburg, Alta.	5-19-63	Montana	0	0	0
Wilson, Rik	6:00	180	Long Beach, Calif.	6-17-62	Montana-St. Louis	7	14	21

GOALTENDERS	Hgt.	Wgt.	Place of Birth	Date	1983-84 Club	Mins.	GA.	SO.
Heinz, Rick	5:10	165	Essex, Ont.	5-30-55	St. Louis	1118	80	0
Liut, Mike	6:02	195	Weston, Ont.	1- 7-56	St. Louis	3425	197	3
Perry, Alan	5:08	155	Providence, R.I.	8-30-66	Mt. St. Charles H.S.	900	28	1
Wamsley, Richard	5:11	185	Simcoe, Ont.	5-25-59	Montreal	2333	144	2

Toronto Maple Leafs
Norris Division

President, Governor and Managing Director	Harold E. Ballard
Chairman of the Board	Paul McNamara
Vice-President	Frank "King" Clancy
General Manager	Gerry McNamara
Coach	Dan Maloney
Executive Assistant	Gord Stellick
Scouts	Johnny Bower, Frank Currie, Jacques Toupin, Dick Duff, Floyd Smith, Jack Faulkner, Jim Easdell, Anders Bengston
Publicity Director	Stan Obodiac
Treasurer	Donald Crump
Box Office Manager	Gordon Finn
Trainers	Guy Kinnear, Dan Lemelin
Home Ice	Maple Leaf Gardens
Address	60 Carlton Street, Toronto, Ont. M5B 1L1
Capacity for Hockey	16,382 (including standees)
Club Colors	Blue and White
Phone	(416) 977-1641

Harold Ballard

Gerry McNamara

Dan Maloney

Toronto Maple Leafs 1984-85 Roster

FORWARDS

Name	Hgt.	Wgt.	Place of Birth	Date	1983-84 Club	G.	A.	Pts.
Anderson, John	5:11	190	Toronto, Ont.	3-28-57	Toronto	37	31	68
Aubin, Normand	6:00	185	St. Leonard, Que.	7-26-60	St. Catharines	47	47	94
Boudreau, Bruce	5:09	175	Toronto, Ont.	1- 9-56	St. Catharines	47	62	109
Britz, Greg	6:00	180	Buffalo, N.Y.	1- 3-61	St. Catharines-Toronto	23	16	39
Costello, Rich	6:00	175	Framingham, Mass.	6-27-63	St. Catharines-Toronto	2	1	3
Courtnall, Russ	5:11	175	Duncan, B.C.	1- 2-65	Victoria-Can. Oly.-Toronto	3	9	12
Daoust, Dan	5:11	165	Montreal, Que.	2-29-60	Toronto	18	56	74
Derlago, Bill	5:10	194	Birtle, Man.	8-25-58	Toronto	40	20	60
Fenton, Jeff	6:03	192	Edmonton Alta.	10-13-63	Kelowna	32	58	90
Frycer, Miroslav	6:00	198	Opava, Czechoslovakia	9-27-59	Toronto	10	16	26
Gavin, Stewart	6:00	180	Ottawa, Ont.	3-15-60	Toronto	10	22	32
Graham, Pat	6:01	180	Toronto, Ont.	5-25-61	Toronto-St. Catharines	4	4	8
Hodgson, Dan	5:09	173	Ft. Vermillion, Alta.	8-29-65	Prince Albert	62	119	181
Ihnacak, Miroslav	6:00	185	Poprad, Czech.	2-19-62	Czech National Team	..	..	..
Ihnacak Peter	6:01	195	Poprad, Czech.	5- 3-57	Toronto	10	13	23
Jackson, Jeff	6:00	193	Catham, Ont.	4-24-65	Brantford	22	42	64
Joseph, Fabian	5:08	165	Sydney, N.S.	12- 5-65	Victoria	52	75	127
Kaszycki, Mike	5:09	190	Milton, Ont.	2-27-56	St. Catharines	39	71	110
Lavers, Mike	6:04	195	St. John, Nfld.	5-17-63	Loyola University	..	..	..
Laxdal, Derek	6:01	176	St. Boniface, Man.	2-21-66	Brandon	23	20	43
Lefrancois, Normand	5:11	181	Montreal, Que.	4-20-62	Muskegon	13	20	33
MacInnis, Joseph	6:00	165	Cambridge, Mass.	5-25-66	Watertown H.S. (Mass.)	28	18	46
Maguire, Kevin	6:02	200	Toronto, Ont.	1- 5-63	Orillia (Ont.) Tier II	35	42	77
Martin, Terry	5:11	195	Barrie, Ont.	10-25-55	Toronto	15	10	25
McRae, Basil	6:02	200	Orillia, Ont.	1- 1-61	St. Catharines-Toronto	14	25	39
Perlini, Fred	6:02	175	Sault Ste. Marie, Ont.	4-12-62	St. Catharines-Toronto	21	31	52
Poddubny, Walt	6:01	203	Thunder Bay, Ont.	2-14-60	Toronto	11	14	25
Rolston, Greg	6:01	180	Flint, Mich.	2-27-65		..	..	..
Ruzicka, Vladimir	6:01	175	Czechoslovakia	6- 6-63	C.H.Z. Litvinov	..	..	..
Strong, Ken	5:11	185	Toronto, Ont.	5- 9-63	St. Catharines-Toronto	27	45	72
Terrion, Greg	5:11	190	Marmora, Ont.	5- 2-60	Toronto	15	24	39
Thomas, Steve	5:10	185	Stockport, England	7-15-63	Toronto Jrs.	51	54	105
Turner, Dan	6:03	200	Flin Flon, Man.	3-18-64	Medicine Hat	17	22	39
Vaive, Rick	6:00	180	Ottawa, Ont.	5-14-59	Toronto	52	41	93
Verstraete, Leigh	5:11	183	Pincher Creek, Alta.	1- 6-62	St. Catharines	0	7	7
Wurst, Mike	6:04	210	Edina, Minn.	10- 5-64	Ohio State University	..	..	..
Yaremchuk, Gary	6:00	183	Edmonton, Alta.	8-15-61	St. Catharines-Toronto	24	37	61

DEFENSEMEN

Name	Hgt.	Wgt.	Place of Birth	Date	1983-84 Club	G.	A.	Pts.
Albrecht, Cliff	6:00	185	Bramalea, Ont.	5-24-63	Princeton University	9	9	18
Benning, Jim	6:00	183	Edmonton, Alta.	4-29-63	Toronto	12	39	51
Buckley, David	6:04	195	Newton, Mass.	1-27-66	Trinity-Pawling H.S.	10	17	27
Campedelli, Dom	6:01	195	Cohasset, Me.	4- 3-64	Boston College	10	19	29
Capuano, Jack	6:02	210	Cranston, R.I.	7- 7-66	Kent High School	10	8	18
Farrish, Dave	6:01	195	Wingham, Ont.	8- 1-56	St. Catharines-Toronto	4	19	23
Gill, Todd	6:01	175	Brockville, Ont.	11- 9-65	Windsor	9	48	57
Gingras, Gaston	6:00	191	Temiscaming, Que.	2-13-59	Toronto	7	20	27
Iafrate, Al	6:03	190	Dearborn, Mich.	3-21-66	Team USA-Belleville	6	21	27
Korn, Jim	6:03	210	Hopkins, Minn.	7-28-57	Toronto	12	14	26
Leeman, Gary	5:11	170	Toronto, Ont.	2-19-64	Toronto	4	8	12
Loven, Tim	6:00	189	Red River, N.D.	10-14-63	U. of North Dakota	0	7	7
McGill, Bob	6:00	200	Edmonton, Alta.	4-27-62	St. Catharines-Toronto	1	15	16
Muni, Craig	6:02	201	Toronto, Ont.	7-19-62	St. Catharines	4	16	20
Nylund, Gary	6:04	200	Surrey, B.C.	10-28-63	Toronto	2	14	16
Plante, Cam	6:00	190	Brandon, Man.	3-12-64	Brandon	22	118	140
Salming, Borje	6:01	185	Kiruna, Sweden	4-17-51	Toronto	5	38	43
Slanina, Peter	..	..	Czechoslovakia	..-..-..		..	..	..
Spezza, George	6:00	187	Toronto, Ont.	1-27-64	Toronto Jrs.	..	..	..
Stewart, Bill	6:02	180	Toronto, Ont.	10- 6-57	Toronto	2	17	19
Triano, Jeff	6:00	180	Niagara Falls, Ont.	4-11-64	Toronto Jrs.	7	27	34
Uvira, Edourd	..	..	Czechoslovakia	......	Czechoslovakia National Team..	..	..	..

GOALTENDERS

Name	Hgt.	Wgt.	Place of Birth	Date	1983-84 Club	Mins.	GA.	SO.
Bester, Allan	5:07	152	Hamilton, Ont.	3-26-63	Brantford-Toronto	3119	205	1
Dowie, Bruce	5:08	165	Oakville, Ont.	12- 9-62	Muskegon-St. Cath.-Toronto	1788	145	2
Palmateer, Mike	5:09	170	Toronto, Ont.	1-13-54	Toronto	1831	149	0
Reese, Jeff	5:09	150	Brantford, Ont.	3-24-66	London	2308	173	0
St. Croix, Rick	5:10	160	Kenora, Ont.	1- 3-55	Toronto-St. Catharines	1421	109	0
Wregget, Ken	6:01	182	Brandon, Man.	3-25-64	Toronto-Lethbridge	3218	175	0

Vancouver Canucks
Smythe Division

Chairman of the Board	Frank A. Griffiths
Assistant to the Chairman	Arthur R. Griffiths
Senior Vice-President	John C. "Jake" Milford
Vice-President and General Manager	Harry Neale
Vice-President, Finance	John Chesman
Vice President, Marketing	John Whitman
Assistant General Manager	Jack Gordon
Coach	Bill LaForge
Associate Coach	Ron Smith
Director of Player Personnel	Larry Popein
Chief Scout	Jack MacDonald
Scouts	Mike Penny, George Wood, Jack McCartan, Paul Allen
Public Relations Director	Norm Jewison
Public Relations Assistants	Frank Bohmer, Walter "Babe" Pratt
Trainers	Ken Fleger and Larry Ashley
Home Ice	Pacific Coliseum
Address	100 North Renfrew St., Vancouver, B.C. V5K 3N7
Capacity for Hockey	16,553
Club Colors	Black, Red and Yellow
Phone	(604) 254-5141

Frank A. Griffiths

Jake Milford

Harry Neale

Bill LaForge

Vancouver Canucks 1984-85 Roster

FORWARDS

Name	Hgt.	Wgt.	Place of Birth	Date	1983-84 Club	G.	A.	Pts.
Bertuzzi, Brian	5:11	172	Vancouver, B.C.	1-24-66	Kamloops	29	21	50
Bruce, Dave	5:11	168	Thunder Bay, Ont.	10-7-64	Kitchener	52	40	92
Chaulk, Landis	6:01	198	Swift Current, Sask.	5-17-66	Calgary Jrs.	21	28	49
Coxe, Craig	6:04	195	Chula Vista, Calif.	1-21-64	Belleville	17	28	45
Crawford, Marc	5:11	185	Belleville, Ont.	2-13-64	Vancouver-Fredericton	9	23	32
Delorme, Ron	6:02	185	North Battleford, Sask.	9-3-55	Vancouver	2	2	4
Driscoll, Steve	5:09	175	Montreal, Que.	6-7-64	Cornwall-Fredericton	38	51	89
Gillis, Jere	6:00	190	Bend, Ore.	1-18-57	Fredericton-Vancouver	31	41	72
Gradin, Thomas	5:11	170	Solleftea, Sweden	2-18-56	Vancouver	21	57	78
Hall, Taylor	5:11	185	Regina, Sask.	2-20-64	Regina-Vancouver	64	79	143
Kirton, Mark	5:10	170	Regina, Sask.	2-3-58	Vancouver-Fredericton	10	13	23
Kulak, Stu	5:10	180	Edmonton, Alta.	3-10-63	Fredericton	12	16	28
Lanthier, Jean-Marc	6:02	195	Montreal, Que.	3-27-63	Vancouver-Fredericton	27	18	45
Lemay, Moe	5:11	185	Saskatoon, Sask.	2-18-62	Fredericton-Vancouver	21	25	46
Lowry, Dave	6:01	185	Sudbury, Ont.	1-14-65	London	29	47	76
Lupul, Gary	5:08	170	Powell River, B.C.	4-20-59	Vancouver	17	27	44
MacAdam, Al	6:00	175	Charlottetown, P.E.I.	3-16-52	Minnesota	22	13	35
Martin, Grant	5:10	190	Sm. Rock Falls, Ont.	3-13-62	Vancouver-Fredericton	36	26	62
McClanahan, Rob	5:10	180	St. Paul, Minn.	1-9-58	N.Y. Rangers-Tulsa	10	18	28
McNab, Peter	6:03	205	Vancouver, B.C.	5-8-52	Boston-Vancouver	15	22	37
Morrison, Dave	6:01	185	Toronto, Ont.	6-12-62	New Haven-Fredericton	..	..	..
Neely, Cam	6:01	185	Comox, B.C.	6-6-65	Portland-Vancouver	24	33	57
Rohlicek, Jeff	6:00	175	Park Ridge, Ill.	1-27-66	Portland	44	53	97
Rota, Darcy	5:11	178	Vancouver, B.C.	2-16-53	Vancouver	28	20	48
Skriko, Petri	5:10	172	Laapeenranta, Finland	3-12-62	Saipa (Finland)	25	26	51
Smyl, Stan	5:09	185	Glendon, Alta.	1-28-58	Vancouver	24	43	67
Stevens, Mike	5:11	193	Kitchener, Ont.	12-30-65	Kitchener	19	21	40
Sundstrom, Patrik	6:00	203	Skelleftea, Sweden	12-14-61	Vancouver	38	53	91
Tanti, Tony	5:09	185	Toronto, Ont.	9-7-63	Vancouver	45	41	86
Tottle, Scott	5:11	175	Brantford, Ont.	1-30-65	Peterborough	63	47	110
Vignola, Rejean	5:10	186	Baie-Comeau, Que.	1-27-62	Fredericton	25	13	38

DEFENSEMEN

Name	Hgt.	Wgt.	Place of Birth	Date	1983-84 Club	G.	A.	Pts.
Belland, Neil	5:11	180	Parry Sound, Ont.	4-3-61	Fredericton-Vancouver	10	28	38
Bubla, Jiri	5:11	198	Usti nad Labem, Czech.	1-27-50	Vancouver	6	33	39
Butcher, Garth	6:00	200	Regina, Sask.	1-8-63	Vancouver-Fredericton	6	13	19
Daigneault, Jean-Jacques	5:11	180	Montreal, Que.	10-12-65	Team Canada-Longueuil	8	26	34
Halward, Doug	6:01	197	Toronto, Ont.	11-1-55	Vancouver	7	16	23
Holloway, Bruce	6:00	200	Revelstoke, B.C.	6-27-63	Fredericton	3	30	33
Kayser, Steve	6:02	200	Ottawa, Ont.	2-7-65	Univ. of Vermont	3	7	10
Lanz, Rick	6:02	193	Karlouyvary, Czech.	9-16-61	Vancouver	18	39	57
Lidster, Doug	6:01	195	Kamloops, B.C.	10-18-60	Team Canada-Vancouver	6	20	26
Measures, Allan	5:11	165	Barrhead, Alta.	5-8-65	Calgary Jrs.	17	36	53
Petit, Michel	6:01	191	St. Malo, Que.	2-12-64	Team Canada-Vancouver	9	19	28
Schliebener, Andy	6:00	196	Ottawa, Ont.	8-16-62	Fredericton-Vancouver	3	16	19

GOALTENDERS

Name	Hgt.	Wgt.	Place of Birth	Date	1983-84 Club	Mins.	GA.	SO.
Brodeur, Richard	5:07	185	Longueuil, Que.	9-15-52	Vancouver	2110	141	1
Caprice, Frank	5:09	160	Hamilton, Ont.	5-2-62	Fredericton-Vancouver	2187	111	3
Garrett, John	5:08	175	Trenton, Ont.	6-17-51	Vancouver	1653	113	0
Kilroy, Shawn	5:11	175	Ottawa, Ont.	4-22-64	Peterborough	2784	193	0
Young, Wendell	5:08	185	Halifax, N.S.	8-1-63	Fred-Milwaukee-SLC	2003	136	1

Washington Capitals
Patrick Division

Chairman of the Board, President and Governor	Abe Pollin
Executive Vice-President and Alternate Governor	Richard M. Patrick
Legal Counsel and Alternate Governors	Peter F. O'Malley, David M. Osnos
Vice-President and General Manager	David Poile
Comptroller	Ed Stelzer
Coach	Bryan Murray
Assistant Coach	Terry Murray
Director of Player Personnel and Recruitment	Jack Button
Assistant Director of Player Recruitment	David Conte
Scouts	Bob Carpenter Sr., Claude Carrier, Glen Dirk, Ron Lapointe, Bob Russel, Dick Todd, Wink Wilson
Special Assistant to Hockey Department	Jim Loria
Executive Director of Marketing	Lew Strudler
Director of Public Relations	Lou Corletto
Administrative Assistant	Sharon Sylvester
Trainer	Dick Young
Assistant Trainer	Doug Shearer
Home Ice	Capital Centre
Address	Landover, Md. 20785
Seating Capacity	18,130
Club Colors	Red, White and Blue
Phone	(301) 350-3400

Abe Pollin

David Poile

Jack Button

Bryan Murray

Washington Capitals 1984-85 Roster

FORWARDS

Name	Hgt.	Wgt.	Place of Birth	Date	1983-84 Club	G.	A.	Pts.
Adams, Greg	6:01	190	Duncan, B.C.	5-31-60	Washington	2	6	8
Carpenter, Bobby	6:01	190	Beverly, Mass.	7-13-63	Washington	28	40	68
Christian, Dave	5:11	170	Warroad, Minn.	5-13-59	Washington	29	52	81
Currie, Glen	6:02	180	Montreal, Que.	7-18-58	Washington	12	24	36
Duchesne, Gaetan	6:00	190	Quebec City, Que.	7-11-62	Washington	17	19	36
Erickson, Bryan	5:09	170	Roseau, Minn.	3- 7-60	Washington-Hershey	28	29	57
Evason, Dean	5:10	175	Flin Flon, Man.	8-22-60	Kamloops	49	88	137
Franceschetti, Lou	6:00	190	Toronto, Ont.	3-28-58	Washington-Hershey	26	34	60
Gardner, Paul	6:00	195	Fort Erie, Ont.	3- 5-56	Pittsburgh-Baltimore	32	54	86
Gartner, Mike	6:00	185	Ottawa, Ont.	10-29-57	Washington	40	45	85
Gould, Bob	5:11	190	Petrolia, Ont.	9- 2-57	Washington	21	19	40
Gustafsson, Bengt	6:00	190	Karlskoga, Sweden	3-23-58	Washington	32	43	75
Haworth, Alan	5:10	190	Drummondville, Que.	9- 1-60	Washington	24	31	55
Hidi, Andre	6:02	205	Toronto, Ont.	6- 5-60	University of Toronto	30	31	61
Jarvis, Doug	5:09	170	Brantford, Ont.	3-24-55	Washington	13	29	42
Kastelic, Ed	6:03	210	Toronto, Ont.	1-29-64	London	17	16	33
Laughlin, Craig	6:00	190	Toronto, Ont.	5- 4-58	Washington	20	32	52
McGeough, Jim	5:08	170	Regina, Sask.	4-13-63	Hershey	40	36	76
Sampson, Gary	6:00	190	Atikokan, Ont.	8-24-59	U.S. Olympic-Washington	23	22	45
Siltala, Mike	5:09	170	Toronto, Ont.	8- 5-63	Hershey	15	17	32

DEFENSEMEN

Name	Hgt.	Wgt.	Place of Birth	Date	1983-84 Club	G.	A.	Pts.
Andersson, Peter	6:02	200	Federtalve, Sweden	3- 2-61	Washington	3	7	10
Blomqvist, Timo	6:00	200	Helsinki, Finland	1-23-61	Washington	1	19	20
Calder, Eric	6:01	185	Kitchener, Ont.	6-26-63	Hershey	2	6	8
Chorney, Marc	6:00	200	Sudbury, Ont.	11- 8-59	Pittsburgh-Los Angeles	3	10	13
Langway, Rod	6:03	215	Maag, Taiwan	5- 3-57	Washington	9	24	33
Murphy, Larry	6:00	200	Toronto, Ont.	9-12-60	Los Angeles-Washington	13	36	49
Shand, Dave	6:02	200	Cold Lake, Alta.	8-11-56	Washington-Hershey	4	16	20
Stevens, Scott	6:00	200	Kitchener, Ont.	4- 1-64	Washington	13	32	45
Veitch, Darren	6:00	190	Saskatoon, Sask.	4-24-60	Washington-Hershey	7	24	31

GOALTENDERS

Name	Hgt.	Wgt.	Place of Birth	Date	1983-84 Club	Mins.	GA.	SO.
Jensen, Al	5:10	180	Hamilton, Ont.	11-27-58	Washington-Hershey	2594	133	4
Mason, Bob	6:01	180	Int'national Falls, Minn.	4-22-61	U.S. Olym.-Hershey-Washington	402	29	0
Riggin, Pat	5:09	170	Kinkardine, Ont.	5-26-59	Washington-Hershey	2484	109	4
Sidorkiewicz, Peter	5:09	165	Dabrown B'stocka, Pol.	6-29-63	Oshawa	2966	205	1

Winnipeg Jets

Smythe Division

Chairman of the Board	R. G. (Bob) Graham
President and Governor	Barry Shenkarow
Vice-President and General Manager	John Ferguson
Assistant G.M. and Director of Player Personnel	Mike Doran
Vice-President, Finance and Administration	Romeo Verrier
Coach	Barry Long
Assistant Coaches	Bill Sutherland, Rick Bowness
Director of Recruiting	Mike Smith
Chief Scout	Les Binkley
Eastern Scout	Tom Savage
Western Scout	Charlie Hodge
Special Assignments	Bill Lesuk
Scouts	Joe Yanetti, Dave Peterson, Ken Chisholm
Director of Hockey and Media Information	Ralph Carter
Director of Corporate Marketing	Madeline Hanson-Pierce
Athletic Therapist	Chuck Badcock
Home Ice	Winnipeg Arena
Address	15-1430 Maroons Road, Winnipeg, Man. R3G 0L5
Capacity for Hockey	15,250
Club Colors	Red, White and Blue
Phone	(204) 772-9491

Bob Graham

John Ferguson

Barry Long

Winnipeg Jets 1984-85 Roster

FORWARDS

Name	Hgt.	Wgt.	Place of Birth	Date	1983-84 Club	G.	A.	Pts.
Arniel, Scott	6:01	190	Kingston, Ont.	9-17-62	Winnipeg	21	35	56
Boschman, Laurie	6:00	183	Major, Sask.	6- 4-60	Winnipeg	28	46	74
Douglas, Jordy	6:00	200	Winnipeg, Man.	1-20-58	Winnipeg	7	6	13
Eaves, Murray	5:10	185	Calgary, Alta.	5-10-60	Winnipeg-Sherbrooke	47	68	115
Hawerchuk, Dale	5:11	185	Toronto, Ont.	4- 4-63	Winnipeg	37	65	102
Lauen, Mike	6:01	185	Edina, Minn.	2- 9-61	Sherbrooke	23	29	52
Lukowich, Morris	5:09	175	Speers, Sask.	6- 1-56	Winnipeg	30	25	55
Lundholm, Bengt	6:00	180	Falun, Sweden	8- 4-55	Winnipeg	5	14	19
MacLean, Paul	6:00	205	Grostenquin, France	3- 9-58	Winnipeg	40	31	71
McBain, Andrew	6:01	195	Toronto, Ont.	2-18-65	Winnipeg	11	19	30
McCaskill, Kirk	6:01	195	Phoenix, Ariz.	4- 9-61	Sherbrooke	10	12	22
Mishler, Tim	6:00	180	Grand Forks, Minn.	10- 3-63	Des Moines	..	..	..
Mullen, Brian	5:10	180	New York, N.Y.	3-16-62	Winnipeg	21	41	62
Pooley, Paul	6:00	175	Exeter, Ont.	8- 2-60	Ohio State	32	64	96
Pooley, Perry	6:00	175	Exeter, Ont.	8- 2-60	Ohio State	39	40	79
Smail, Doug	5:09	175	Moose Jaw, Sask.	9- 2-57	Winnipeg	20	17	37
Steen, Thomas	5:10	195	Tockmark, Sweden	6- 8-60	Winnipeg	20	45	65
Turnbull, Perry	6:02	200	Rimbey, Alta.	3- 9-59	St. Louis-Montreal	20	15	35
Wilson, Ron	5:09	175	Toronto, Ont.	5-13-56	Winnipeg	3	12	15
Young, Tim	6:01	190	Scarborough, Ont.	2-22-55	Winnipeg	15	19	34

DEFENSEMEN

Name	Hgt.	Wgt.	Place of Birth	Date	1983-84 Club	G.	A.	Pts.
Babych, David	6:01	215	Edmonton, Alta.	5-23-61	Winnipeg	18	39	57
Campbell, Wade	6:04	220	Peace River, Alta.	1- 2-61	Winnipeg	7	14	21
Carlyle, Randy	5:10	200	Sudbury, Ont.	4-19-56	Pittsburgh-Winnipeg	3	26	29
Channell, Craig	5:11	190	Moncton, N.B.	4-24-62	Sherbrooke	5	18	23
Dollas, Bob	6:02	220	Montreal, Que.	1-31-65	Laval	12	33	45
Elcombe, Kelly	5:11	195	Winnipeg, Man.	3-14-60	Sherbrooke	2	21	23
Ellett, Dave	6:01	200	Cleveland, Ohio	3-30-64	Bowling Green	15	39	54
Kyte, Jim	6:05	210	Ottawa, Ont.	3-21-64	Winnipeg	1	2	3
Picard, Robert	6:02	205	Montreal, Que.	5-25-57	Montreal-Winnipeg	6	16	22
Seppa, Jyrki	6:01	189	Tamperes, Finland	11-14-61	Sherbrooke-Winnipeg	5	35	40
Spring, Don	5:11	195	Maracaibo, Venezuela	6-15-59	Winnipeg-Sherbrooke	0	2	2
Watters, Tim	5:11	180	Kamloops, B.C.	7-25-59	Winnipeg	3	20	23

GOALTENDERS

Name	Hgt.	Wgt.	Place of Birth	Date	1983-84 Club	Mins.	GA.	SO.
Behrend, Marc	6:01	185	Madison, Wis.	1-11-61	Winnipeg	351	32	0
Dick, Greg	5:08	160	Minneapolis, Minn.	3- 8-62	St. Mary's	840	72	0
Hayward, Brian	5:10	175	Georgetown, Ont.	6-25-60	Winnipeg-Sherbrooke	2311	193	0
Soetaert, Doug	6:01	185	Edmonton, Alta.	4-21-56	Winnipeg	2536	182	0
Veisor, Mike	5:09	160	Toronto, Ont.	8-25-52	Hart.-Sherbrooke-Winnipeg	919	70	0

Rick Middleton

Wayne Gretzky

Michel Goulet

The Sporting News
1983-84 NHL All-Star Team

First Team	Position	Second Team
Wayne Gretzky, Edmonton	Center	Bryan Trottier, N.Y. Islanders
Rick Middleton, Boston	Right Wing	Mike Bossy, N.Y. Islanders
Michel Goulet, Quebec	Left Wing	John Ogrodnick, Detroit
Ray Bourque, Boston	Defense	Paul Coffey, Edmonton
Rod Langway, Washington	Defense	Denis Potvin, N.Y. Islanders
Pat Riggin, Washington	Goalie	Tom Barrasso, Buffalo

THE SPORTING NEWS NHL Player of the Year: Wayne Gretzky, Edmonton.
THE SPORTING NEWS NHL Rookie of the Year: Steve Yzerman, Detroit.
NOTE: THE SPORTING NEWS All-Star Team is selected by the NHL Players.

Ray Bourque

Pat Riggin

Rod Langway

Wayne Gretzky continued to pile up individual awards and records in 1983-84. He won the Hart Trophy (most valuable player) for the fifth straight year, the Ross Trophy (leading scorer) for the fourth straight, and compiled an NHL-record 51-game scoring streak (breaking his own league mark) before being shut out by Los Angeles goaltender Markus Mattsson on January 28.

Washington goaltenders Pat Riggin (above) and Al Jensen combined to allow just 219 goals last season in capturing the Bill Jennings Trophy.

1983-84 FINAL NHL STANDINGS

Prince of Wales Conference
Charles F. Adams Division

	G.	W.	L.	T.	Pts.	GF.	GA.
Boston Bruins	80	49	25	6	104	336	261
Buffalo Sabres	80	48	25	7	103	315	257
Quebec Nordiques	80	42	28	10	94	360	278
Montreal Canadiens	80	35	40	5	75	286	295
Hartford Whalers	80	28	42	10	66	288	320

Lester Patrick Division

	G.	W.	L.	T.	Pts.	GF.	GA.
New York Islanders	80	50	26	4	104	357	269
Washington Capitals	80	48	27	5	101	308	226
Philadelphia Flyers	80	44	26	10	98	350	290
New York Rangers	80	42	29	9	93	314	304
New Jersey Devils	80	17	56	7	41	231	350
Pittsburgh Penguins	80	16	58	6	38	254	390

Clarence Campbell Conference
James Norris Division

	G.	W.	L.	T.	Pts.	GF.	GA.
Minnesota North Stars	80	39	31	10	88	345	344
St. Louis Blues	80	32	41	7	71	293	316
Detroit Red Wings	80	31	42	7	69	298	323
Chicago Black Hawks	80	30	42	8	68	277	311
Toronto Maple Leafs	80	26	45	9	61	303	387

Conn Smythe Division

	G.	W.	L.	T.	Pts.	GF.	GA.
Edmonton Oilers	80	57	18	5	119	446	314
Calgary Flames	80	34	32	14	82	311	314
Vancouver Canucks	80	32	39	9	73	306	328
Winnipeg Jets	80	31	38	11	73	340	374
Los Angeles Kings	80	23	44	13	59	309	376

Top 20 Scorers for the Art Ross Memorial Trophy

*Indicates league-leading figure.

	Games	G.	A.	Pts.	Pen.
1. Wayne Gretzky, Edmonton	74	*87	*118	*205	39
2. Paul Coffey, Edmonton	80	40	86	126	104
3. Michel Goulet, Quebec	75	56	65	121	76
4. Peter Stastny, Quebec	80	46	73	119	73
5. Mike Bossy, New York Islanders	67	51	67	118	8
6. Barry Pederson, Boston	80	39	77	116	64
7. Jari Kurri, Edmonton	64	52	61	113	14
8. Bryan Trottier, New York Islanders	68	40	71	111	59
9. Bernie Federko, St. Louis	79	41	66	107	43
10. Rick Middleton, Boston	80	47	58	105	14
11. Dale Hawerchuk, Winnipeg	80	37	65	102	73
12. Mark Messier, Edmonton	73	37	64	101	165
13. Glenn Anderson, Edmonton	80	54	45	99	65
14. Ray Bourque, Boston	78	31	65	96	57
15. Bernie Nicholls, Los Angeles	78	41	54	95	83
16. Denis Savard, Chicago	75	37	57	94	71
17. Tim Kerr, Philadelphia	79	54	39	93	29
Rick Vaive, Toronto	76	52	41	93	114
19. Mike Bullard, Pittsburgh	76	51	41	92	57
Charlie Simmer, Los Angeles	79	44	48	92	78
Marcel Dionne, Los Angeles	66	39	53	92	28
Brian Propp, Philadelphia	79	39	53	92	37

National Hockey League Team-by-Team Individual Scoring

*Indicates league-leading figure.

Boston Bruins

	Games	G.	A.	Pts.	Pen.
Barry Pederson	80	39	77	116	64
Rick Middleton	80	47	58	105	14
Ray Bourque	78	31	65	96	57
Tom Fergus	69	25	36	61	12
Mike O'Connell	75	18	42	60	42
Keith Crowder	63	24	28	52	128
Mike Krushelnyski	66	25	20	45	55
Craig MacTavish	70	20	23	43	35
Gord Kluzak	80	10	27	37	135
Nevin Markwart	70	14	16	30	121
Dave Silk	35	13	17	30	64
Terry O'Reilly	58	12	18	30	124
Jim Nill, Vancouver	51	9	6	15	78
Boston	27	3	2	5	81
Totals	78	12	8	20	159
Bruce Crowder	74	6	14	20	44
Mike Milbury	74	2	17	19	159
Guy Lapointe	45	2	16	18	34
Mike Gillis	50	6	11	17	35
Randy Hillier	69	3	12	15	125
Steve Kasper	27	3	11	14	19
Luc Dufour	41	6	4	10	47
Dave Donnelly	16	3	4	7	2
Lyndon Byers	10	2	4	6	32
Doug Kostynski	9	3	1	4	2
Greg Johnston	15	2	1	3	2
John Blum, Edmonton	4	0	1	1	2
Boston	12	1	1	2	30
Totals	16	1	2	3	32
Brian Curran	16	1	1	2	57
Jim Schoenfeld	39	0	2	2	20
Dave Reid	8	1	0	1	2
Mike Moffat (Goalie)	4	0	0	0	0
Geoff Courtnall	5	0	0	0	0
Doug Keans (Goalie)	33	0	0	0	2
Pete Peeters (Goalie)	50	0	0	0	36

Buffalo Sabres

	Games	G.	A.	Pts.	Pen.
Gil Perreault	73	31	59	90	32
Dave Andreychuk	78	38	42	80	42
Phil Housley	75	31	46	77	33
Mike Foligno	70	32	31	63	151
Real Cloutier	77	24	36	60	25
Lindy Ruff	58	14	31	45	101
Gilles Hamel	75	21	23	44	37
Paul Cyr	71	16	27	43	52
Hannu Virta	70	6	30	36	12
Ric Seiling	78	13	22	35	42
Mike Ramsey	72	9	22	31	82
Sean McKenna	78	20	10	30	45
Bill Hajt	79	3	24	27	32
Craig Ramsay	76	9	17	26	17
Brent Peterson	70	9	12	21	52
Jim Wiemer	64	5	15	20	48
John Tucker	21	12	4	16	4
Mike Moller	59	5	11	16	27
Larry Playfair	76	5	11	16	209
Jerry Korab	48	2	9	11	82
Claude Verret	11	2	5	7	2

Buffalo Sabres defenseman Phil Housley

	Games	G.	A.	Pts.	Pen.
Steve Patrick	11	1	4	5	6
Adam Creighton	7	2	2	4	4
Mark Renaud	10	1	3	4	6
Dave Fenyves	10	0	4	4	9
Mal Davis	11	2	1	3	4
Tom Barrasso (Goalie)	42	0	2	2	20
Chris Langevin	6	1	0	1	2
Bob Sauve (Goalie)	40	0	0	0	2

Calgary Flames

	Games	G.	A.	Pts.	Pen.
Kent Nilsson	67	31	49	80	22
Ed Beers	73	36	39	75	88
Lanny McDonald	65	33	33	66	64
Hakan Loob	77	30	25	55	22
Dan Quinn	54	19	33	52	20
Doug Risebrough	77	23	28	51	161
Mike Eaves	61	14	36	50	20
Allan MacInnis	51	11	34	45	42
Kari Eloranta	78	5	34	39	44
Jim Peplinski	74	11	22	33	114
Jamie Macoun	72	9	23	32	97
Colin Patterson	56	13	14	27	15
Paul Baxter	74	7	20	27	182
Steve Tambellini	73	15	10	25	16
Richard Kromm	53	11	12	23	27
Paul Reinhart	27	6	15	21	10
Steve Bozek	46	10	10	20	16
Jim Jackson	49	6	14	20	13
Steve Konroyd	80	1	13	14	94
Dave Hindmarch	29	6	5	11	2
Tony Stiles	30	2	7	9	20
Jamie Hislop	27	1	8	9	2
Tim Hunter	43	4	4	8	130
Carey Wilson	15	2	5	7	2
Mickey Volcan	19	1	4	5	18
Charles Bourgeois	17	1	3	4	35
Bruce Eakin	7	2	1	3	4
Rejean Lemelin (Goalie)	51	0	3	3	6
Keith Hanson	25	0	2	2	77
Don Edwards (Goalie)	41	0	2	2	2
Neil Sheehy	1	1	0	1	2
Danny Bolduc	2	0	1	1	0
Mike Vernon (Goalie)	1	0	0	0	0
Jeff Brubaker	4	0	0	0	19

Chicago Black Hawks

	Games	G.	A.	Pts.	Pen.
Denis Savard	75	37	57	94	71
Steve Larmer	80	35	40	75	34
Doug Wilson	66	13	45	58	64
Bill Gardner	79	27	21	48	12
Bob Murray	78	11	37	48	78
Tom Lysiak	54	17	30	47	35
Jeff Larmer, New Jersey	40	6	13	19	8
Chicago	36	9	13	22	20
Totals	76	15	26	41	28
Darryl Sutter	59	20	20	40	44
Keith Brown	74	10	25	35	94
Behn Wilson	59	10	22	32	143
Troy Murray	61	15	15	30	45
Steve Ludzik	80	9	20	29	73
Rich Preston	75	10	18	28	50
Denis Cyr	46	12	13	25	19
Curt Fraser	29	5	12	17	26
Jack O'Callahan	70	4	13	17	67

Chicago Black Hawks right wing Steve Larmer

	Games	G.	A.	Pts.	Pen.
Rick Paterson	72	7	6	13	41
Dave Feamster	46	6	7	13	42
Ken Yaremchuk	47	6	7	13	19
Peter Marsh	43	4	6	10	44
Al Secord	14	4	4	8	77
Don Dietrich	17	0	5	5	0
Randy Boyd, Pittsburgh	5	0	1	1	6
Chicago	23	0	4	4	16
Totals	28	0	5	5	22
Tom McMurchy	27	3	1	4	42
Jerome Dupont	36	2	2	4	116
Murray Bannerman (Goalie)	56	0	4	4	17
Tony Esposito (Goalie)	18	0	3	3	0
Darrel Anholt	1	0	0	0	0
Jim Camazzola	1	0	0	0	0
Bruce Cassidy	1	0	0	0	0
Dan Frawley	3	0	0	0	0
Perry Pelensky	4	0	0	0	5
Bob Janecyk (Goalie)	8	0	0	0	2
Florent Robidoux	9	0	0	0	0

Detroit Red Wings

	Games	G.	A.	Pts.	Pen.
Steve Yzerman	80	39	48	87	33
Ivan Boldirev	75	35	48	83	20
Ron Duguay	80	33	47	80	34
John Ogrodnick	64	42	36	78	14
Reed Larson	78	23	39	62	122
Kelly Kisio	70	23	37	60	34
Brad Park	80	5	53	58	85
Lane Lambert	73	20	15	35	115
Rick MacLeish, Philadelphia	29	8	14	22	4
Detroit	25	2	8	10	4
Totals	54	10	22	32	8
Blake Dunlop, St. Louis	17	1	10	11	4
Detroit	57	6	14	20	20
Totals	74	7	24	31	24
Danny Gare	63	13	13	26	147
Ed Johnstone	46	12	11	23	54
Greg Smith	75	3	20	23	108
Bob Manno	62	9	13	22	60
Dwight Foster	52	9	12	21	50
Randy Ladouceur	71	3	17	20	58
Claude Loiselle	28	4	6	10	32
John Barrett	78	2	8	10	78
Pierre Aubry, Quebec	23	1	1	2	17
Detroit	14	4	1	5	8
Totals	37	5	2	7	25
Colin Campbell	68	3	4	7	108
Joe Paterson	41	2	5	7	148
Paul Woods	57	2	5	7	18
Andre St. Laurent, Pittsburgh	8	2	0	2	21
Detroit	19	1	3	4	17
Totals	27	3	3	6	38
Murray Craven	15	0	4	4	6
Brad Smith	8	2	1	3	36
Ted Nolan	19	1	2	3	26
Greg Stefan (Goalie)	50	0	3	3	14
Corrado Micalef (Goalie)	14	0	1	1	2
Barry Melrose	21	0	1	1	74
Eddie Mio (Goalie)	24	0	1	1	0
Jody Gage	3	0	0	0	0
Ken Holland (Goalie)	3	0	0	0	0
Brian Johnson	3	0	0	0	5

Detroit Red Wings left wing John Ogrodnick

Edmonton Oilers

	Games	G.	A.	Pts.	Pen.
Wayne Gretzky	74	*87	*118	*205	39
Paul Coffey	80	40	86	126	104
Jari Kurri	64	52	61	113	14
Mark Messier	73	37	64	101	165
Glenn Anderson	80	54	45	99	65
Ken Linseman	72	18	49	67	119
Pat Hughes	77	27	28	55	61
Dave Hunter	80	22	26	48	90
Kevin Lowe	80	4	42	46	59
Charlie Huddy	75	8	34	42	43
Randy Gregg	80	13	27	40	56
Willy Lindstrom	73	22	16	38	38
Kevin McClelland, Pittsburgh	24	2	4	6	62
Edmonton	52	8	20	28	127
Totals	76	10	24	34	189
Jaroslav Pouzar	67	13	19	32	44
Dave Lumley	56	6	15	21	68
Lee Fogolin	80	5	16	21	125
Don Jackson	64	8	12	20	120
Dave Semenko	52	6	11	17	118
Grant Fuhr (Goalie)	45	0	14	14	6
Pat Conacher	45	2	8	10	31
Rick Chartraw, New York Rangers	4	0	0	0	4
Edmonton	24	2	6	8	21
Totals	28	2	6	8	25
Ken Berry	13	2	3	5	10
Raimo Summanen	2	1	4	5	2
Kari Jalonen, Calgary	9	0	3	3	0
Edmonton	3	0	0	0	0
Totals	12	0	3	3	0
Jim Playfair	2	1	1	2	2
Tom Gorence	12	1	1	2	0
Gord Sherven	2	1	0	1	0
Marc Habscheid	9	1	0	1	6
Todd Strueby	1	0	1	1	2
Andy Moog (Goalie)	38	0	1	1	4
Dean Clark	1	0	0	0	0
Steve Graves	2	0	0	0	0
Reg Kerr	3	0	0	0	0
Ray Cote	13	0	0	0	2

Hartford Whalers

	Games	G.	A.	Pts.	Pen.
Mark Johnson	79	35	52	87	27
Ron Francis	72	23	60	83	45
Sylvain Turgeon	76	40	32	72	55
Ray Neufeld	80	27	42	69	97
Bob Crawford	80	36	25	61	32
Greg Malone	78	17	37	54	56
Risto Siltanen	75	15	38	53	34
Tony Currie, Vancouver	18	3	3	6	2
Hartford	32	12	16	28	4
Totals	50	15	19	34	6
Mike Zuke	75	6	23	29	36
Richie Dunn	63	5	20	25	30
Norm Dupont	40	7	15	22	12
Torrie Robertson	66	7	14	21	198
Doug Sulliman	67	6	12	18	20
Chris Kotsopoulos	72	5	13	18	118
Dan Bourbonnais	35	0	16	16	0
Joel Quenneville	80	5	8	13	95
Jack Brownschidle, St. Louis	51	1	7	8	19
Hartford	13	2	2	4	10
Totals	64	3	9	12	29
Marty Howe	69	0	11	11	34

Edmonton Oilers defenseman Paul Coffey

	Games	G.	A.	Pts.	Pen.
Randy Pierce	17	6	3	9	9
Ed Hospodar	59	0	9	9	163
Steve Stoyanovich	23	3	5	8	11
Dave Tippett	17	4	2	6	2
Mike Crombeen	56	1	4	5	25
Mark Fusco	17	0	4	4	2
Paul Lawless	6	0	3	3	0
Greg Millen (Goalie)	60	0	3	3	10
Mark Paterson	9	2	0	2	4
Ross Yates	7	1	1	2	4
Paul MacDermid	3	0	1	1	0
Ed Staniowski, Winnipeg (Goalie)	1	0	1	1	0
Hartford (Goalie)	18	0	0	0	2
Totals	19	0	1	1	2
Bob Hess	3	0	0	0	0
Gerry McDonald	5	0	0	0	4
Reid Bailey	12	0	0	0	25

Los Angeles Kings

	Games	G.	A.	Pts.	Pen.
Bernie Nicholls	78	41	54	95	83
Charlie Simmer	79	44	48	92	78
Marcel Dionne	66	39	53	92	28
Jim Fox	80	30	42	72	26
Dave Taylor	63	20	49	69	91
Brian MacLellan	72	25	29	54	45
Mark Hardy	79	8	41	49	122
Doug Smith	72	16	20	36	28
Mike McEwen, New York Islanders	15	0	2	2	6
Los Angeles	47	10	24	34	14
Totals	62	10	26	36	20
Anders Hakansson	80	15	17	32	41
Terry Ruskowski	77	7	25	32	92
Brian Engblom, Washington	6	0	1	1	8
Los Angeles	74	2	27	29	59
Totals	80	2	28	30	67
Billy Harris, Toronto	50	7	10	17	14
Los Angeles	21	2	4	6	6
Totals	71	9	14	23	20
Wes Jarvis	61	9	13	22	36
John Paul (J.P.) Kelly	72	7	14	21	73
Jay Wells	69	3	18	21	141
Russ Anderson	70	5	12	17	126
Ken Houston, Washington	4	0	0	0	4
Los Angeles	33	8	8	16	11
Totals	37	8	8	16	15
Steve Christoff	58	8	7	15	13
Marc Chorney, Pittsburgh	4	0	1	1	8
Los Angeles	71	3	9	12	58
Totals	75	3	10	13	66
Kevin Lavallee	19	3	3	6	2
Dean Kennedy	37	1	5	6	50
Fred Barrett	15	2	0	2	8
Marco Baron (Goalie)	21	0	2	2	10
Bob Laforest	5	1	0	1	2
Daryl Evans	4	0	1	1	0
Mike Heidt	6	0	1	1	7
Mike Blake (Goalie)	29	0	1	1	6
Dan Brennan	2	0	0	0	0
Warren Holmes	3	0	0	0	0
Phil Sykes	3	0	0	0	2
Dean Jenkins	5	0	0	0	2
Bill O'Dwyer	5	0	0	0	0
Mario Lessard (Goalie)	6	0	0	0	0
Gary Laskoski (Goalie)	13	0	0	0	0
Markus Mattsson (Goalie)	19	0	0	0	0

Los Angeles Kings center Bernie Nicholls

Minnesota North Stars

	Games	G.	A.	Pts.	Pen.
Neal Broten	76	28	61	89	43
Brian Bellows	78	41	42	83	66
Brad Maxwell	78	19	54	73	225
Dino Ciccarelli	79	38	33	71	58
Tom McCarthy	66	39	31	70	49
Keith Acton, Montreal	9	3	7	10	4
Minnesota	62	17	38	55	60
Totals	71	20	45	65	64
Dennis Maruk	71	17	43	60	42
Steve Payne	78	28	31	59	49
Gordie Roberts	77	8	45	53	132
Mark Napier, Montreal	5	3	2	5	0
Minnesota	58	13	28	41	17
Totals	63	16	30	46	17
Willi Plett	73	15	23	38	316
Al MacAdam	80	22	13	35	23
Brian Lawton	58	10	21	31	33
Paul Holmgren, Philadelphia	52	9	13	22	105
Minnesota	11	2	5	7	46
Totals	63	11	18	29	151
Curt Giles	70	6	22	28	59
Craig Levie	37	6	13	19	44
Lars Lindgren, Vancouver	7	1	2	3	4
Minnesota	59	2	14	16	33
Totals	66	3	16	19	37
Brent Ashton	68	7	10	17	54
George Ferguson	63	6	10	16	19
Craig Hartsburg	26	7	7	14	37
Dan Mandich	31	2	7	9	77
Dave Richter	42	2	3	5	132
Randy Velischek	33	2	2	4	10
Tom Hirsch	15	1	3	4	20
Dirk Graham	6	1	1	2	0
David H. Jensen	8	0	1	1	0
Gilles Meloche (Goalie)	52	0	1	1	2
Bob Rouse	1	0	0	0	0
Jon Casey (Goalie)	2	0	0	0	0
Tim Coulis	2	0	0	0	4
Jim Craig (Goalie)	3	0	0	0	0
Scott Bjugstad	5	0	0	0	2
Don Beaupre (Goalie)	33	0	0	0	17

Montreal Canadiens

	Games	G.	A.	Pts.	Pen.
Bobby Smith, Minnesota	10	3	6	9	9
Montreal	70	26	37	63	62
Totals	80	29	43	72	71
Guy Lafleur	80	30	40	70	19
Mats Naslund	77	29	35	64	4
Guy Carbonneau	78	24	30	54	75
Ryan Walter	73	20	29	49	83
John Chabot	56	18	25	43	13
Larry Robinson	74	9	34	43	39
Bob Gainey	77	17	22	39	41
Mario Tremblay	67	14	25	39	112
Pierre Mondou	52	15	22	37	8
Steve Shutt	63	14	23	37	29
Perry Turnbull, St. Louis	32	14	8	22	81
Montreal	40	6	7	13	59
Totals	72	20	15	35	140
Chris Nilan	76	16	10	26	*338
Craig Ludwig	80	7	18	25	52
Bill Root	72	4	13	17	45
Alfie Turcotte	30	7	7	14	10
Jean Hamel	79	1	12	13	92

Minnesota North Stars center Neal Broten

	Games	G.	A.	Pts.	Pen.
Ric Nattress	34	0	12	12	15
Mark Hunter	22	6	4	10	42
Kent Carlson	65	3	7	10	73
Mike McPhee	14	5	2	7	41
Rick Wamsley (Goalie)	42	0	3	3	6
Claude Lemieux	8	1	1	2	12
Chris Chelios	12	0	2	2	12
Rick Green	7	0	1	1	7
Mark Holden (Goalie)	1	0	0	0	0
Sergio Momesso	1	0	0	0	0
Jocelyn Gauvreau	2	0	0	0	0
Larry Landon	2	0	0	0	0
Dave Allison	3	0	0	0	12
Bill Kitchen	3	0	0	0	2
John Newberry	3	0	0	0	0
Normand Baron	4	0	0	0	12
Steve Penney (Goalie)	4	0	0	0	0
Richard Sevigny (Goalie)	40	0	0	0	12

New Jersey Devils

	Games	G.	A.	Pts.	Pen.
Mel Bridgman	79	23	38	61	121
Jan Ludvig	74	22	32	54	70
Pat Verbeek	79	20	27	47	158
Joe Cirella	79	11	33	44	137
Bob MacMillan	71	17	23	40	23
Aaron Broten	80	13	23	36	36
Tim Higgins, Chicago	32	1	4	5	21
New Jersey	37	18	10	28	27
Totals	69	19	14	33	48
Don Lever	70	14	19	33	44
Paul Gagne	66	14	18	32	33
Phil Russell	76	9	22	31	96
Rick Meagher	52	14	14	28	16
Gary McAdam, Washington	24	1	5	6	12
New Jersey	38	9	6	15	15
Totals	62	10	11	21	27
Dave Cameron	67	9	12	21	85
Murray Brumwell	42	7	13	20	14
Bob Hoffmeyer	58	4	12	16	61
Bob Lorimer	72	2	10	12	62
Mike Antonovich	38	3	5	8	16
Yvon Vautour	42	3	4	7	78
Dave Lewis	66	2	5	7	63
Ken Daneyko	11	1	4	5	17
Mike Kitchen	43	1	4	5	24
Rob Palmer	38	0	5	5	10
Hector Marini	32	2	2	4	47
Larry Floyd	7	1	3	4	7
Rich Chernomaz	7	2	1	3	2
Grant Mulvey	12	1	2	3	19
Kevin Maxwell	14	0	3	3	2
Rocky Trottier	5	1	1	2	0
Bruce Driver	4	0	2	2	0
Glenn (Chico) Resch (Goalie)	51	0	2	2	12
Glenn Merkosky	5	1	0	1	0
John MacLean	23	1	0	1	10
Alan Hepple	1	0	0	0	7
John Johannson	5	0	0	0	0
Garry Howatt	6	0	0	0	14
Ron Low (Goalie)	44	0	0	0	4

New York Islanders

	Games	G.	A.	Pts.	Pen.
Mike Bossy	67	51	67	118	8
Bryan Trottier	68	40	71	111	59

New York Islanders right wing Mike Bossy

	Games	G.	A.	Pts.	Pen.
Denis Potvin	78	22	63	85	87
John Tonelli	73	27	40	67	66
Greg Gilbert	79	31	35	66	59
Bob Bourne	78	22	34	56	75
Brent Sutter	69	34	15	49	69
Tomas Jonsson	72	11	36	47	54
Butch Goring	71	22	24	46	8
Bob Nystrom	74	15	29	44	80
Duane Sutter	78	17	23	40	94
Stefan Persson	75	9	24	33	65
Clark Gillies	76	12	16	28	65
Anders Kallur	65	9	14	23	24
Pat LaFontaine	15	13	6	19	6
Dave Langevin	69	3	16	19	53
Ken Morrow	63	3	11	14	45
Gord Dineen	43	1	11	12	32
Wayne Merrick	31	6	5	11	10
Paul Boutilier	28	0	11	11	36
Pat Flatley	16	2	7	9	6
Billy Carroll	39	5	2	7	12
Mats Hallin	40	2	5	7	27
Gord Lane	38	0	3	3	70
Roland Melanson (Goalie)	37	0	2	2	10
Billy Smith (Goalie)	42	0	2	2	23
Garth MacGuigan	3	0	1	1	0
Darcy Regier	5	0	1	1	0
Bruce Affleck	1	0	0	0	0
Kelly Hrudey (Goalie)	12	0	0	0	0

New York Rangers

	Games	G.	A.	Pts.	Pen.
Mark Pavelich	77	29	53	82	96
Pierre Larouche	77	48	33	81	22
Anders Hedberg	79	32	35	67	16
Don Maloney	79	24	42	66	62
Mike Rogers	78	23	38	61	45
Reijo Ruotsalainen	74	20	39	59	26
Ron Greschner	77	12	44	56	117
Mark Osborne	73	23	28	51	88
Blaine Stoughton, Hartford	54	23	14	37	4
New York Rangers	14	5	2	7	4
Totals	68	28	16	44	8
Peter Sundstrom	77	22	22	44	24
Barry Beck	72	9	27	36	132
Dave Maloney	68	7	26	33	168
Jan Erixon	75	5	25	30	16
Mikko Leinonen	28	3	23	26	28
Willie Huber	42	9	14	23	60
Mike Allison	45	8	12	20	64
Kent-Erik Andersson	63	5	15	20	8
Tom Laidlaw	79	3	15	18	62
Rob McClanahan	41	6	8	14	21
Nick Fotiu	40	7	6	13	115
Mike Blaisdell	36	5	6	11	31
Jim Patrick	12	1	7	8	2
Steve Richmond	26	2	5	7	110
Robbie Ftorek	31	3	2	5	22
Larry Patey, St. Louis	17	0	1	1	8
New York Rangers	9	1	2	3	4
Totals	26	1	3	4	12
Bob Brooke	9	1	2	3	4
George McPhee	9	1	1	2	11
Scot Kleinendorst	23	0	2	2	35
Glen Hanlon (Goalie)	50	0	2	2	30
Chris Kontos	6	0	1	1	8
Mike Backman	8	0	1	1	8
Mark Morrison	1	0	0	0	0

New York Rangers center Pierre Larouche

	Games	G.	A.	Pts.	Pen.
John Vanbiesbrouck (Goalie)	3	0	0	0	2
Ron Scott (Goalie)	9	0	0	0	0
Steve Weeks (Goalie)	26	0	0	0	4

Philadelphia Flyers

	Games	G.	A.	Pts.	Pen.
Tim Kerr	79	54	39	93	29
Brian Propp	79	39	53	92	37
Dave Poulin	73	31	45	76	47
Darryl Sittler	76	27	36	63	38
Bobby Clarke	73	17	43	60	70
Bill Barber	63	22	32	54	36
Mark Howe	71	19	34	53	44
Ron Sutter	79	19	32	51	101
Ilkka Sinisalo	73	29	17	46	29
Thomas Eriksson	68	11	33	44	37
Doug Crossman	78	7	28	35	63
Len Hachborn	38	11	21	32	4
Miroslav Dvorak	66	4	27	31	27
Rich Sutter, Pittsburgh	5	0	0	0	0
Philadelphia	70	16	12	28	93
Totals	75	16	12	28	93
Brad McCrimmon	71	0	24	24	76
Glen Cochrane	67	7	16	23	225
Ray Allison	37	8	13	21	47
Brad Marsh	77	3	14	17	83
Paul Guay	14	2	6	8	14
Ross Fitzpatrick	12	4	2	6	0
Dave Brown	19	1	5	6	98
Darryl Stanley	23	1	4	5	71
Lindsay Carson	16	1	3	4	10
Bob Froese (Goalie)	48	0	2	2	10
Pelle Lindbergh (Goalie)	36	0	1	1	6
Randy Holt	26	0	0	0	74

Pittsburgh Penguins

	Games	G.	A.	Pts.	Pen.
Mike Bullard	76	51	41	92	57
Doug Shedden	67	22	35	57	20
Mark Taylor, Philadelphia	1	0	0	0	0
Pittsburgh	59	24	31	55	24
Totals	60	24	31	55	24
Ron Flockhart, Philadelphia	8	0	3	3	4
Pittsburgh	68	27	18	45	40
Totals	76	27	21	48	44
Rick Kehoe	57	18	27	45	8
Tom Roulston, Edmonton	24	5	7	12	16
Pittsburgh	53	11	17	28	8
Totals	77	16	24	40	24
Pat Boutette	73	14	26	40	142
Andy Brickley	50	18	20	38	9
Kevin McCarthy, Vancouver	47	2	14	16	61
Pittsburgh	31	4	16	20	52
Totals	78	6	30	36	113
Greg Hotham	76	5	25	30	59
Bob Errey	65	9	13	22	29
Norm Schmidt	34	6	12	18	12
Bryan Maxwell, Winnipeg	3	0	3	3	27
Pittsburgh	45	3	12	15	84
Totals	48	3	15	18	111
Gary Rissling	47	4	13	17	297
Tom O'Regan	51	4	10	14	8
Greg Fox, Chicago	24	0	5	5	31
Pittsburgh	49	2	5	7	66
Totals	73	2	10	12	97
Tim Hrynewich	25	4	5	9	34

Philadelphia Flyers left wing Brian Propp

	Games	G.	A.	Pts.	Pen.
Marty McSorley	72	2	7	9	224
Tim Thornbury	14	1	8	9	16
Warren Young	15	1	7	8	19
Steve Gatzos	23	3	3	6	15
Rod Buskas	47	2	4	6	60
Bob Gladney	13	1	5	6	2
Ted Bulley	26	3	2	5	12
Dave Hannan	24	2	3	5	33
Paul Gardner	16	0	5	5	6
Jim Hamilton	11	2	2	4	4
Rod Schutt	11	1	3	4	4
Rocky Saganiuk	29	1	3	4	37
Darren Lowe	8	1	2	3	0
Mitch Lamoureux	8	1	1	2	6
Tim Tookey	8	0	2	2	2
Dean Defazio	22	0	2	2	28
Greg Tebbutt	24	0	2	2	31
Phil Bourque	5	0	1	1	12
Michel Dion (Goalie)	30	0	1	1	2
Grant Sasser	3	0	0	0	0
Vincent Tremblay	4	0	0	0	2
Todd Charlesworth	10	0	0	0	8
Troy Loney	13	0	0	0	9
Roberto Romano (Goalie)	18	0	0	0	0
Denis Herron (Goalie)	38	0	0	0	21

Quebec Nordiques

	Games	G.	A.	Pts.	Pen.
Michel Goulet	75	56	65	121	76
Peter Stastny	80	46	73	119	73
Dale Hunter	77	24	55	79	232
Wilf Paiement	80	39	37	76	121
Anton Stastny	69	25	37	62	14
Marian Stastny	68	20	32	52	26
Tony McKegney	75	24	27	51	23
Mario Marois	80	13	36	49	151
Andre Savard	60	20	24	44	38
Alain Cote	77	19	24	43	41
Bo Berglund	75	16	27	43	20
Louis Sleigher	44	15	19	34	32
Andre Dore, St. Louis	55	3	12	15	58
Quebec	25	1	16	17	25
Totals	80	4	28	32	83
Pat Price	72	3	25	28	188
Jean-Francois (J.F.) Sauve	39	10	17	27	2
Normand Rochefort	75	2	22	24	47
Randy Moller	74	4	14	18	147
Paul Gillis	57	8	9	17	59
Rick Lapointe	22	2	10	12	12
Blake Wesley	46	2	8	10	75
John Van Boxmeer	18	5	3	8	12
Wally Weir	25	2	3	5	17
Gord Donnelly	38	0	5	5	60
Jimmy Mann, Winnipeg	16	0	1	1	54
Quebec	22	1	1	2	42
Totals	38	1	2	3	96
Dan Bouchard (Goalie)	57	0	3	3	19
Clint Malarchuk (Goalie)	23	0	1	1	9
Jim Dobson	1	0	0	0	0
Jean Marc Gaulin	2	0	0	0	0
Brian Ford (Goalie)	3	0	0	0	0
Mario Gosselin (Goalie)	3	0	0	0	2
David Shaw	3	0	0	0	0

Quebec Nordiques center Dale Hunter

St. Louis Blues

	Games	G.	A.	Pts.	Pen.
Bernie Federko	79	41	66	107	43
Joe Mullen	80	41	44	85	19
Brian Sutter	76	32	51	83	162
Jorgen Pettersson	77	28	34	62	29
Rob Ramage	80	15	45	60	121
Doug Gilmour	80	25	28	53	57
Guy Chouinard	64	12	34	46	10
Wayne Babych	70	13	29	42	52
Doug Wickenheiser, Montreal	27	5	5	10	6
St. Louis	46	7	21	28	19
Totals	73	12	26	38	25
Mark Reeds	65	11	14	25	23
Pat Hickey	67	9	11	20	24
Dave Pichette, Quebec	23	2	7	9	12
St. Louis	23	0	11	11	6
Totals	46	2	18	20	18
Greg Paslawski, Montreal	26	1	4	5	4
St. Louis	34	8	6	14	17
Totals	60	9	10	19	21
Rik Wilson	48	7	11	18	53
Tim Bothwell	62	2	13	15	65
Jack Carlson	58	6	8	14	85
Dwight Schofield	70	4	10	14	219
Gilbert Delorme, Montreal	27	2	7	9	8
St. Louis	44	0	5	5	41
Totals	71	2	12	14	49
Perry Anderson	50	7	5	12	195
Alain Lemieux	17	4	5	9	6
Terry Johnson	65	2	6	8	141
Mike Liut (Goalie)	58	0	4	4	0
Jim Pavese	4	0	1	1	19
Perry Ganchar	1	0	0	0	0
John Markell	2	0	0	0	0
Ralph Klassen	5	0	0	0	0
Michel Larocque (Goalie)	5	0	0	0	2
Dave Barr, New York Rangers	6	0	0	0	2
St. Louis	1	0	0	0	0
Totals	7	0	0	0	2
Rick Heinz (Goalie)	22	0	0	0	4

Toronto Maple Leafs

	Games	G.	A.	Pts.	Pen.
Rick Vaive	76	52	41	93	114
Dan Daoust	78	18	56	74	88
John Anderson	73	37	31	68	22
Bill Derlago	79	40	20	60	50
Jim Benning	79	12	39	51	66
Dale McCourt, Buffalo	5	1	3	4	0
Toronto	72	19	24	43	10
Totals	77	20	27	47	10
Borje Salming	68	5	38	43	92
Greg Terrion	79	15	24	39	36
Stewart Gavin	80	10	22	32	90
Gaston Gingras	59	7	20	27	16
Jim Korn	65	12	14	26	257
Miroslav Frycer	47	10	16	26	55
Terry Martin	63	15	10	25	51
Walt Poddubny	38	11	14	25	48
Peter Ihnacak	47	10	13	23	24
Dave Farrish	59	4	19	23	57
Bill Stewart	56	2	17	19	116
Gary Nylund	47	2	14	16	103
Gary Leeman	52	4	8	12	31
Russ Courtnall	14	3	9	12	6
Pat Graham	41	4	4	8	65

St. Louis Blues center Bernie Federko

	Games	G.	A.	Pts.	Pen.
Frank Nigro	17	2	3	5	16
Rich Costello	10	2	1	3	2
Dave Hutchison	47	0	3	3	137
Ken Strong	2	0	2	2	2
Bob McGill	11	0	2	2	51
Mike Palmateer (Goalie)	34	0	2	2	28
Fred Perlini	1	0	0	0	0
Gary Yaremchuk	1	0	0	0	0
Bruce Dowie (Goalie)	2	0	0	0	0
Basil McRae	3	0	0	0	19
Ken Wregget (Goalie)	3	0	0	0	0
Greg Britz	6	0	0	0	2
Rick St. Croix (Goalie)	20	0	0	0	0
Allan Bester (Goalie)	32	0	0	0	6

Vancouver Canucks

	Games	G.	A.	Pts.	Pen.
Patrik Sundstrom	78	38	53	91	37
Tony Tanti	79	45	41	86	50
Thomas Gradin	75	21	57	78	32
Stan Smyl	80	24	43	67	136
Rick Lanz	79	18	39	57	45
Darcy Rota	59	28	20	48	73
Gary Lupul	69	17	27	44	51
Jiri Bubla	62	6	33	39	43
Peter McNab, Boston	52	14	16	30	10
Vancouver	13	1	6	7	10
Totals	65	15	22	37	20
Cam Neely	56	16	15	31	57
Dave Williams	67	15	16	31	294
Moe Lemay	56	12	18	30	38
Doug Halward	54	7	16	23	35
Jere Gillis	37	9	13	22	7
Neil Belland	44	7	13	20	24
Harold Snepsts	79	4	16	20	152
Michel Petit	44	6	9	15	53
Lars Molin	42	6	7	13	4
Andy Schliebener	51	2	10	12	48
Mark Kirton	26	2	3	5	2
Ron Delorme	64	2	2	4	68
Jean-Marc Lanthier	11	2	1	3	2
Garth Butcher	28	2	0	2	34
Grant Martin	12	0	2	2	6
Richard Brodeur (Goalie)	36	0	2	2	0
Taylor Hall	4	1	0	1	0
Marc Crawford	19	0	1	1	9
Doug Lidster	8	0	0	0	4
Gerry Minor	9	0	0	0	0
Frank Caprice (Goalie)	19	0	0	0	2
John Garrett (Goalie)	29	0	0	0	9

Washington Capitals

	Games	G.	A.	Pts.	Pen.
Mike Gartner	80	40	45	85	90
Dave Christian	80	29	52	81	28
Bengt Gustafsson	69	32	43	75	16
Bobby Carpenter	80	28	40	68	51
Alan Haworth	75	24	31	55	52
Craig Laughlin	80	20	32	52	69
Larry Murphy, Los Angeles	6	0	3	3	0
Washington	72	13	33	46	50
Totals	78	13	36	49	50
Scott Stevens	78	13	32	45	201
Doug Jarvis	80	13	29	42	12
Bobby Gould	78	21	19	40	74
Gaetan Duchesne	79	17	19	36	29

Washington Capitals center Dave Christian

	Games	G.	A.	Pts.	Pen.
Glen Currie	80	12	24	36	20
Rod Langway	80	9	24	33	61
Bryan Erickson	45	12	17	29	16
Darren Veitch	46	6	18	24	17
Timo Blomqvist	65	1	19	20	84
Dave Shand	72	4	15	19	124
Chris Valentine	22	6	5	11	21
Peter Andersson	42	3	7	10	20
Greg Adams	57	2	6	8	133
Greg Theberge	13	1	2	3	4
Gary Sampson	15	1	1	2	6
Paul MacKinnon	12	0	1	1	4
Andre Hidi	1	0	0	0	0
Dave Parro (Goalie)	1	0	0	0	0
Dean Evason	2	0	0	0	2
Lou Franceschetti	2	0	0	0	0
Bob Mason (Goalie)	2	0	0	0	0
Pat Riggin (Goalie)	41	0	0	0	4
Al Jensen (Goalie)	43	0	0	0	22

Winnipeg Jets

	Games	G.	A.	Pts.	Pen.
Dale Hawerchuk	80	37	65	102	73
Lucien DeBlois	80	34	45	79	50
Laurie Boschman	61	28	46	74	234
Paul MacLean	76	40	31	71	155
Thomas Steen	78	20	45	65	69
Brian Mullen	75	21	41	62	28
Dave Babych	66	18	39	57	62
Scott Arniel	80	21	35	56	68
Morris Lukowich	80	30	25	55	71
Moe Mantha	72	16	38	54	67
Doug Smail	66	20	17	37	62
Tim Young	44	15	19	34	25
Andrew McBain	78	11	19	30	37
Randy Carlyle, Pittsburgh	50	3	23	26	82
Winnipeg	5	0	3	3	2
Totals	55	3	26	29	84
Robert Picard, Montreal	7	0	2	2	0
Winnipeg	62	6	16	22	34
Totals	69	6	18	24	34
Tim Watters	74	3	20	23	169
Wade Campbell	79	7	14	21	147
Bengt Lundholm	57	5	14	19	20
Ron Wilson	51	3	12	15	12
Jordy Douglas, Minnesota	14	3	4	7	10
Winnipeg	17	4	2	6	8
Totals	31	7	6	13	18
Don Spring	21	0	4	4	4
Jim Kyte	58	1	2	3	55
Doug Soetaert (Goalie)	47	0	3	3	14
Jyrki Seppa	13	0	2	2	6
Mike Lauen	3	0	1	1	0
Brian Hayward (Goalie)	28	0	1	1	2
Bob Dollas	1	0	0	0	0
Murray Eaves	2	0	0	0	0
Tim Trimper	5	0	0	0	0
Marc Behrend (Goalie)	6	0	0	0	0
John Gibson	11	0	0	0	14
Mike Veisor, Hartford (Goalie)	4	0	0	0	0
Winnipeg (Goalie)	8	0	0	0	0
Totals	12	0	0	0	0

Winnipeg Jets center Dale Hawerchuk

Complete Goaltending Records

	Games	Mins.	Goals	SO.	Avg.
Dave Parro, Washington	1	1	0	0	0.00
Bob Mason, Washington	2	120	3	0	1.50
Pat Riggin, Washington	41	2299	102(1)	*4	*2.66
Al Jensen, Washington	43	2414	117(3)	*4	2.91
WASHINGTON TOTALS	80	4834	226	8	2.81
Tom Barrasso, Buffalo	42	2475	117(2)	2	2.84
Bob Sauve, Buffalo	40	2375	138	0	3.49
BUFFALO TOTALS	80	4850	257	2	3.18
Doug Keans, Boston	33	1779	92(2)	2	3.10
Pete Peeters, Boston	50	2868	151(1)	0	3.16
Mike Moffat, Boston	4	186	15	0	4.84
BOSTON TOTALS	80	4833	261	2	3.24
Kelly Hrudey, New York Islanders	12	535	28	0	3.14
Roland Melanson, New York Islanders	37	2019	110(1)	0	3.27
Billy Smith, New York Islanders	42	2279	130	2	3.42
NEW YORK ISLANDERS TOTALS	80	4833	269	2	3.34
Mario Gosselin, Quebec	3	148	3	1	1.22
Dan Bouchard, Quebec	57	3373	180(2)	1	3.20
Clint Malarchuk, Quebec	23	1215	80	0	3.95
Brian Ford, Quebec	3	123	13	0	6.34
QUEBEC TOTALS	80	4859	278	2	3.43
Bob Froese, Philadelphia	48	2863	150(2)	2	3.14
Pelle Lindbergh, Philadelphia	36	1999	135(3)	1	4.05
PHILADELPHIA TOTALS	80	4862	290	3	3.58
Richard Sevigny, Montreal	40	2203	124(3)	1	3.38
Rick Wamsley, Montreal	42	2333	144(1)	2	3.70
Mark Holden, Montreal	1	52	4	0	4.62
Steve Penney, Montreal	4	240	19	0	4.75
MONTREAL TOTALS	80	4828	295	3	3.67
John Vanbiesbrouck, New York Rangers	3	180	10(1)	0	3.33
Glen Hanlon, New York Rangers	50	2837	166(5)	1	3.51
Ron Scott, New York Rangers	9	485	29(1)	0	3.59
Steve Weeks, New York Rangers	26	1361	90(2)	0	3.97
NEW YORK RANGERS TOTALS	80	4863	304	1	3.75
Murray Bannerman, Chicago	56	3335	188(4)	2	3.38
Bob Janecyk, Chicago	8	412	28	0	4.08
Tony Esposito, Chicago	18	1095	88(3)	1	4.82
CHICAGO TOTALS	80	4842	311	3	3.85
Rejean Lemelin, Calgary	51	2568	150	0	3.50
Don Edwards, Calgary	41	2303	157(3)	0	4.09
Mike Vernon, Calgary	1	11	4	0	21.82
CALGARY TOTALS	80	4882	314	0	3.86
Andy Moog, Edmonton	38	2212	139(2)	1	3.77
Grant Fuhr, Edmonton	45	2625	171(2)	1	3.91
EDMONTON TOTALS	80	4837	314	2	3.89
Mike Liut, St. Louis	58	3425	197(6)	3	3.45
Rick Heinz, St. Louis	22	1118	80(1)	0	4.29
Michel Larocque, St. Louis	5	300	31(1)	0	6.20
ST. LOUIS TOTALS	80	4843	316	3	3.91
Greg Millen, Hartford	*60	*3583	*221(5)	2	3.70
Ed Staniowski, Hartford (a)	18	1041	74	0	4.27
Mike Veisor, Hartford (b)	4	240	20	0	5.00
HARTFORD TOTALS	80	4864	320	2	3.95
Greg Stefan, Detroit	50	2600	152(5)	2	3.51
Corrado Micalef, Detroit	14	808	52(4)	0	3.86
Ken Holland, Detroit	3	146	10(2)	0	4.11
Eddie Mio, Detroit	24	1295	95(3)	1	4.40
DETROIT TOTALS	80	4849	323	3	4.00
Frank Caprice, Vancouver	19	1099	62(2)	1	3.38
Richard Brodeur, Vancouver	36	2107	141(7)	1	4.02
John Garrett, Vancouver	29	1652	113(3)	0	4.10
VANCOUVER TOTALS	80	4858	328	2	4.05

Just one year after completing an outstanding career at a Massachusetts high school, Buffalo's Tom Barrasso won the Vezina Trophy, the Calder Trophy and was named to the NHL's All-Star first team.

	Games	Mins.	Goals	SO.	Avg.
Don Beaupre, Minnesota	33	1791	123(2)	0	4.12
Gilles Meloche, Minnesota	52	2883	201(3)	2	4.18
Jon Casey, Minnesota	2	84	6	0	4.29
Jim Craig, Minnesota	3	110	9	0	4.91
MINNESOTA TOTALS	80	4868	344	2	4.24
Glenn Resch, New Jersey	51	2641	184(4)	1	4.18
Ron Low, New Jersey	44	2218	161(1)	0	4.36
NEW JERSEY TOTALS	80	4859	350	+2	4.32
Mike Veisor, Winnipeg (b)	8	420	26	0	3.71
Doug Soetaert, Winnipeg	47	2536	182(1)	0	4.31
Brian Hayward, Winnipeg	28	1530	124(1)	0	4.86
Marc Behrend, Winnipeg	6	351	32	0	5.47
Ed Staniowski, Winnipeg (a)	1	40	8	0	12.00
WINNIPEG TOTALS	80	4877	374	0	4.60
Marco Baron, Los Angeles	21	1211	87(5)	0	4.31
Markus Mattsson, Los Angeles	19	1101	79(1)	1	4.31
Mike Blake, Los Angeles	29	1634	118(1)	0	4.33
Gary Laskoski, Los Angeles	13	665	55(2)	0	4.96
Mario Lessard, Los Angeles	6	266	26(2)	0	5.86
LOS ANGELES TOTALS	80	4877	376	1	4.63
Bruce Dowie, Toronto	2	72	4	0	3.33
Allan Bester, Toronto	32	1848	134(1)	0	4.35
Mike Palmateer, Toronto	34	1831	149(3)	0	4.88
Ken Wregget, Toronto	3	165	14	0	5.09
Rick St. Croix, Toronto	20	939	80(2)	0	5.11
TORONTO TOTALS	80	4855	387	0	4.78
Denis Herron, Pittsburgh	38	2028	138(7)	1	4.08
Roberto Romano, Pittsburgh	18	1020	78	1	4.59
Michel Dion, Pittsburgh	30	1553	138(4)	0	5.33
Vincent Tremblay, Pittsburgh	4	240	24(1)	0	6.00
PITTSBURGH TOTALS	80	4841	390	2	4.83

( )—Empty Net Goals. Do not count against an individual average.
+—Combined shutout by Resch and Low vs. Detroit, Dec. 4, 1983.
(a)—Staniowski played for Winnipeg and Hartford.
(b)—Veisor played for Hartford and Winnipeg.

Individual Leaders (1983-84)

Goals	Wayne Gretzky, Edmonton—	87
Assists	Wayne Gretzky, Edmonton—	118
Points	Wayne Gretzky, Edmonton—	205
Goaltender's Average (25 Games)	Pat Riggin, Washington—	2.66
Shutouts	Pat Riggin, Washington—	4
	Al Jensen, Washington—	4

NHL Miscellaneous Statistics

(Players are listed alphabetically)

Player — Team	Games	Shots	Goals	Shooting Pct.	PPG	SHG	+/−
Keith Acton, Montreal	9	14	3	21.4	2	0	− 5
Minnesota	62	151	17	11.3	4	2	+ 2
Totals	71	165	20	12.1	6	2	− 3
Greg Adams, Washington	57	37	2	5.4	0	0	+ 1
Bruce Affleck, N.Y. Islanders	1	2	0	....	0	0	− 1
Dave Allison, Montreal	3	2	0	....	0	0	− 2
Mike Allison, N.Y. Rangers	45	52	8	15.4	0	0	+ 5
Ray Allison, Philadelphia	37	73	8	11.0	0	0	+ 11
Glenn Anderson, Edmonton	80	277	54	19.5	11	4	+ 41
John Anderson, Toronto	73	192	37	19.3	14	0	− 12
Perry Anderson, St. Louis	50	49	7	14.3	0	0	− 13
Russ Anderson, Los Angeles	70	47	5	10.6	0	0	− 30
Kent-Erik Andersson, N.Y. Rangers	63	70	5	7.1	0	0	+ 5
Peter Andersson, Washington	42	49	3	6.1	2	0	+ 12
Dave Andreychuk, Buffalo	78	178	38	21.3	10	0	+ 20
Darrel Anholt, Chicago	1	0	0	....	0	0	+ 2
Mike Antonovich, New Jersey	38	47	3	6.4	0	0	− 15
Scott Arniel, Winnipeg	80	140	21	15.0	6	0	− 10
Brent Ashton, Minnesota	68	82	7	8.5	0	0	− 13
Pierre Aubry, Quebec	23	9	1	11.1	0	0	− 3
Detroit	14	13	4	30.8	0	0	− 1
Totals	37	22	5	22.7	0	0	− 4
Dave Babych, Winnipeg	66	233	18	7.7	10	0	− 31
Wayne Babych, St. Louis	70	115	13	11.3	3	0	+ 1
Mike Backman, N.Y. Rangers	8	6	0	....	0	0	+ 8
Reid Bailey, Hartford	12	8	0	....	0	0	− 2
Bill Barber, Philadelphia	63	203	22	10.8	3	0	+ 4
Normand Baron, Montreal	4	2	0	....	0	0	− 2
Dave Barr, N.Y. Rangers	6	9	0	....	0	0	Even
St. Louis	1	0	0	....	0	0	− 1
Totals	7	0	0	....	0	0	− 1
Fred Barrett, Los Angeles	15	4	2	50.0	0	0	− 2
John Barrett, Detroit	78	63	2	3.2	0	0	Even
Paul Baxter, Calgary	74	87	7	8.0	1	0	− 1
Barry Beck, N.Y. Rangers	72	159	9	5.7	2	1	+ 12
Ed Beers, Calgary	73	189	36	19.0	16	0	+ 7
Neil Belland, Vancouver	44	84	7	8.3	2	0	− 8
Brian Bellows, Minnesota	78	236	41	17.4	14	5	− 2
Jim Benning, Toronto	79	136	12	8.8	6	0	− 4
Bo Berglund, Quebec	75	83	16	19.3	1	0	+ 6
Ken Berry, Edmonton	13	18	2	11.1	0	1	+ 6
Scott Bjugstad, Minnesota	5	5	0	....	0	0	− 1
Mike Blaisdell, N.Y. Rangers	36	63	5	7.9	0	0	Even
Timo Blomqvist, Washington	65	69	1	1.4	0	0	+ 17
John Blum, Edmonton	4	3	0	....	0	0	Even
Boston	12	9	1	11.1	0	0	+ 5
Totals	16	12	1	8.3	0	0	+ 5
Ivan Boldirev, Detroit	75	185	35	18.9	12	0	+ 3
Danny Bolduc, Calgary	2	4	0	....	0	0	+ 1
Laurie Boschman, Winnipeg	61	138	28	20.3	9	0	− 4
Mike Bossy, N.Y. Islanders	67	246	51	10.7	6	0	+ 66
Tim Bothwell, St. Louis	62	59	2	3.4	1	0	+ 22
Dan Bourbonnais, Hartford	35	42	0	....	0	0	+ 3
Charles Bourgeois, Calgary	17	20	1	5.0	0	0	Even
Bob Bourne, N.Y. Islanders	78	140	22	15.7	5	5	+ 12
Phil Bourque, Pittsburgh	5	6	0	....	0	0	− 2
Ray Bourque, Boston	78	*340	31	9.1	12	1	+ 51
Pat Boutette, Pittsburgh	73	107	14	13.1	10	0	− 58
Paul Boutilier, N.Y. Islanders	28	31	0	....	0	0	+ 18
Randy Boyd, Pittsburgh	5	14	0	....	0	0	− 2
Chicago	23	21	0	....	0	0	Even
Totals	28	35	0	....	0	0	− 2
Steve Bozek, Calgary	46	76	10	13.2	0	0	− 16
Dan Brennan, Los Angeles	2	1	0	....	0	0	− 1
Andy Brickley, Pittsburgh	50	75	18	24.0	7	1	− 7
Mel Bridgman, New Jersey	79	127	23	18.1	9	1	− 27
Greg Britz, Toronto	6	1	0	....	0	0	− 1

Player — Team	Games	Shots	Goals	Shooting Pct.	PPG	SHG	+/−
Bob Brooke, N.Y. Rangers	9	10	1	10.0	0	0	+ 1
Aaron Broten, New Jersey	80	102	13	12.7	3	0	− 28
Neal Broten, Minnesota	76	185	28	15.1	8	3	+ 16
Dave Brown, Philadelphia	19	9	1	11.1	0	0	+ 4
Keith Brown, Chicago	74	148	10	6.8	3	0	− 18
Jack Brownschidle, St. Louis	51	50	1	2.0	1	0	− 21
Hartford	13	17	2	11.8	0	0	− 5
Totals	64	67	3	4.5	1	0	− 26
Jeff Brubaker, Calgary	4	2	0	....	0	0	− 1
Murray Brumwell, New Jersey	42	55	7	12.7	5	0	− 5
Jiri Bubla, Vancouver	62	84	6	7.1	2	0	− 10
Mike Bullard, Pittsburgh	76	213	51	23.9	15	0	− 33
Ted Bulley, Pittsburgh	26	27	3	11.1	0	0	− 14
Rod Buskas, Pittsburgh	47	39	2	5.1	1	0	− 18
Garth Butcher, Vancouver	28	33	2	6.1	0	0	− 12
Lyndon Byers, Boston	10	11	2	18.2	0	0	+ 3
Jim Camazzola, Chicago	1	1	0	....	0	0	Even
Dave Cameron, New Jersey	67	79	9	11.4	2	0	− 11
Colin Campbell, Detroit	68	48	3	6.3	0	0	Even
Wade Campbell, Winnipeg	79	89	7	7.9	0	0	− 2
Guy Carbonneau, Montreal	78	166	24	14.5	3	7	+ 5
Jack Carlson, St. Louis	58	35	6	17.1	0	0	+ 9
Kent Carlson, Montreal	65	41	3	7.3	0	0	− 15
Randy Carlyle, Pittsburgh	50	107	3	2.8	0	0	− 25
Winnipeg	5	5	0	....	0	0	+ 2
Totals	55	112	3	2.7	0	0	− 23
Bob Carpenter, Washington	80	228	28	12.3	8	0	Even
Billy Carroll, N.Y. Islanders	39	39	5	12.8	0	0	− 1
Lindsay Carson, Philadelphia	16	16	1	6.3	0	0	− 7
Bruce Cassidy, Chicago	1	1	0	....	0	0	Even
John Chabot, Montreal	56	69	18	26.1	4	1	− 2
Todd Charlesworth, Pittsburgh	10	6	0	....	0	0	− 7
Rick Chartraw, N.Y. Rangers	4	0	0	....	0	0	− 3
Edmonton	24	23	2	8.7	0	0	+ 5
Totals	28	23	2	8.7	0	0	+ 2
Chris Chelios, Montreal	12	23	0	....	0	0	− 5
Rich Chernomaz, New Jersey	7	7	2	28.6	0	0	− 3
Marc Chorney, Pittsburgh	4	5	0	....	0	0	− 4
Los Angeles	71	57	3	5.3	0	0	− 24
Totals	75	62	3	4.8	0	0	− 28
Guy Chouinard, St. Louis	64	117	12	10.3	4	0	− 15
Dave Christian, Washington	80	164	29	17.7	9	0	+ 26
Steve Christoff, Los Angeles	58	74	8	10.8	0	0	− 19
Dino Ciccarelli, Minnesota	79	211	38	18.0	16	0	+ 1
Joe Cirella, New Jersey	79	156	11	7.1	6	0	− 43
Dean Clark, Edmonton	1	0	0	....	0	0	Even
Bobby Clarke, Philadelphia	73	129	17	13.2	3	1	+ 23
Real Cloutier, Buffalo	77	169	24	14.2	9	0	− 1
Glen Cochrane, Philadelphia	67	69	7	10.1	0	0	+ 16
Paul Coffey, Edmonton	80	258	40	15.5	14	1	+ 52
Pat Conacher, Edmonton	45	18	2	11.1	0	0	− 2
Rich Costello, Toronto	10	7	2	28.6	1	0	− 5
Alain Cote, Quebec	77	116	19	16.4	0	1	+ 21
Ray Cote, Edmonton	13	12	0	....	0	0	− 5
Tim Coulis, Minnesota	2	0	0	....	0	0	− 1
Geoff Courtnall, Boston	5	0	0	....	0	0	− 1
Russ Courtnall, Toronto	14	29	3	10.3	1	0	Even
Murray Craven, Detroit	15	8	0	....	0	0	+ 2
Bob Crawford, Hartford	80	179	36	20.1	5	0	− 1
Marc Crawford, Vancouver	19	13	0	....	0	0	Even
Adam Creighton, Buffalo	7	8	2	25.0	0	0	Even
Mike Crombeen, Hartford	56	46	1	2.2	0	0	− 13
Doug Crossman, Philadelphia	78	160	7	4.4	2	0	+ 23
Bruce Crowder, Boston	74	65	6	9.2	0	0	+ 1
Keith Crowder, Boston	63	110	24	21.8	4	0	+ 12
Brian Curran, Boston	16	6	1	16.7	0	0	Even
Glen Currie, Washington	80	71	12	16.9	0	2	+ 9
Tony Currie, Vancouver	18	22	3	13.6	1	0	− 1
Hartford	32	54	12	22.2	6	0	− 2
Totals	50	76	15	19.7	7	0	− 3

Player — Team	Games	Shots	Goals	Shooting Pct.	PPG	SHG	+/-
Denis Cyr, Chicago	46	72	12	16.7	6	0	Even
Paul Cyr, Buffalo	71	142	16	11.3	5	0	− 3
Ken Daneyko, New Jersey	11	17	1	5.9	0	0	− 1
Dan Daoust, Toronto	78	154	18	11.7	8	0	− 16
Mal Davis, Buffalo	11	12	2	16.7	1	0	− 1
Lucien DeBlois, Winnipeg	80	195	34	17.4	8	1	− 14
Dean Defazio, Pittsburgh	22	12	0	....	0	0	− 11
Gilbert Delorme, Montreal	27	37	2	5.4	0	0	− 4
St. Louis	44	68	0	....	0	0	− 7
Totals	71	105	2	1.9	0	0	− 11
Ron Delorme, Vancouver	64	18	2	11.1	0	0	− 2
Bill Derlago, Toronto	79	210	40	19.0	8	2	− 7
Don Dietrich, Chicago	17	22	0	....	0	0	− 1
Gord Dineen, N. Y. Islanders	43	37	1	2.7	0	0	+ 10
Marcel Dionne, Los Angeles	66	278	39	14.0	13	0	+ 8
Jim Dobson, Quebec	1	1	0	....	0	0	− 1
Bob Dollas, Winnipeg	1	0	0	....	0	0	− 2
Dave Donnelly, Boston	16	22	3	13.6	0	0	+ 13
Gord Donnelly, Quebec	38	14	0	....	0	0	− 1
Andre Dore, St. Louis	55	51	3	5.8	0	0	+ 3
Quebec	25	30	1	3.3	0	0	+ 1
Totals	80	81	4	4.9	0	0	+ 4
Jordy Douglas, Minnesota	14	21	3	14.3	0	0	− 2
Winnipeg	17	14	4	28.6	1	0	− 9
Totals	31	35	7	20.0	1	0	− 11
Bruce Driver, New Jersey	4	5	0	....	0	0	− 2
Gaetan Duchesne, Washington	79	116	17	14.7	3	2	+ 15
Luc Dufour, Boston	41	39	6	15.4	0	0	+ 2
Ron Duguay, Detroit	80	215	33	15.3	13	1	− 26
Blake Dunlop, St. Louis	17	18	1	5.6	0	0	− 1
Detroit	57	67	6	9.0	1	1	− 13
Totals	74	85	7	8.2	1	1	− 14
Richie Dunn, Hartford	63	82	5	6.1	0	0	− 20
Jerome Dupont, Chicago	36	28	2	7.1	0	0	− 11
Norm Dupont, Hartford	40	85	7	8.2	2	0	− 16
Miroslav Dvorak, Philadelphia	66	85	4	4.7	0	1	+ 19
Bruce Eakin, Calgary	7	8	2	25.0	0	0	− 1
Mike Eaves, Calgary	61	118	14	11.9	3	0	+ 9
Murray Eaves, Winnipeg	2	1	0	....	0	0	Even
Kari Eloranta, Calgary	78	59	5	8.5	2	0	+ 12
Brian Engblom, Washington	6	15	0	....	0	0	− 4
Los Angeles	74	127	2	1.6	2	0	− 9
Totals	80	142	2	1.4	2	0	− 13
Bryan Erickson, Washington	45	66	12	18.2	4	0	+ 10
Thomas Eriksson, Philadelphia	68	110	11	10.0	2	0	+ 28
Jan Erixon, N. Y. Rangers	75	94	5	5.8	1	0	+ 14
Bob Errey, Pittsburgh	65	84	9	10.7	1	0	− 20
Daryl Evans, Los Angeles	4	6	0	....	0	0	+ 1
Dean Evason, Washington	2	0	0	....	0	0	Even
Dave Farrish, Toronto	59	77	4	5.2	1	0	− 13
Dave Feamster, Chicago	46	44	6	13.6	0	0	− 8
Bernie Federko, St. Louis	79	198	41	20.7	14	0	− 3
Dave Fenyves, Buffalo	10	4	0	....	0	0	+ 7
Tom Fergus, Boston	69	123	25	20.3	6	0	+ 8
George Ferguson, Minnesota	63	57	6	10.5	0	0	− 6
Ross Fitzpatrick, Philadelphia	12	21	4	19.0	0	0	+ 4
Pat Flatley, N. Y. Islanders	16	17	2	11.8	1	0	+ 3
Ron Flockhart, Philadelphia	8	12	0	....	0	0	+ 1
Pittsburgh	68	202	27	13.4	5	0	− 19
Totals	76	214	27	12.6	5	0	− 18
Larry Floyd, New Jersey	7	15	1	6.7	0	0	− 4
Lee Fogolin, Edmonton	80	73	5	6.8	0	0	+ 33
Mike Foligno, Buffalo	70	183	32	17.5	6	0	+ 32
Dwight Foster, Detroit	52	75	9	12.0	0	2	− 4
Nick Fotiu, N. Y. Rangers	40	40	7	17.5	0	0	+ 8
Greg Fox, Chicago	24	15	0	....	0	0	Even
Pittsburgh	49	27	2	7.4	0	0	− 42
Totals	73	42	2	4.8	0	0	− 42
Jim Fox, Los Angeles	80	153	30	19.6	10	0	− 12
Lou Franceschetti, Washington	2	2	0	....	0	0	− 2
Ron Francis, Hartford	72	202	23	11.4	5	0	− 10

Player — Team	Games	Shots	Goals	Shooting Pct.	PPG	SHG	+/−
Curt Fraser, Chicago	29	45	5	11.1	1	0	+ 9
Dan Frawley, Chicago	3	2	0	....	0	0	− 1
Miroslav Frycer, Toronto	47	83	10	12.0	1	0	− 23
Robbie Ftorek, N. Y. Rangers	31	7	3	42.9	0	0	+ 2
Mark Fusco, Hartford	17	17	0	....	0	0	− 6
Jody Gage, Detroit	3	1	0	....	0	0	Even
Paul Gagne, New Jersey	66	109	14	12.8	3	0	− 22
Bob Gainey, Montreal	77	125	17	13.6	0	0	+ 10
Perry Ganchar, St. Louis	1	0	0	....	0	0	+ 1
Paul Gardner, Pittsburgh	16	21	0	....	0	0	− 4
Bill Gardner, Chicago	79	114	27	23.7	3	3	+ 1
Danny Gare, Detroit	63	148	13	8.8	1	0	+ 3
Mike Gartner, Washington	80	286	40	14.0	8	0	+ 22
Steve Gatzos, Pittsburgh	23	29	3	10.3	0	0	− 9
Jean-Marc Gaulin, Quebec	2	0	0	....	0	0	− 1
Jocelyn Gauvreau, Montreal	2	0	0	....	0	0	− 2
Stewart Gavin, Toronto	80	96	10	10.4	0	1	− 6
John Gibson, Winnipeg	11	4	0	....	0	0	+ 2
Greg Gilbert, N. Y. Islanders	79	118	31	26.3	6	0	+ 51
Curt Giles, Minnesota	70	78	6	7.7	2	0	+ 2
Clark Gillies, N. Y. Islanders	76	138	12	8.7	3	0	+ 5
Jere Gillis, Vancouver	37	55	9	16.4	0	1	+ 2
Mike Gillis, Boston	50	59	6	10.2	0	0	− 7
Paul Gillis, Quebec	57	58	8	13.8	0	0	+ 10
Doug Gilmour, St. Louis	80	157	25	15.9	3	1	+ 6
Gaston Gingras, Toronto	59	125	7	5.6	4	0	− 30
Bob Gladney, Pittsburgh	13	15	1	6.7	0	0	− 1
Tom Gorence, Edmonton	12	7	1	14.3	0	0	Even
Butch Goring, N. Y. Islanders	71	89	22	24.7	0	5	+ 8
Bobby Gould, Washington	78	155	21	13.5	4	0	− 2
Michel Goulet, Quebec	75	239	56	23.4	11	2	+ 62
Thomas Gradin, Vancouver	75	170	21	12.4	11	1	− 2
Dirk Graham, Minnesota	6	10	1	10.0	0	0	+ 1
Pat Graham, Toronto	41	46	4	8.7	0	0	− 8
Steve Graves, Edmonton	2	2	0	....	0	0	Even
Rick Green, Montreal	7	10	0	....	0	0	− 5
Randy Gregg, Edmonton	80	91	13	14.3	2	1	+ 40
Ron Greschner, N. Y. Rangers	77	130	12	9.2	5	0	+ 5
Wayne Gretzky, Edmonton	74	324	*87	26.9	*20	*12	*+ 76
Paul Guay, Philadelphia	14	19	2	10.5	0	0	+ 1
Bengt-Ake Gustafsson, Washington	69	146	32	21.9	8	0	+ 29
Marc Habscheid, Edmonton	6	6	1	16.7	0	0	− 3
Len Hachborn, Philadelphia	38	69	11	15.9	1	0	+ 8
Bill Hajt, Buffalo	79	53	3	5.7	0	1	+ 26
Anders Hakansson, Los Angeles	80	117	15	12.8	0	1	− 7
Taylor Hall, Vancouver	4	3	1	33.3	0	0	− 2
Mats Hallin, N. Y. Islanders	40	31	2	6.5	0	0	− 2
Doug Halward, Vancouver	54	108	7	6.5	2	0	+ 1
Gilles Hamel, Buffalo	75	135	21	15.6	4	2	+ 4
Jean Hamel, Montreal	79	68	1	1.5	0	0	+ 7
Jim Hamilton, Pittsburgh	11	21	2	9.5	1	0	+ 2
Dave Hannan, Pittsburgh	24	21	2	9.5	0	1	− 2
Keith Hanson, Calgary	25	19	0	....	0	0	− 13
Mark Hardy, Los Angeles	79	175	8	4.6	5	0	− 30
Billy Harris, Toronto	50	68	7	10.3	0	0	− 20
Los Angeles	21	19	2	10.5	0	0	− 3
Totals	71	87	9	10.3	0	0	− 23
Craig Hartsburg, Minnesota	26	54	7	13.0	5	0	− 2
Dale Hawerchuk, Winnipeg	80	256	37	14.5	10	0	− 14
Alan Haworth, Washington	75	164	24	14.6	7	0	+ 14
Anders Hedberg, N. Y. Rangers	79	209	32	15.3	6	0	+ 18
Mike Heidt, Los Angeles	6	1	0	....	0	0	− 1
Alan Hepple, New Jersey	1	0	0	....	0	0	− 1
Bob Hess, Hartford	3	3	0	....	0	0	+ 1
Pat Hickey, St. Louis	67	77	9	11.7	0	0	− 3
Tim Higgins, Chicago	32	21	1	4.8	0	0	+ 1
New Jersey	37	72	18	25.0	3	1	− 4
Totals	69	93	19	20.4	3	1	− 3
Randy Hillier, Boston	69	62	3	4.8	0	0	− 5
Dave Hindmarch, Calgary	29	49	6	12.2	0	0	− 2
Tom Hirsch, Minnesota	15	24	1	4.2	0	1	− 3

Player — Team	Games	Shots	Goals	Shooting Pct.	PPG	SHG	+/−
Jamie Hislop, Calgary	27	18	1	5.6	0	0	Even
Bob Hoffmeyer, New Jersey	58	80	4	5.0	0	0	− 20
Warren Holmes, Los Angeles	3	3	0	....	0	0	− 3
Paul Holmgren, Philadelphia	52	75	9	12.0	1	0	+ 1
Minnesota	11	17	2	11.8	0	0	− 2
Totals	63	92	11	12.0	1	0	− 1
Randy Holt, Philadelphia	26	4	0	....	0	0	− 1
Ed Hospodar, Hartford	59	55	0	....	0	0	− 17
Greg Hotham, Pittsburgh	76	120	5	4.2	3	0	− 25
Phil Housley, Buffalo	75	234	31	13.2	13	2	+ 4
Ken Houston, Washington	4	3	0	....	0	0	− 2
Los Angeles	33	35	8	22.9	0	0	− 3
Totals	37	38	8	21.1	0	0	− 5
Garry Howatt, New Jersey	6	5	0	....	0	0	− 1
Mark Howe, Philadelphia	71	184	19	10.3	3	3	+ 30
Marty Howe, Hartford	69	58	0	....	0	0	+ 1
Tim Hrynewich, Pittsburgh	25	24	4	16.7	0	0	− 10
Willie Huber, N.Y. Rangers	42	92	9	9.8	4	1	− 14
Charlie Huddy, Edmonton	75	161	8	5.0	3	0	+ 50
Pat Hughes, Edmonton	77	164	27	16.5	2	3	+ 18
Dale Hunter, Quebec	77	123	24	19.5	7	2	+ 35
Dave Hunter, Edmonton	80	117	22	18.8	1	1	+ 25
Mark Hunter, Montreal	22	24	6	25.0	1	0	− 2
Tim Hunter, Calgary	43	22	4	18.2	0	0	Even
Dave Hutchison, Toronto	47	16	0	....	0	0	+ 5
Peter Ihnacak, Toronto	47	76	10	13.2	5	0	− 21
Don Jackson, Edmonton	64	57	8	14.0	0	1	+ 28
Jim Jackson, Calgary	49	66	6	9.1	0	1	+ 1
Kari Jalonen, Calgary	9	4	0	....	0	0	− 1
Edmonton	3	0	0	....	0	0	− 2
Totals	12	4	0	....	0	0	− 3
Doug Jarvis, Washington	80	122	13	10.7	12	0	+ 7
Wes Jarvis, Los Angeles	61	63	9	14.3	1	1	− 7
Dean Jenkins, Los Angeles	5	3	0	....	0	0	− 1
David H. Jensen, Minnesota	8	5	0	....	0	0	+ 2
John Johannson, New Jersey	5	4	0	....	0	0	− 2
Brian Johnson, Detroit	3	4	0	....	0	0	− 3
Mark Johnson, Hartford	79	184	35	19.0	13	1	− 14
Terrance Johnson, St. Louis	65	38	2	5.3	0	0	+ 5
Greg Johnston, Boston	15	15	2	13.3	0	0	− 3
Ed Johnstone, Detroit	46	50	12	24.0	4	0	+ 3
Tomas Jonsson, N.Y. Islanders	72	122	11	9.0	2	0	+ 12
Anders Kallur, N.Y. Islanders	65	70	9	12.9	2	3	Even
Steve Kasper, Boston	27	39	3	7.7	0	0	+ 3
Rick Kehoe, Pittsburgh	57	156	18	11.5	7	0	− 20
John Paul Kelly, Los Angeles	72	86	7	8.1	0	0	− 34
Dean Kennedy, Los Angeles	37	22	1	4.5	0	0	− 5
Reg Kerr, Edmonton	3	3	0	....	0	0	− 3
Tim Kerr, Philadelphia	79	286	54	18.9	9	0	+ 30
Mark Kirton, Vancouver	26	26	2	7.7	0	0	− 8
Kelly Kisio, Detroit	70	146	23	15.8	1	0	+ 16
Bill Kitchen, Montreal	3	3	0	....	0	0	Even
Mike Kitchen, New Jersey	43	37	1	2.7	0	0	− 15
Ralph Klassen, St. Louis	5	5	0	....	0	0	− 5
Scot Kleinendorst, N.Y. Rangers	23	13	0	....	0	0	− 10
Gord Kluzak, Boston	80	125	10	8.0	5	0	+ 9
Steve Konroyd, Calgary	80	94	1	1.1	0	1	− 8
Chris Kontos, N.Y. Rangers	6	1	0	....	0	0	Even
Jerry Korab, Buffalo	48	41	2	4.9	1	0	+ 4
Jim Korn, Toronto	65	94	12	12.8	0	0	− 33
Doug Kostynski, Boston	9	8	3	37.5	0	0	+ 2
Chris Kotsopoulos, Hartford	72	96	5	5.2	3	0	− 2
Richard Kromm, Calgary	53	66	11	16.7	0	0	+ 14
Mike Krushelnyski, Boston	66	152	25	16.4	3	2	+ 9
Jari Kurri, Edmonton	64	194	52	26.8	10	5	+ 38
Jim Kyte, Winnipeg	58	7	1	14.3	0	0	− 7
Randy Ladouceur, Detroit	71	89	3	3.4	0	0	− 12
Guy Lafleur, Montreal	80	217	30	13.8	6	0	− 14
Pat LaFontaine, N.Y. Islanders	15	35	13	37.1	1	0	+ 9
Bob Laforest, Los Angeles	5	15	1	6.7	1	0	− 3
Tom Laidlaw, N.Y. Rangers	79	61	3	4.9	0	0	− 10

Player — Team	Games	Shots	Goals	Shooting Pct.	PPG	SHG	+/−
Lane Lambert, Detroit	73	88	20	22.7	1	0	− 5
Mitch Lamoureux, Pittsburgh	8	13	1	7.7	0	0	− 6
Larry Landon, Montreal	2	5	0	....	0	0	+ 2
Gord Lane, N.Y. Islanders	38	16	0	....	0	0	+ 6
Chris Langevin, Buffalo	6	4	1	25.0	0	0	− 2
Dave Langevin, N.Y. Islanders	69	89	3	3.4	0	0	+ 26
Rod Langway, Washington	80	168	9	5.4	1	2	+ 14
Jean-Marc Lanthier, Vancouver	11	9	2	22.2	0	0	− 2
Rick Lanz, Vancouver	79	230	18	7.8	14	0	− 3
Guy Lapointe, Boston	45	57	2	3.5	1	0	− 3
Rick Lapointe, Quebec	22	24	2	8.3	0	0	+ 9
Jeff Larmer, New Jersey	40	57	6	10.5	0	0	− 17
Chicago	36	62	9	14.5	2	0	+ 3
Totals	76	119	15	12.6	2	0	− 14
Steve Larmer, Chicago	80	206	35	17.0	13	0	− 1
Pierre Larouche, N.Y. Rangers	77	241	48	19.9	19	0	− 15
Reed Larson, Detroit	78	262	23	8.8	10	0	− 10
Mike Lauen, Winnipeg	3	3	0	....	0	0	Even
Craig Laughlin, Washington	80	111	20	18.0	7	0	+ 4
Kevin Lavallee, Los Angeles	19	41	3	7.3	0	0	− 5
Paul Lawless, Hartford	6	7	0	....	0	0	− 5
Brian Lawton, Minnesota	58	74	10	13.5	0	0	Even
Gary Leeman, Toronto	52	41	4	9.8	1	0	− 14
Mikko Leinonen, N.Y. Rangers	28	39	3	7.7	0	0	+ 4
Moe Lemay, Vancouver	56	109	12	11.0	1	0	+ 4
Alain Lemieux, St. Louis	17	14	4	28.6	1	0	Even
Claude Lemieux, Montreal	8	7	1	14.3	0	0	− 2
Don Lever, New Jersey	70	111	14	12.6	3	0	− 21
Craig Levie, Minnesota	37	55	6	10.9	0	0	+ 9
Dave Lewis, New Jersey	66	38	2	5.3	0	0	− 19
Doug Lidster, Vancouver	8	7	0	....	0	0	− 7
Lars Lindgren, Vancouver	7	4	1	25.0	0	0	Even
Minnesota	59	66	2	3.0	0	0	− 3
Totals	66	70	3	4.3	0	0	− 3
Willy Lindstrom, Edmonton	73	116	22	19.0	2	0	+ 17
Ken Linseman, Edmonton	72	105	18	17.1	5	1	+ 30
Claude Loiselle, Detroit	28	20	4	20.0	0	0	+ 4
Troy Loney, Pittsburgh	13	5	0	....	0	0	− 7
Hakan Loob, Calgary	77	178	30	16.9	3	0	+ 11
Bob Lorimer, New Jersey	72	65	2	3.1	1	0	− 28
Darren Lowe, Pittsburgh	8	14	1	7.1	0	0	− 5
Kevin Lowe, Edmonton	80	81	4	4.9	1	0	+ 37
Jan Ludvig, New Jersey	74	176	22	12.5	7	0	− 18
Craig Ludwig, Montreal	80	116	7	6.0	0	0	− 10
Steve Ludzik, Chicago	80	102	9	8.8	0	0	− 5
Morris Lukowich, Winnipeg	80	155	30	19.4	4	0	+ 10
Dave Lumley, Edmonton	56	44	6	13.6	0	0	+ 14
Bengt Lundholm, Winnipeg	57	48	5	10.4	1	0	− 7
Gary Lupul, Vancouver	69	128	17	13.3	6	0	− 16
Tom Lysiak, Chicago	54	103	17	16.5	5	1	− 13
Al MacAdam, Minnesota	80	104	22	21.2	1	4	− 5
Paul MacDermid, Hartford	3	2	0	....	0	0	+ 1
Garth MacGuigan, N.Y. Islanders	3	2	0	....	0	0	Even
Allan MacInnis, Calgary	51	160	11	6.9	7	0	+ 1
Paul MacKinnon, Washington	12	3	0	....	0	0	− 7
John MacLean, New Jersey	23	22	1	4.5	0	0	− 7
Paul MacLean, Winnipeg	76	158	40	25.3	13	0	− 15
Rick MacLeish, Philadelphia	29	70	8	11.4	3	0	− 4
Detroit	25	26	2	7.7	0	0	− 4
Totals	54	96	10	10.4	3	0	Even
Brian MacLellan, Los Angeles	72	106	25	23.6	3	1	− 21
Bob MacMillan, New Jersey	71	114	17	14.9	2	0	− 21
Jamie Macoun, Calgary	72	165	9	5.5	0	1	+ 3
Craig MacTavish, Boston	70	135	20	14.8	7	0	+ 9
Greg Malone, Hartford	78	124	17	13.7	3	0	− 10
Dave Maloney, N.Y. Rangers	68	76	7	9.2	2	0	+ 11
Don Maloney, N.Y. Rangers	79	129	24	18.6	5	3	− 5
Dan Mandich, Minnesota	31	29	2	6.9	0	0	− 6
Jimmy Mann, Winnipeg	16	5	0	....	0	0	Even
Quebec	22	15	1	6.7	0	0	− 3
Totals	38	20	1	5.0	0	0	− 3

Player — Team	Games	Shots	Goals	Shooting Pct.	PPG	SHG	+/−
Bob Manno, Detroit	62	70	9	12.9	0	1	− 1
Moe Mantha, Winnipeg	72	228	16	7.0	3	0	− 14
Hector Marini, New Jersey	32	33	2	6.1	0	0	− 2
John Markell, St. Louis	2	0	0	....	0	0	− 4
Nevin Markwart, Boston	70	66	14	21.2	0	0	+ 2
Mario Marois, Quebec	80	186	13	7.0	4	0	+ 51
Brad Marsh, Philadelphia	77	90	3	3.6	0	0	+ 24
Peter Marsh, Chicago	43	86	4	4.7	0	0	− 11
Grant Martin, Vancouver	12	7	0	....	0	0	− 2
Terry Martin, Toronto	63	62	15	24.2	1	2	− 8
Dennis Maruk, Minnesota	71	130	17	13.1	7	0	− 17
Brad Maxwell, Minnesota	78	228	19	8.3	8	0	− 7
Bryan Maxwell, Winnipeg	3	6	0	....	0	0	+ 1
Pittsburgh	45	55	3	5.5	0	0	+ 2
Totals	48	61	3	4.9	0	0	+ 3
Kevin Maxwell, New Jersey	14	8	0	....	0	0	− 9
Gary McAdam, Washington	24	23	1	4.3	0	0	Even
New Jersey	38	68	9	13.2	0	2	− 7
Totals	62	91	10	11.0	0	2	− 7
Andrew McBain, Winnipeg	78	93	11	11.8	0	0	− 6
Kevin McCarthy, Vancouver	47	44	2	4.5	0	0	− 8
Pittsburgh	31	57	4	7.0	1	0	− 32
Totals	78	101	6	5.9	1	0	− 40
Tom McCarthy, Minnesota	66	165	39	23.6	16	2	+ 17
Rob McClanahan, N. Y. Rangers	41	52	6	11.5	0	0	Even
Kevin McClelland, Pittsburgh	24	40	2	5.0	0	2	− 7
Edmonton	52	65	8	12.3	0	2	+ 9
Totals	76	105	10	9.5	0	4	+ 2
Dale McCourt, Buffalo	5	5	1	20.0	0	0	− 2
Toronto	72	98	19	19.4	8	2	− 16
Totals	77	103	20	19.4	8	2	− 18
Brad McCrimmon, Philadelphia	71	106	0	....	0	0	+ 19
Gerry McDonald, Hartford	5	7	0	....	0	0	− 3
Lanny McDonald, Calgary	65	245	33	13.5	10	0	− 15
Mike McEwen, N. Y. Islanders	15	27	0	....	0	0	− 5
Los Angeles	47	133	10	7.5	7	0	− 12
Totals	62	160	10	6.3	7	0	− 17
Bob McGill, Toronto	11	3	0	....	0	0	+ 1
Tony McKegney, Quebec	75	171	24	14.0	4	0	+ 4
Sean McKenna, Buffalo	78	107	20	18.7	0	0	Even
Tom McMurchy, Chicago	27	21	3	14.3	0	0	− 7
Peter McNab, Boston	52	81	14	17.3	2	0	+ 7
Vancouver	13	20	1	5.0	1	0	− 2
Totals	65	101	15	14.9	3	0	+ 5
George McPhee, N. Y. Rangers	9	1	1	100.0	0	0	Even
Mike McPhee, Montreal	14	22	5	22.7	0	0	+ 4
Basil McRae, Toronto	3	7	0	....	0	0	− 3
Marty McSorley, Pittsburgh	72	75	2	2.7	0	0	− 39
Rick Meagher, New Jersey	52	125	14	11.2	2	0	− 9
Barry Melrose, Detroit	21	8	0	....	0	0	Even
Glen Merkosky, New Jersey	5	6	1	16.7	0	0	Even
Wayne Merrick, N. Y. Islanders	31	32	6	18.8	0	0	+ 2
Mark Messier, Edmonton	73	219	37	16.9	7	4	+ 40
Rick Middleton, Boston	80	209	47	22.5	16	4	+ 26
Mike Milbury, Boston	74	66	2	3.0	0	0	+ 2
Gerry Minor, Vancouver	9	2	0	....	0	0	Even
Lars Molin, Vancouver	42	47	6	12.8	0	1	− 9
Mike Moller, Buffalo	59	43	5	11.6	0	0	+ 2
Randy Moller, Quebec	74	78	4	5.1	0	0	+ 26
Sergio Momesso, Montreal	1	0	0	....	0	0	+ 1
Pierre Mondou, Montreal	52	105	15	14.3	3	1	+ 9
Mark Morrison, N. Y. Rangers	1	5	0	....	0	0	Even
Ken Morrow, N. Y. Islanders	63	71	3	11.5	0	0	+ 26
Brian Mullen, Winnipeg	75	164	21	12.8	4	4	− 11
Joe Mullen, St. Louis	80	228	41	18.0	13	0	− 8
Grant Mulvey, New Jersey	12	15	1	6.7	0	0	− 5
Larry Murphy, Los Angeles	6	11	0	....	0	0	− 4
Washington	72	138	13	9.4	2	0	+ 12
Totals	78	149	13	8.7	2	0	+ 8
Bob Murray, Chicago	78	190	11	5.8	3	1	+ 1
Troy Murray, Chicago	61	119	15	12.6	0	1	+ 10

Player — Team	Games	Shots	Goals	Shooting Pct.	PPG	SHG	+/−
Mark Napier, Montreal	5	11	3	27.3	0	0	Even
Minnesota	58	83	13	15.7	0	0	+ 2
Totals	63	94	16	17.0	0	0	+ 2
Mats Naslund, Montreal	77	146	29	19.9	3	0	+ 5
Ric Nattress, Montreal	34	33	0	....	0	0	− 11
Cam Neely, Vancouver	56	87	16	18.4	3	0	Even
Ray Neufeld, Hartford	80	163	27	16.6	5	0	− 18
John Newberry, Montreal	3	2	0	....	0	0	Even
Bernie Nicholls, Los Angeles	78	255	41	16.1	8	4	− 21
Frank Nigro, Toronto	17	18	2	11.1	0	0	− 4
Chris Nilan, Montreal	76	98	16	16.3	4	0	− 4
Jim Nill, Vancouver	51	53	9	17.0	0	0	− 7
Boston	27	19	3	15.8	0	0	− 5
Totals	78	72	12	16.7	0	0	− 12
Kent Nilsson, Calgary	67	181	31	17.1	7	9	− 24
Ted Nolan, Detroit	19	15	1	6.7	0	0	− 11
Gary Nylund, Toronto	47	71	2	2.8	0	0	− 27
Bob Nystrom, N. Y. Islanders	74	134	15	11.2	1	0	+ 9
Jack O'Callahan, Chicago	70	88	4	4.5	0	0	− 6
Mike O'Connell, Boston	75	194	18	9.3	9	0	+ 18
Bill O'Dwyer, Los Angeles	5	2	0	....	0	0	+ 1
John Ogrodnick, Detroit	64	252	42	16.7	19	3	− 16
Tom O'Regan, Pittsburgh	51	44	4	9.1	0	0	− 22
Terry O'Reilly, Boston	58	48	12	25.0	2	0	+ 9
Mark Osborne, N. Y. Rangers	73	139	23	16.5	6	0	+ 1
Wilf Paiement, Quebec	80	207	39	18.8	8	3	+ 28
Rob Palmer, New Jersey	38	18	0	....	0	0	− 10
Brad Park, Detroit	80	140	5	3.6	4	0	− 29
Greg Paslawski, Montreal	26	27	1	3.7	0	0	− 5
St. Louis	34	36	8	22.2	1	0	+ 4
Totals	60	63	9	14.3	1	0	− 1
Joe Paterson, Detroit	41	26	2	7.7	0	0	Even
Mark Paterson, Hartford	9	10	2	20.0	0	0	+ 4
Rick Paterson, Chicago	72	64	7	10.9	0	0	− 13
Larry Patey, St. Louis	17	9	0	....	0	0	− 12
N. Y. Rangers	9	6	1	16.7	0	1	Even
Totals	26	15	1	6.7	0	1	− 12
Jim Patrick, N. Y. Rangers	12	15	1	6.7	0	0	+ 6
Steve Patrick, Buffalo	11	11	1	9.1	0	0	− 2
Colin Patterson, Calgary	56	87	13	14.9	0	1	+ 17
Mark Pavelich, N. Y. Rangers	77	164	29	17.7	12	1	+ 11
Jim Pavese, St. Louis	4	1	0	....	0	0	− 1
Steve Payne, Minnesota	78	174	28	16.1	7	0	− 2
Barry Pederson, Boston	80	236	39	16.5	10	3	+ 27
Perry Pelensky, Chicago	4	4	0	....	0	0	Even
Jim Peplinski, Calgary	74	149	11	7.4	0	0	− 21
Fred Perlini, Toronto	1	3	0	....	0	0	Even
Gilbert Perreault, Buffalo	73	165	31	18.8	8	2	+ 19
Stefan Persson, N. Y. Islanders	75	95	9	9.5	4	0	+ 30
Brent Peterson, Buffalo	70	81	9	11.1	0	0	+ 3
Michel Petit, Vancouver	44	78	6	7.7	5	0	− 6
Jorgen Pettersson, St. Louis	77	212	28	13.2	7	0	− 2
Robert Picard, Montreal	7	7	0	....	0	0	− 1
Winnipeg	62	126	6	4.8	1	1	+ 9
Totals	69	133	6	4.5	1	1	+ 8
Dave Pichette, Quebec	23	34	2	5.8	0	0	+ 2
St. Louis	23	37	0	....	0	0	− 5
Totals	46	71	2	2.8	0	0	− 3
Randy Pierce, Hartford	17	25	6	24.0	0	1	+ 5
Jim Playfair, Edmonton	2	2	1	50.0	0	0	+ 4
Larry Playfair, Buffalo	76	67	5	7.5	0	0	+ 4
Willi Plett, Minnesota	73	103	15	14.6	1	0	− 6
Walt Poddubny, Toronto	38	77	11	14.3	4	0	− 12
Denis Potvin, N. Y. Islanders	78	246	22	8.9	11	1	+ 55
Dave Poulin, Philadelphia	73	185	31	16.8	6	3	+ 31
Jaroslav Pouzar, Edmonton	67	87	13	14.9	2	0	+ 17
Rich Preston, Chicago	75	109	10	9.2	3	1	− 21
Pat Price, Quebec	72	59	3	5.1	0	0	+ 20
Brian Propp, Philadelphia	79	301	39	13.0	11	1	+ 49
Joel Quenneville, Hartford	80	67	5	7.5	0	2	− 11
Dan Quinn, Calgary	54	103	19	18.4	11	0	− 1

Player — Team	Games	Shots	Goals	Shooting Pct.	PPG	SHG	+/−
Rob Ramage, St. Louis	80	267	15	5.6	9	0	− 11
Craig Ramsay, Buffalo	76	97	9	9.3	0	0	+ 3
Mike Ramsey, Buffalo	72	134	9	6.7	1	0	+ 26
Mark Reeds, St. Louis	65	72	11	15.3	3	1	− 3
Darcy Regier, N. Y. Islanders	5	6	0	....	0	0	+ 2
Dave Reid, Boston	8	4	1	25.0	0	0	+ 1
Paul Reinhart, Calgary	27	92	6	6.5	3	0	− 10
Mark Renaud, Buffalo	10	11	1	9.1	0	0	+ 1
Steve Richmond, N. Y. Rangers	26	16	2	12.5	0	0	+ 6
Dave Richter, Minnesota	42	22	2	9.1	0	0	− 8
Doug Risebrough, Calgary	77	161	23	14.3	0	1	+ 11
Gary Rissling, Pittsburgh	47	40	4	10.0	1	0	− 9
Gordie Roberts, Minnesota	77	131	8	6.1	1	1	+ 14
Torrie Robertson, Hartford	66	61	7	11.5	0	0	− 9
Florent Robidoux, Chicago	9	2	0	....	0	0	− 3
Larry Robinson, Montreal	74	141	9	6.4	4	0	+ 4
Normand Rochefort, Quebec	75	84	2	2.4	0	0	+ 41
Mike Rogers, N. Y. Rangers	78	186	23	12.4	6	3	− 24
Bill Root, Montreal	72	71	4	5.6	1	1	+ 26
Darcy Rota, Vancouver	59	127	28	22.0	6	0	− 12
Tom Roulston, Edmonton	24	38	5	13.2	1	0	Even
Pittsburgh	53	110	11	10.0	3	0	− 31
Totals	77	148	16	10.8	4	0	− 31
Bob Rouse, Minnesota	1	0	0	....	0	0	Even
Lindy Ruff, Buffalo	58	126	14	11.1	3	0	+ 15
Reijo Ruotsalainen, N. Y. Rangers	74	287	20	7.0	5	0	+ 17
Terry Ruskowski, Los Angeles	77	51	7	13.7	0	2	− 24
Phil Russell, New Jersey	76	123	9	7.3	0	0	− 27
Rocky Saganiuk, Pittsburgh	29	30	1	3.3	0	0	− 12
Andre St. Laurent, Pittsburgh	8	13	2	15.4	0	1	− 3
Detroit	19	24	1	4.2	0	1	− 3
Totals	27	37	3	8.1	0	2	− 6
Borje Salming, Toronto	68	160	5	3.1	2	1	− 34
Gary Sampson, Washington	15	17	1	5.9	0	0	+ 1
Grant Sasser, Pittsburgh	3	2	0	....	0	0	− 2
Jean-Francois (J.F.) Sauve, Quebec	39	43	10	23.8	5	0	+ 4
Andre Savard, Quebec	60	100	20	20.0	0	2	+ 17
Denis Savard, Chicago	75	210	37	17.6	12	0	− 13
Andy Schliebener, Vancouver	51	62	2	3.2	0	0	− 9
Norm Schmidt, Pittsburgh	34	56	6	10.7	0	0	− 1
Jim Schoenfeld, Boston	39	35	0	....	0	0	+ 18
Dwight Schofield, St. Louis	70	46	4	8.7	0	0	− 3
Rod Schutt, Pittsburgh	11	13	1	7.7	0	0	Even
Al Secord, Chicago	14	35	4	11.4	1	0	+ 7
Ric Seiling, Buffalo	78	135	13	9.6	0	3	+ 10
Dave Semenko, Edmonton	52	39	6	15.4	0	0	+ 9
Jyrki Seppa, Winnipeg	13	7	0	....	0	0	− 9
Dave Shand, Washington	72	53	4	7.5	0	0	+ 23
Dave Shaw, Quebec	3	3	0	....	0	0	+ 2
Doug Shedden, Pittsburgh	67	159	22	13.8	6	1	− 38
Neil Sheehy, Calgary	1	1	1	100.0	0	0	Even
Gord Sherven, Edmonton	2	5	1	20.0	0	0	+ 1
Steve Shutt, Montreal	63	146	14	9.6	4	0	− 18
Dave Silk, Boston	35	62	13	21.0	5	0	+ 11
Risto Siltanen, Hartford	75	163	15	9.2	12	0	− 21
Charlie Simmer, Los Angeles	79	188	44	23.4	13	1	+ 7
Ilkka Sinisalo, Philadelphia	73	165	29	17.6	2	3	+ 22
Darryl Sittler, Philadelphia	76	212	27	12.7	11	1	+ 13
Louis Sleigher, Quebec	44	74	15	20.3	3	1	+ 23
Doug Smail, Winnipeg	66	122	20	16.4	1	4	− 5
Brad Smith, Detroit	8	10	2	20.0	0	0	− 2
Doug Smith, Los Angeles	72	146	16	11.0	6	0	− 33
Greg Smith, Detroit	75	63	3	4.8	0	0	+ 6
Bobby Smith, Minnesota	10	21	3	14.3	1	0	− 1
Montreal	70	179	26	14.5	6	1	− 7
Totals	80	200	29	14.5	7	1	− 8
Stan Smyl, Vancouver	80	205	24	11.7	8	0	− 21
Harold Snepsts, Vancouver	79	77	4	5.2	0	0	− 19
Don Spring, Winnipeg	21	10	0	....	0	0	− 5
Darryl Stanley, Philadelphia	23	14	1	7.1	0	0	+ 4
Anton Stastny, Quebec	69	145	25	17.2	7	0	+ 12

Player — Team	Games	Shots	Goals	Shooting Pct.	PPG	SHG	+/−
Marian Stastny, Quebec	68	113	20	17.7	4	0	+ 1
Peter Stastny, Quebec	80	189	46	24.3	11	0	+ 22
Thomas Steen, Winnipeg	78	181	20	11.0	5	3	− 5
Scott Stevens, Washington	78	155	13	8.4	7	0	+ 26
Bill Stewart, Toronto	56	42	2	4.8	0	0	− 1
Tony Stiles, Calgary	30	19	2	10.5	0	0	+ 14
Blaine Stoughton, Hartford	54	103	23	22.3	7	0	− 13
N. Y. Rangers	14	27	5	18.5	1	0	− 12
Totals	68	130	28	21.5	8	0	− 25
Steve Stoyanovich, Hartford	23	60	3	5.0	0	0	− 1
Ken Strong, Toronto	2	3	0	....	0	0	Even
Todd Strueby, Edmonton	1	1	0	....	0	0	+ 2
Doug Sulliman, Hartford	67	130	6	4.6	0	0	− 11
Raimo Summanen, Edmonton	2	3	1	33.5	0	0	+ 4
Patrik Sundstrom, Vancouver	78	216	38	17.6	7	0	− 11
Peter Sundstrom, N. Y. Rangers	77	153	22	14.4	0	2	+ 3
Brent Sutter, N. Y. Islanders	69	154	34	22.1	7	0	+ 4
Brian Sutter, St. Louis	76	193	32	16.6	14	2	− 6
Darryl Sutter, Chicago	59	135	20	14.8	8	0	− 18
Duane Sutter, N. Y. Islanders	78	137	17	12.4	2	0	+ 2
Rich Sutter, Pittsburgh	5	2	0	....	0	0	− 2
Philadelphia	70	133	16	12.0	2	0	+ 10
Totals	75	135	16	11.9	2	0	+ 8
Ron Sutter, Philadelphia	79	145	19	13.1	5	3	+ 4
Phil Sykes, Los Angeles	3	2	0	....	0	0	− 1
Steve Tambellini, Calgary	73	99	15	15.2	1	0	− 8
Tony Tanti, Vancouver	79	247	45	18.2	19	1	− 12
Dave Taylor, Los Angeles	63	150	20	13.3	6	0	− 3
Mark Taylor, Philadelphia	1	0	0	....	0	0	Even
Pittsburgh	59	107	24	22.4	9	1	− 20
Totals	60	107	24	22.4	9	1	− 20
Greg Tebbutt, Pittsburgh	24	38	0	....	0	0	− 26
Greg Terrion, Toronto	79	92	15	16.3	0	2	− 6
Greg Theberge, Washington	13	19	1	5.3	1	0	− 4
Tom Thornbury, Pittsburgh	14	44	1	2.3	0	0	− 19
Dave Tippett, Hartford	17	25	4	16.0	0	0	− 1
John Tonelli, N. Y. Islanders	73	105	27	25.7	5	1	+ 21
Tim Tookey, Pittsburgh	8	7	0	....	0	0	− 2
Mario Tremblay, Montreal	67	133	14	10.5	3	0	+ 2
Tim Trimper, Winnipeg	5	1	0	....	0	0	+ 1
Bryan Trottier, N. Y. Islanders	68	194	40	20.6	7	3	+ 70
Rockey Trottier, New Jersey	5	2	1	50.0	0	0	− 1
John Tucker, Buffalo	21	40	12	30.0	5	0	+ 2
Alfie Turcotte, Montreal	30	33	7	21.2	5	0	− 9
Sylvain Turgeon, Hartford	76	237	40	16.9	18	0	− 11
Perry Turnbull, St. Louis	32	84	14	16.7	1	0	− 2
Montreal	40	67	6	9.0	2	0	− 12
Totals	72	151	20	13.2	3	0	− 14
Rick Vaive, Toronto	76	261	52	19.9	17	0	− 14
Chris Valentine, Washington	22	33	6	18.2	2	0	− 8
John Van Boxmeer, Quebec	18	33	5	15.2	4	0	− 1
Yvon Vautour, New Jersey	42	44	3	6.8	0	0	− 18
Darren Veitch, Washington	46	120	6	5.0	4	0	Even
Randy Velischek, Minnesota	33	15	2	13.3	0	0	− 6
Pat Verbeek, New Jersey	79	167	20	12.0	5	1	− 19
Claude Verret, Buffalo	11	14	2	14.3	1	0	− 3
Hannu Virta, Buffalo	70	98	6	6.1	4	0	+ 14
Mickey Volcan, Calgary	19	13	1	7.7	0	0	− 2
Ryan Walter, Montreal	73	117	20	17.1	7	1	− 11
Tim Watters, Winnipeg	74	66	3	4.5	1	0	+ 7
Wally Weir, Quebec	25	15	2	13.3	0	0	+ 5
Jay Wells, Los Angeles	69	96	3	3.1	0	0	− 10
Blake Wesley, Quebec	46	40	2	5.0	0	0	+ 14
Doug Wickenheiser, Montreal	27	26	5	19.2	0	0	+ 1
St. Louis	46	116	7	6.0	2	0	+ 10
Totals	73	142	12	8.5	2	0	+ 11
Jim Wiemer, Buffalo	64	91	5	5.5	0	1	+ 1
Dave Williams, Vancouver	67	119	15	12.6	2	0	− 11
Behn Wilson, Chicago	59	141	10	7.1	3	0	− 5
Carey Wilson, Calgary	15	11	2	18.2	0	0	− 1
Doug Wilson, Chicago	66	199	13	6.5	4	1	− 11

Player — Team	Games	Shots	Goals	Shooting Pct.	PPG	SHG	+/−
Ron Wilson, Winnipeg	51	52	3	5.8	0	0	− 3
Rik Wilson, St. Louis	48	72	7	9.7	2	0	+ 4
Paul Woods, Detroit	57	33	2	6.1	0	0	− 16
Gary Yaremchuk, Toronto	1	1	0	....	0	0	− 1
Ken Yaremchuk, Chicago	47	49	6	12.7	0	0	− 7
Ross Yates, Hartford	7	6	1	16.7	0	0	Even
Tim Young, Winnipeg	44	77	15	19.5	3	0	− 11
Warren Young, Pittsburgh	15	12	1	8.3	0	0	− 2
Steve Yzerman, Detroit	80	177	39	22.0	13	0	− 17
Mike Zuke, Hartford	75	84	6	7.1	1	0	− 18

Wayne Gretzky's 51-game scoring streak

Oct. 5 (at Edmonton): 1 goal, 1 assist; Edmonton 5, Toronto 4.
Oct. 7 (at Winnipeg): 2 goals, 1 assist; Edmonton 8, Winnipeg 6.
Oct. 9 (at Edmonton): 1 goal, 2 assists; Edmonton 4, Minnesota 3.
Oct. 12 (at Edmonton): 2 goals, 3 assists; Edmonton 8, Detroit 3.
Oct. 15 (at Calgary): 1 goal, 1 assist; Edmonton 4, Calgary 3.
Oct. 16 (at Edmonton): 1 goal, 2 assists; Edmonton 5 Calgary 1.
Oct. 19 (at Vancouver): 2 goals, 0 assists; Edmonton 10, Vancouver 7.
Oct. 20 (at Los Angeles): 1 goal, 0 assists; Los Angeles 7, Edmonton 2.
Oct. 22 (at Edmonton): 0 goals, 3 assists; Vancouver 5, Edmonton 5.
Oct. 26 (at Toronto): 1 goal, 0 assists; Toronto 8, Edmonton 3.
Oct. 29 (at Montreal): 0 goals, 1 assist; Edmonton 3, Montreal 1.
Oct. 30 (at New York): 1 goal, 0 assists; Edmonton 5, New York Rangers 4.
Nov. 2 (at Edmonton): 2 goals, 3 assists; Edmonton 11, Washington 3.
Nov. 5 (at Edmonton): 0 goals, 1 assist; Edmonton 7, Pittsburgh 3.
Nov. 6 (at Winnipeg): 4 goals, 3 assists; Edmonton 8, Winnipeg 5.
Nov. 8 (at Quebec): 1 goal, 1 assist; Edmonton 7, Quebec 4.
Nov. 9 (at Washington): 1 goal, 3 assists; Edmonton 7, Washington 4.
Nov. 12 (at Detroit): 3 goals, 2 assists; Edmonton 7, Detroit 3.
Nov. 13 (at Chicago): 0 goals, 1 assist; Chicago 5, Edmonton 3.
Nov. 18 (at Edmonton): 0 goals, 3 assists; Edmonton 7, Buffalo 0.
Nov. 19 (at Edmonton): 3 goals, 5 assists; Edmonton 13, New Jersey 4.
Nov. 21 (at Edmonton): 1 goal, 0 assists; Edmonton 7, Winnipeg 6.
Nov. 23 (at Los Angeles): 0 goals, 2 assists; Edmonton 7, Los Angeles 3.
Nov. 25 (at Minnesota): 1 goal, 0 assists; Edmonton 2, Minnesota 2.
Nov. 26 (at St. Louis); 0 goals, 5 assists; St. Louis 8, Edmonton 6.
Nov. 30 (at Edmonton): 1 goal, 1 assist; Philadelphia 3, Edmonton 3.
Dec. 3 (at Edmonton): 0 goals, 3 assists; Edmonton 7, Los Angeles 3.
Dec. 4 (at Edmonton): 0 goals, 1 assist; New York Islanders 4, Edmonton 2.
Dec. 7 (at Edmonton): 0 goals, 2 assists; Edmonton 5, Vancouver 4.
Dec. 10 (at Vancouver): 0 goals, 1 assist; Vancouver 3, Edmonton 2.
Dec. 13 (at Uniondale, N.Y.): 1 goal, 1 assist; New York Islanders 8, Edmonton 5.
Dec. 14 (at New York): 3 goals, 2 assists; Edmonton 9, New York Rangers 4.
Dec. 17 (at Edmonton): 1 goal, 5 assists; Edmonton 8, Quebec 1.
Dec. 18 (at Winnipeg): 2 goals, 2 assists; Edmonton 7, Winnipeg 5.
Dec. 21 (at Edmonton): 3 goals, 2 assists; Edmonton 7, Winnipeg 4.
Dec. 23 (at Edmonton): 1 goal, 1 assist; Edmonton 5, Calgary 5.
Dec. 26 (at Calgary): 1 goal, 2 assists; Edmonton 6, Calgary 3.
Dec. 28 (at Vancouver): 0 goals, 2 assists; Edmonton 4, Vancouver 2.
Dec. 30 (at Edmonton): 0 goals, 1 assist; Edmonton 2, Boston 0.
Jan. 3 (at Calgary): 1 goal, 3 assists; Edmonton 9, Calgary 6.
Jan. 4 (at Edmonton): 4 goals, 4 assists; Edmonton 12, Minnesota 8.
Jan. 7 (at Edmonton): 3 goals, 0 assists; Edmonton 5, Hartford 3.
Jan. 9 (at Detroit): 2 goals, 1 assist; Edmonton 7, Detroit 3.
Jan. 11 (at Chicago): 1 goal, 0 assists; Edmonton 5, Chicago 3.
Jan. 13 (at Buffalo): 0 goals, 1 assist; Buffalo 3, Edmonton 1.
Jan. 15 (at New Jersey): 0 goals, 3 assists; Edmonton 5, New Jersey 4.
Jan. 18 (at Edmonton): 3 goals, 2 assists; Edmonton 7, Vancouver 5.
Jan. 20 (at Edmonton): 2 goals, 3 assists; Edmonton 7, Los Angeles 5.
Jan. 21 (at Los Angeles): 0 goals, 2 assists; Edmonton 6, Los Angeles 3.
Jan. 25 (at Vancouver): 2 goals, 2 assists; Edmonton 6, Vancouver 4.
Jan. 27 (at Edmonton): 1 goal, 0 assists; Edmonton 3, New Jersey 3.
Jan. 28 (at Edmonton): Did not score vs. Los Angeles.

NHL Departmental Leaders

Power-Play Goal Leaders
1. Wayne Gretzky, Edmonton 20
2. Pierre Larouche, N. Y. Rangers 19
   John Ogrodnick, Detroit 19
   Tony Tanti, Vancouver 19
5. Sylvain Turgeon, Hartford 18
6. Rick Vaive, Toronto 17
7. Rick Middleton, Boston 16
   Ed Beers, Calgary 16
   Dino Ciccarelli, Minnesota 16
   Tom McCarthy, Minnesota 16

Shorthanded Goal Leaders
1. Wayne Gretzky, Edmonton 12
2. Kent Nilsson, Calgary 9
3. Guy Carbonneau, Montreal 7
4. Brian Bellows, Minnesota 5
   Bob Bourne, N. Y. Islanders 5
   Butch Goring, N. Y. Islanders 5
   Jari Kurri, Edmonton 5
8. Rick Middleton, Boston 4
   Mark Messier, Edmonton 4
   Glenn Anderson, Edmonton 4
   Bernie Nicholls, Los Angeles 4
   Brian Mullen, Winnipeg 4
   Doug Smail, Winnipeg 4

Shots On Goal Leaders
1. Ray Bourque, Boston 340
2. Wayne Gretzky, Edmonton 324
3. Brian Propp, Philadelphia 301
4. Reijo Ruotsalainen, N. Y. Rangers 287
5. Mike Gartner, Washington 286
   Tim Kerr, Philadelphia 286
7. Marcel Dionne, Los Angeles 278
8. Glenn Anderson, Edmonton 277
9. Rob Ramage, St. Louis 267
10. Reed Larson, Detroit 262

Shooting Percentage Leaders
(At least 80 shots)
1. Wayne Gretzky, Edmonton 26.85
2. Jari Kurri, Edmonton 26.80
3. Greg Gilbert, N. Y. Islanders 26.27
4. John Tonelli, N. Y. Islanders 25.71
5. Paul MacLean, Winnipeg 25.32
6. Butch Goring, N. Y. Islanders 24.72
7. Peter Stastny, Quebec 24.34
8. Mike Bullard, Pittsburgh 23.94
9. Bill Gardner, Chicago 23.68
10. Tom McCarthy, Minnesota 23.64

Plus/Minus Leaders
1. Wayne Gretzky, Edmonton .... +76
2. Bryan Trottier, N. Y. Islanders .... +70
3. Mike Bossy, N. Y. Islanders .... +66
4. Michel Goulet, Quebec .... +62
5. Denis Potvin, N. Y. Islanders .... +55
6. Paul Coffey, Edmonton .... +52
7. Ray Bourque, Boston .... +51
   Greg Gilbert, N. Y. Islanders .... +51
   Mario Marois, Quebec .... +51
10. Charlie Huddy, Edmonton .... +50

Miscellaneous Goaltending Statistics

	Games	W.	L.	T.	Goals	Saves	Sv. Pct.	Goal Interval
Murray Bannerman, Chicago	56	23	29	4	188	1475	88.7	17:44
Marco Baron, Los Angeles	21	3	14	4	87	541	86.1	13:55
Tom Barrasso, Buffalo	42	26	12	3	117	979	89.3	21:09
Don Beaupre, Minnesota	33	16	13	2	123	846	87.3	14:34
Marc Behrend, Winnipeg	6	2	4	0	32	152	82.6	10:58
Allan Bester, Toronto	32	11	16	4	134	1009	88.3	13:47
Mike Blake, Los Angeles	29	9	11	5	118	772	86.7	13:51
Dan Bouchard, Quebec	57	29	18	8	180	1341	88.2	18:44
Richard Brodeur, Vancouver	36	10	21	5	141	919	86.7	14:57
Frank Caprice, Vancouver	19	8	8	2	62	461	88.1	17:44
Jon Casey, Minnesota	2	1	0	0	6	53	89.8	14:00
Jim Craig, Minnesota	3	1	1	0	9	47	83.9	12:13
Michel Dion, Pittsburgh	30	2	19	4	138	795	85.2	11:15
Bruce Dowie, Toronto	2	0	1	0	4	39	90.7	18:00
Don Edwards, Calgary	41	13	19	5	157	1057	87.1	14:40
Tony Esposito, Chicago	18	5	10	3	88	531	85.8	12:27
Brian Ford, Quebec	3	1	1	0	13	57	81.4	9:28
Bob Froese, Philadelphia	48	28	13	7	150	1174	88.7	19:05
Grant Fuhr, Edmonton	45	30	10	4	171	1290	88.3	15:21
John Garrett, Vancouver	29	14	10	2	113	642	85.0	14:37
Mario Gosselin, Quebec	3	2	0	0	3	64	95.5	49:20
Glen Hanlon, N.Y. Rangers	50	28	14	4	166	1337	89.0	17:06
Brian Hayward, Winnipeg	28	7	18	2	124	735	85.6	12:20
Rick Heinz, St. Louis	22	7	7	3	80	458	85.1	13:59
Denis Herron, Pittsburgh	38	8	24	2	138	1055	88.4	14:42
Mark Holden, Montreal	1	0	1	0	4	13	76.5	13:00
Ken Holland, Detroit	3	0	1	1	10	41	80.4	14:36
Kelly Hrudey, N.Y. Islanders	12	7	2	0	28	261	90.3	19:07
Bob Janecyk, Chicago	8	2	3	1	28	209	88.2	14:43
Al Jensen, Washington	43	25	13	3	117	875	88.2	20:38
Doug Keans, Boston	33	19	8	3	92	697	88.3	19:20

	Games	W.	L.	T.	Goals	Saves	Sv. Pct.	Goal Interval
Michel Larocque, St. Louis	5	0	5	0	31	132	81.0	9:41
Gary Laskoski, Los Angeles	13	4	7	1	55	264	82.8	12:05
Rejean Lemelin, Calgary	51	21	12	9	150	1255	89.3	17:07
Mario Lessard, Los Angeles	6	0	4	1	26	132	83.5	10:14
Pelle Lindbergh, Philadelphia	36	16	13	3	135	828	86.0	14:48
Mike Liut, St. Louis	58	25	29	4	197	1494	88.4	17:23
Ron Low, New Jersey	44	8	25	4	161	971	85.8	13:47
Clint Malarchuk, Quebec	23	10	9	2	80	511	86.5	15:11
Bob Mason, Washington	2	2	0	0	3	43	93.5	40:00
Markus Mattsson, Los Angeles	19	7	8	2	79	450	85.1	13:56
Roland Melanson, N.Y. Islanders	37	20	11	2	110	1018	90.2	18:21
Gilles Meloche, Minnesota	52	21	17	8	201	1320	86.8	14:21
Corrado Micalef, Detroit	14	5	8	1	52	305	85.4	15:32
Greg Millen, Hartford	60	21	30	9	*221	1591	87.8	16:13
Ed Mio, Detroit	24	7	11	3	95	579	85.9	13:38
Mike Moffat, Boston	4	1	1	1	15	66	81.5	12:24
Andy Moog, Edmonton	38	27	8	1	139	1038	88.2	15:55
Mike Palmateer, Toronto	34	9	17	4	149	834	84.8	12:17
Dave Parro, Washington	1	0	0	0	0	0	....	....
Peter Peeters, Boston	50	29	16	2	151	1070	87.6	19:00
Steve Penney, Montreal	4	0	4	0	19	96	83.5	12:38
Glenn Resch, New Jersey	51	9	31	3	184	1238	87.1	14:21
Pat Riggin, Washington	41	21	14	2	102	821	88.9	22:32
Roberto Romano, Pittsburgh	18	6	11	0	78	551	87.6	13:05
Rick St. Croix, Toronto	20	5	10	0	80	449	84.9	11:44
Bob Sauve, Buffalo	40	22	13	4	138	912	86.9	17:13
Ron Scott, N.Y. Rangers	9	2	3	3	29	224	88.5	16:43
Richard Sevigny, Montreal	40	16	18	2	124	819	86.9	17:46
Billy Smith, N.Y. Islanders	42	23	13	2	130	1122	89.6	17:32
Doug Soetaert, Winnipeg	47	18	15	7	182	1202	86.8	13:56
Ed Staniowski, Winnipeg	1	0	0	0	8	12	60.0	5:00
Hartford	18	6	9	1	74	482	86.7	14:04
Totals	19	6	9	1	82	494	85.8	13:11
Greg Stefan, Detroit	50	19	22	2	152	1066	87.5	17:06
Vincent Tremblay, Pittsburgh	4	0	4	0	24	117	83.0	10:00
John Vanbiesbrouck, N.Y. Rangers	3	2	1	0	10	74	88.1	18:00
Mike Veisor, Hartford	4	1	3	0	20	94	82.5	12:00
Winnipeg	8	4	1	2	26	146	84.9	16:09
Totals	12	5	4	2	46	240	83.9	14:21
Mike Vernon, Calgary	1	0	1	0	4	6	33.3	2:45
Rick Wamsley, Montreal	42	19	17	3	144	832	85.2	16:12
Steve Weeks, N.Y. Rangers	26	10	11	2	90	575	86.5	15:07

Note: Goal Interval is the average time between goals allowed (Empty net goals not counted).

Goaltending Departmental Leaders

Games Played Leaders
1. Greg Millen, Hartford ... 60
2. Mike Liut, St. Louis ... 58
3. Dan Bouchard, Quebec ... 57
4. Murray Bannerman, Chicago ... 56
5. Gilles Meloche, Minnesota ... 52

Minutes Played Leaders
1. Greg Millen, Hartford ... 3583
2. Mike Liut, St. Louis ... 3425
3. Dan Bouchard, Quebec ... 3373
4. Murray Bannerman, Chicago ... 3335
5. Gilles Meloche, Minnesota ... 2883

NHL Goalie-Win Leaders
1. Grant Fuhr, Edmonton ... 30
2. Peter Peeters, Boston ... 29
   Dan Bouchard, Quebec ... 29
4. Bob Froese, Philadelphia ... 28
   Glen Hanlon, N. Y. Rangers ... 28

Goalie Saves Leaders
1. Greg Millen, Hartford ... 1591
2. Mike Liut, St. Louis ... 1494
3. Murray Bannerman, Chicago ... 1475
4. Dan Bouchard, Quebec ... 1341
5. Glen Hanlon, N. Y. Rangers ... 1337

Goalie Save-Percentage Leaders
(At least 500 shots faced)
1. Roland Melanson, N. Y. Islanders ... 90.2%
2. Billy Smith, N. Y. Islanders ... 89.6%
3. Tom Barrasso, Buffalo ... 89.3%
   Rejean Lemelin, Calgary ... 89.3%
5. Glen Hanlon, N. Y. Rangers ... 89.0%

Goal Interval Leaders
(Average amount of time between goals; 20-game minimum)
1. Pat Riggin, Washington ... 22:32
2. Tom Barrasso, Buffalo ... 21:09
3. Al Jensen, Washington ... 20:38
4. Doug Keans, Boston ... 19:20
5. Bob Froese, Philadelphia ... 19:05

1984 Stanley Cup Playoffs

Top 10 Playoff Scoring Leaders

	Games	G.	A.	Pts.	Pen.
Wayne Gretzky, Edmonton	19	13	*22	*35	12
Jari Kurri, Edmonton	19	*14	14	28	13
Mark Messier, Edmonton	19	8	18	26	19
Paul Coffey, Edmonton	19	8	14	22	21
Clark Gillies, New York Islanders	21	12	7	19	19
Mike Bossy, New York Islanders	21	8	10	18	4
Paul Reinhart, Calgary	11	6	11	17	2
Glenn Anderson, Edmonton	19	6	11	17	33
Pat Flatley, New York Islanders	21	9	6	15	14
Ken Linseman, Edmonton	19	10	4	14	65
Bryan Trottier, New York Islanders	21	8	6	14	49
Mats Naslund, Montreal	15	6	8	14	4
Brent Sutter, New York Islanders	20	4	10	14	18
Allan MacInnis, Calgary	11	2	12	14	13
Brian Bellows, Minnesota	16	2	12	14	6

*Indicates a league-leading figure.

Preliminary Rounds
(Division Semifinals)
(Best-of-five series)

ADAMS DIVISION

	W.	L.	Pts.	GF.	GA.
Montreal Canadiens	3	0	6	10	2
Boston Bruins	0	3	0	2	10

(Montreal won Adams Division semifinals, 3-0)
Wed. April 4—Montreal 2, at Boston 1
Thur. April 5—Montreal 3, at Boston 1
Sat. April 7—Boston 0, at Montreal 5

	W.	L.	Pts.	GF.	GA.
Quebec Nordiques	3	0	6	13	5
Buffalo Sabres	0	3	0	5	13

(Quebec Nordiques won Adams Division semifinals, 3-0)
Wed. April 4—Quebec 3, at Buffalo 2
Thur. April 5—Quebec 6, at Buffalo 2
Sat. April 7—Buffalo 1, at Quebec 4

PATRICK DIVISION

	W.	L.	Pts.	GF.	GA.
New York Islanders	3	2	6	13	14
New York Rangers	2	3	4	14	13

(New York Islanders won Patrick Division semifinals, 3-2)
Wed. April 4—N.Y. Rangers 1, at N.Y. Islanders 4
Thru. April 5—N.Y. Rangers 3, at N.Y. Islanders 0
Sat. April 7—N.Y. Islanders 2, at N.Y. Rangers 7
Sun. April 8—N.Y. Islanders 4, at N.Y. Rangers 1
Tue. April 10—N.Y. Rangers 2, at N.Y. Islanders 3 (a)
  (a)—Ken Morrow scored at 8:56 of overtime for N.Y. Islanders.

	W.	L.	Pts.	GF.	GA.
Washington Capitals	3	0	6	15	5
Philadelphia Flyers	0	3	0	5	15

(Washington Caps won Patrick Division semifinals, 3-0)
Wed. April 4—Philadelphia 2, at Washington 4
Thur. April 5—Philadelphia 2, at Washington 6
Sat. April 7—Washington 5, at Philadelphia 1

NORRIS DIVISION

	W.	L.	Pts.	GF.	GA.
Minnesota North Stars	3	2	6	18	14
Chicago Black Hawks	2	3	4	14	18

(Minnesota North Stars won Division semifinals, 3-2)
Wed. April 4—Chicago 3, at Minnesota 1
Thur. April 5—Chicago 5, at Minnesota 6
Sat. April 7—Minnesota 4, at Chicago 1
Sun. April 8—Minnesota 3, at Chicago 4
Tue. April 10—Chicago 1, at Minnesota 4

	W.	L.	Pts.	GF.	GA.
St. Louis Blues	3	1	6	13	12
Detroit Red Wings	1	3	2	12	13

(St. Louis Blues won Division semifinals, 3-1)
Wed. April 4—Detroit 2, at St. Louis 3
Thur. April 5—Detroit 5, at St. Louis 3
Sat. April 7—St. Louis 1, at Detroit 3 (b)
Sun. April 8—St. Louis 3, at Detroit 2 (c)
  (b)—Mark Reeds scored at 17:07 of second overtime for St. Louis.
  (c)—Jorgen Pettersson scored at 2:42 of overtime for St. Louis.

SMYTHE DIVISION

	W.	L.	Pts.	GF.	GA.
Edmonton Oilers	3	0	6	18	7
Winnipeg Jets	0	3	0	7	18

(Edmonton Oilers won Division semifinals, 3-0)
Wed. April 4—Winnipeg 2, at Edmonton 9
Thur. April 5—Winnipeg 4, at Edmonton 5 (d)
Sat. April 7—Edmonton 4, at Winnipeg 1
  (d)—Randy Gregg scored at 0:21 of overtime for Edmonton.

	W.	L.	Pts.	GF.	GA.
Calgary Flames	3	1	6	14	13
Vancouver Canucks	1	3	2	13	14

(Calgary Flames won Division semifinals, 3-1)
Wed. April 4—Vancouver 3, at Calgary 5
Thur. April 5—Vancouver 2, at Calgary 4
Sat. April 7—Calgary 0, at Vancouver 7
Sun. April 8—Calgary 5, at Vancouver 1

Quarterfinal Rounds

(Divisional Finals)
(Best-of-seven series)

ADAMS DIVISION

	W.	L.	Pts.	GF.	GA.
Montreal Canadiens	4	2	8	20	13
Quebec Nordiques	2	4	4	13	20

(Montreal Canadiens won Division finals, 4-2)

Thur. April 12—Montreal 2, at Quebec 4
Fri. April 13—Montreal 4, at Quebec 1
Sun. April 15—Quebec 1, at Montreal 2
Mon. April 16—Quebec 4, at Montreal 3 (e)
Wed. April 18—Montreal 4, at Quebec 0
Fri. April 20—Quebec 3, at Montreal 5

(e)—Bo Berglund scored at 3:00 of overtime for Quebec.

PATRICK DIVISION

	W.	L.	Pts.	GF.	GA.
New York Islanders	4	1	8	20	13
Washington Capitals	1	4	2	13	20

(New York Islanders won Division finals, 4-1)

Thur. April 12—Washington 3, at N.Y. Islanders 2
Fri. April 13—Washington 4, at N.Y. Islanders 5 (f)
Sun. April 15—N.Y. Islanders 3, at Washington 1
Mon. April 16—N.Y. Islanders 5, at Washington 2
Wed. April 18—Washington 3, at N.Y. Islanders 5

(f)—Anders Kallur scored at 7:35 of overtime for N.Y. Islanders.

NORRIS DIVISION

	W.	L.	Pts.	GF.	GA.
Minnesota North Stars	4	3	8	19	17
St. Louis Blues	3	4	6	17	19

(Minnesota North Stars won Division finals, 4-3)

Thur. April 12—St. Louis 1, at Minnesota 2
Fri. April 13—St. Louis 4, at Minnesota 3 (g)
Sun. April 15—Minnesota 1, at St. Louis 3
Mon. April 16—Minnesota 3, at St. Louis 2
Wed. April 18—St. Louis 0, at Minnesota 6
Fri. April 20—Minnesota 0, at St. Louis 4
Sun. April 22—St. Louis 3, at Minnesota 4 (h)

(g)—Doug Gilmour scored at 16:16 of overtime for St. Louis.

(h)—Steve Payne scored at 6:00 of overtime for Minnesota.

SMYTHE DIVISION

	W.	L.	Pts.	GF.	GA.
Edmonton Oilers	4	3	8	33	27
Calgary Flames	3	4	6	27	33

(Edmonton Oilers won Division finals, 4-3)

Thur. April 12—Calgary 2, at Edmonton 5
Fri. April 13—Calgary 6, at Edmonton 5 (i)
Sun. April 15—Edmonton 3, at Calgary 2
Mon. April 16—Edmonton 5, at Calgary 3
Wed. April 18—Calgary 5, at Edmonton 4
Fri. April 20—Edmonton 4, at Calgary 5 (j)
Sun. April 22—Calgary 4, at Edmonton 7

(i)—Carey Wilson scored at 3:42 of overtime for Calgary.

(j)—Lanny MacDonald scored at 1:04 of overtime for Calgary.

Semifinal Rounds

(Conference Championships)
(Best-of-seven series)

PRINCE OF WALES CONFERENCE

	W.	L.	Pts.	GF.	GA.
New York Islanders	4	2	8	17	12
Montreal Canadiens	2	4	4	12	17

(New York Islanders won Conference Title, 4-2)

Tue. April 24—N.Y. Islanders 0, at Montreal 3
Thur. April 26—N.Y. Islanders 2, at Montreal 4
Sat. April 28—Montreal 2, at N.Y. Islanders 5
Tue. May 1—Montreal 1, at N.Y. Islanders 3
Thur. May 3—N.Y. Islanders 3, at Montreal 1
Sat. May 5—Montreal 1, at N.Y. Islanders 4

CLARENCE CAMPBELL CONFERENCE

	W.	L.	Pts.	GF.	GA.
Edmonton Oilers	4	0	8	22	10
Minnesota North Stars	0	4	0	10	22

(Edmonton Oilers won Conference Title, 4-0)

Tue. April 24—Minnesota 1, at Edmonton 7
Thur. April 26—Minnesota 3, at Edmonton 4
Sat. April 28—Edmonton 8, at Minnesota 5
Tue. May 1—Edmonton 3, at Minnesota 1

Finals for the Stanley Cup

(Best-of-seven series)

	W.	L.	Pts.	GF.	GA.
Edmonton Oilers	4	1	8	21	12
New York Islanders	1	4	2	12	21

(Edmonton Oilers won Stanley Cup Championship Series, 4-1)

Thur. May 10—Edmonton 1, at New York Islanders 0
Sat. May 12—Edmonton 1, at New York Islanders 6
Tue. May 15—New York Islanders 2, at Edmonton 7
Thur. May 17—New York Islanders 2, at Edmonton 7
Sat. May 19—New York Islanders 2, at Edmonton 5

Game 1—Tuesday, May 10 at New York Islanders (Edmonton won, 1-0)

FIRST PERIOD: No Scoring. Penalties: Lowe (Edm.) 8:40; Potvin (N.Y.) 11:34; Hunter (Edm.) 14:09; Potvin (N.Y.) 14:51; Jackson (Edm.) 15:47.

SECOND PERIOD: No Scoring. Penalties: Dineen (N.Y.) 11:52; Jackson (Edm.) 14:37.

THIRD PERIOD: 1. Edmonton, McClelland (Hughes, Hunter) 1:55. Penalties: Hunter (Edm.) 9:06; Jonsson (N.Y.) 15:42.

Shots Against:
Fuhr (Edmonton) 14	12	8 —	34
Smith (New York Islanders) 10	12	16 —	38

Attendance: 15,861

Game 2—Saturday, May 12 at New York Islanders (N.Y. Islanders won, 6-1)

FIRST PERIOD: 1. Islanders, Trottier (Bossy, Boutilier) 0:53; 2. Islanders, Gilbert, (LaFontaine) 5:48 (PPG); 3. Edmonton, Gregg (McClelland) 15:06; 4. Islanders, Gillies (Kallur) 18:31. Penalties: Anderson (Edm.) 0:09; Tonelli (N.Y.) 0:09; Huddy (Edm.) 4:14; Jackson (Edm.) 6:29; Hughes (Edm.) 6:29; D. Sutter (N.Y.) 6:29; Hughes (Edm.) 8:31; B. Sutter (N.Y.) 9:12; Jackson (Edm.) 12:11; Gilbert (N.Y.) 12:11; Jonsson (N.Y.) 12:52; McClelland (Edm.) minor/major 15:42; D. Sutter (N.Y.) minor/major 15:42.

SECOND PERIOD: 5. Islanders, Trottier (B. Sutter, Flatley) 4:52; 6. Islanders, Gillies (Potvin, Bossy) 16:48 (PPG). Penalties: Jonsson (N.Y.) 5:37; Anderson (Edm.) 16:05.

THIRD PERIOD: 7. Islanders, Gillies (Trottier, Boutilier) 17:04 (PPG). Penalties: Messier (Edm.) minor/major 6:52; Dineen (N.Y.) minor/major 6:52; Gretzky (Edm.) 8:30; Semenko (Edm.) 15:16; Lumley (Edm.) major/game misconduct 17:25; Linseman (Edm.) minor/major/game misconduct 17:25; Dineen (N.Y.) major/game misconduct 17:25; Gilbert (N.Y.) double minor/major/misconduct 17:25.

Shots Against:
Fuhr (Edmonton) 12	9	5 —	26
Smith (New York Islanders) 12	6	5 —	23

Attendance: 15,861

Game 3—Tuesday, May 15 at Edmonton (Edmonton won, 7-2)

FIRST PERIOD: 1. Islanders Gillies (Flatley, B. Sutter) 1:32; 2. Edmonton, Lowe (Anderson, Lindstrom) 13:49. Penalties: D. Sutter (N.Y.) 2:27; Linseman (Edm.) 2:27; B. Sutter (N.Y.) 6:30; McClelland (Edm.) 8:49; Jonsson (N.Y.) 10:59; Fogolin (Edm.) 14:32; Flatley (N.Y.) double minor 15:16; Gilbert (N.Y.) major 15:16; Gregg (Edm.) 15:16; Jackson (Edm.) major 15:16; Tonelli (N.Y.) 17:53; Linseman (Edm.) 17:53.

SECOND PERIOD: 3. Islanders, Gillies (Trottier, Bossy) 2:54 (PPG); 4. Edmonton, Messier (Fogolin) 8:38; 5. Edmonton, Anderson (Huddy, Gretzky) 19:12; 6. Edmonton, Coffey (Hughes, Linseman) 19:29. Penalties: Hunter (Edm.) 1:55; B. Sutter (N.Y.) 3:34; Pouzar (Edm.) 10:00; Trottier (N.Y.) 14:22; Pouzar (Edm.) 14:22; D. Sutter (N.Y.) double minor 17:53; Fogolin (Edm.) double minor 17:53.

THIRD PERIOD: 7. Edmonton, Messier (Hughes) 5:32; 8. Edmonton, McClelland (Lumley) 5:52; 9. Edmonton, Semenko (Kurri, Gretzky) 9:41. Penalties: Pouzar (Edm.) 6:16; Anderson (Edm.) 6:56; Morrow (N.Y.) 14:19; Anderson (Edm.) 14:19; Melanson (N.Y.) 19:37; McClelland (Edm.) 19:37.

Shots Against:
Fuhr and Moog (Edmonton) 10	8	8 —	26
Smith and Melanson (New York Islanders) 11	12	17 —	40

Attendance: 17,498

Game 4—Thursday, May 17 at Edmonton (Edmonton won, 7-2)

FIRST PERIOD: 1. Edmonton, Gretzky (Semenko, Kurri) 1:53; 2. Edmonton, Lindstrom (Anderson) 3:22; 3. Islanders, B. Sutter (Gilbert, Morrow) 14:03; 4. Edmonton, Messier (Unassisted) 17:54. Penalties: Nystrom (N.Y.) 4:41; Potvin (N.Y.) 13:20; Lumley (Edm.) 13:20; Langevin (N.Y.) major 15:53; Morrow (N.Y.) 17:31; Kurri (Edm.) 17:31; Gretzky (Edm.) 17:31; Lowe (Edm.) 18:25; Linseman (Edm.) major 18:51.

SECOND PERIOD: 5. Edmonton, Lindstrom (Messier, Coffey) 5:21; 6. Edmonton, Conacher (Hughes) 7:58; 7. Edmonton, Coffey (Kurri, Semenko) 10:52; 8. Islanders, Flatley (Gillies, Persson) 19:44. Penalties: Nystrom (N.Y.) 4:47; D. Sutter (N.Y.) minor/major 13:47; McClelland (Edm.) major 13:47.

THIRD PERIOD: 9. Edmonton, Gretzky (Unassisted) 14:11. Penalties: Huddy (Edm.) 6:36.

Shots Against:
Smith (New York Islanders) 16	10	12 —	38
Moog (Edmonton) 7	7	7 —	21

Attendance: 17,498

Game 5—Saturday, May 19 at Edmonton (Edmonton won 5-2)

  FIRST PERIOD: 1. Edmonton, Gretzky (Kurri) 12:08; 2. Edmonton, Gretzky (Kurri) 17:26. Penalties: Bench (Edm.) s/b Lindstrom, 0:47; Flatley (N.Y.) 4:09; Persson (N.Y.) 7:43; D. Sutter (N.Y.) 18:47.
  SECOND PERIOD: 3. Edmonton, Linseman (Huddy, Gretzky) 0:38 (PPG); 4. Edmonton, Kurri (Coffey, Anderson) 4:59 (PPG). Penalties: D. Sutter (N.Y.) 4:19; Semenko (Edm.) 10:22.
  THIRD PERIOD: 5. Islanders, LaFontaine (Flatley, Gillies) 0:13; 6. Islanders, LaFontaine (Gillies) 0:35; 7. Edmonton, Lumley (Unassisted) 19:47 (Empty Net). Penalties: Flatley (N.Y.) 16:45.

Shots Against:
  Smith and Melanson (New York Islanders) .... 9 5   9 — 23
  Moog (Edmonton) .... 8 6 11 — 25
Attendance: 17,498.

Team-by-Team Playoff Scoring

Boston Bruins
(Lost Adams Division semifinals to Montreal, 3-0)

	Games	G.	A.	Pts.	Pen.
Tom Fergus	3	2	0	2	9
Ray Bourque	3	0	2	2	0
Barry Pederson	3	0	1	1	2
Craig MacTavish	1	0	0	0	0
Mike Krushelnyski	2	0	0	0	0
John Blum	3	0	0	0	4
Bruce Crowder	3	0	0	0	0
Keith Crowder	3	0	0	0	2
Brian Curran	3	0	0	0	7
Dave Donnelly	3	0	0	0	0
Mike Gillis	3	0	0	0	2
Steve Kasper	3	0	0	0	7
Gord Kluzak	3	0	0	0	0
Rick Middleton	3	0	0	0	0
Mike Milbury	3	0	0	0	12
Jim Nill	3	0	0	0	4
Mike O'Connell	3	0	0	0	0
Terry O'Reilly	3	0	0	0	14
Pete Peeters (Goalie)	3	0	0	0	2
Dave Silk	3	0	0	0	7

Buffalo Sabres
(Lost Adams Division semifinals to Quebec, 3-0)

	Games	G.	A.	Pts.	Pen.
Mike Foligno	3	2	1	3	19
Gilles Hamel	3	0	2	2	2
Sean McKenna	3	1	0	1	2
Lindy Ruff	3	1	0	1	9
John Tucker	3	1	0	1	0
Dave Andreychuk	2	0	1	1	2
Paul Cyr	3	0	1	1	0
Brent Peterson	3	0	1	1	0
Craig Ramsay	3	0	1	1	0
Mike Ramsey	3	0	1	1	6
Mal Davis	1	0	0	0	0
Bob Mongrain	1	0	0	0	2
Steve Patrick	1	0	0	0	0
Real Cloutier	2	0	0	0	0
Dave Fenyves	2	0	0	0	7
Bob Sauve (Goalie)	2	0	0	0	0
Tom Barrasso (Goalie)	3	0	0	0	7
Bill Hajt	3	0	0	0	0
Phil Housley	3	0	0	0	6
Jerry Korab	3	0	0	0	5
Larry Playfair	3	0	0	0	0
Ric Seiling	3	0	0	0	2
Hannu Virta	3	0	0	0	2

Calgary Flames
(Lost Smythe Division finals to Edmonton, 4-3)

	Games	G.	A.	Pts.	Pen.
Paul Reinhart	11	6	11	17	2
Allan MacInnis	11	2	12	14	13
Lanny McDonald	11	6	7	13	6
Mike Eaves	11	4	4	8	2
Dave Quinn	8	3	5	8	4
Jim Peplinski	11	3	4	7	21
Ed Beers	11	2	5	7	12
Hakan Loob	11	2	3	5	2
Carey Wilson	6	3	1	4	2
Steve Bozek	10	3	1	4	15
Doug Risebrough	11	2	1	3	25
Steve Konroyd	8	1	2	3	8
Jim Jackson	6	1	1	2	4
Richard Kromm	11	1	1	2	9
Colin Patterson	11	1	1	2	6
Kari Eloranta	6	0	2	2	2
Paul Baxter	11	0	2	2	37
Jim Macoun	11	1	0	1	0
Steve Tambellini	2	0	1	1	0
Charles Bourgeois	8	0	1	1	27
Danny Bolduc	1	0	0	0	0
Neil Sheehy	4	0	0	0	4
Don Edwards (Goalie)	6	0	0	0	0
Tim Hunter	7	0	0	0	21
Rejean Lemelin (Goalie)	8	0	0	0	0

Chicago Black Hawks
(Lost Norris Division semifinals to Minnesota, 3-2)

	Games	G.	A.	Pts.	Pen.
Al Secord	5	3	4	7	28
Bob Murray	5	3	1	4	6
Steve Larmer	5	2	2	4	7
Denis Savard	5	1	3	4	9
Doug Wilson	5	0	3	3	0
Tom Lysiak	5	1	1	2	2
Rick Paterson	5	1	1	2	6
Darryl Sutter	5	1	1	2	0
Jeff Larmer	5	1	0	1	2
Troy Murray	5	1	0	1	7
Steve Ludzik	4	0	1	1	9
M. Bannerman (Goalie)	5	0	1	1	5
Keith Brown	5	0	1	1	10
Dave Feamster	5	0	1	1	4
Bill Gardner	5	0	1	1	0
Rich Preston	5	0	1	1	4
Ken Yaremchuk	1	0	0	0	0
Jack O'Callahan	2	0	0	0	2
Jerome Dupont	4	0	0	0	15
Behn Wilson	4	0	0	0	4
Curt Fraser	5	0	0	0	14

Detroit Red Wings
(Lost Norris Division semifinals to St. Louis, 3-1)

	Games	G.	A.	Pts.	Pen.
Steve Yzerman	4	3	3	6	0
Ron Duguay	4	2	3	5	2
Ivan Boldirev	4	0	5	5	4
Brad Park	3	0	3	3	0
Bob Manno	4	0	3	3	0
Danny Gare	4	2	0	2	38
Reed Larson	4	2	0	2	21
Kelly Kisio	4	1	0	1	4
Randy Ladouceur	4	1	0	1	6
Greg Smith	4	1	0	1	8
Dwight Foster	3	0	1	1	0
Blake Dunlop	4	0	1	1	4
Rick MacLeish	1	0	0	0	0
C. Micalef (Goalie)	1	0	0	0	0
Eddie Mio (Goalie)	1	0	0	0	0
Ed Johnstone	2	0	0	0	0
Pierre Aubry	3	0	0	0	2
Joe Paterson	3	0	0	0	7
Greg Stefan (Goalie)	3	0	0	0	0
John Barrett	4	0	0	0	4
Colin Campbell	4	0	0	0	21
Lane Lambert	4	0	0	0	10
John Ogrodnick	4	0	0	0	0

Edmonton Oilers
(Winners of 1984 Stanley Cup Playoffs)

	Games	G.	A.	Pts.	Pen.
Wayne Gretzky	19	13	*22	*35	12
Jari Kurri	19	*12	14	28	13
Mark Messier	19	8	18	26	19
Paul Coffey	19	8	14	22	21
Glenn Anderson	19	6	11	17	33
Ken Linseman	19	10	4	14	65
Pat Hughes	19	2	11	13	12
Dave Hunter	17	5	5	10	14
Willy Lindstrom	19	5	5	10	10
Dave Semenko	19	5	5	10	44
Kevin McClelland	18	4	6	10	42
Randy Gregg	19	3	7	10	21
Kevin Lowe	19	3	7	10	16
Charlie Huddy	12	1	9	10	8
Dave Lumley	19	2	5	7	44
Raimo Summanen	5	1	4	5	0
Lee Fogolin	19	1	4	5	23
Jaroslav Pouzar	14	1	2	3	12
Don Jackson	19	1	2	3	32
Grant Fuhr (Goalie)	16	0	3	3	4
Pat Conacher	3	1	0	1	2
Larry Melnyk	6	0	1	1	2
Rick Chartraw	1	0	0	0	2
Andy Moog (Goalie)	7	0	0	0	2

Minnesota North Stars
(Lost Campbell Conference finals to Edmonton, 4-0)

	Games	G.	A.	Pts.	Pen.
Brian Bellows	16	2	12	14	6
Brad Maxwell	16	2	11	13	40
Keith Acton	15	4	7	11	12
Neal Broten	16	5	5	10	4
Dennis Maruk	16	5	5	10	8
Gordie Roberts	15	3	7	10	23
Dino Ciccarelli	16	4	5	9	27
Steve Payne	15	3	6	9	18
Willi Plett	16	6	2	8	51
Mark Napier	12	3	2	5	0
Craig Levie	15	2	3	5	32
Tom McCarthy	8	1	4	5	6
Al MacAdam	16	1	4	5	7
Curt Giles	16	1	3	4	25
Brent Ashton	12	1	2	3	22
George Ferguson	13	2	0	2	2
Lars Lindgren	15	2	0	2	6
Paul Holmgren	12	0	1	1	6
Don Beaupre (Goalie)	13	0	1	1	0
Dirk Graham	1	0	0	0	2
Randy Velischek	1	0	0	0	0
Gilles Meloche (Goalie)	4	0	0	0	0
Brian Lawton	5	0	0	0	10
Dave Richter	8	0	0	0	20
Tom Hirsch	12	0	0	0	6

Montreal Canadiens
(Lost Wales Conference finals to N.Y. Islanders, 4-2)

	Games	G.	A.	Pts.	Pen.
Mats Naslund	15	6	8	14	4
Chris Chelios	15	1	9	10	17
Steve Shutt	11	7	2	9	8
Pierre Mondou	14	6	3	9	2
Mario Tremblay	15	6	3	9	31
Bobby Smith	15	2	7	9	8
Guy Charbonneau	15	4	3	7	12
Bob Gainey	15	1	5	6	9
John Chabot	11	1	4	5	0
Larry Robinson	15	0	5	5	22
Mark Hunter	14	2	1	3	69
Ryan Walter	15	2	1	3	4
Perry Turnbull	9	1	2	3	10
Rick Green	15	1	2	3	33
Guy Lafleur	12	0	3	3	5
Craig Ludwig	15	0	3	3	23
Jean Hamel	15	0	2	2	16
Steve Penney (Goalie)	15	0	2	2	2
Mike McPhee	15	1	0	1	31
Chris Nilan	15	1	0	1	*81
Rick Wamsley (Goalie)	1	0	0	0	0
Richard Sevigny (Goalie)	2	0	0	0	32
Normand Baron	3	0	0	0	22

New York Islanders
(Lost Stanley Cup finals to Edmonton, 4-1)

	Games	G.	A.	Pts.	Pen.
Clark Gillies	21	12	7	19	19
Mike Bossy	21	8	10	18	4
Pat Flatley	21	9	6	15	14
Bryan Trottier	21	8	6	14	49
Brent Sutter	20	4	10	14	18
Greg Gilbert	21	5	7	12	39
Pat LaFontaine	16	3	6	9	8
Tomas Jonsson	21	3	5	8	22
Paul Boutilier	21	1	7	8	10
Denis Potvin	20	1	5	6	28
Butch Goring	21	1	5	6	2
Stefan Persson	16	0	6	6	2
Anders Kallur	17	2	2	4	2
John Tonelli	17	1	3	4	31
Duane Sutter	21	1	3	4	48
Dave Langevin	12	0	4	4	18
Ken Morrow	20	1	2	3	20

	Games	G.	A.	Pts.	Pen.
Bob Bourne..................	8	1	1	2	7
Gord Dineen.................	9	1	1	2	28
Bob Nystrom................	15	0	2	2	8
Wayne Merrick..............	1	0	0	0	0
Gord Lane...................	4	0	0	0	2
Billy Carroll.................	5	0	0	0	0
Mats Hallin..................	6	0	0	0	7
R. Melanson (Goalie).....	6	0	0	0	2
Billy Smith (Goalie)........	21	0	0	0	17

New York Rangers
(Lost Patrick Division semifinals to N.Y. Islanders, 3-2)

	Games	G.	A.	Pts.	Pen.
Mark Pavelich...............	5	2	4	6	0
Don Maloney................	5	1	4	5	0
Pierre Larouche.............	5	3	1	4	2
Peter Sundstrom............	5	1	3	4	0
Jim Patrick..................	5	0	3	3	2
Jan Erixon...................	5	2	0	2	4
Willie Huber.................	4	1	1	2	9
Reijo Ruotsalainen.........	5	1	1	2	2
Mikko Leinonen.............	5	0	2	2	4
Ron Greschner..............	2	1	0	1	2
Barry Beck...................	4	1	0	1	6
Anders Hedberg............	5	1	0	1	0
Larry Patey..................	4	0	1	1	6
Mike Allison.................	5	0	1	1	6
Kent-Erik Andersson.......	5	0	1	1	0
Mark Osborne...............	5	0	1	1	7
Dave Maloney...............	1	0	0	0	2
Mike Rogers.................	1	0	0	0	0
J. Vanbiesbrouck (G.).....	1	0	0	0	0
Steve Richmond............	4	0	0	0	12
Bob Brooke..................	5	0	0	0	7
Glen Hanlon (Goalie).....	5	0	0	0	6
Tom Laidlaw.................	5	0	0	0	8

Philadelphia Flyers
(Lost Patrick Division semifinals to Washington, 3-0)

	Games	G.	A.	Pts.	Pen.
Bobby Clarke................	3	2	1	3	6
Ilkka Sinisalo................	2	2	0	2	0
Brad Marsh..................	3	1	1	2	2
Darryl Sittler................	3	0	2	2	7
Ray Allison..................	3	0	1	1	4
Thomas Eriksson...........	3	0	1	1	0
Brian Propp..................	3	0	1	1	6
Frank Bathe..................	1	0	0	0	2
Lindsay Carson.............	1	0	0	0	5
Brad McCrimmon...........	1	0	0	0	4
Dave Brown..................	2	0	0	0	12
Miroslav Dvorak............	2	0	0	0	2
Pelle Lindbergh (Goalie)	2	0	0	0	0
Doug Crossman............	3	0	0	0	0
Bob Froese (Goalie).......	3	0	0	0	0
Paul Guay....................	3	0	0	0	4
Len Hachborn...............	3	0	0	0	7
Mark Howe...................	3	0	0	0	2
Tim Kerr......................	3	0	0	0	0
Dave Poulin..................	3	0	0	0	2
Darryl Stanley...............	3	0	0	0	19
Rich Sutter...................	3	0	0	0	15
Ron Sutter...................	3	0	0	0	22

Quebec Nordiques
(Lost Adams Division finals to Montreal, 4-2)

	Games	G.	A.	Pts.	Pen.
Peter Stastny................	9	2	7	9	31
Jean-Francois Sauve......	9	2	5	7	2
Anton Stastny...............	9	2	5	7	7
Michel Goulet...............	9	2	4	6	17
Dale Hunter..................	9	2	3	5	41
Marian Stastny..............	9	2	3	5	2
Mario Marois.................	9	1	4	5	6
Wilf Paiement...............	9	3	1	4	24
Andre Savard................	9	3	0	3	2
Blake Wesley................	9	1	2	3	20
Bo Berglund..................	7	2	0	2	4
Louis Sleigher...............	7	1	1	2	42
Alain Cote....................	9	0	2	2	17
Normand Rochefort.......	6	1	0	1	6
Randy Moller................	9	1	0	1	45
Pat Price.....................	9	1	0	1	10
Paul Gillis...................	1	0	0	0	2
Clint Malarchuk (Goalie)	1	0	0	0	15
Wally Weir...................	1	0	0	0	17
Rick Lapointe...............	3	0	0	0	0
Jimmy Mann.................	3	0	0	0	22
Tony McKegney.............	7	0	0	0	0
Dan Bouchard (Goalie)..	9	0	0	0	2
Andre Dore...................	9	0	0	0	8

St. Louis Blues
(Lost Norris Division finals to Minnesota, 4-3)

	Games	G.	A.	Pts.	Pen.
Doug Gilmour...............	11	2	9	11	10
Jorgen Pettersson..........	11	7	3	10	2
Rob Ramage.................	11	1	8	9	32
Bernie Federko.............	11	4	4	8	10
Mark Reeds..................	11	3	3	6	15
Brian Sutter.................	11	1	5	6	22
Wayne Babych..............	10	1	4	5	4
Perry Ganchar..............	7	3	1	4	0
Doug Wickenheiser........	11	2	2	4	2
Gilbert Delorme............	11	1	3	4	11
Dave Pichette...............	9	1	2	3	18
Joe Mullen...................	6	2	0	2	0
Pat Hickey...................	11	1	1	2	6
Guy Chouinard..............	5	0	2	2	0
Tim Bothwell................	11	0	2	2	14
Greg Paslawski.............	9	1	0	1	2
Terry Johnson...............	11	0	1	1	25
Rick Heinz (Goalie)........	1	0	0	0	0
Jim Pavese...................	2	0	0	0	0
Dwight Schofield...........	4	0	0	0	26
Jack Carlson................	5	0	0	0	2
Perry Anderson.............	9	0	0	0	27
Mike Liut (Goalie)..........	11	0	0	0	0
Rik Wilson...................	11	0	0	0	9

Vancouver Canucks
(Lost Smythe Division semifinals to Calgary, 3-1)

	Games	G.	A.	Pts.	Pen.
Doug Halward...............	4	3	1	4	2
Rick Lanz.....................	4	0	4	4	2
Jere Gillis...................	4	2	1	3	0
Stan Smyl....................	4	2	1	3	4
Neil Belland.................	4	1	2	3	7
Tony Tanti...................	4	1	2	3	0
Cam Neely...................	4	2	0	2	2

	Games	G.	A.	Pts.	Pen.
Ron Delorme	4	1	0	1	8
Dave Williams	4	1	0	1	13
Doug Lidster	2	0	1	1	0
Darcy Rota	3	0	1	1	0
Thomas Gradin	4	0	1	1	2
Gary Lupul	4	0	1	1	7
Harold Snepsts	4	0	1	1	15
Patrik Sundstrom	4	0	1	1	7
Michel Petit	1	0	0	0	0
Jiri Bubla	2	0	0	0	0
John Garrett (Goalie)	2	0	0	0	0
Lars Molin	2	0	0	0	0
Peter McNab	3	0	0	0	0
Andy Schliebener	3	0	0	0	0
R. Brodeur (Goalie)	4	0	0	0	2
Moe Lemay	4	0	0	0	12

Washington Capitals
(Lost Patrick Division finals to N.Y. Islanders, 4-1)

	Games	G.	A.	Pts.	Pen.
Mike Gartner	8	3	7	10	16
Dave Christian	8	5	4	9	5
Scott Stevens	8	1	8	9	21
Craig Laughlin	8	4	2	6	6
Alan Haworth	8	3	2	5	4
Bengt-Ake Gustafsson	5	2	3	5	0
Bryan Erickson	8	2	3	5	7
Doug Jarvis	8	2	3	5	6
Rod Langway	8	0	5	5	7
Bobby Carpenter	8	2	1	3	25
Gaetan Duchesne	8	2	1	3	2
Larry Murphy	8	0	3	3	6
Bobby Gould	5	0	2	2	4
Glen Currie	8	1	0	1	0
Gary Sampson	8	1	0	1	0
Peter Andersson	3	0	1	1	2

	Games	G.	A.	Pts.	Pen.
Darren Veitch	5	0	1	1	15
Al Jensen (Goalie)	6	0	1	1	2
Dave Shand	8	0	1	1	13
Greg Adams	1	0	0	0	0
Andre Hidi	2	0	0	0	0
Lou Franceschetti	3	0	0	0	8
Pat Riggin (Goalie)	5	0	0	0	2
Timo Blomqvist	8	0	0	0	8

Winnipeg Jets
(Lost Smythe Division semifinals to Edmonton, 3-0)

	Games	G.	A.	Pts.	Pen.
Brian Mullen	3	0	3	3	6
Andrew McBain	3	2	0	2	0
Dave Babych	3	1	1	2	0
Dale Hawerchuk	3	1	1	2	0
Randy Carlyle	3	0	2	2	4
Paul MacLean	3	1	0	1	0
Moe Mantha	3	1	0	1	0
Tim Watters	3	1	0	1	2
Tim Young	1	0	1	1	0
Laurie Boschman	3	0	1	1	5
Lucien DeBlois	3	0	1	1	4
Doug Smail	3	0	1	1	7
Thomas Steen	3	0	1	1	9
Jordy Douglas	1	0	0	0	2
Doug Soetaert (Goalie)	1	0	0	0	0
Mike Veisor (Goalie)	1	0	0	0	0
Scott Arniel	2	0	0	0	5
Marc Behrend (Goalie)	2	0	0	0	0
Murray Eaves	2	0	0	0	2
Wade Campbell	3	0	0	0	7
Jim Kyte	3	0	0	0	11
Morris Lukowich	3	0	0	0	0
Robert Picard	3	0	0	0	12

Complete Stanley Cup Goaltending

	Games	Mins.	Goals	SO.	Avg.
Rick Wamsley	1	32	0	0	0.00
Steve Penney	15	871	32	*3	*2.20
MONTREAL TOTALS	15	903	32	3	2.13
John Vanbiesbrouck	1	1	0	0	0.00
Glen Hanlon	5	308	13	1	2.53
NEW YORK RANGERS TOTALS	5	309	13	1	2.52
Mike Liut	11	714	29(1)	1	2.44
Rick Heinz	1	8	1	0	7.50
ST. LOUIS TOTALS	11	722	31	1	2.58
Dan Bouchard	9	543	25	0	2.76
QUEBEC TOTALS	9	543	25	0	2.76
Greg Stefan	3	210	8	0	2.29
Eddie Mio	1	63	3	0	2.86
Corrado Micalef	1	7	2	0	17.14
DETROIT TOTALS	4	280	13	0	2.79
Billy Smith	*21	*1190	*54	0	2.72
Roland Melanson	6	87	5(1)	0	3.45
NEW YORK ISLANDERS TOTALS	21	1277	60	0	2.82
Andy Moog	7	263	12	0	2.74
Grant Fuhr	16	883	44	1	2.99
EDMONTON TOTALS	19	1146	56	1	2.93
Pat Riggin	5	230	9(1)	0	2.35
Al Jensen	6	258	14(1)	0	3.26
WASHINGTON TOTALS	8	488	25	0	3.07

	Games	Mins.	Goals	SO.	Avg.
Don Beaupre	13	782	40	1	3.07
Gilles Meloche	4	200	11(2)	0	3.30
MINNESOTA TOTALS	16	982	53	1	3.24
Pete Peeters	3	180	10	0	3.33
BOSTON TOTALS	3	180	10	0	3.33
John Garrett	2	18	0(1)	0	0.00
Richard Brodeur	4	222	12(1)	1	3.24
VANCOUVER TOTALS	4	240	14	1	3.50
Murray Bannerman	5	300	17(1)	0	3.40
CHICAGO TOTALS	5	300	18	0	3.60
Don Edwards	6	217	12(1)	0	3.32
Rejean Lemelin	8	448	32(1)	0	4.29
CALGARY TOTALS	11	665	46	0	4.15
Tom Barrasso	3	139	8	0	3.45
Bob Sauve	2	41	5	0	7.32
BUFFALO TOTALS	3	180	13	0	4.33
Bob Froese	3	154	11(1)	0	4.29
Pelle Lindbergh	2	26	3	0	6.92
PHILADELPHIA TOTALS	3	180	15	0	5.00
Marc Behrend	2	121	9	0	4.46
Mike Veisor	1	40	4	0	6.00
Doug Soetaert	1	20	5	0	15.00
WINNIPEG TOTALS	3	181	18	0	5.97

( )—Empty Net Goals. Not counted against an individual goalies' average.

Individual Stanley Cup Leaders

Goals	Jari Kurri, Edmonton—	14
Assists	Wayne Gretzky, Edmonton—	22
Points	Wayne Gretzky, Edmonton—	35
Penalty Minutes	Chris Nilan, Montreal—	81
Goaltender's average (360 Minutes)	Steve Penney, Montreal—	2.20
Shutouts	Steve Penney, Montreal—	3

Individual 1983-84 NHL Trophy Winners

ART ROSS TROPHY (Scoring Leader)	Wayne Gretzky, Edmonton
HART MEMORIAL TROPHY (Most Valuable)	Wayne Gretzky, Edmonton
JAMES NORRIS MEMORIAL TROPHY (Top Defenseman)	Rod Langway, Washington
VEZINA TROPHY (Top Goaltender)	Tom Barrasso, Buffalo
BILL JENNINGS TROPHY (Goaltending Trophy)	Pat Riggin, Washington
	Al Jensen, Washington
CALDER MEMORIAL TROPHY (Top Rookie)	Tom Barrasso, Buffalo
LADY BYNG TROPHY (Most Gentlemanly)	Mike Bossy, N.Y. Islanders
CONN SMYTHE TROPHY (Playoff MVP)	Mark Messier, Edmonton
BILL MASTERTON MEMORIAL TROPHY (Perseverance, Sportsmanship and Dedication)	Brad Park, Detroit
FRANK J. SELKE TROPHY (Best Defensive Forward)	Doug Jarvis, Washington
JACK ADAMS AWARD (Coach of the Year)	Bryan Murray, Washington

Year-By-Year NHL Standings

From 1917-18 through the 1925-26 season, National Hockey League champions played against the Pacific Coast Hockey League for the Stanley Cup. So, only Stanley Cup championships are designated in the following club records for that period.

Key to standings: *—Missed playoffs. †—Eliminated in first round of new playoff format (1974-75). a—Eliminated in quarterfinal round. b—Eliminated in semifinal round. c—Eliminated in final round. xx—Stanley Cup champion.

NOTE: Records for Edmonton Oilers, Hartford Whalers, Quebec Nordiques and Winnipeg Jets include World Hockey Association results prior to their entrance into NHL in 1979-80. Key to WHA standings: *—Missed playoffs. †—Preliminary round (established for 1975-76 season). a—Eliminated in quarterfinal round. b—Eliminated in semifinal round. c—Eliminated in final round. xx—Avco World Cup champion.

Boston Bruins

Season	W.	L.	T.	Pts.	GF.	GA.	Position
1924-25	6	24	0	12	49	119	Sixth
1925-26	17	15	4	38	92	85	Fourth
1926-27	21	20	3	45	97	89	Second—c
1927-28	20	13	11	51	77	70	First—b
1928-29	26	13	5	57	89	52	First—xx
1929-30	38	5	1	77	179	98	First—c
1930-31	28	10	6	62	143	90	First—b
1931-32	15	21	12	42	122	117	Fourth—*
1932-33	25	15	8	58	124	88	First—b
1933-34	18	25	5	41	111	130	Fourth—*
1934-35	26	16	6	58	129	112	First—b
1935-36	22	20	6	50	92	83	Second—a
1936-37	23	18	7	53	120	110	Second—a
1937-38	30	11	7	67	142	89	First—b
1938-39	36	10	2	74	156	76	First—xx
1939-40	31	12	5	67	170	98	First—b
1940-41	27	8	13	67	168	102	First—xx
1941-42	25	17	6	56	160	118	Third—b
1942-43	24	17	9	57	195	176	Second—c
1943-44	19	26	5	43	223	268	Fifth—*
1944-45	16	30	4	36	179	219	Fourth—b
1945-46	24	18	8	56	167	156	Second—c
1946-47	26	23	11	63	190	175	Third—b
1947-48	23	24	13	59	167	168	Third—b
1948-49	29	23	8	66	178	163	Second—b
1949-50	22	32	16	60	198	228	Fifth—*
1950-51	22	30	18	62	178	197	Fourth—b
1951-52	25	29	16	66	162	176	Fourth—b
1952-53	28	29	13	69	152	172	Third—c
1953-54	32	28	10	74	177	181	Fourth—b
1954-55	23	26	21	67	169	188	Fourth—b
1955-56	23	34	13	59	147	185	Fifth—*
1956-57	34	24	12	80	195	174	Third—c
1957-58	27	28	15	69	199	194	Fourth—c
1958-59	32	29	9	73	205	215	Second—b
1959-60	28	34	8	64	220	241	Fifth—*
1960-61	15	42	13	43	176	254	Sixth—*
1961-62	15	47	8	38	177	306	Sixth—*
1962-63	14	39	17	45	198	281	Sixth—*
1963-64	18	40	12	48	170	212	Sixth—*
1964-65	21	43	6	48	166	253	Sixth—*
1965-66	21	43	6	48	174	275	Fifth—*
1966-67	17	43	10	44	182	253	Sixth—*
1967-68	37	27	10	84	259	216	Third—a
1968-69	42	18	16	100	303	221	Second—b
1969-70	40	17	19	99	277	216	Second—xx
1970-71	57	14	7	121	399	207	First—a
1971-72	54	13	11	119	330	204	First—xx
1972-73	51	22	5	107	330	235	Second—a
1973-74	52	17	9	113	349	221	First—c
1974-75	40	26	14	94	345	245	Second—†
1975-76	48	15	17	113	313	237	First—b
1976-77	49	23	8	106	312	240	First—c
1977-78	51	18	11	113	333	218	First—c
1978-79	43	23	14	100	316	270	First—b
1979-80	46	21	13	105	310	234	Second—a
1980-81	37	30	13	87	316	272	Second—†

Season	W.	L.	T.	Pts.	GF.	GA.	Position
1981-82	43	27	10	96	323	285	Second—a
1982-83	50	20	10	110	327	228	First—b
1983-84	49	25	6	104	336	261	First—†
	1801	1410	581	4183	11972	11046	

Buffalo Sabres

Season	W.	L.	T.	Pts.	GF.	GA.	Position
1970-71	24	39	15	63	217	291	Fifth—*
1971-72	16	43	19	51	203	289	Sixth—*
1972-73	37	27	14	88	257	219	Fourth—a
1973-74	32	34	12	76	242	250	Fifth—*
1974-75	49	16	15	113	354	240	First—c
1975-76	46	21	13	105	339	240	Second—a
1976-77	48	24	8	104	301	220	Second—a
1977-78	44	19	17	105	288	215	Second—a
1978-79	36	28	16	88	280	263	Second—†
1979-80	47	17	16	110	318	201	First—b
1980-81	39	20	21	99	327	250	First—a
1981-82	39	26	15	93	307	273	Third—†
1982-83	38	29	13	89	318	285	Third—a
1983-84	48	25	7	103	315	257	Second—†
	543	368	201	1277	4066	3493	

Calgary Flames

Season	W.	L.	T.	Pts.	GF.	GA.	Position
1972-73	25	38	15	65	191	239	Seventh—*
1973-74	30	34	14	74	214	238	Fourth—a
1974-75	34	31	15	83	243	233	Fourth—*
1975-76	35	33	12	82	262	237	Third—†
1976-77	34	34	12	80	264	265	Third—†
1977-78	34	27	19	87	274	252	Third—†
1978-79	41	31	8	90	327	280	Fourth—†
1979-80	35	32	13	83	282	269	Fourth—†
1980-81	39	27	14	92	329	298	Third—b
1981-82	29	34	17	75	334	345	Third—†
1982-83	32	34	14	78	321	317	Second—a
1983-84	34	32	14	82	311	314	Second—a
	402	387	167	971	3352	3287	

Chicago Black Hawks

Season	W.	L.	T.	Pts.	GF.	GA.	Position
1926-27	19	22	3	41	115	116	Third—a
1927-28	7	34	3	17	68	134	Fifth—*
1928-29	7	29	8	22	33	85	Fifth—*
1929-30	21	18	5	47	117	111	Second—a
1930-31	24	17	3	51	108	78	Second—c
1931-32	18	19	11	47	86	101	Second—a
1932-33	16	20	12	44	88	101	Fourth—*
1933-34	20	17	11	51	88	83	Second—xx
1934-35	26	17	5	57	118	88	Second—a
1935-36	21	19	8	50	93	92	Third—a
1936-37	14	27	7	35	99	131	Fourth—*
1937-38	14	25	9	37	97	139	Third—xx
1938-39	12	28	8	32	91	132	Seventh—*
1939-40	23	19	6	52	112	120	Fourth—a
1940-41	16	25	7	39	112	139	Fifth—b
1941-42	22	23	3	47	145	155	Fourth—a
1942-43	17	18	15	49	179	180	Fifth—*
1943-44	22	23	5	49	178	187	Fourth—c
1944-45	13	30	7	33	141	194	Fifth—*
1945-46	23	20	7	53	200	178	Third—b
1946-47	19	37	4	42	193	274	Sixth—*
1947-48	20	34	6	46	195	225	Sixth—*
1948-49	21	31	8	50	173	211	Fifth—*
1949-50	22	38	10	54	203	244	Sixth—*
1950-51	13	47	10	36	171	280	Sixth—*
1951-52	17	44	9	43	158	241	Sixth—*
1952-53	27	28	15	69	169	175	Fourth—b
1953-54	12	51	7	31	133	242	Sixth—*

Season	W.	L.	T.	Pts.	GF.	GA.	Position
1954-55	13	40	17	43	161	235	Sixth—*
1955-56	19	39	12	50	155	216	Sixth—*
1956-57	16	39	15	47	169	225	Sixth—*
1957-58	24	39	7	55	163	202	Fifth—*
1958-59	28	29	13	69	197	208	Third—b
1959-60	28	29	13	69	191	180	Third—b
1960-61	29	24	17	75	198	180	Third—xx
1961-62	31	26	13	75	217	186	Third—c
1962-63	32	21	17	81	194	178	Second—b
1963-64	36	22	12	84	218	169	Second—b
1964-65	34	28	8	76	224	176	Third—c
1965-66	37	25	8	82	240	187	Second—b
1966-67	41	17	12	94	264	170	First—b
1967-68	32	26	16	80	212	222	Fourth—b
1968-69	34	33	9	77	280	246	Sixth—*
1969-70	45	22	9	99	250	170	First—b
1970-71	49	20	9	107	277	184	First—c
1971-72	46	17	15	107	256	166	First—b
1972-73	42	27	9	93	284	225	First—c
1973-74	41	14	23	105	272	164	Second—b
1974-75	37	35	8	82	268	241	Third—a
1975-76	32	30	18	82	254	261	First—a
1976-77	26	43	11	63	240	298	Third—†
1977-78	32	29	19	83	230	220	First—a
1978-79	29	36	15	73	244	277	First—a
1979-80	34	27	19	87	241	250	First—a
1980-81	31	33	16	78	304	315	Second—†
1981-82	30	38	12	72	332	363	Fourth—b
1982-83	47	23	10	104	338	268	First—b
1983-84	30	42	8	68	277	311	Fourth—†
	1491	1633	603	3584	10813	11129	

Detroit Red Wings

Season	W.	L.	T.	Pts.	GF.	GA.	Position
1926-27	12	28	4	28	76	105	Fifth—*
1927-28	19	19	6	44	88	79	Fourth—*
1928-29	19	16	9	47	72	63	Third—a
1929-30	14	24	6	34	117	133	Fourth—*
1930-31	16	21	7	39	102	105	Fourth—*
1931-32	18	20	10	46	95	108	Third—a
1932-33	25	15	8	58	111	93	Second—b
1933-34	24	14	10	58	113	98	First—c
1934-35	19	22	7	45	127	114	Fourth—*
1935-36	24	16	8	56	124	103	First—xx
1936-37	25	14	9	59	128	102	First—xx
1937-38	12	25	11	35	99	133	Fourth—*
1938-39	18	24	6	42	107	128	Fifth—b
1939-40	16	26	6	38	90	126	Fifth—b
1940-41	21	16	11	53	112	102	Third—c
1941-42	19	25	4	42	140	147	Fifth—c
1942-43	25	14	11	61	169	124	First—xx
1943-44	26	18	6	58	214	177	Second—b
1944-45	31	14	5	67	218	161	Second—c
1945-46	20	20	10	50	146	159	Fourth—b
1946-47	22	27	11	55	190	193	Fourth—b
1947-48	30	18	12	72	187	148	Second—c
1948-49	34	19	7	75	195	145	First—c
1949-50	37	19	14	88	229	164	First—xx
1950-51	44	13	13	101	236	139	First—b
1951-52	44	14	12	100	215	133	First—xx
1952-53	36	16	18	90	222	133	First—b
1953-54	37	19	14	88	191	132	First—xx
1954-55	42	17	11	95	204	134	First—xx
1955-56	30	24	16	76	183	148	Second—c
1956-57	38	20	12	88	198	157	First—b
1957-58	29	29	12	70	176	207	Third—b
1958-59	25	37	8	58	167	218	Sixth—*
1959-60	26	29	15	67	186	197	Fourth—b
1960-61	25	29	16	66	195	215	Fourth—c
1961-62	23	33	14	60	184	219	Fifth—*

Season	W.	L.	T.	Pts	GF.	GA.	Position
1962-63	32	25	13	77	200	194	Fourth—c
1963-64	30	29	11	71	191	204	Fourth—c
1964-65	40	23	7	87	224	175	First—b
1965-66	31	27	12	74	221	194	Fourth—c
1966-67	27	39	4	58	212	241	Fifth—*
1967-68	27	35	12	66	245	257	Sixth—*
1968-69	33	31	12	78	239	221	Fifth—*
1969-70	40	21	15	95	246	199	Third—a
1970-71	22	45	11	55	209	308	Seventh—*
1971-72	33	35	10	76	261	262	Fifth—*
1972-73	37	29	12	86	265	243	Fifth—*
1973-74	29	39	10	68	255	319	Sixth—*
1974-75	23	45	12	58	259	335	Fourth—*
1975-76	26	44	10	62	226	300	Fourth—*
1976-77	16	55	9	41	183	309	Fifth—*
1977-78	32	34	14	78	252	266	Second—a
1978-79	23	41	16	62	252	295	Fifth—*
1979-80	26	43	11	63	268	306	Fifth—*
1980-81	19	43	18	56	252	339	Fifth—*
1981-82	21	47	12	54	270	351	Sixth—*
1982-83	21	44	15	57	263	344	Fifth—*
1983-84	31	42	7	69	298	323	Third—†
	1544	1570	612	3700	10897	11027	

Edmonton Oilers

Season	W.	L.	T.	Pts	GF.	GA.	Position
1972-73	38	37	3	79	269	256	Fifth—*
1973-74	38	37	3	79	268	269	Third—a
1974-75	36	38	4	76	279	279	Fifth—*
1975-76	27	49	5	59	268	345	Fourth—a
1976-77	34	43	4	72	243	304	Fourth—a
1977-78	38	39	3	79	309	307	Fifth—a
1978-79	48	30	2	98	340	266	First—c
1979-80	28	39	13	69	301	322	Fourth—†
1980-81	29	35	16	74	328	327	Fourth—a
1981-82	48	17	15	111	417	295	First—†
1982-83	47	21	12	106	424	315	First—c
1983-84	57	18	5	119	446	314	First—xx
	468	403	85	1021	3892	3599	

Hartford Whalers

Season	W.	L.	T.	Pts	GF.	GA.	Position
1972-73	46	30	2	94	318	263	First—xx
1973-74	43	31	4	90	291	260	First—a
1974-75	43	30	5	91	274	279	First—a
1975-76	33	40	7	73	255	290	Third—b
1976-77	35	40	6	76	275	290	Fourth—a
1977-78	44	31	5	93	335	269	Second—c
1978-79	37	34	9	83	298	287	Fourth—b
1979-80	27	34	19	73	303	312	Fourth—†
1980-81	21	41	18	60	292	372	Fourth—*
1981-82	21	41	18	60	264	351	Fifth—*
1982-83	19	54	7	45	261	403	Fifth—*
1983-84	28	42	10	66	288	320	Fifth—*
	397	448	110	904	3459	3696	

Los Angeles Kings

Season	W.	L.	T.	Pts	GF.	GA.	Position
1967-68	31	33	10	72	200	224	Second—a
1968-69	24	42	10	58	185	260	Fourth—b
1969-70	14	52	10	38	168	290	Sixth—*
1970-71	25	40	13	63	239	303	Fifth—*
1971-72	20	49	9	49	206	305	Seventh—*
1972-73	31	36	11	73	232	245	Sixth—*
1973-74	33	33	12	78	233	231	Third—a
1974-75	42	17	21	105	269	185	Second-†
1975-76	38	33	9	85	263	265	Second—a
1976-77	34	31	15	83	271	241	Second—a
1977-78	31	34	15	77	243	245	Third—†
1978-79	34	34	12	80	292	286	Third—†

Season	W.	L.	T.	Pts.	GF.	GA.	Position
1979-80	30	36	14	74	290	313	Second—†
1980-81	43	24	13	99	337	290	Second—†
1981-82	24	41	15	63	314	369	Fourth—a
1982-83	27	41	12	66	308	365	Fifth—*
1983-84	23	44	13	59	309	376	Fifth—*
	504	520	214	1222	4359	4793	

Minnesota North Stars

Season	W.	L.	T.	Pts.	GF.	GA.	Position
1967-68	27	32	15	69	191	226	Fourth—b
1968-69	18	43	15	51	189	270	Sixth—*
1969-70	19	35	22	60	224	257	Third—a
1970-71	28	34	16	72	191	223	Fourth—b
1971-72	37	29	12	86	212	191	Second—a
1972-73	37	30	11	85	254	230	Third—a
1973-74	23	38	17	63	235	275	Seventh—*
1974-75	23	50	7	53	221	341	Fourth—*
1975-76	20	53	7	47	195	303	Fourth—*
1976-77	23	39	18	64	240	310	Second—†
1977-78	18	53	9	45	218	325	Fifth—*
1978-79	28	40	12	68	257	289	Fourth—*
1979-80	36	28	16	88	311	253	Third—b
1980-81	35	28	17	87	291	263	Third—c
1981-82	37	23	20	94	346	288	First—†
1982-83	40	24	16	96	321	290	Second—a
1983-84	39	31	10	88	345	344	First—b
	488	610	240	1216	4241	4678	

Montreal Canadiens

Season	W.	L.	T.	Pts.	GF.	GA.	Position
1917-18	13	9	0	26	115	84	First and Third
1918-19	10	8	0	20	88	78	Second
1919-20	13	11	0	26	129	113	Second
1920-21	13	11	0	26	112	99	Third
1921-22	12	11	1	25	88	94	Third
1922-23	13	9	2	28	73	61	Second
1923-24	13	11	0	26	59	48	Second—xx
1924-25	17	11	2	36	93	56	Third
1925-26	11	24	1	23	79	108	Seventh
1926-27	28	14	2	58	99	67	Second—c
1927-28	26	11	7	59	116	48	First—b
1928-29	22	7	15	59	71	43	First—b
1929-30	21	14	9	51	142	114	Second—xx
1930-31	26	10	8	60	129	89	First—xx
1931-32	25	16	7	57	128	111	First—b
1932-33	18	25	5	41	92	115	Third—a
1933-34	22	20	6	50	99	101	Second—a
1934-35	19	23	6	44	110	145	Third—a
1935-36	11	26	11	33	82	123	Fourth—*
1936-37	24	18	6	54	115	111	First—b
1937-38	18	17	13	49	123	128	Third—a
1938-39	15	24	9	39	115	146	Sixth—a
1939-40	10	33	5	25	90	167	Seventh—*
1940-41	16	26	6	38	121	147	Sixth—a
1941-42	18	27	3	39	134	173	Sixth—a
1942-43	19	19	12	50	181	191	Fourth—b
1943-44	38	5	7	83	234	109	First—xx
1944-45	38	8	4	80	228	121	First—b
1945-46	28	17	5	61	172	134	First—xx
1946-47	34	16	10	78	189	138	First—c
1947-48	20	29	11	51	147	169	Fifth—*
1948-49	28	23	9	65	152	126	Third—b
1949-50	29	22	19	77	172	150	Second—b
1950-51	25	30	15	65	173	184	Third—c
1951-52	34	26	10	78	195	164	Second—c
1952-53	28	23	19	75	155	148	Second—xx
1953-54	35	24	11	81	195	141	Second—c
1954-55	41	18	11	93	228	157	Second—c
1955-56	45	15	10	100	222	131	First—xx
1956-57	35	23	12	82	210	155	Second—xx
1957-58	43	17	10	96	250	158	First—xx

Season	W.	L.	T.	Pts.	GF.	GA.	Position
1958-59	39	18	13	91	258	158	First—xx
1959-60	40	18	12	92	255	178	First—xx
1960-61	41	19	10	92	254	188	First—b
1961-62	42	14	14	98	259	166	First—b
1962-63	28	19	23	79	225	183	Third—b
1963-64	36	21	13	85	209	167	First—b
1964-65	36	23	11	83	211	185	Second—xx
1965-66	41	21	8	90	239	173	First—xx
1966-67	32	25	13	77	202	188	Second—c
1967-68	42	22	10	94	236	167	First—xx
1968-69	46	19	11	103	271	202	First—xx
1969-70	38	22	16	92	244	201	Fifth—*
1970-71	42	23	13	97	291	216	Third—xx
1971-72	46	16	16	108	307	205	Third—a
1972-73	52	10	16	120	329	184	First—xx
1973-74	45	24	9	99	293	240	Second—a
1974-75	47	14	19	113	374	225	First—b
1975-76	58	11	11	127	337	174	First—xx
1976-77	60	8	12	132	387	171	First—xx
1977-78	59	10	11	129	359	183	First—xx
1978-79	52	17	11	115	337	204	First—xx
1979-80	47	20	13	107	328	240	First—a
1980-81	45	22	13	103	332	232	First—†
1981-82	46	17	17	109	360	223	First—†
1982-83	42	24	14	98	350	286	Second—†
1983-84	35	40	5	75	286	295	Fourth—b
	2091	1228	633	4815	13238	10179	

New Jersey Devils

(Franchise transferred from Colorado after 1981-82 season.)

Season	W.	L.	T.	Pts.	GF.	GA.	Position
1974-75	15	54	11	41	184	328	Fifth—*
1975-76	12	56	12	36	190	351	Fifth—*
1976-77	20	46	14	54	226	307	Fifth—*
1977-78	19	40	21	59	257	305	Second—†
1978-79	15	53	12	42	210	331	Fourth—*
1979-80	20	48	13	51	234	308	Sixth—*
1980-81	22	45	13	57	258	344	Fifth—*
1981-82	18	49	13	49	241	362	Fifth—*
1982-83	17	49	14	48	230	338	Fifth—*
1983-84	17	56	7	41	231	350	Fifth—*
	175	496	130	478	2261	3727	

New York Islanders

Season	W.	L.	T.	Pts.	GF.	GA.	Position
1972-73	12	60	6	30	170	347	Eighth—*
1973-74	19	41	18	56	182	247	Eighth—*
1974-75	33	25	22	88	264	221	Third—b
1975-76	42	21	17	101	297	190	Second—b
1976-77	47	21	12	106	288	193	Second—b
1977-78	48	17	15	111	334	210	First—a
1978-79	51	15	14	116	358	214	First—b
1979-80	39	28	13	91	281	247	Second—xx
1980-81	48	18	14	110	355	260	First—xx
1981-82	54	16	10	118	385	250	First—xx
1982-83	42	26	12	96	302	226	Second—xx
1983-84	50	26	4	104	357	269	First—c
	485	314	157	1127	3573	2874	

New York Rangers

Season	W.	L.	T.	Pts.	GF.	GA.	Position
1926-27	25	13	6	56	95	72	First—a
1927-28	19	16	9	47	94	79	Second—xx
1928-29	21	13	10	52	72	65	Second—c
1929-30	17	17	10	44	136	143	Third—b
1930-31	19	16	9	47	106	87	Third—b
1931-32	23	17	8	54	134	112	First—c
1932-33	23	17	8	54	135	107	Third—xx
1933-34	21	19	8	50	120	113	Third—a
1934-35	22	20	6	50	137	139	Third—b

Season	W.	L.	T.	Pts.	GF.	GA.	Position
1935-36	19	17	12	50	91	96	Fourth—*
1936-37	19	20	9	47	117	106	Third—c
1937-38	27	15	6	60	149	96	Second—a
1938-39	26	16	6	58	149	105	Second—b
1939-40	27	11	10	64	136	77	Second—xx
1940-41	21	19	8	50	143	125	Fourth—a
1941-42	29	17	2	60	177	143	First—b
1942-43	11	31	8	30	161	253	Sixth—*
1943-44	6	39	5	17	162	310	Sixth—*
1944-45	11	29	10	32	154	247	Sixth—*
1945-46	13	28	9	35	144	191	Sixth—*
1946-47	22	32	6	50	167	186	Fifth—*
1947-48	21	26	13	55	176	201	Fourth—b
1948-49	18	31	11	47	133	172	Sixth—*
1949-50	28	31	11	67	170	189	Fourth—c
1950-51	20	29	21	61	169	201	Fifth—*
1951-52	23	34	13	59	192	219	Fifth—*
1952-53	17	37	16	50	152	211	Sixth—*
1953-54	29	31	10	68	161	182	Fifth—*
1954-55	17	35	18	52	150	210	Fifth—*
1955-56	32	28	10	74	204	203	Third—b
1956-57	26	30	14	66	184	227	Fourth—b
1957-58	32	25	13	77	195	188	Second—b
1958-59	26	32	12	64	201	217	Fifth—*
1959-60	17	38	15	49	187	247	Sixth—*
1960-61	22	38	10	54	204	248	Fifth—*
1961-62	26	32	12	64	195	207	Fourth—b
1962-63	22	36	12	56	211	233	Fifth—*
1963-64	22	38	10	54	186	242	Fifth—*
1964-65	20	38	12	52	179	246	Fifth—*
1965-66	18	41	11	47	195	261	Sixth—*
1966-67	30	28	12	72	188	189	Fourth—b
1967-68	39	23	12	90	226	183	Second—a
1968-69	41	26	9	91	231	196	Third—a
1969-70	38	22	16	92	246	189	Fourth—a
1970-71	49	18	11	109	259	177	Second—b
1971-72	48	17	13	109	317	192	Second—c
1972-73	47	23	8	102	297	208	Third—b
1973-74	40	24	14	94	300	251	Third—b
1974-75	37	29	14	88	319	276	Second—†
1975-76	29	42	9	67	262	333	Fourth—*
1976-77	29	37	14	72	272	310	Fourth—*
1977-78	30	37	13	73	279	280	Fourth—†
1978-79	40	29	11	91	316	292	Third—c
1979-80	38	32	10	86	308	284	Third—a
1980-81	30	36	14	74	312	317	Fourth—b
1981-82	39	27	14	92	316	306	Second—a
1982-83	35	35	10	80	306	287	Fourth—a
1983-84	42	29	9	93	314	304	Fourth—†
	1538	1566	622	3698	11291	11530	

Philadelphia Flyers

Season	W.	L.	T.	Pts.	GF.	GA.	Position
1967-68	31	32	11	73	173	179	First—a
1968-69	20	35	21	61	174	225	Third—a
1969-70	17	35	24	58	197	225	Fifth—*
1970-71	28	33	17	73	207	225	Third—a
1971-72	26	38	14	66	200	236	Fifth—*
1972-73	37	30	11	85	296	256	Second—b
1973-74	50	16	12	112	273	164	First—xx
1974-75	51	18	11	113	293	181	First—xx
1975-76	51	13	16	118	348	209	First—c
1976-77	48	16	16	112	323	213	First—b
1977-78	45	20	15	105	296	200	Second—b
1978-79	40	25	15	95	281	248	Second—a
1979-80	48	12	20	116	327	254	First—c
1980-81	41	24	15	97	313	249	Second—a
1981-82	38	31	11	87	325	313	Third—†
1982-83	49	23	8	106	326	240	First—†
1983-84	44	26	10	98	350	290	Third—†
	664	427	247	1575	4702	4007	

Pittsburgh Penguins

Season	W.	L.	T.	Pts.	GF.	GA.	Position
1967-68	27	34	13	67	195	216	Fifth—*
1968-69	20	45	11	51	189	252	Fifth—*
1969-70	26	38	12	64	182	238	Second—b
1970-71	21	37	20	62	221	240	Sixth—*
1971-72	26	38	14	66	220	258	Fourth—a
1972-73	32	37	9	73	257	265	Fifth—*
1973-74	28	41	9	65	242	273	Fifth—*
1974-75	37	28	15	89	326	289	Third—a
1975-76	35	33	12	82	339	303	Third—†
1976-77	34	33	13	81	240	252	Third—†
1977-78	25	37	18	68	254	321	Fourth—*
1978-79	36	31	13	85	281	279	Second—a
1979-80	30	37	13	73	251	303	Third—†
1980-81	30	37	13	73	302	345	Third—†
1981-82	31	36	13	75	310	337	Fourth—†
1982-83	18	53	9	45	257	394	Sixth—*
1983-84	16	58	6	38	254	390	Sixth—*
	472	653	213	1157	4078	4955	

Quebec Nordiques

Season	W.	L.	T.	Pts.	GF.	GA.	Position
1972-73	33	40	5	71	276	313	Fifth—*
1973-74	38	36	4	80	306	280	Fifth—*
1974-75	46	32	0	92	331	299	First—c
1975-76	50	27	4	104	371	316	Second—a
1976-77	47	31	3	97	353	295	First—xx
1977-78	40	37	3	83	349	347	Fourth—b
1978-79	41	34	5	87	288	271	Second—b
1979-80	25	44	11	61	248	313	Fifth—*
1980-81	30	32	18	78	314	318	Fourth—†
1981-82	33	31	16	82	356	345	Fourth—b
1982-83	34	34	12	80	343	336	Fourth—†
1983-84	42	28	10	94	360	278	Third—a
	459	403	91	1009	3895	3711	

St. Louis Blues

Season	W.	L.	T.	Pts.	GF.	GA.	Position
1967-68	27	31	16	70	177	191	Third—c
1968-69	37	25	14	88	204	157	First—c
1969-70	37	27	12	86	224	179	First—c
1970-71	34	25	19	87	223	208	Second—a
1971-72	28	39	11	67	208	247	Third—b
1972-73	32	34	12	76	233	251	Fourth—a
1973-74	26	40	12	64	206	248	Sixth—*
1974-75	35	31	14	84	269	267	Second—†
1975-76	29	37	14	72	249	290	Third—†
1976-77	32	39	9	73	239	276	First—a
1977-78	20	47	13	53	195	304	Fourth—*
1978-79	18	50	12	48	249	348	Third—*
1979-80	34	34	12	80	266	278	Second—†
1980-81	45	18	17	107	352	281	First—a
1981-82	32	40	8	72	315	349	Third—a
1982-83	25	40	15	65	285	316	Fourth—†
1983-84	32	41	7	71	293	316	Second—a
	523	598	217	1263	4187	4506	

Toronto Maple Leafs

Season	W.	L.	T.	Pts.	GF.	GA.	Position
1917-18	13	9	0	26	108	109	Second, First
1918-19	5	13	0	10	64	92	Third
1919-20	12	12	0	24	119	106	Third
1920-21	15	9	0	30	105	100	First
1921-22	13	10	1	27	98	97	Second—xx
1922-23	13	10	1	27	82	88	Third
1923-24	10	14	0	20	59	85	Third
1924-25	19	11	0	38	90	84	Second
1925-26	12	21	3	27	92	114	Sixth
1926-27	15	24	5	35	79	94	Fifth—*
1927-28	18	18	8	44	89	88	Fourth—*

— 117 —

Season	W.	L.	T.	Pts.	GF.	GA.	Position
1928-29	21	18	5	47	85	69	Third—b
1929-30	17	21	6	40	116	124	Fourth—*
1930-31	22	13	9	53	118	99	Second—a
1931-32	23	18	7	53	155	127	Second—xx
1932-33	24	18	6	54	119	111	First—c
1933-34	26	13	9	61	174	119	First—b
1934-35	30	14	4	64	157	111	First—c
1935-36	23	19	6	52	126	106	Second—c
1936-37	22	21	5	49	119	115	Third—a
1937-38	24	15	9	57	151	127	First—c
1938-39	19	20	9	47	114	107	Third—c
1939-40	25	17	6	56	134	110	Third—c
1940-41	28	14	6	62	145	99	Second—b
1941-42	27	18	3	57	158	136	Second—xx
1942-43	22	19	9	53	198	159	Third—b
1943-44	23	23	4	50	214	174	Third—b
1944-45	24	22	4	52	183	161	Third—xx
1945-46	19	24	7	45	174	185	Fifth—*
1946-47	31	19	10	72	209	172	Second—xx
1947-48	32	15	13	77	182	143	First—xx
1948-49	22	25	13	57	147	161	Fourth—xx
1949-50	31	27	12	74	176	173	Third—b
1950-51	41	16	13	95	212	138	Second—xx
1951-52	29	25	16	74	168	157	Third—b
1952-53	27	30	13	67	156	167	Fifth—*
1953-54	32	24	14	78	152	131	Third—b
1954-55	24	24	22	70	147	135	Third—b
1955-56	24	33	13	61	153	181	Fourth—b
1956-57	21	34	15	57	174	192	Fifth—*
1957-58	21	38	11	53	192	226	Sixth—*
1958-59	27	32	11	65	189	201	Fourth—c
1959-60	35	26	9	79	199	195	Second—c
1960-61	39	19	12	90	234	176	Second—b
1961-62	37	22	11	85	232	180	Second—xx
1962-63	35	23	12	82	221	180	First—xx
1963-64	33	25	12	78	192	172	Third—xx
1964-65	30	26	14	74	204	173	Fourth—b
1965-66	34	25	11	79	208	187	Third—b
1966-67	32	27	11	75	204	211	Third—xx
1967-68	33	31	10	76	209	176	Fifth—*
1968-69	35	26	15	85	234	217	Fourth—a
1969-70	29	34	13	71	222	242	Sixth—*
1970-71	37	33	8	82	248	211	Fourth—a
1971-72	33	31	14	80	209	208	Fourth—a
1972-73	27	41	10	64	247	279	Sixth—*
1973-74	35	27	16	86	274	230	Fourth—a
1974-75	31	33	16	78	280	309	Third—a
1975-76	34	31	15	83	294	276	Third—b
1976-77	33	32	15	81	301	285	Third—b
1977-78	41	29	10	92	271	237	Third—b
1978-79	34	33	13	81	267	252	Third—a
1979-80	35	40	5	75	304	327	Fourth—†
1980-81	28	37	15	71	322	367	Fifth—†
1981-82	20	44	16	56	298	380	Fifth—*
1982-83	28	40	12	68	293	330	Third—†
1983-84	26	45	9	61	303	387	Fifth—*
	1740	1600	612	4092	12152	11660	

Vancouver Canucks

Season	W.	L.	T.	Pts.	GF.	GA.	Position
1970-71	24	46	8	56	229	296	Sixth—*
1971-72	20	50	8	48	203	297	Seventh—*
1972-73	22	47	9	53	233	339	Seventh—*
1973-74	24	43	11	59	224	296	Seventh—*
1974-75	38	32	10	86	271	254	First—a
1975-76	33	32	15	81	271	272	Second—†
1976-77	25	42	13	63	235	294	Fourth—*
1977-78	20	43	17	57	239	320	Third—*
1978-79	25	42	13	63	217	291	Second—†
1979-80	27	37	16	70	256	281	Third—†
1980-81	28	32	20	76	289	301	Third—†

Season	W.	L.	T.	Pts.	GF.	GA.	Position
1981-82	30	33	17	77	290	286	Second—c
1982-83	30	35	15	75	303	309	Third—†
1983-84	32	39	9	73	306	328	Third—†
	378	553	181	937	3566	4164	

Washington Capitals

Season	W.	L.	T.	Pts.	GF.	GA.	Position
1974-75	8	67	5	21	181	446	Fifth—*
1975-76	11	59	10	32	224	394	Fifth—*
1976-77	24	42	14	62	221	307	Fourth—*
1977-78	17	49	14	48	195	321	Fifth—*
1978-79	24	41	15	63	273	338	Fourth—*
1979-80	27	40	13	67	261	293	Fifth—*
1980-81	26	36	18	70	286	317	Fifth—*
1981-82	26	41	13	65	319	338	Fifth—*
1982-83	39	25	16	94	306	283	Third—†
1983-84	48	27	5	101	308	226	Second—a
	250	427	123	623	2574	3263	

Winnipeg Jets

Season	W.	L.	T.	Pts.	GF.	GA.	Position
1972-73	43	31	4	90	285	249	First—c
1973-74	34	39	5	73	264	296	Fourth—a
1974-75	38	35	5	81	322	293	Third—*
1975-76	52	27	2	106	345	254	First—xx
1976-77	46	32	2	94	366	291	Second—c
1977-78	50	28	2	102	381	270	First—xx
1978-79	39	35	6	84	307	306	Third—xx
1979-80	20	49	11	51	214	314	Fifth—*
1980-81	9	57	14	32	246	400	Sixth—*
1981-82	33	33	14	80	319	332	Second—†
1982-83	33	39	8	74	311	333	Fourth—†
1983-84	31	38	11	73	340	374	Third—†
	428	443	84	940	3700	3712	

NHL Stanley Cup Winners

SEASON	TEAM	COACH
1917-18	Toronto Arenas	Dick Carroll
1919-20	Ottawa Senators	Pete Green
1920-21	Ottawa Senators	Pete Green
1921-22	Toronto St. Pats	Eddie Powers
1922-23	Ottawa Senators	Pete Green
1923-24	Montreal Canadiens	Leo Dandurand
1924-25	Victoria Cougars	Lester Patrick
1925-26	Montreal Maroons	Eddie Gerard
1926-27	Ottawa Senators	Dave Gill
1927-28	New York Rangers	Lester Patrick
1928-29	Boston Bruins	Cy Denneny
1929-30	Montreal Canadiens	Cecil Hart
1930-31	Montreal Canadiens	Cecil Hart
1931-32	Toronto Maple Leafs	Dick Irvin
1932-33	New York Rangers	Lester Patrick
1933-34	Chicago Black Hawks	Tommy Gorman
1934-35	Montreal Maroons	Tommy Gorman
1935-36	Detroit Red Wings	Jack Adams
1936-37	Detroit Red Wings	Jack Adams
1937-38	Chicago Black Hawks	Bill Stewart
1938-39	Boston Bruins	Art Ross
1939-40	New York Rangers	Frank Boucher
1940-41	Boston Bruins	Cooney Weiland
1941-42	Toronto Maple Leafs	Hap Day
1942-43	Detroit Red Wings	Jack Adams
1943-44	Montreal Canadiens	Dick Irvin
1944-45	Toronto Maple Leafs	Hap Day
1945-46	Montreal Canadiens	Dick Irvin
1946-47	Toronto Maple Leafs	Hap Day
1947-48	Toronto Maple Leafs	Hap Day
1948-49	Toronto Maple Leafs	Hap Day
1949-50	Detroit Red Wings	Tommy Ivan
1950-51	Toronto Maple Leafs	Joe Primeau
1951-52	Detroit Red Wings	Tommy Ivan
1952-53	Montreal Canadiens	Dick Irvin
1953-54	Detroit Red Wings	Tommy Ivan
1954-55	Detroit Red Wings	Jimmy Skinner
1955-56	Montreal Canadiens	Toe Blake
1956-57	Montreal Canadiens	Toe Blake
1957-58	Montreal Canadiens	Toe Blake
1958-59	Montreal Canadiens	Toe Blake
1959-60	Montreal Canadiens	Toe Blake
1960-61	Chicago Black Hawks	Rudy Pilous
1961-62	Toronto Maple Leafs	Punch Imlach
1962-63	Toronto Maple Leafs	Punch Imlach
1963-64	Toronto Maple Leafs	Punch Imlach
1964-65	Montreal Canadiens	Toe Blake
1965-66	Montreal Canadiens	Toe Blake
1966-67	Toronto Maple Leafs	Punch Imlach
1967-68	Montreal Canadiens	Toe Blake
1968-69	Montreal Canadiens	Claude Ruel
1969-70	Boston Bruins	Harry Sinden
1970-71	Montreal Canadiens	Al MacNeil
1971-72	Boston Bruins	Tom Johnson
1972-73	Montreal Canadiens	Scotty Bowman
1973-74	Philadelphia Flyers	Fred Shero
1974-75	Philadelphia Flyers	Fred Shero
1975-76	Montreal Canadiens	Scotty Bowman
1976-77	Montreal Canadiens	Scotty Bowman
1977-78	Montreal Canadiens	Scotty Bowman
1978-79	Montreal Canadiens	Scotty Bowman
1979-80	New York Islanders	Al Arbour
1980-81	New York Islanders	Al Arbour
1981-82	New York Islanders	Al Arbour
1982-83	New York Islanders	Al Arbour
1983-84	Edmonton Oilers	Glen Sather

NOTE: 1918-19 series between Montreal and Seattle cancelled after five games because of influenza epidemic.

Stanley Cup Playoff Records

Team

1—Most Stanley Cup Championships: Montreal Canadiens (20).
2—Most Final Series Appearances: Montreal Canadiens (26).
3—Most Years in Playoffs: Montreal Canadiens (54).
4—Most Consecutive Stanley Cup Championships: Montreal Canadiens (5).
5—Most Consecutive Playoff Appearances: Montreal Canadiens (21).
6—Most Goals, One Team, One Game: Montreal Canadiens (11) vs. Toronto, March 30, 1944.
7—Most Goals, One Team, One Period: Montreal Canadiens (7) vs. Toronto, March 30, 1944—3rd period.
8—Most Consecutive Playoff Game Victories: Montreal Canadiens (11); Boston Bruins (11).

Individual

1—Most Years in Playoffs: Gordie Howe (Detroit 19, Hartford 1)—20.
2—Most Consecutive Years in Playoffs: Jean Beliveau (Montreal)—16.
3—Most Playoff Games: Henri Richard (Montreal)—180.
4—Most Points in Playoffs: Jean Beliveau (Montreal)—176.
5—Most Goals in Playoffs: Maurice Richard (Montreal)—82.
6—Most Assists in Playoffs: Denis Potvin (N.Y. Islanders)—99.
7—Most Shutouts in Playoffs: Jacques Plante (Montreal, St. Louis)—14.
8—Most Games Played by Goaltender: Bill Smith (N.Y. Islanders)—123.
9—Most Points One Year:
    Wayne Gretzky (Edmonton)—38 in 1982-83.
10—Most Goals One Year: Reggie Leach (Philadelphia)—19 in 1975-76.
11—Most Assists One Year: Wayne Gretzky (Edmonton)—26 in 1982-83.
12—Most Points By Defenseman One Year: Denis Potvin (N.Y. Islanders)—25 in 1980-81.
13—Most Goals By Defenseman One Year: Bobby Orr (Boston)—9 in 1969-70.
14—Most Assists By Defenseman One Year: Bobby Orr (Boston)—19 in 1971-72.
15—Most Penalty Minutes One Year: Dave Schultz (Philadelphia)—139 in 1973-74.
16—Most Shutouts One Year:
    Clint Benedict (Montreal Maroons)—4 in 1927-28.
    Dave Kerr (N.Y. Rangers)—4 in 1936-37.
    Frank McCool (Toronto)—4 in 1944-45.
    Terry Sawchuk (Detroit)—4 in 1951-52.
    Bernie Parent (Philadelphia)—4 in 1974-75.
    Ken Dryden (Montreal)—4 in 1976-77.
17—Most Consecutive Shutouts: Frank McCool (Toronto)—3 in 1944-45.
18—Most Points One Game:
    Wayne Gretzky (Edmonton)—7 vs. Calgary, April 17, 1983.
19—Most Goals One Game:
    Maurice Richard (Montreal)—5 vs. Toronto, March 23, 1944.
    Darryl Sittler (Toronto)—5 vs. Philadelphia, April 22, 1976.
    Reggie Leach (Philadelphia)—5 vs. Boston, May 6, 1976.
20—Most Assists One Game:
    Mikko Leinonen (N.Y. Rangers)—6 vs. Philadelphia, April 8, 1982.
21—Most Penalty Minutes in Playoffs: Dave (Tiger) Williams (Toronto, Vancouver)—421.

Individual Awards
Art Ross Trophy
(Leading Scorer—Regular Season)

Season	Player	Games	G.	A.	Pts.
1917-18	Joe Malone, Montreal	20	44	**	44
1918-19	Newsy Lalonde, Montreal	17	23	9	32
1919-20	Joe Malone, Quebec Bulldogs	24	39	6	45
1920-21	Newsy Lalonde, Montreal	24	33	8	41
1921-22	Punch Broadbelt, Ottawa	24	32	14	46
1922-23	Babe Dye, Toronto	22	26	11	37
1923-24	Cy Denneny, Ottawa	21	22	1	23
1924-25	Babe Dye, Toronto	29	38	6	44
1925-26	Nels Stewart, Montreal Maroons	36	34	8	42
1926-27	Bill Cook, New York Rangers	44	33	4	37
1927-28	Howie Morenz, Montreal	43	33	18	51
1928-29	Ace Bailey, Toronto	44	22	10	32
1929-30	Cooney Weiland, Boston	44	43	30	73
1930-31	Howie Morenz, Montreal	39	28	23	51
1931-32	Harvey Jackson, Toronto	48	28	25	53
1932-33	Bill Cook, New York Rangers	48	28	22	50
1933-34	Charlie Conacher, Toronto	42	32	20	52
1934-35	Charlie Conacher, Toronto	48	36	21	57
1935-36	Dave Schriner, New York Americans	48	19	26	45
1936-37	Dave Schriner, New York Americans	48	21	25	46
1937-38	Gordie Drillon, Toronto	48	26	26	52
1938-39	Toe Blake, Montreal	48	24	23	47
1939-40	Milt Schmidt, Boston	48	22	30	52
1940-41	Bill Cowley, Boston	46	17	45	62
1941-42	Bryan Hextall, New York Rangers	48	24	32	56
1942-43	Doug Bentley, Chicago	50	33	40	73
1943-44	Herbie Cain, Boston	48	36	46	82
1944-45	Elmer Lach, Montreal	50	26	54	80
1945-46	Max Bentley, Chicago	47	31	30	61
1946-47	Max Bentley, Chicago	60	29	43	72
1947-48	Elmer Lach, Montreal	60	30	31	61
1948-49	Roy Conacher, Chicago	60	26	42	68
1949-50	Ted Lindsay, Detroit	69	23	55	78
1950-51	Gordie Howe, Detroit	70	43	43	86
1951-52	Gordie Howe, Detroit	70	47	39	86
1952-53	Gordie Howe, Detroit	70	49	46	95
1953-54	Gordie Howe, Detroit	70	33	48	81
1954-55	Bernie Geoffrion, Montreal	70	38	37	75
1955-56	Jean Beliveau, Montreal	70	47	41	88
1956-57	Gordie Howe, Detroit	70	44	45	89
1957-58	Dickie Moore, Montreal	70	36	48	84
1958-59	Dickie Moore, Montreal	70	41	55	96
1959-60	Bobby Hull, Chicago	70	39	42	81
1960-61	Bernie Geoffrion, Montreal	64	50	45	95
1961-62	Bobby Hull, Chicago	70	50	34	84
1962-63	Gordie Howe, Detroit	70	38	48	86
1963-64	Stan Mikita, Chicago	70	39	50	89
1964-65	Stan Mikita, Chicago	70	28	59	87
1965-66	Bobby Hull, Chicago	65	54	43	97
1966-67	Stan Mikita, Chicago	70	35	62	97
1967-68	Stan Mikita, Chicago	72	40	47	87
1968-69	Phil Esposito, Boston	74	49	77	126
1969-70	Bobby Orr, Boston	76	33	87	120
1970-71	Phil Esposito, Boston	78	76	76	152
1971-72	Phil Esposito, Boston	76	66	67	133
1972-73	Phil Esposito, Boston	78	55	75	130
1973-74	Phil Esposito, Boston	78	68	77	145
1974-75	Bobby Orr, Boston	80	46	89	135
1975-76	Guy Lafleur, Montreal	80	56	69	125
1976-77	Guy Lafleur, Montreal	80	56	80	136
1977-78	Guy Lafleur, Montreal	78	60	72	132
1978-79	Bryan Trottier, New York Islanders	76	47	87	134
1979-80	Marcel Dionne, Los Angeles	80	53	84	137
1980-81	Wayne Gretzky, Edmonton	80	55	109	164
1981-82	Wayne Gretzky, Edmonton	80	92	120	212
1982-83	Wayne Gretzky, Edmonton	80	71	125	196
1983-84	Wayne Gretzky, Edmonton	74	87	118	205

**—Number of assists not recorded.

Hart Memorial Trophy
(Most Valuable Player)

1923-24—Frank Nighbor, Ottawa
1924-25—Billy Burch, Hamilton
1925-26—Nels Stewart, Montreal Maroons
1926-27—Herb Gardiner, Montreal
1927-28—Howie Morenz, Montreal
1928-29—Roy Worters, N.Y. Americans
1929-30—Nels Stewart, Montreal Maroons
1930-31—Howie Morenz, Montreal
1931-32—Howie Morenz, Montreal
1932-33—Eddie Shore, Boston
1933-34—Aurel Joliat, Montreal
1934-35—Eddie Shore, Boston
1935-36—Eddie Shore, Boston
1936-37—Babe Siebert, Montreal
1937-38—Eddie Shore, Boston
1938-39—Toe Blake, Montreal
1939-40—Ebbie Goodfellow, Detroit
1940-41—Bill Cowley, Boston
1941-42—Tom Anderson, N.Y. Americans
1942-43—Bill Cowley, Boston
1943-44—Babe Pratt, Toronto
1944-45—Elmer Lach, Montreal
1945-46—Max Bentley, Chicago
1946-47—Maurice Richard, Montreal
1947-48—Buddy O'Connor, N.Y. Rangers
1948-49—Sid Abel, Detroit
1949-50—Chuck Rayner, N.Y. Rangers
1950-51—Milt Schmidt, Boston
1951-52—Gordie Howe, Detroit
1952-53—Gordie Howe, Detroit
1953-54—Al Rollins, Chicago
1954-55—Ted Kennedy, Toronto
1955-56—Jean Beliveau, Montreal
1956-57—Gordie Howe, Detroit
1957-58—Gordie Howe, Detroit
1958-59—Andy Bathgate, N.Y. Rangers
1959-60—Gordie Howe, Detroit
1960-61—Bernie Geoffrion, Montreal
1961-62—Jacques Plante, Montreal
1962-63—Gordie Howe, Detroit
1963-64—Jean Beliveau, Montreal
1964-65—Bobby Hull, Chicago
1965-66—Bobby Hull, Chicago
1966-67—Stan Mikita, Chicago
1967-68—Stan Mikita, Chicago
1968-69—Phil Esposito, Boston
1969-70—Bobby Orr, Boston
1970-71—Bobby Orr, Boston
1971-72—Bobby Orr, Boston
1972-73—Bobby Clarke, Philadelphia
1973-74—Phil Esposito, Boston
1974-75—Bobby Clarke, Philadelphia
1975-76—Bobby Clarke, Philadelphia
1976-77—Guy Lafleur, Montreal
1977-78—Guy Lafleur, Montreal
1978-79—Bryan Trottier, N.Y. Islanders
1979-80—Wayne Gretzky, Edmonton
1980-81—Wayne Gretzky, Edmonton
1981-82—Wayne Gretzky, Edmonton
1982-83—Wayne Gretzky, Edmonton
1983-84—Wayne Gretzky, Edmonton

Penalty Leaders

	Games	Penalty Minutes
1926-27—Nels Stewart, Montreal Maroons	44	133
1927-28—Eddie Shore, Boston	44	165
1928-29—Merv "Red" Dutton, Montreal Maroons	44	139
1929-30—Joe Lamb, Ottawa Senators	44	119
1930-31—Harvey Rockburn, Detroit	42	118
1931-32—Merv "Red" Dutton, N.Y. Americans	47	107
1932-33—Red Horner, Toronto	47	144
1933-34—Red Horner, Toronto	42	126*
1934-35—Red Horner, Toronto	46	125
1935-36—Red Horner, Toronto	43	167
1936-37—Red Horner, Toronto	48	124
1937-38—Red Horner, Toronto	47	82*
1938-39—Red Horner, Toronto	48	85
1939-40—Red Horner, Toronto	30	87
1940-41—Jimmy Orlando, Detroit	48	99
1941-42—Jimmy Orlando, Detroit	48	81**
1942-43—Jimmy Orlando, Detroit	40	89*
1943-44—Mike McMahon, Montreal Canadiens	42	98
1944-45—Pat Egan, Boston	48	86
1945-46—Jack Stewart, Detroit	47	73
1946-47—Gus Mortson, Toronto	60	133
1947-48—Bill Barilko, Toronto	57	147
1948-49—Bill Ezinicki, Toronto	52	145
1949-50—Bill Ezinicki, Toronto	67	144
1950-51—Gus Mortson, Toronto	60	142
1951-52—Walter "Gus" Kyle, Boston	69	127
1952-53—Maurice Richard, Montreal Canadiens	70	112
1953-54—Gus Mortson, Chicago	68	132
1954-55—Fernie Flaman, Boston	70	150
1955-56—Lou Fontinato, N.Y. Rangers	70	202
1956-57—Gus Mortson, Chicago	70	147
1957-58—Lou Fontinato, N.Y. Rangers	70	152
1958-59—Ted Lindsay, Chicago	70	184
1959-60—Carl Brewer, Toronto	67	150

	Games	Penalty Minutes
1960-61—Pierre Pilote, Chicago	70	165
1961-62—Lou Fontinato, Montreal Canadiens	54	167
1962-63—Howie Young, Detroit	64	273
1963-64—Vic Hadfield, N.Y. Rangers	69	151
1964-65—Carl Brewer, Toronto	70	177
1965-66—Reg Fleming, N.Y. Rangers	69	166
1966-67—John Ferguson, Montreal Canadiens	67	177
1967-68—Barclay Plager, St. Louis Blues	49	153
1968-69—Forbes Kennedy, Philadelphia-Toronto	77	219
1969-70—Keith Magnuson, Chicago	76	213
1970-71—Keith Magnuson, Chicago	76	291
1971-72—Bryan Watson, Pittsburgh Penguins	75	212
1972-73—Dave Schultz, Philadelphia Flyers	76	259
1973-74—Dave Schultz, Philadelphia Flyers	73	348
1974-75—Dave Schultz, Philadelphia Flyers	76	472
1975-76—Steve Durbano, Pittsburgh-Kansas City	69	370
1976-77—Dave Williams, Toronto	77	338
1977-78—Dave Schultz, Los Angeles-Pittsburgh	74	405
1978-79—Dave Williams, Toronto	77	298
1979-80—Jimmy Mann, Winnipeg	72	287
1980-81—Dave Williams, Vancouver	77	333
1981-82—Paul Baxter, Pittsburgh	76	407
1982-83—Randy Holt, Washington	70	275
1983-84—Chris Nilan, Montreal	76	338

*—Match Misconduct penalty not included in total minutes.
**—Three Match misconduct penalties not included in total minutes. 1946-47 was first season that Match penalties were automatically included in penalty totals.

James Norris Memorial Trophy
(Outstanding Defenseman)

1953-54—Red Kelly, Detroit
1954-55—Doug Harvey, Montreal
1955-56—Doug Harvey, Montreal
1956-57—Doug Harvey, Montreal
1957-58—Doug Harvey, Montreal
1958-59—Tom Johnson, Montreal
1959-60—Doug Harvey, Montreal
1960-61—Doug Harvey, Montreal
1961-62—Doug Harvey, N.Y. Rangers
1962-63—Pierre Pilote, Chicago
1963-64—Pierre Pilote, Chicago
1964-65—Pierre Pilote, Chicago
1965-66—Jacques Laperriere, Montreal
1966-67—Harry Howell, N.Y. Rangers
1967-68—Bobby Orr, Boston
1968-69—Bobby Orr, Boston
1969-70—Bobby Orr, Boston
1970-71—Bobby Orr, Boston
1971-72—Bobby Orr, Boston
1972-73—Bobby Orr, Boston
1973-74—Bobby Orr, Boston
1974-75—Bobby Orr, Boston
1975-76—Denis Potvin, N.Y. Islanders
1976-77—Larry Robinson, Montreal
1977-78—Denis Potvin, N.Y. Islanders
1978-79—Denis Potvin, N.Y. Islanders
1979-80—Larry Robinson, Montreal
1980-81—Randy Carlyle, Pittsburgh
1981-82—Doug Wilson, Chicago
1982-83—Rod Langway, Washington
1983-84—Rod Langway, Washington

Vezina Trophy

(Awarded to goalkeeper(s) having played a minimum 25 games for the team with fewest goals scored against. Beginning with 1981-82 season, awarded to outstanding goaltender.)

	Games	Goals	SO.	Avg.
1926-27—George Hainsworth, Montreal	44	67	14	1.52
1927-28—George Hainsworth, Montreal	44	48	13	1.09
1928-29—George Hainsworth, Montreal	44	43	22	0.98
1929-30—Tiny Thompson, Boston	44	98	3	2.23
1930-31—Roy Worters, New York Americans	44	74	8	1.68
1931-32—Charlie Gardiner, Chicago	48	101	4	2.10
1932-33—Tiny Thompson, Boston	48	88	11	1.83
1933-34—Charlie Gardiner, Chicago	48	83	10	1.73
1934-35—Lorne Chabot, Chicago	48	88	8	1.83
1935-36—Tiny Thompson, Boston	48	82	10	1.71
1936-37—Normie Smith, Detroit	48	102	6	2.13
1937-38—Tiny Thompson, Boston	48	89	7	1.85
1938-39—Frank Brimsek, Boston	43	69	10	1.60
1939-40—Dave Kerr, New York Rangers	48	77	8	1.60
1940-41—Turk Broda, Toronto	48	99	4	2.06
1941-42—Frank Brimsek, Boston	47	112	3	2.38

Season	Goaltender	Games	Goals	SO.	Avg.
1942-43	Johnny Mowers, Detroit	50	124	6	2.48
1943-44	Bill Durnan, Montreal	50	109	2	2.18
1944-45	Bill Durnan, Montreal	50	121	1	2.42
1945-46	Bill Durnan, Montreal	40	104	4	2.60
1946-47	Bill Durnan, Montreal	60	138	4	2.30
1947-48	Turk Broda, Toronto	60	143	5	2.38
1948-49	Bill Durnan, Montreal	60	126	10	2.10
1949-50	Bill Durnan, Montreal	64	141	8	2.20
1950-51	Al Rollins, Toronto	40	70	5	1.75
1951-52	Terry Sawchuk, Detroit	70	139	11	1.98
1952-53	Terry Sawchuk, Detroit	70	133	12	1.94
1953-54	Harry Lumley, Toronto	69	128	13	1.85
1954-55	Terry Sawchuk, Detroit	68	132	12	1.94
1955-56	Jacques Plante, Montreal	64	119	7	1.86
1956-57	Jacques Plante, Montreal	61	123	9	2.02
1957-58	Jacques Plante, Montreal	57	119	9	2.09
1958-59	Jacques Plante, Montreal	67	144	9	2.15
1959-60	Jacques Plante, Montreal	69	175	3	2.54
1960-61	John Bower, Toronto	58	145	2	2.50
1961-62	Jacques Plante, Montreal	70	166	4	2.37
1962-63	Glenn Hall, Chicago	66	166	5	2.51
1963-64	Charlie Hodge, Montreal	62	140	8	2.26
1964-65	Terry Sawchuk, Toronto	36	92	1	2.56
	John Bower, Toronto	34	81	3	2.38
1965-66	Lorne Worsley, Montreal	48	114	2	2.36
	Charlie Hodge, Montreal	21	56	1	2.58
1966-67	Glenn Hall, Chicago	32	66	2	2.38
	Denis DeJordy, Chicago	44	104	4	2.46
1967-68	Lorne Worsley, Montreal	40	73	6	1.98
	Rogatien Vachon, Montreal	39	92	4	2.48
1968-69	Glenn Hall, St. Louis	41	85	8	2.17
	Jacques Plante, St. Louis	37	70	5	1.96
1969-70	Tony Esposito, Chicago	63	136	15	2.17
1970-71	Ed Giacomin, New York Rangers	45	95	8	2.15
	Gilles Villemure, N.Y. Rangers	34	78	4	2.29
1971-72	Tony Esposito, Chicago	48	82	9	1.76
	Gary Smith, Chicago	28	62	5	2.41
1972-73	Ken Dryden, Montreal	54	119	6	2.26
1973-74	Bernie Parent, Philadelphia	73	136	12	1.89
	Tony Esposito, Chicago	70	141	10	2.04
1974-75	Bernie Parent, Philadelphia	68	137	12	2.03
1975-76	Ken Dryden, Montreal	62	121	8	2.03
1976-77	Ken Dryden, Montreal	56	117	10	2.14
	Michel Larocque, Montreal	26	53	4	2.09
1977-78	Ken Dryden, Montreal	52	105	5	2.05
	Michel Larocque, Montreal	30	77	1	2.67
1978-79	Ken Dryden, Montreal	47	108	5	2.30
	Michel Larocque, Montreal	34	94	3	2.84
1979-80	Bob Sauve, Buffalo	32	74	4	2.36
	Don Edwards, Buffalo	49	125	4	2.57
1980-81	Richard Sevigny, Montreal	33	71	2	2.40
	Michel Larocque, Montreal	28	82	1	3.03
	Denis Herron, Montreal	25	67	1	3.50
1981-82	Bill Smith, New York Islanders	46	133	0	2.97
1982-83	Pete Peeters, Boston	62	142	8	2.36
1983-84	Tom Barrasso, Buffalo	42	117	2	2.84

Bill Jennings Trophy

(Awarded to goalkeeper(s) having played a minimum of 25 games for the team with fewest goals scored against, beginning with 1981-82 season.)

Season	Goaltender	Games	Goals	SO.	Avg.
1981-82	Denis Herron, Montreal	27	68	3	2.64
	Rick Wamsley, Montreal	38	101	2	2.75
1982-83	Roland Melanson, N.Y. Islanders	44	109	1	2.66
	Billy Smith, N.Y. Islanders	41	112	1	2.87
1983-84	Pat Riggin, Washington	41	102	4	2.66
	—Al Jensen, Washington	43	117	4	2.91

Calder Memorial Trophy
(Rookie of the Year)

1932-33—Carl Voss, Detroit
1933-34—Russ Blinco, Montreal Maroons
1934-35—Dave Schriner, N.Y. Americans
1935-36—Mike Karakas, Chicago
1936-37—Syl Apps, Toronto
1937-38—Cully Dahlstrom, Chicago
1938-39—Frank Brimsek, Boston
1939-40—Kilby Macdonald, N.Y. Rangers
1940-41—John Quilty, Montreal
1941-42—Grant Warwick, N.Y. Rangers
1942-43—Gaye Stewart, Toronto
1943-44—Gus Bodnar, Toronto
1944-45—Frank McCool, Toronto
1945-46—Edgar Laprade, N.Y. Rangers
1946-47—Howie Meeker, Toronto
1947-48—Jim McFadden, Detroit
1948-49—Pentti Lund, N.Y. Rangers
1949-50—Jack Gelineau, Boston
1950-51—Terry Sawchuk, Detroit
1951-52—Bernie Geoffrion, Montreal
1952-53—Lorne Worsley, N.Y. Rangers
1953-54—Camille Henry, N.Y. Rangers
1954-55—Ed Litzenberger, Chicago
1955-56—Glenn Hall, Detroit
1956-57—Larry Regan, Boston
1957-58—Frank Mahovlich, Toronto
1958-59—Ralph Backstrom, Montreal
1959-60—Bill Hay, Chicago
1960-61—Dave Keon, Toronto
1961-62—Bobby Rousseau, Montreal
1962-63—Kent Douglas, Toronto
1963-64—Jacques Laperriere, Montreal
1964-65—Roger Crozier, Detroit
1965-66—Brit Selby, Toronto
1966-67—Bobby Orr, Boston
1967-68—Derek Sanderson, Boston
1968-69—Danny Grant, Minnesota
1969-70—Tony Esposito, Chicago
1970-71—Gilbert Perreault, Buffalo
1971-72—Ken Dryden, Montreal
1972-73—Steve Vickers, N.Y. Rangers
1973-74—Denis Potvin, N.Y. Islanders
1974-75—Eric Vail, Atlanta
1975-76—Bryan Trottier, N.Y. Islanders
1976-77—Willi Plett, Atlanta
1977-78—Mike Bossy, N.Y. Islanders
1978-79—Bobby Smith, Minnesota
1979-80—Ray Bourque, Boston
1980-81—Peter Stastny, Quebec
1981-82—Dale Hawerchuk, Winnipeg
1982-83—Steve Larmer, Chicago
1983-84—Tom Barrasso, Buffalo

(Award was originally Leading Rookie Award. Named Calder Trophy in 1936-37 and became Calder Memorial Trophy when NHL President Frank Calder passed away—1942-43 season.)

Lady Byng Memorial Trophy
(Most Gentlemanly Player)

1924-25—Frank Nighbor, Ottawa
1925-26—Frank Nighbor, Ottawa
1926-27—Billy Burch, N.Y. Americans
1927-28—Frank Boucher, N.Y. Rangers
1928-29—Frank Boucher, N.Y. Rangers
1929-30—Frank Boucher, N.Y. Rangers
1930-31—Frank Boucher, N.Y. Rangers
1931-32—Joe Primeau, Toronto
1932-33—Frank Boucher, N.Y. Rangers
1933-34—Frank Boucher, N.Y. Rangers
1934-35—Frank Boucher, N.Y. Rangers
1935-36—Doc Romnes, Chicago
1936-37—Marty Barry, Detroit
1937-38—Gordie Drillon, Toronto
1938-39—Clint Smith, N.Y. Rangers
1939-40—Bobby Bauer, Boston
1940-41—Bobby Bauer, Boston
1941-42—Syl Apps, Toronto
1942-43—Max Bentley, Chicago
1943-44—Clint Smith, Chicago
1944-45—Bill Mosienko, Chicago
1945-46—Toe Blake, Montreal
1946-47—Bobby Bauer, Boston
1947-48—Buddy O'Connor, N.Y. Rangers
1948-49—Bill Quackenbush, Detroit
1949-50—Edgar Laprade, N.Y. Rangers
1950-51—Red Kelly, Detroit
1951-52—Sid Smith, Toronto
1952-53—Red Kelly, Detroit
1953-54—Red Kelly, Detroit
1954-55—Sid Smith, Toronto
1955-56—Earl Reibel, Detroit
1956-57—Andy Hebenton, N.Y. Rangers
1957-58—Camille Henry, N.Y. Rangers
1958-59—Alex Delvecchio, Detroit
1959-60—Don McKenney, Boston
1960-61—Red Kelly, Toronto
1961-62—Dave Keon, Toronto
1962-63—Dave Keon, Toronto
1963-64—Ken Wharram, Chicago
1964-65—Bobby Hull, Chicago
1965-66—Alex Delvecchio, Detroit
1966-67—Stan Mikita, Chicago
1967-68—Stan Mikita, Chicago
1968-69—Alex Delvecchio, Detroit
1969-70—Phil Goyette, St. Louis
1970-71—John Bucyk, Boston
1971-72—Jean Ratelle, N.Y. Rangers
1972-73—Gil Perreault, Buffalo
1973-74—John Bucyk, Boston
1974-75—Marcel Dionne, Detroit
1975-76—Jean Ratelle, N.Y. R.-Boston
1976-77—Marcel Dionne, Los Angeles
1977-78—Butch Goring, Los Angeles
1978-79—Bob MacMillan, Atlanta
1979-80—Wayne Gretzky, Edmonton
1980-81—Butch Goring, N.Y. Islanders
1981-82—Rick Middleton, Boston
1982-83—Mike Bossy, N.Y. Islanders
1983-84—Mike Bossy, N.Y. Islanders

(Originally Lady Byng Trophy. After winning award seven times, Frank Boucher received permanent possession and a new trophy was donated to NHL in 1936. After Lady Byng's death in 1949, NHL changed name to Lady Byng Memorial Trophy.)

Conn Smythe Trophy
(Most Valuable Player in Playoffs)

1964-65—Jean Beliveau, Montreal
1965-66—Roger Crozier, Detroit
1966-67—Dave Keon, Toronto
1967-68—Glenn Hall, St. Louis
1968-69—Serge Savard, Montreal
1969-70—Bobby Orr, Boston
1970-71—Ken Dryden, Montreal
1971-72—Bobby Orr, Boston
1972-73—Yvan Cournoyer, Montreal
1973-74—Bernie Parent, Philadelphia
1974-75—Bernie Parent, Philadelphia
1975-76—Reggie Leach, Philadelphia
1976-77—Guy Lafleur, Montreal
1977-78—Larry Robinson, Montreal
1978-79—Bob Gainey, Montreal
1979-80—Bryan Trottier, N.Y. Islanders
1980-81—Butch Goring, N.Y. Islanders
1981-82—Mike Bossy, N. Y. Islanders
1982-83—Billy Smith, N.Y. Islanders
1983-84—Mark Messier, Edmonton

Bill Masterton Memorial Trophy
(Presented by Professional Hockey Writers' Association to player who best exemplifies the qualities of perseverance, sportsmanship and dedication to hockey.)

1967-68—Claude Provost, Montreal
1968-69—Ted Hampson, Oakland
1969-70—Pit Martin, Chicago
1970-71—Jean Ratelle, N.Y. Rangers
1971-72—Bobby Clarke, Philadelphia
1972-73—Lowell MacDonald, Pittsburgh
1973-74—Henri Richard, Montreal
1974-75—Don Luce, Buffalo
1975-76—Rod Gilbert, N.Y. Rangers
1976-77—Ed Westfall, N.Y. Islanders
1977-78—Butch Goring, Los Angeles
1978-79—Serge Savard, Montreal
1979-80—Al MacAdam, Minnesota
1980-81—Blake Dunlop, St. Louis
1981-82—Glenn Resch, Colorado
1982-83—Lanny McDonald, Calgary
1983-84—Brad Park, Detroit

Frank J. Selke Trophy
(Best Defensive Forward)

1977-78—Bob Gainey, Montreal
1978-79—Bob Gainey, Montreal
1979-80—Bob Gainey, Montreal
1980-81—Bob Gainey, Montreal
1981-82—Steve Kasper, Boston
1982-83—Bobby Clarke, Philadelphia
1983-84—Doug Jarvis, Washington

Jack Adams Award
(Coach of the Year)

1973-74—Fred Shero, Philadelphia
1974-75—Bob Pulford, Los Angeles
1975-76—Don Cherry, Boston
1976-77—Scotty Bowman, Montreal
1977-78—Bobby Kromm, Detroit
1978-79—Al Arbour, N.Y. Islanders
1979-80—Pat Quinn, Philadelphia
1980-81—Red Berenson, St. Louis
1981-82—Tom Watt, Winnipeg
1982-83—Orval Tessier, Chicago
1983-84—Bryan Murray, Washington

NHL Entry Draft—June 10, 1984

(*Indicates an 18-year-old pick. †Indicates a 19-year-old pick)
(18 year old—born between Sept. 1, 1965 and Aug. 31, 1966)
(19 year old—born between Sept. 1, 1964 and Aug. 31, 1965)

First Round

NHL Club	PLAYER	(Pos)	1983-84 CLUB (League)
1—Pittsburgh	*Mario Lemieux	(C)	Laval Voisins (QHL)
2—New Jersey	*Kirk Muller	(C)	Guelph Platers (OHL)
3—Chicago (from Los Angeles)	*Ed Olczyk	(RW)	U.S. Olympic Team
4—Toronto	*Al Iafrate	(D)	U.S. Olympic/Belleville Bulls (OHL)
5—Montreal (from Hartford)	*Petr Svoboda	(D)	Czechoslovakia
6—Los Angeles (from Chicago)	*Craig Redmond	(D)	Canadian Olympic Team
7—Detroit	*Shawn Burr	(C)	Kitchener Rangers (OHL)
8—Montreal (from St. Louis)	*Shayne Corson	(C)	Brantford Alexanders (OHL)
9—Pittsburgh (from Winnipeg)	*Doug Bodger	(D)	Kamloops Jr. Oilers (WHL)
10—Vancouver	*J.J. Daigneault	(D)	Canadian Oly./Langueuil (QHL)
11—Hartford (from Montreal)	*Sylvain Cote	(D)	Quebec Remparts (QHL)
12—Calgary	*Gary Roberts	(LW)	Ottawa 67's (OHL)
13—Minnesota	*David Quinn	(D)	Kent H.S. (Conn. H.S.)
14—N.Y. Rangers	*Terry Carkner	(D)	Peterborough Petes (OHL)
15—Quebec	*Trevor Stienburg	(RW)	Guelph Platers (OHL)
16—Pittsburgh (from Philadelphia)	*Roger Belanger	(C)	Kingston Canadians (OHL)
17—Washington	*Kevin Hatcher	(D)	North Bay Centennials (OHL)
18—Buffalo	*Bo Mikael Andersson	(C)	Vastra Frolunda (Sweden)
19—Boston	*Dave Pasin	(RW)	Prince Albert Raiders (WHL)
20—N.Y. Islanders	*Duncan MacPherson	(D)	Saskatoon Blades (WHL)
21—Edmonton	*Selmar Odelein	(D)	Regina Pats (WHL)

Second Round

NHL Club	PLAYER	(Pos)	1983-84 CLUB (League)
22—Philadelphia (from Pittsburgh)	*Greg Smyth	(D)	London Knights (OHL)
23—New Jersey	*Craig Billington	(G)	Belleville Bulls (OHL)
24—Los Angeles	*Brian Wilks	(C)	Kitchener Rangers (OHL)
25—Toronto	*Todd Gill	(D)	Windsor Spitfires (OHL)
26—St. Louis (from Hart. & Mont.)	*Brian Benning	(D)	Portland Winter Hawks (WHL)
27—Philadelphia (from Chicago)	*Scott Mellanby	(RW)	Henry Carr H.S. (Toronto Jr. B)
28—Detroit	*Doug Houda	(D)	Calgary Wranglers (WHL)
29—Montreal (from St. Louis)	*Stephane Richer	(C)	Granby Bisons (QHL)
30—Winnipeg	*Peter Douris	(C)	Univ. of New Hampshire (ECAC)
31—Vancouver	*Jeff Rohlicek	(LW)	Portland Winter Hawks (WHL)
32—St. Louis (from Montreal)	*Anthony Hrkac	(C)	Orillia Junior 'A' (Ontario)
33—Calgary	*Ken Sabourin	(D)	S. S. Marie Greyhounds (OHL)
34—Washington (from Minnesota)	*Stephen Leach	(RW)	Matignon H.S. (Mass.)
35—N.Y. Rangers	Raimo Helminen	(C)	Ilves Tampere (Finland)
36—Quebec	*Jeff Brown	(D)	Sudbury Wolves (OHL)
37—Philadelphia	*Jeff Chychrun	(D)	Kingston Canadians (OHL)
38—Calgary (from Washington)	*Paul Ranheim	(C)	Edina H.S. (Minn.)
39—Buffalo	*Doug Trapp	(LW)	Regina Pats (WHL)
40—Boston	*Ray Podloski	(C)	Portland Winter Hawks (WHL)
41—N.Y. Islanders	*Bruce Melanson	(RW)	Oshawa Generals (OHL)
42—Edmonton	†Daryl Reaugh	(G)	Kamloops Jr. Oilers (WHL)

Third Round

NHL Club	PLAYER	(Pos)	1983-84 CLUB (League)
43—Philadelphia (from Pittsburgh)	*David McLay	(LW)	Kelowna Wings (WHL)
44—New Jersey	*Neil Davey	(D)	Michigan State Univ. (CCHA)
45—Chicago (from Los Angeles)	*Trent Yawney	(D)	Saskatoon Blades (WHL)
46—Minnesota (from Toronto)	*Kenneth Hodge Jr.	(C)	St. John's Prep. (Mass.)
47—Philadelphia (from Hartford)	*John Stevens	(D)	Oshawa Generals (OHL)
48—Los Angeles (from Chicago)	*John English	(D)	S. S. Marie Greyhounds (OHL)
49—Detroit	Milan Chalupa	(D)	Czechoslovakia Nat.
50—St. Louis	*Toby Ducolon	(RW)	Bellows H.S. (Vt.)
51—Montreal (from Winnipeg)	*Roy Patrick	(G)	Granby Bisons (OHL)
52—Vancouver	*David Saunders	(LW)	St. Lawrence Univ. (CCHA)
53—St. Louis (from Montreal)	*Robert Dirk	(D)	Regina Pats (WHL)
54—Montreal (from Calgary)	*Grame Bonar	(RW)	S. S. Marie Greyhounds (WHL)
55—Vancouver (from Minnesota)	*Landis Chaulk	(LW)	Calgary Wranglers (WHL)
56—St. Louis (from N.Y. Rangers)	*Alan Perry	(G)	Mt. St. Charles H.S. (R.I.)
57—Quebec	*Steven Finn	(D)	Laval Voisins (QHL)
58—Vancouver (from Philadelphia)	*Mike Stevens	(C)	Kitchener Rangers (OHL)

NHL Club	PLAYER	(Pos)	1983-84 CLUB (League)
59—Washington	*Michael Pivonka	(C)	Kladno Poldi (Czechoslovakia)
60—Buffalo	*Ray Sheppard	(RW)	Cornwall Royals (OHL)
61—Boston	*Jeff Cornelius	(D)	Toronto Marlboros (OHL)
62—N.Y. Islanders	*Jeff Norton	(D)	Cushing Academy
63—Edmonton	*Todd Norman	(C)	Hill Murray H.S. (Minn.)

Fourth Round

NHL Club	PLAYER	(Pos)	1983-84 CLUB (League)
64—Pittsburgh	*Mark Teevans	(RW)	Peterborough Petes (OHL)
65—Montreal (from New Jersey)	*Lee Brodeur	(RW)	Grafton H.S. (No. Dak.)
66—Chicago	*Tony Eriksson	(C)	Ornskoldsvik Mo Do AIK (Sweden)
67—Toronto	†Jeff Reese	(G)	London Knights (OHL)
68—Winnipeg (from Hartford)	*Chris Mills	(D)	Bramalea Jr. B. (Ontario)
69—Los Angeles (from Chicago)	*Thomas Glavine	(C)	Billerica H.S. (Mass.)
70—N.Y. Islanders	†Doug Wieck	(LW)	Rochester Mayo H.S. (Minn.)
71—St. Louis	*Graham Herring	(D)	Longueuil Chevaliers (QHL)
72—Winnipeg	*Sean Clement	(D)	Brockville Jr. A (Ontario)
73—Vancouver	*Brian Bertuzzi	(C)	Kamloops Jr. Oilers (WHL)
74—New Jersey (from Montreal)	*Paul Ysebaert	(C)	Petrolia Jr. B (Ontario)
75—Calgary	Peter Rosol	(LW)	Dukla Jihlava (Czechoslovakia)
76—Minnesota	Miroslav Maly	(D)	Bayreuth (West Germany)
77—N.Y. Rangers	*Paul Broten	(C)	Roseau H.S. (Minn.)
78—Quebec	*Terry Perkins	(RW)	Portland Winter Hawks (WHL)
79—Philadelphia	*Dave Hanson	(C)	Grand Forks H.S. (No. Dak.)
80—Washington	*Kris King	(C)	Peterborough Petes (OHL)
81—Buffalo	*Bob Halkidis	(D)	London Knights (OHL)
82—Boston	*Robert Joyce	(C)	Notre Dame H.S. (Sask.)
83—N.Y. Islanders	*Ari Eerik Haanpaa	(RW)	Ilves Tampere (Finland)
84—Edmonton	*Rich Novak	(RW)	Richmond Tier II (B.C.)

Fifth Round

NHL Club	PLAYER	(Pos)	1983-84 CLUB (League)
85—Pittsburgh	Arto Javanainen	(RW)	Assat Pori (Finland)
86—New Jersey	*Jon Morris	(C)	Chelmsford H.S. (Mass.)
87—Los Angeles	*David Grannis	(RW)	South St. Paul H.S. (Minn.)
88—Toronto	*Jack Capuano	(D)	Kent H.S. (Conn.)
89—Minnesota (from Hartford)	Jiri Poner	(RW)	EV Landshut (W. Germany)
90—Chicago	*Timo Lehkonen	(G)	Jokerit Helsinki (Finland)
91—Detroit	*Mats Lundstrom	(LW)	Sweden Jr. Nat.
92—St. Louis	*Scott Paluch	(D)	Chicago Jets
93—Winnipeg	†Scott Schneider	(C)	Colorado College (WCHA)
94—Vancouver	*Brett MacDonald	(D)	North Bay Centennials (OHL)
95—Montreal	*Gerald Johannson	(D)	Swift Current
96—Calgary	Joel Paunio	(LW)	Ifk (Finland)
97—Minnesota	Kari Takko	(G)	Assat Pori (Finland)
98—N.Y. Rangers	*Clark Donatelli	(LW)	Stratford Jr. A (Ontario)
99—Winnipeg (from Quebec)	*Brent Severyn	(D)	Seattle Breakers (WHL)
100—Philadelphia	*Brian Dobbin	(RW)	London Knights (OHL)
101—Chicago (from Washington)	*Darin Sceviour	(RW)	Lethbridge Broncos (WHL)
102—Buffalo	*Joe Rampton	(LW)	S. S. Marie Greyhounds (OHL)
103—Boston	†Mike Bishop	(G)	London Knights (OHL)
104—N.Y. Islanders	*Mike Murray	(C)	London Knights (OHL)
105—Edmonton	*Richard Lambert	(LW)	Henry Carr H.S. (Ontario)

Sixth Round

NHL Club	PLAYER	(Pos)	1983-84 CLUB (League)
106—Edmonton (from Pittsburgh)	*Emanuel Viveiros	(D)	Prince Albert Raiders (WHL)
107—New Jersey	*Kirk McLean	(G)	Oshawa Generals (OHL)
108—Los Angeles	†Greg Strome	(G)	Univ. North Dakota (WCHA)
109—Toronto	*Fabian Joseph	(C)	Victoria Cougars (WHL)
110—Hartford	†Mike Millar	(RW)	Brantford Alexanders (OHL)
111—Chicago	*Chris Clifford	(G)	Kingston Canadians (OHL)
112—Detroit	*Randy Hansch	(G)	Victoria Cougars (WHL)
113—St. Louis	*Steve Tuttle	(RW)	Richmond Tier II (B.C.)
114—Winnipeg	*Gary Lorden	(D)	Bishop Hendricken (R.I.)
115—Vancouver	*Jeff Korchinski	(D)	Clarkson College (ECAC)
116—Montreal	*Jim Nesich	(RW/C)	Verdun Juniors (QHL)
117—Calgary	Brett Hull	(RW)	Penticton Knights (BCJHL)
118—Minnesota	*Gary McColgan	(LW)	Oshawa Generals (OHL)
119—N.Y. Rangers	Kjell Samuelson	(D)	Leksands IF (Sweden)

NHL Club	PLAYER	(Pos)	1983-84 CLUB (League)
120—Quebec	*Darren Cota	(RW)	Kelowna Wings (WHL)
121—Philadelphia	*John Dzikowski	(LW)	Brandon Wheat Kings (WHL)
122—Washington	*Vito Cramarossa	(RW)	Toronto Marlboros (OHL)
123—Buffalo	*James Gasseau	(D)	Drummondville Voltigeurs (QHL)
124—Boston	*Randy Oswald	(D)	Michigan Tech. Univ. (CCHA)
125—N.Y. Islanders	*Jim Wilharm	(D)	Minnetonka H.S. (Minn.)
126—Edmonton	Ivan Dornic	(LW)	Dukla Trencin (Czechoslovakia)

Seventh Round

NHL Club	PLAYER	(Pos)	1983-84 CLUB (League)
127—Pittsburgh	*Tom Ryan	(D)	Newton North H.S. (Mass.)
128—New Jersey	*Ian Ferguson	(D)	Oshawa Generals (OHL)
129—Los Angeles	†Timothy Hanley	(C)	Deerfield Academy (Mass.)
130—Toronto	*Joseph MacInnis	(C)	Watertown H.S.
131—Hartford	*Mark Vellucci	(D)	Belleville Bulls (OHL)
132—Chicago	*Mike Stapleton	(C)	Cornwall Royals (OHL)
133—Detroit	†Stefan Larson	(D)	Fastra Frolunda (Sweden)
134—St. Louis	*Cliff Ronning	(C)	New Westminister Bruins (WHL)
135—Winnipeg	*Luciano Borsato	(C)	Bramalea Jr. B (Ont.)
136—Vancouver	*Blaine Chrest	(C)	Portland Winter Hawks (WHL)
137—Montreal	*Scott MacTavish	(D)	Fredericton H.S. (New Brun.)
138—Calgary	*Kevan Melrose	(D)	Red Deer Rustlers (AJHL)
139—Minnesota	Vladimir Kyhos	(LW)	Litvinov CHZ (Czechoslovakia)
140—N.Y. Rangers	*Thomas Hussey	(LW)	St. Andrews H.S. (Ont.)
141—Quebec	Henrik Cedergren	(RW)	Gavle Brynas IF (Sweden)
142—Philadelphia	*Tom Allen	(D)	Kitchener Rangers (OHL)
143—Washington	*Timo Kalevi Iljima	(C)	Karpat Oulu (Finland)
144—Buffalo	*Darcy Wakaluk	(G)	Kelowna Wings (AJHL)
145—Boston	*Mark Thietke	(C)	Saskatoon Blades (WHL)
146—N.Y. Islanders	*Kelly Murphy	(D)	Notre Dame H.S. (Sask.)
147—Edmonton	*Heikki Riihijarvi	(D)	Kiekkoreipas Lahti (Finland)

Eighth Round

NHL Club	PLAYER	(Pos)	1983-84 CLUB (League)
148—St. Louis	*Don Porter	(LW)	Michigan Tech. Univ. (CCHA)
149—New Jersey	*Vladimir Kames	(C)	Dukla Jihlava (Czechoslovakia)
150—Los Angeles	Shannon Deegan	(C)	Univ. of Vermont (ECAC)
151—Toronto	*Derek Laxdal	(RW)	Brandon Wheat Kings (WHL)
152—Detroit	*Lars Karlsson	(LW)	Karlstad Farjestads BK (Sweden)
153—Chicago	*Glenn Greenough	(RW)	Sudbury Wolves (OHL)
154—Detroit	Urban Nordin	(C)	Ornskoldsvik Mo Do AIK (Sweden)
155—St. Louis	*Jim Vesey	(C)	Columbus H.S. (Mass.)
156—Winnipeg	†Brad Jones	(C)	Univ. of Michigan (CCHA)
157—Vancouver	*Jim Agnew	(D)	Brandon Wheat Kings (WHL)
158—Montreal	*Brad McCaughey	(RW)	Ann Arbour H.S. (Mich.)
159—Calgary	Jurri Hrdina	(RW)	Czechoslovakia Olympic Team
160—Minnesota	*Darin MacInnis	(G)	Kent H.S. (Conn.)
161—N.Y. Rangers	*Brian Nelson	(C)	Willmar H.S. (Minn.)
162—Quebec	*Jyrki Maki	(D)	Simley H.S. (Minn.)
163—Philadelphia	*Luke Vitale	(C)	Henry Carr H.S. (Ontario)
164—Washington	*Frank Joo	(D)	Regina Pats (WHL)
165—Buffalo	Orwar Stambert	(D)	Stockholm Djurgardens IF (Swd.)
166—Boston	*Don Sweeney	(D)	St. Paul's H.S. (N.H.)
167—N.Y. Islanders	*Franco Desantis	(D)	Verdun Juniors (QHL)
168—Edmonton	*Todd Ewen	(RW)	New Westminster Bruins (WHL)

Ninth Round

NHL Club	PLAYER	(Pos)	1983-84 CLUB (League)
169—Pittsburgh	†John Del Col	(LW)	Toronto Marlboros (OHL)
170—New Jersey	*Mike Roth	(D)	Hill Murray H.S. (Minn.)
171—Los Angeles	*Luc Robitaille	(LW)	Hull Olympiques (QHL)
172—Toronto	Dan Turner	(LW)	Medicine Hat Tigers (WHL)
173—Hartford	†John Devereaux	(C)	Scituate H.S. (Mass.)
174—Chicago	†Ralph Difiore	(D)	Shawinigan Cataracts (QHL)
175—Detroit	Bill Shibicky	(C)	Michigan State Univ. (CCHA)
176—St. Louis	*Daniel Jomphe	(LW)	Granby Bisons (OHL)
177—Winnipeg	*Gord Whitaker	(RW)	Colorado College (WCHA)
178—Vancouver	*Rex Grant	(G)	Kamloops Jr. Oilers (WHL)
179—Montreal	*Eric Demers	(LW)	Shawinigan Cataracts (QHL)
180—Calgary	Gary Suter	(D)	Univ. of Wisconsin (WCHA)
181—Minnesota	†Duane Wahlin	(RW)	St. Paul Johnson H.S. (Minn.)

NHL Club	PLAYER	(Pos)	1983-84 CLUB (League)
182—N.Y. Rangers	*Ville Kentala	(LW)	IFK Helsinki (Finland)
183—Quebec	*Guy Ouellette	(C)	Quebec Remparts (QHL)
184—Philadelphia	*Billy Powers	(C)	Matignon H.S. (Mass.)
185—Washington	*Jim Thomson	(RW)	Toronto Marlboros (OHL)
—Buffalo (Under Dispute)			
186—Boston	*Kevin Heffernan	(C)	Weymouth H.S. (Mass.)
187—N.Y. Islanders	*Tom Warden	(D)	North Bay Centennials (OHL)
188—N.Y. Rangers (from Edmonton)	*Heinz Ehlers	(C)	Leksands IF (Sweden)

Tenth Round

NHL Club	PLAYER	(Pos)	1983-84 CLUB (League)
189—Pittsburgh	*Steve Hurt	(RW)	Hill Murray H.S. (Minn.)
190—New Jersey	*Mike Peluso	(D)	Greenway H.S. (Minn.)
191—Los Angeles	†Jeff Crossman	(C)	Western Michigan Univ. (CCHA)
192—Toronto	*David Buckley	(D)	Trinity Pawling H.S. (Mass.)
193—Hartford	*Brent Regan	(RW)	St. Albert Saints (AJHL)
194—Chicago	*Joakim Persson	(RW)	Gavle Brynas IF (Sweden)
195—Detroit	*Jay Rose	(D)	New Prep School (Mass.)
196—St. Louis	†Tom Tilley	(D)	Orillia Tier II (Ont.)
197—Winnipeg	†Rick Forest	(LW)	Melville Jr. A (Sask.)
198—Vancouver	†Ed Lowney	(RW)	Boston University (ECAC)
199—Montreal	†Ron Annear	(D)	San Diego University
200—Calgary	*Petr Rucka	(C)	Sparta Praha (Czechoslovakia)
201—Minnesota	*Michael Oen	(C)	Stillwater H.S. (Minn.)
202—N.Y. Rangers	*Redford Royals	(C)	Redford Royals (Mich.)
203—Quebec	†Ken Quinney	(RW)	Calgary Wranglers (WHL)
204—Philadelphia	*Daryn Fersovich	(C)	St. Albert Saints (AJHL)
205—Washington	*Paul Cavallini	(D)	Henry Carr H.S. (Toronto Jr. B.)
206—Buffalo	†Brian McKinnon	(C)	Ottawa 67's (OHL)
207—Boston	*J.D. Urbanic	(LW)	Windsor Spitfires (OHL)
208—N.Y. Islanders	David Volek	(RW)	Slavia Praha (Czechoslovakia)
209—Edmonton	*Joel Curtis	(LW)	Oshawa Generals (OHL)

Eleventh Round

NHL Club	PLAYER	(Pos)	1983-84 CLUB (League)
210—Pittsburgh	*Jim Steen	(C)	Morhead H.S. (Minn.)
211—New Jersey	*Jartto Piipatinen	(C)	Kiekkoreipas Lahti (Finland)
212—Los Angeles	†Paul Kenny	(G)	Cornwall Royals (OHL)
213—Toronto	†Mikael Wurst	(LW)	Ohio State University (CCHA)
214—Hartford	Jim Culhane	(D)	Western Michigan Univ. (CCHA)
215—Chicago	*Bill Brown	(C)	Simley H.S. (Minn.)
216—Detroit	*Tim Kaiser	(RW/D)	Guelph Platers (OHL)
217—St. Louis	*Mark Cupolo	(LW)	Guelph Platers (OHL)
218—Winnipeg	†Mike Warus	(RW)	Lake Superior St. Col. (CCHA)
219—Vancouver	Doug Clarke	(D)	Colorado College (WCHA)
220—Montreal	*Dave Tanner	(D)	Notre Dame H.S. (Sask.)
221—Calgary	†Stefan Jonsson	(D)	Sodertalje (Sweden)
222—Minnesota	*Tom Terwilliger	(D)	Edina H.S. (Minn.)
223—N.Y. Rangers	*Tom Lorentz	(C)	Brady H.S. (Minn.)
224—Chicago	*David MacKey	(LW)	Victoria Cougars (WHL)
—Philadelphia (invalid claim)			
225—Washington	*Mikhail Tatarinow	(D)	Sokol Kiev (USSR)
226—Buffalo	*Grant Delcourt	(RW)	Kelowna Wings (BCJHL)
227—Boston	*Bill Kopecky	(C)	Austin Prep H.S. (Mass.)
228—N.Y. Islanders	*Russ Becker	(D)	Virginia H.S. (Minn.)
229—Edmonton	*Simon Wheeldon	(C)	Victoria Cougars (WHL)

Twelfth Round

NHL Club	PLAYER	(Pos)	1983-84 CLUB (League)
230—Pittsburgh	*Mark Ziliotto	(LW)	Streetsville Jr. B (Ont.)
231—New Jersey	*Chris Kiene	(D)	Springfield Olympics (NEJHL)
232—Los Angeles	*Brian Martin	(C)	Belleville Bulls (OHL)
233—Toronto	Peter Slanina	(D)	Czechoslovakia Olympic Team
234—Hartford	†Peter Abric	(G)	North Bay Centennials (OHL)
235—Chicago	*Dan Williams	(D)	Chicago Jets
236—Detroit	*Tom Nickolau	(C)	Guelph Platers (OHL)
237—St. Louis	†Mark Lanigan	(D)	Waterloo (Ia.)
238—Winnipeg	†Jim Edmons	(G)	Cornell University (ECAC)
239—Vancouver	*Ed Kister	(D)	London Knights (OHL)
240—Montreal	*Troy Crosby	(G)	Verdun Juniors (QHL)

The top two picks in the '84 NHL draft were center Mario Lemieux (right), taken No. 1 by the Pittsburgh Penguins, and center Kirk Muller, taken No. 2 by the New Jersey Devils.

NHL Club	PLAYER	(Pos)	1983-84 CLUB (League)
241—Calgary	Rudolf Suchanek	(D)	Czechoslovakia Olympic Team
242—Minnesota	*Mike Nightengale	(D)	Simley H.S. (Minn.)
243—N.Y. Rangers	†Scott Brower	(G)	Lloydminster Tier II (B.C.)
244—Quebec	Peter Loob	(D)	Sodertalje (Sweden)
245—Philadelphia	Juraj Bakos	(D)	VSZ Kosice (Czechoslovakia)
246—Washington	*Per Schedrin	(D)	Gavle Brynas IF (Sweden)
247—Buffalo	*Sean Baker	(LW)	Seattle Breakers (WHL)
248—Boston	*Jim Newhouse	(LW)	Matignon H.S. (Mass.)
249—N.Y. Islanders	*Allister Brown	(D)	Univ. of New Hampshire (ECAC)
250—Edmonton	*Darren Gani	(D)	Belleville Bulls (OHL)

INDIVIDUAL RECORDS

SINGLE SEASON RECORDS

1—GOALS
- **NHL**—Wayne Gretzky, Edmonton Oilers—92 (1981-82 season).
- **WHA**—Bobby Hull, Winnipeg Jets—77 (1974-75 season).
- **CHL**—Alain Caron, St. Louis Braves—77 (1963-64 season).
- **AHL**—Mitch Lamoreaux, Baltimore Skipjacks—57 (1982-83 season).
- **IHL**—Merv Dubchak, Fort Wayne Komets—72 (1965-66 season).

2—ASSISTS
- **NHL**—Wayne Gretzky, Edmonton Oilers—125 (1982-83 season).
- **WHA**—Andre Lacroix, San Diego Mariners—106 (1974-75 season).
- **CHL**—Richie Hansen, Salt Lake Golden Eagles—81 (1981-82 season).
- **AHL**—George "Red" Sullivan, Hershey Bears—89 (1953-54 season).
- **IHL**—Chick Chalmers, Louisville Rebels—93 (1959-60 season).
  - Len Thornson, Fort Wayne Komets—93 (1966-67 season).

3—POINTS
- **NHL**—Wayne Gretzky, Edmonton Oilers—212 (1981-82 season).
- **WHA**—Marc Tardif, Quebec Nordiques—154 (1977-78 season).
- **CHL**—Alain Caron, St. Louis Braves—125 (1963-64 season).
- **AHL**—Ross Yates, Binghamton Whalers—125 (1982-83 season).
- **IHL**—Gary Ford, Muskegon Mohawks—141 (1972-73 season).

4—PENALTY MINUTES
- **NHL**—Dave Schultz, Philadelphia Flyers—472 (1974-75 season).
- **WHA**—Curt Brackenbury, Minnesota Fighting Saints and Quebec Nordiques—365 (1975-76 season).
- **CHL**—Randy Holt, Dallas Black Hawks—411 (1974-75 season).
- **AHL**—Dave Brown, Maine Mariners—418 (1982-83 season).
- **IHL**—Len Ircandia, Kalamazoo Wings—446 (1976-77 season).

5—SHUTOUTS
- **NHL**—George Hainsworth, Montreal Canadiens—22 (1928-29 season).

Modern Era
- **NHL**—Tony Esposito, Chicago Black Hawks—15 (1969-70 season).
- **WHA**—Gerry Cheevers, Cleveland Crusaders—5 (1972-73 season).
  - Joe Daley, Winnipeg Jets—5 (1975-76 season).
- **CHL**—Marcel Pelletier, St. Paul Rangers—9 (1963-64 season).
- **AHL**—Gordie Bell, Buffalo Bisons—9 (1942-43 season).
- **IHL**—Charlie Hodge, Cincinnati Mohawks—10 (1953-54 season).

6—GOALS AGAINST AVERAGE
- **NHL**—George Hainsworth, Montreal Canadiens—0.98 (1928-29 season).
- **WHA**—Don McLeod, Houston Aeros—2.57 (1973-74 season).
- **CHL**—Russ Gillow, Oklahoma City Blazers—2.16 (1967-68 season).
- **AHL**—Frank Brimsek, Providence Reds—1.79 (1937-38 season).
- **IHL**—Glenn Ramsay, Cincinnati Mohawks—1.88 (1956-57 season).

CAREER (Regular Season Only)
(No WHA Records Listed for Most Seasons Played.)

1—MOST SEASONS
- **NHL**—Gordie Howe, Detroit Red Wings and Hartford Whalers—26 (1946-47 through 1970-71 and 1979-80).
- **CHL**—Richie Hansen, Fort Worth Texans, Salt Lake Golden Eagles, Wichita Wind—9 (1975-76 through 1983-84 seasons).
- **AHL**—Fred Glover, Indianapolis Caps, St. Louis Flyers, Cleveland Barons—20.
  - Willie Marshall, Pittsburgh Hornets, Rochester Americans, Hershey Bears, Providence Reds, Baltimore Clippers—20.
- **IHL**—Glenn Ramsay, Cincinnati Mohawks, Troy Bruins, Toledo Blades, St. Paul Saints, Omaha Knights, Des Moines Oak Leafs, Toledo Hornets—17 (1956-57 through 1972-73).

2—GAMES PLAYED
- **NHL**—Gordie Howe, Detroit Red Wings and Hartford Whalers—1,767 (26 seasons).
- **WHA**—Andre Lacroix, Philadelphia Blazers, New York Golden Blades, Jersey Knights, San Diego Mariners, Houston Aeros and New England Whalers—551 (7 seasons).
- **CHL**—Richie Hansen, Fort Worth Texans, Salt Lake Golden Eagles, Wichita Wind—575 (9 seasons).
- **AHL**—Willie Marshall, Pittsburgh Hornets, Rochester Americans, Hershey Bears, Providence Reds, Baltimore Clippers—1,205 (20 seasons).
- **IHL**—Glenn Ramsay, Cincinnati Mohawks, Troy Bruins, Toledo Blades, St. Paul Saints, Omaha Knights, Des Moines Oak Leafs, Toledo Hornets—997 (17 seasons).

3—GOALS SCORED
NHL—Gordie Howe, Detroit Red Wings, Hartford Whalers—801 (26 seasons).
WHA—Marc Tardif, Quebec Nordiques—316 (6 seasons).
CHL—Richie Hansen, Fort Worth Texans, Salt Lake Golden Eagles, Wichita Wind—204 (9 seasons).
AHL—Willie Marshall, Pittsburgh Hornets, Rochester Americans, Hershey Bears, Providence Reds, Baltimore Clippers—523 (20 seasons).
IHL—Joe Kastelic, Fort Wayne Komets, Troy Bruins, Louisville Rebels, Muskegon Zephyrs, Muskegon Mohawks—526 (15 seasons).

4—ASSISTS
NHL—Gordie Howe, Detroit Red Wings, Hartford Whalers—1,049.
WHA—Andre Lacroix, Philadelphia Blazers, Jersey Knights, San Diego Mariners, Houston Aeros, New England Whalers—547 (7 seasons).
CHL—Richie Hansen, Fort Worth Texans, Salt Lake Golden Eagles, Wichita Wind—374 (9 seasons).
AHL—Willie Marshall, Pittsburgh Hornets, Hershey Bears, Rochester Americans, Providence Reds, Baltimore Clippers—852 (20 seasons).
IHL—Len Thornson, Huntington Hornets, Indianapolis Chiefs, Fort Wayne Komets—826 (13 seasons).

5—TOTAL POINTS
NHL—Gordie Howe, Detroit Red Wings, Hartford Whalers—1,850 (26 seasons).
WHA—Andre Lacroix, Philadelphia Blazers, Jersey Knights, San Diego Mariners, Houston Aeros, New England Whalers—798 (7 seasons).
CHL—Richie Hansen, Fort Worth Texans, Salt Lake Golden Eagles, Wichita Wind—578 (9 seasons).
AHL—Willie Marshall, Pittsburgh Hornets, Hershey Bears, Rochester Americans, Providence Reds, Baltimore Clippers—1,375 (20 seasons).
IHL—Len Thornson, Huntington Hornets, Indianapolis Chiefs, Fort Wayne Komets—1,252 (13 seasons).

6—PENALTY MINUTES
NHL—Dave (Tiger) Williams, Toronto Maple Leafs, Vancouver Canucks—2,994 (9 seasons).
WHA—Paul Baxter, Cleveland Crusaders, Quebec Nordiques—962 (5 seasons).
CHL—Brad Gassoff, Tulsa Oilers, Dallas Black Hawks—899 (5 seasons).
AHL—Fred Glover, Indianapolis Caps, St. Louis Flyers, Cleveland Barons—2,402 (20 seasons).
IHL—Lynn Margarit, Muskegon Mohawks—1,895 (8 seasons).

7—SHUTOUTS
NHL—Terry Sawchuk, Detroit Red Wings, Boston Bruins, Los Angeles Kings, New York Rangers, Toronto Maple Leafs—103 (20 seasons).
WHA—Ernie Wakely, Winnipeg Jets, San Diego Mariners, Houston Aeros—16 (6 seasons).
CHL—Michel Dumas, Dallas Black Hawks—12 (4 seasons).
Mike Veisor, Dallas Black Hawks—12 (5 seasons).
AHL—Johnny Bower, Cleveland Barons, Providence Reds—45 (11 seasons).
IHL—Glenn Ramsay, Cincinnati Mohawks, Fort Wayne Komets, Troy Bruins, Toledo Blades, St. Paul Saints, Omaha Knights, Des Moines Oak Leafs, Toledo Hornets—45 (17 seasons).

SINGLE GAME RECORDS

1—GOALS
NHL—Joe Malone, Quebec Bulldogs (January 31, 1920 vs. Toronto St. Pats)—7.

Modern Era
NHL—Syd Howe, Detroit Red Wings (Feb. 3, 1944 vs. N.Y. Rangers)—6.
Gordon Berenson, St. Louis Blues (Nov. 7, 1968 vs. Philadelphia)—6.
Darryl Sittler, Toronto Maple Leafs (Feb. 7, 1976 vs. Boston Bruins)—6.
WHA—Ron Ward, New York Raiders (January 4, 1973 vs. Ottawa)—5.
Ron Climie, Edmonton Oilers (vs. N.Y. Golden Blades, November 6, 1973)—5.
Andre Hinse, Houston Aeros (Jan. 16, 1975 vs. Edmonton)—5.
Vaclav Nedomansky, Toronto Toros (Nov. 13, 1975 vs. Denver Spurs)—5.
Wayne Connelly, Minnesota Fighting Saints (Nov. 27, 1975 vs. Cincinnati Stingers)—5.
Ron Ward, Cleveland Crusaders (Nov. 30, 1975 vs. Toronto Toros)—5.
Real Cloutier, Quebec Nordiques (Oct. 26, 1976 vs. Phoenix Roadrunners)—5.
CHL—Jim Mayer, Dallas Black Hawks (February 23, 1979)—6.
AHL—Bob Heron, Pittsburgh Hornets (1941-42)—6.
Harry Pidhirny, Springfield Indians (1953-54)—6.
Camille Henry, Providence Reds (1955-56)—6.
IHL—Pierre Brillant, Indianapolis Chiefs (Feb. 18, 1959)—6.
Bryan McLay, Muskegon Zephyrs (Mar. 8, 1961)—6.
Elliott Chorley, St. Paul Saints (Jan. 17, 1962)—6.
Joe Kastelic, Muskegon Zephyrs (Mar. 1, 1962)—6.

2—ASSISTS
NHL—Billy Taylor, Detroit Red Wings (Mar. 16, 1947 vs. Chicago)—7.
Wayne Gretzky, Edmonton Oilers (Feb. 15, 1980 vs. Washington)—7.
WHA—Jim Harrison, Alberta Oilers (January 30, 1973 vs. New York)—7.
Jim Harrison, Cleveland Crusaders (Nov. 30, 1975 vs. Toronto Toros)—7.

CHL—Art Stratton, St. Louis Braves (1966-67)—6.
Ron Ward, Tulsa Oilers (1967-68)—6.
Bill Hogaboam, Omaha Knights, January 15, 1972—6.
Jim Wiley, Tulsa Oilers, (1974-75)—6.
AHL—Art Stratton, Buffalo Bisons (Mar. 17, 1963 vs. Pittsburgh)—9.
IHL—Jean-Paul Denis, St. Paul Saints (Jan. 17, 1962)—9.

3—POINTS

NHL—Darryl Sittler, Toronto Maple Leafs (Feb. 7, 1976 vs. Boston Bruins)—10.
WHA—Jim Harrison, Alberta Oilers (January 30, 1973 vs. New York)—10.
CHL—Steve Vickers, Omaha Knights (Jan. 15, 1972 vs. Kansas City)—8.
AHL—Art Stratton, Buffalo Bisons (Mar. 17, 1963 vs. Pittsburgh)—9.
IHL—Elliott Chorley, St. Paul Saints (Jan. 17, 1962)—11.
Jean-Paul Denis, St. Paul Saints (Jan. 17, 1962)—11.

4—PENALTY MINUTES

NHL—Randy Holt, Los Angeles Kings (March 11, 1979 vs. Philadelphia)—67.
WHA—Dave Hanson, Birmingham Bulls (Feb. 5, 1978 vs. Indianapolis)—46.
CHL—Gary Rissling, Birmingham Bulls (Dec. 5, 1980 vs. Salt Lake)—49.
AHL—Wally Weir, Rochester Americans (Jan. 16, 1981 vs. New Brunswick)—54.
IHL—Bob Kelly, Port Huron Flags (Dec. 31, 1967)—42.
Lynn Margarit, Muskegon Mohawks (Dec. 31, 1973 vs. Saginaw)—42.
Carlo Torresan, Muskegon Mohawks (1976-77)—42.

DEFENSEMEN'S RECORDS
SINGLE SEASON

1—GOALS

NHL—Bobby Orr, Boston Bruins (1974-75 season)—46.
WHA—Kevin Morrison, Jersey Knights (1973-74 season)—24.
CHL—Dan Poulin, Nashville South Stars (1981-82 season)—29.
AHL—Greg Tebbutt, Baltimore Skipjacks (1982-83 season)—28.
IHL—Roly McLenahan, Cincinnati Mohawks (1955-56 season)—34.

2—ASSISTS

NHL—Bobby Orr, Boston Bruins (1970-71 season)—102.
WHA—J. C. Tremblay, Quebec Nordiques (1975-76 season)—77.
CHL—Barclay Plager, Omaha Knights (1963-64 season)—61.
AHL—Craig Levie, Nova Scotia Voyageurs (1980-81 season)—62.
IHL—Gerry Glaude, Muskegon Zephyrs (1962-63 season)—86.

3—POINTS

NHL—Bobby Orr, Boston Bruins (1970-71 season)—139.
WHA—J. C. Tremblay, Quebec Nordiques (1972-73 and 1975-76 seasons)—89.
CHL—Dan Poulin, Nashville South Stars (1981-82 season)—85.
AHL—Greg Tebbutt, Baltimore Skipjacks (1982-83 season)—84.
IHL—Gerry Glaude, Muskegon Zephyrs (1962-63 season)—101.

American Hockey League

218 Memorial Avenue, P.O. Box 100, West Springfield, Mass. 01090
Phone— (413) 781-2030

Chairman of the Board—Robert W. Clarke
President and Treasurer—Jack Butterfield
Vice-President and General Counsel—Richard F. Canning
Vice-President, Secretary—Gordon C. Anziano

Board Of Governors

Adirondack—Jim Devellano
Baltimore—John M. Haas
Binghamton—Emile Francis
Fredericton—Gilles Leger
Hershey—Frank Mathers
Maine—Ed Anderson
Moncton—To be announced
New Haven—Macgregor Kilpatrick
Nova Scotia—To be announced
Rochester—Seymour Knox III
St. Catharines—Gerry McNamara
Sherbrooke—John Ferguson
Springfield—Peter Cooney
Honorary Governors—Edward W. Shore, Sr.,
    George Sage

Adirondack Red Wings

President—Michael Ilitch
Vice-President—To be announced
General Manager—Jim Devellano
Dir. of Operations—Jack Kelley
Dir. of Player Personnel and Coach—Bill Dineen
Dir. of P.R./Marketing—David Strader
Trainer—David Casey
Home Ice—Glens Falls Civic Center
Address—1 Civic Center Plaza,
    Glens Falls, N.Y. 12801
Capacity—5,600
NHL Affiliation—Detroit Red Wings
Phone— (518) 761-3856

Baltimore Skipjacks

President—John M. Haas
Alternate Governor—Ken Schinkel
Vice-President—James S. Watson
Secretary-Treasurer—Robert A. Pinkner
Exec. Vice-Pres.—Walter R. Freeman
V.P. Communications—Walter Gutowski
Coach—Gene Ubriaco
Trainer—Tim Ringler
Home Ice—Baltimore Civic Center
Address—Civic Center-Suite 412,
    201 W. Baltimore St.
    Baltimore, Md. 21201
Seating Capacity—10,200
NHL Affiliation—Pittsburgh Penguins
Phone— (301) 727-0703

Binghamton Whalers

Managing General Partner—Howard Baldwin
President and G.M.—Emile Francis
Alt. Gov., Dir. of Oper.—George Ducharme
Coach—Larry Pleau
Trainer—Jon R. Smith
Marketing Director/P.R.—Phil Jacobs
Director of Media Relations—Ed Finocchiaro
Executive Assistant—Karen Mikolasko
Home Ice—Broome County
    Veterans Memorial Arena
Address—P.O. Box 996,
    Binghamton, N.Y. 13902
Seating Capacity—4,855
NHL Affiliation—Hartford Whalers
Phone— (607) 723-8937

Fredericton Express

President—Gilles Leger
Director of Operations—Michael Doyle
General Manager-Coach—Earl Jessiman
Comptroller—Larry Gagnon
Dir. Media Relations—Ernie Fitzsimmons
Trainer—Marty Flynn
Equipment Manager—Scott Beckingham
Executive Secretary—Cathy Belmore
Home Ice—Aitken Center, University
    of New Brunswick
Seating Capacity—3,458
NHL Affiliations—Quebec Nordiques
    and Vancouver Canucks
Address—Aitken Center, Box 9900
    Fredericton, N.B. E3B 5G4
Phone— (506) 455-0861

Hershey Bears

Board Chairman—Edward R. Book
President—Kenneth V. Hatt
President & Gen. Mgr.—Frank Mathers
Coach—Gary Inness
Trainer—Bernie Beauchamp
Promotions Dir.—Doug Yingst
Publicity Director—Dennis Miller
Home Ice—Hersheypark Arena
Address—P.O. Box 866
    Hershey, Pa. 17033
Seating Capacity—7,286
NHL Affiliations—Philadelphia Flyers
    and Boston Bruins
Phone— (717) 534-3983

Maine Mariners

Chairman—John J. McMullen
President—Ed Anderson
Director of Hockey Oper.—Max McNab
General Manager—To be announced
Coach—Tom McVie
V.P., Media—Dale Arnold
Bus. Manager-Controller—Gordon Corkum
Marketing Director—To be announced
Home Ice—Cumberland County
    Civic Center
Address—P.O. Box 1219
    Portland, Me. 04104
Seating Capacity—6,734
NHL Affiliation—New Jersey Devils
Phone— (207) 775-3411

Moncton Golden Flames

Governor—To be announced
General Manager—To be announced
Coach—Pierre Page
Assistant General Manager—To be announced
Media Relations—To be announced
Marketing and P.R. Director—To be announced
Home Ice—Moncton Coliseum
Address—Moncton, N.B.
    E1C 8P2
Seating Capacity—6,904
NHL Affiliation—Calgary Flames
Phone—To be announced

New Haven Nighthawks

Governor—Macgregor Kilpatrick
President—To be announced
General Manager—Roy Mlakar
Coach—Nick Beverley
Dir. of Player Personnel—To be announced
Dir. of Press Relations—Jim Slattery
Office Manager—Henry Bradbury
Home Ice—Veterans Mem. Coliseum
Address—P.O. Box 1444,
         New Haven, Conn. 06506
Seating Capacity—6,156
NHL Affiliation—New York Rangers
Phone—(203) 787-0101

Nova Scotia Oilers

Chairman—Ron Corey
President—R.F. Tiny Titus
Governor—To be announced
Manager—Larry Kish
Coach—To be announced
Vice-President—Peter Green
Dir. of Marketing/P.R.—Joel Jacobson
Dir. of Player Personnel—Claude Ruel
Director of Admin. and Tickets—Paula Barrett
Trainer—Brian Patafie
Home Ice—Halifax Metro-Centre
Address—5284 Duke Street
         Halifax, N.S. B3J 3L2
Seating Capacity—9,552
NHL Affiliation—Edmonton Oilers
Phone—(902) 429-7600

Rochester Americans

Board Chairman—R. Bruce Davey
General Manager—George Bergantz
Coach—To be announced
P.R. Director—Rick Peckham
Dir. of Marketing—Randy S
Sales Director—Vince Pettr
Business Manager—Ellen Champion
Trainer—Jim Pizzutelli
Home Ice—War Memorial Auditorium
Address—War Memorial Auditorium,
         100 Exchange Street
         Rochester, N.Y. 14614
Seating Capacity—7,109
NHL Affiliation—Buffalo Sabres
Phone—(716) 454-5335

St. Catharines Saints

Chairman of the Board—Harold Ballard
Governor—Gerry McNamara
Dir. of Operations—Rudy Pilous
Coach—Claire Alexander
Trainer—Ken Garrett
Dir. of Public Relations—Stan Nieraoka
Home Ice—Garden City Arena
Address—145 King Street
         St. Catharines, Ont., L2R 3J2
Seating Capacity—3,093
NHL Affiliation—Toronto Maple Leafs
Phone—(416) 684-4551

Sherbrooke Canadiens

Exec. Com. Chairman—Barry Shenkarow
Governor—John B. Ferguson
President—Barry Shenkarow
General Manager—George Guilbault
Coach—To be announced
Dir. of Marketing-Sales—Yvon Robert
Dir. of Public Relations—Marc Desmarais
Group Tickets—Rock Guertin
Trainer—Pierre Gervais
Home Ice—Sherbrooke Sports Palace
Address—360 Park Street
         Sherbrooke, Que. J1E 2J9
NHL Affiliations—Montreal Canadiens and
         Winnipeg Jets
Phone—(819) 566-2114

Springfield Indians

President-Governor—Peter R. Cooney
Alternate Governors—James J. Coogan
General Manager—Bruce Landon
Business Manager—Martha Dailey
Coach—To be announced
Trainer—Ed Tyburski
Home Ice—Springfield Civic Center
Address—58 Dwight St.,
         Springfield, Mass. 01103
Seating Capacity—7,417
NHL Affiliations—New York Islanders and
         Minnesota North Stars
Phone—(413) 736-4546

1983-84 Final AHL Standings

North Division

	G.	W.	L.	T.	Pts.	GF.	GA.
Fredericton Express	80	45	30	5	95	340	262
Adirondack Red Wings	80	37	29	14	88	344	330
Maine Mariners	80	33	36	11	77	310	312
Nova Scotia Voyageurs	80	32	37	11	75	277	288
Moncton Alpines	80	32	40	8	72	251	278
Sherbrooke Jets	80	22	53	5	49	301	419

South Division

	G.	W.	L.	T.	Pts.	GF.	GA.
Baltimore Skipjacks	80	46	24	10	102	384	304
Rochester Americans	80	46	32	2	94	363	300
St. Catharines Saints	80	43	31	6	92	364	346
Springfield Indians	80	39	35	6	84	344	340
New Haven Nighthawks	80	36	40	4	76	365	371
Binghamton Whalers	80	33	43	4	70	359	388
Hershey Bears	80	28	42	10	66	320	384

Top 20 Scorers for the John B. Sollenberger Trophy

	Games	G.	A.	Pts.	Pen.
1. Claude Larose, Sherbrooke	80	53	67	*120	6
2. Murray Eaves, Sherbrooke	78	47	68	115	40
3. Mike Kaszycki, St. Catharines	72	39	71	110	51
4. Bruce Boudreau, St. Catharines	80	47	62	109	44
5. Ross Yates, Binghamton	68	35	*73	108	82
6. Mal Davis, Rochester	71	*55	48	103	53
7. Mark Lofthouse, New Haven	79	37	64	101	45
8. Norm Aubin, St. Catharines	80	47	47	94	63
9. Geordie Robertson, Rochester	64	37	54	91	103
10. Claude Verret, Rochester	65	39	51	90	4
11. Daryl Evans, New Haven	69	51	35	86	14
Larry Floyd, Maine	69	37	49	86	40
John Goodwin, Nova Scotia/New Haven	79	24	62	86	46
14. Bob Mongrain, Rochester	78	41	44	85	154
15. Roberto Lavoie, Binghamton	80	34	50	84	68
16. Dean Hopkins, New Haven	79	35	47	82	162
17. Paul Gardner, Baltimore	54	32	49	81	14
18. Bob Sullivan, Binghamton	76	33	47	80	48
Steve Tsujiura, Springfield	78	24	56	80	27
Wayne Thompson, Nova Scotia	80	23	57	80	30

Adirondack Red Wings

	Games	G.	A.	Pts.	Pen.		Games	G.	A.	Pts.	Pen.
Jody Gage	73	40	32	72	32	Claude Loiselle	29	13	16	29	59
Andre St. Laurent	50	26	43	69	129	Ted Nolan	31	10	16	26	76
Gerrard Gallant	77	31	33	64	195	Joe Paterson	20	10	15	25	43
Wayne Crawford	67	28	25	53	97	Randy MacGregor	45	6	15	21	60
Don Murdoch	59	26	20	46	19	Rory Cava	75	2	19	21	160
Derek Smith	61	16	29	45	10	Bob Manno	12	5	11	16	18
Ken Solheim	61	24	20	44	13	Randy Ladouceur	11	3	5	8	12
Brad Smith	46	15	29	44	128	Ken Holland (Goalie)	42	0	5	5	2
Greg Joly	78	10	33	43	133	John Beukeboom	16	2	2	4	66
Larry Trader	80	13	28	41	89	Kirt Bjork	7	1	3	4	4
Ted Speers	79	15	25	40	27	Dave Korol	2	0	4	4	0
Dennis Polonich	66	14	26	40	122	Barry Melrose	16	2	1	3	37
Rejean Cloutier	77	9	30	39	218	Corrado Micalef (G.)	29	0	3	3	10
Charlie Skjodt	55	11	27	38	32	Mike Corrigan	4	1	0	1	0
Ted Muesing	74	7	31	38	35	Ed Mio (Goalie)	4	0	0	0	0
Brian Johnson	58	4	27	31	233	Mark Laforest (Goalie)	7	0	0	0	2

Baltimore Skipjacks

	Games	G.	A.	Pts.	Pen.
Paul Gardner	54	32	49	81	14
Jim Hamilton	66	34	45	79	54
Mitch Lamoureux	68	30	38	68	136
Warren Young	59	25	38	63	142
Tom Thornbury	65	17	46	63	64
Greg Tebbutt	44	12	42	54	125
Tim Tookey	58	16	28	44	25
Dave Hannan	47	18	24	42	98
Bob Geale	74	17	23	40	50
Steve Carlson	63	9	30	39	70
Ted Bulley	49	16	19	35	82
Rod Schutt	36	15	19	34	48
Steve Gatzos	48	14	19	33	43
Bobby Simpson	71	16	16	32	36
Dean Defazio	46	18	13	31	114
Troy Loney	63	18	13	31	147
Tim Hrynewich	52	13	17	30	65
Tom O'Regan	25	13	14	27	15
Gary Rissling	30	12	13	25	47
Phil Bourque	58	5	17	22	96
Ron Meighan	75	4	16	20	36
Dan McCarthy	27	8	11	19	8
Norm Schmidt	43	4	12	16	31
Bennett Wolf	63	3	13	16	*349
Rod Buskas	33	2	12	14	100
Bob Gladney	9	4	7	11	10
Andy Brickley, Spring.	7	1	5	6	2
Baltimore	4	0	5	5	2
Totals	11	1	10	11	4
Brian Lundberg	47	1	5	6	97
Kevin McClelland	3	1	1	2	0
Rocky Saganiuk	5	1	1	2	0
Rich Sutter	2	0	1	1	0
Vince Tremblay (Goalie)	31	0	1	1	18
J. Ralph, Spring. (G.)	8	0	1	1	2
Baltimore (Goalie)	25	0	0	0	2
Totals	33	0	1	1	4
Dave Goertz	1	0	0	0	2
George Gagnon (G.)	1	0	0	0	0
Tony Feltrin	4	0	0	0	2
Roberto Romano (G.)	31	0	0	0	2

Binghamton Whalers

	Games	G.	A.	Pts.	Pen.
Ross Yates	68	35	*73	108	82
Roberto Lavoie	80	34	50	84	68
Bob Sullivan	76	33	47	80	48
Paul Fenton	78	41	24	65	67
Don Gillen	73	27	37	64	140
Paul MacDermid	70	31	30	61	130
Darren McKay	71	11	40	51	206
Dan Fridgen	77	23	27	50	61
Dan Bourbonnais	38	16	32	48	40
Randy Pierce	46	21	24	45	41
Gerry McDonald	72	4	39	43	34
Norm Dupont	27	15	24	39	6
Paul Crowley	80	14	14	28	90
Mike McDougal	59	11	14	25	56
Stuart Smith	54	3	22	25	95
Mike Hoffman	64	11	13	24	92
John Mokosak	79	3	21	24	80
Reid Bailey, St. Cath.	25	0	8	8	73
Binghamton	33	2	11	13	95
Totals	58	2	19	21	168
Randy Gilhen	73	8	12	20	72

	Games	G.	A.	Pts.	Pen.
Steve Stoyanovich	21	11	8	19	0
Tom Cronin	75	2	12	14	90
Jeff Brownschidle	30	2	7	9	50
Sean Coady	48	0	7	7	192
Gray Weicker (Goalie)	2	0	0	0	2
Paul Fricker (Goalie)	30	0	0	0	6
Rollie Boutin (Goalie)	45	0	0	0	8

Fredericton Express

	Games	G.	A.	Pts.	Pen.
Jim Dobson	75	33	44	77	74
Grant Martin	57	36	24	60	46
Gerry Minor	66	16	42	58	85
Jere Gillis	36	22	28	50	35
Jean-Francois Sauve	26	19	31	50	23
John VanBoxmeer	45	10	34	44	48
Jean-Marc Lanthier	60	25	17	42	29
Jean-Marc Gaulin	62	14	28	42	80
Mike Eagles	68	13	29	42	85
Rejean Vignola	67	25	13	38	40
Dave Morrison, N.H.	8	0	4	4	2
Fredericton	68	14	19	33	51
Totals	76	14	23	37	53
Bruce Holloway	66	3	30	33	29
Marc Crawford	56	9	22	31	96
Rick Lapointe	54	8	22	30	79
Claude Julien	57	7	22	29	58
Stu Kulak	52	12	16	28	55
Mike Hough	69	11	16	27	142
Wally Weir	44	6	17	23	45
Mark Kirton	35	8	10	18	8
Andre Cote	34	6	12	18	4
Neil Belland	17	3	15	18	2
Tony Currie	12	6	11	17	16
Garth Butcher	25	4	13	17	43
Michel Bolduc	70	2	15	17	96
Moe Lemay	23	9	7	16	32
Paul Gillis	18	7	8	15	47
Pierre Aubry	12	4	5	9	4
Andy Schliebener	27	1	6	7	27
Gord Donnelly	30	2	3	5	146
Ed Lee	6	0	4	4	4
Brian Ford (Goalie)	36	0	4	4	8
Dave Pichette	10	2	1	3	13
Christian Tanguay	3	2	0	2	0
Mark Kumpel	16	1	1	2	5
Vin Cameron	4	0	2	2	0
Wendell Young (Goalie)	11	0	2	2	4
Michel Galarneau, Bing.	4	1	0	1	0
Fredericton	2	0	0	0	0
Totals	6	1	0	1	0
Clint Malarchuk (Goalie)	11	0	1	1	5
Richard Turmel	28	0	1	1	40
David Mancusco	2	0	0	0	2
David Bluteau	2	0	0	0	0
Steve Driscoll	2	0	0	0	0
Yves Heroux	4	0	0	0	0
Andre Chartrain	5	0	0	0	2
Michel Dufour (Goalie)	6	0	0	0	2
Frank Caprice (Goalie)	18	0	0	0	2

Hershey Bears

	Games	G.	A.	Pts.	Pen.
Doug Morrison	72	38	40	78	42
Jim McGeough	79	40	36	76	108
Lou Franceschetti	73	26	34	60	130

	Games	G.	A.	Pts.	Pen.
Chris Valentine	47	15	44	59	41
Brad Palmer	62	25	32	57	16
Jim Burton	75	10	33	43	50
Dan Miele	65	23	17	40	18
Doug Kostynski	67	13	27	40	8
Mike Siltala	50	15	17	32	29
Greg Theberge	41	3	27	30	25
Mike Gillis	26	8	21	29	13
Bryan Erickson	31	16	12	28	11
Luc Dufour	37	9	19	28	51
Wayne Prestage	52	12	15	27	65
Bob Laforest	42	11	16	27	10
Geoff Courtnall	74	14	12	26	51
Paul MacKinnon	63	3	19	22	29
Dave Silk	15	11	10	21	22
Scott McLellan	73	9	12	21	14
Tony Camazzola	63	6	10	16	138
Tony Fiore	36	5	8	13	6
Peter Dineen, Moncton	63	0	10	10	120
Hershey	12	0	1	1	32
Totals	75	0	11	11	152
Jay Johnston	70	1	9	10	231
Eric Calder	68	2	6	8	50
Darren Veitch	11	1	6	7	4
Craig Steensen	4	2	1	3	2
Brian Curran	23	0	2	2	94
Doug Rigler	1	1	0	1	0
Vic Morin	2	1	0	1	0
David Shand	2	0	1	1	2
Pat Riggin (Goalie)	3	0	1	1	0
Dan Sanscartier (Goalie)	6	0	1	1	0
Mark Bonneau	7	0	1	1	2
Mike Moffat (Goalie)	30	0	1	1	11
Dave Parro (Goalie)	42	0	1	1	16
Mark Evans (Goalie)	1	0	0	0	0
Al Jensen (Goalie)	3	0	0	0	0
Bob Mason (Goalie)	5	0	0	0	0

Maine Mariners

	Games	G.	A.	Pts.	Pen.
Larry Floyd	69	37	49	86	40
Paul Evans	76	23	36	59	65
Glenn Merkosky	75	28	28	56	56
Mike Hordy	72	11	41	52	31
Bud Stefanski	57	26	23	49	47
Kevin Maxwell	56	21	27	48	59
Rich Chernomaz	69	17	29	46	39
Garry Howatt	63	12	21	33	124
Mike Antonovich	25	17	13	30	8
Yvon Joly	39	12	17	29	25
Murray Brumwell	34	4	25	29	16
Alan Hepple	64	4	23	27	117
Al Hill	51	8	16	24	51
Mike Lekun	63	12	9	21	74
Yvon Vautour	24	8	12	20	117
Maynard F. Schurman	43	5	15	20	40
Roy Sommer	67	7	10	17	202
Rob Palmer	33	5	10	15	10
Grant Mulvey	29	6	8	14	49
Mitch Wilson	71	6	8	14	*349
Mike Stothers	61	2	10	12	109
Hector Marini	17	6	5	11	23
Rick Meagher	10	6	4	10	2
Mike Moher	25	5	5	10	119
John Paddock	17	3	6	9	34
Bruce Driver	12	2	6	8	15

	Games	G.	A.	Pts.	Pen.
Doug McGrath	50	2	6	8	64
Carmine Cirella	24	1	7	8	55
Brent Shaw	24	5	2	7	25
Gary McAdam	10	3	4	7	18
Bob Hoffmeyer	14	3	1	4	27
Jay Miller	15	1	1	2	27
Frank Bathe	4	1	0	1	2
Jeff Bandura	9	1	0	1	6
Mike Busniuk	2	0	1	1	2
Alain Vigneault	11	0	1	1	46
Steve Baker, Bing. (G.)	6	0	0	0	0
Maine (Goalie)	13	0	1	1	2
Totals	19	0	1	1	2
Paul Mercier	22	0	1	1	70
Randy Wilson	2	0	0	0	0
Shawn MacKenzie (G.)	34	0	0	0	6
Sam St. Laurent (Goalie)	38	0	0	0	0

Moncton Alpines

	Games	G.	A.	Pts.	Pen.
Ray Cote	66	26	36	62	99
Bart Yachimec	80	27	32	59	91
Mark Habscheid	71	19	37	56	32
Joe McDonnell	78	12	33	45	44
Tom Rowe	50	28	16	44	86
Todd Strueby	72	17	25	42	38
Reg Kerr	60	13	29	42	43
Ken Berry	53	18	20	38	75
Todd Bidner	66	15	13	28	34
Lowell Loveday	65	7	21	28	24
Tom Gorence	53	13	14	27	17
John Blum	57	3	22	25	202
Pat Conacher	28	7	16	23	30
Ross Lambert	75	6	15	21	61
Larry Melnyk, Hershey	51	0	18	18	156
Moncton	14	0	3	3	17
Totals	65	0	21	21	173
Dwayne Boettger	75	1	18	19	160
Dean Dachyshyn	74	9	7	16	92
Shawn Dineen, N.H.	8	0	1	1	4
Moncton	43	0	11	11	116
Totals	51	0	12	12	120
Paul Miller	46	9	2	11	68
Shawn Babcock	48	2	8	10	163
Steve Smith	64	1	8	9	176
Jeff Crawford	37	1	1	2	159
Chris Smith (Goalie)	39	0	2	2	24
Bill Goldthorpe	1	0	0	0	2
Gordie Gallant	3	0	0	0	10
Steve McKenzie	6	0	0	0	0
Tim Molle	10	0	0	0	0
Marco Baron (Goalie)	16	0	0	0	18
Mike Zanier (Goalie)	31	0	0	0	14

New Haven Nighthawks

	Games	G.	A.	Pts.	Pen.
Mark Lofthouse	79	37	64	101	45
Daryl Evans	69	51	35	86	14
John Goodwin, N.S.	35	12	21	33	11
New Haven	44	12	41	53	35
Totals	79	24	62	86	46
Dean Hopkins	79	35	47	82	162
Phil Sykes	77	29	37	66	101
Don Nachbaur	70	33	32	65	194
Brock Tredway	70	21	42	63	4

	Games	G.	A.	Pts.	Pen.
Warren Holmes	76	26	35	61	25
Bill O'Dwyer	58	15	42	57	39
Kevin Lavallee	47	29	23	52	25
Dean Jenkins	64	24	26	50	131
Carl Mokosak	80	18	21	39	206
Tom Price	77	2	23	25	54
Mike Heidt	54	4	20	24	49
Alan Hangsleben	58	1	23	24	88
Al Teur	78	0	20	20	195
Mike Fidler	16	6	7	13	6
Mike McEwen	9	3	7	10	26
Mark Morris	37	3	7	10	35
Archie Henderson	48	1	8	9	164
Dean Kennedy	26	1	7	8	23
Jim Brown	39	2	4	6	18
Howie Scruton	33	1	4	5	21
Jim Walsh	13	0	5	5	14
Brian MacLellan	2	0	2	2	0
Paul Lohnes	2	0	2	2	2
Nick Beverley	2	0	1	1	0
Mike Blake (Goalie)	16	0	1	1	2
Gary Laskoski (Goalie)	22	0	1	1	2
Markus Mattsson (G.)	31	0	1	1	0
Glenn Goldup	1	0	0	0	0
Craig Hurley	2	0	0	0	6
Ralph Cox	3	0	0	0	0
Mario Lessard (Goalie)	5	0	0	0	0
Darren Eliot (Goalie)	7	0	0	0	0
Randy Turnbull	8	0	0	0	46
Dave Ross (Goalie)	8	0	0	0	4

Nova Scotia Voyageurs

	Games	G.	A.	Pts.	Pen.
Wayne Thompson	80	23	57	80	30
Blair Barnes	80	31	32	63	91
John Newberry	78	25	37	62	116
Dan Bonar, New Haven	35	9	14	23	27
Nova Scotia	44	14	23	37	75
Totals	79	23	37	60	102
Larry Landon	79	26	30	56	21
Mike McPhee	67	22	33	55	101
Bill Riley	78	24	24	48	79
Michel Therrien	73	7	34	41	40
Brian Skrudland	56	13	12	25	55
Remi Gagne	74	7	18	25	178
Bill Kitchen	68	4	20	24	193
Stephen Lefebvre	63	7	16	23	107
Whitney Richardson	47	11	11	22	31
Norman Baron	68	11	11	22	275
Dave Allison	53	2	18	20	155
Steve Marengere	32	6	11	17	14
Steve Lalor	67	5	11	16	80
Dave Orleski	20	6	9	15	14
Ted Fauss	71	4	11	15	123
Jeff Teal	16	8	4	12	2
Dave Stoyanovich	73	6	6	12	126
Stan Hennigan	63	1	3	4	83
Mike Jeffrey	20	1	2	3	8
Alain Heroux	4	1	1	2	2
Jocelyn Gauvreau	1	0	2	2	0
Serge Roy	5	0	2	2	0
Mark Holden (Goalie)	47	0	1	1	10
Gilles Heroux (Goalie)	1	0	0	0	0
Guy Pygeon	5	0	0	0	0
Greg Moffett (Goalie)	10	0	0	0	0
Steven Penney (Goalie)	27	0	0	0	15

Rochester Americans

	Games	G.	A.	Pts.	Pen.
Mal Davis	71	*55	48	103	53
Geordie Robertson	64	37	54	91	103
Claude Verret	65	39	51	90	4
Bob Mongrain	78	41	44	85	154
Yvon Lambert	79	27	43	70	14
Daniel Naud	79	15	44	59	29
Warren Harper	78	25	28	53	56
Ron Fischer	80	10	32	42	94
Mark Renaud	64	9	33	42	48
Randy Cunneyworth	54	18	17	35	85
Norm Lacombe	44	10	16	26	45
Chris Langevin	41	11	14	25	133
Steve Patrick	30	8	14	22	33
Steve Dykstra	64	3	19	22	141
Jim Aldred	64	10	9	19	57
Dave Fenyves	70	3	16	19	55
Kai Suikkanen	15	7	10	17	2
Dirk Rueter	76	0	16	16	95
Gates Orlando	11	8	7	15	2
Jim Wiemer	12	4	11	15	11
Lou Crawford	76	7	6	13	234
Tom St. James	31	6	7	13	8
Rich Goodfellow	20	2	6	8	25
Venci Sebek	41	2	5	7	27
Jeff Eatough	24	1	5	6	5
Rick Hampton	21	1	3	4	7
Jerry Korab	4	0	4	4	2
Bob Bodak	12	2	1	3	6
Val James	62	1	2	3	122
Jacques Cloutier (G.)	51	0	2	2	10
Clint Fehr	10	1	0	1	0
Phil Myre (Goalie)	33	0	1	1	4

St. Catharines Saints

	Games	G.	A.	Pts.	Pen.
Mike Kaszycki	72	39	71	110	51
Bruce Boudreau	80	47	62	109	44
Norm Aubin	80	47	47	94	63
Ken Strong	78	27	45	72	78
Ernie Godden	78	31	36	67	69
Gary Yaremchuk	73	24	37	61	84
Lee Norwood	75	13	46	59	91
Russ Adam	70	32	24	56	76
Fred Perlini	79	21	31	52	67
Garry Lariviere	65	7	35	42	41
Frank Nigro	41	17	24	41	16
Greg Britz	44	23	16	39	25
Basil McRae	78	14	25	39	187
Fred Boimistruck	80	2	28	30	68
Craig Muni	64	4	16	20	79
Ron Zanussi	59	4	15	19	59
Bob McGill	55	1	15	16	217
Pat Graham	25	7	7	14	18
Marc Magnan	54	3	6	9	170
Leigh Verstraete	51	0	7	7	183
Ron Choules	14	1	1	2	26
Dave Farrish	4	0	2	2	6
Bill Harris	2	0	1	1	0
Rick St. Croix (Goalie)	8	0	1	1	0
Bruce Dowie (Goalie)	9	0	0	0	0
Nick Ricci (Goalie)	14	0	0	0	17
Bob Parent (Goalie)	17	0	0	0	8
Rich Costello	20	0	0	0	12
Tim Bernhardt (Goalie)	42	0	0	0	0

Sherbrooke Jets

	Games	G.	A.	Pts	Pen.
Claude Larose	80	53	67	*120	6
Murray Eaves	78	47	68	115	40
Guy Fournier	80	25	28	53	30
Mike Lauen	61	23	29	52	13
Alain Baigle	79	22	26	48	24
Tom Gibson	79	19	29	48	88
Ron Wilson	22	10	30	40	16
Jyrki Seppa	60	5	35	40	43
Tim Trimper	32	10	24	34	26
Brad Tippett	80	14	19	33	60
Dave Chartier	43	13	14	27	59
Michel Lanouette	29	14	10	24	72
Craig Channell	80	5	18	23	112
Kelly Elcombe	58	2	21	23	64
Kirk McCaskill	78	10	12	22	21
Rick Bowness	21	9	11	20	44
Don Spring	50	0	17	17	21
Bill Whelton	67	2	14	16	32
John Gibson	49	4	11	15	174
Steven Fletcher	77	3	7	10	208
Jimmy Mann	20	6	3	9	94
Sandy Beadle	70	2	5	7	8
Kevin Primeau	30	2	1	3	6
Moe Mantha	7	1	1	2	10
Luc Bachand	8	0	1	1	0
Brian Hayward (Goalie)	15	0	1	1	2
Paul Pageau (Goalie)	46	0	1	1	0
Bob O'Connor (Goalie)	5	0	0	0	0
Mike Veisor (Goalie)	5	0	0	0	2
Tom Martin	5	0	0	0	16
Joel Baillargeon	8	0	0	0	26

Springfield Indians

	Games	G.	A.	Pts.	Pen.
Steve Tsujiura	78	24	56	80	27
John Ollson	75	29	43	72	51
Ross Fitzpatrick	45	33	30	63	28
Dave Michayluk	79	18	44	62	37
Len Hachborn	28	18	42	60	15
Dan Frawley	69	22	34	56	137
Florent Robidoux	68	26	22	48	123
Bob Mormina	56	14	27	41	15
Perry Pelensky	73	22	16	38	185
Rod Willard	76	17	19	36	76
Don Dietrich	50	14	21	35	14
Darrell Anholt	80	13	21	34	142
Randy Boyd, Baltimore	20	6	13	19	69
Springfield	27	2	11	13	48
Totals	47	8	24	32	117
Dave Brown	59	17	14	31	150
Tom McMurchy	43	16	14	30	54
Steve Smith	70	4	25	29	77
Alain Lemieux	14	11	14	25	18
Steve Blyth	77	4	20	24	112
Peter Marsh	23	8	13	21	32
Jeff Smith	56	6	13	19	36
Taras Zytnysky	70	1	17	18	55
Dennis Cyr	17	4	13	17	11
Daryl Stanley	52	4	10	14	122
Dan Wood	13	5	8	13	4
Steve Taylor	12	3	6	9	7
Lindsay Carson	5	2	4	6	5
Andre Villeneuve	8	1	5	6	6
Jerome Dupont	12	2	3	5	65
Len Dawes	13	1	4	5	2
Brian Shaw	4	2	2	4	2
Michel Larocque (G.)	5	0	2	2	0
Marc Bergevin	7	0	1	1	2
Bob Janecyk (Goalie)	30	0	1	1	2
Todd Bergen	1	0	0	0	0
Brian Tutt	1	0	0	0	2
Marcel Frere	1	0	0	0	10
Pelle Lindbergh (Goalie)	4	0	0	0	0
Gil Hudon (Goalie)	28	0	0	0	4
W. Skorod'ski, Sh. (G.)	19	0	0	0	12
Springfield (G.)	14	0	0	0	10
Totals	33	0	0	0	22

Complete AHL Goaltending

	Games	Mins.	Goals	SO.	Avg.
Mark Evans, Hershey	1	26	0	0	0.00
Gilles Heroux, Nova Scotia	1	60	2	0	2.00
Pat Riggin, Hershey	3	185	7	0	2.27
Ed Mio, Adirondack	4	250	11	0	2.64
Frank Caprice, Fredericton	18	1089	49	2	2.70
Brian Ford, Fredericton	36	2142	105(6)	2	*2.94
George Gagnon, Baltimore	1	40	2	0	3.00
Pelle Lindbergh, Springfield	4	240	12	0	3.00
Michel Dufour, Fredericton	6	365	19	0	3.12
Marco Baron, Moncton	16	858	45(1)	0	3.15
Mike Zanier, Moncton	31	1743	96(2)	0	3.30
Mark Holden, Nova Scotia	47	2739	153(1)	0	3.35
Bob Janecyk, Springfield	30	1664	94	0	3.39
Phil Myre, Rochester	33	1803	104(2)	*4	3.46
Shawn MacKenzie, Maine	34	1948	113(5)	0	3.48
Chris Smith, Moncton	39	2243	130(4)	0	3.48
Steve Penney, Nova Scotia	27	1571	92(3)	0	3.51
Rick St. Croix, St. Catharines	8	482	29	0	3.61
Clint Malarchuk, Fredericton	11	663	40(3)	0	3.62
Roberto Romano, Baltimore	31	1759	106(1)	0	3.62
Jacques Cloutier, Rochester	*51	*2841	172(7)	1	3.63
Dan Sanscartier, Hershey	6	310	19(1)	0	3.68
Tim Bernhardt, St. Catharines	42	2501	154	0	3.69
Ken Holland, Adirondack	42	2495	154(3)	0	3.70

	Games	Mins.	Goals	SO.	Avg.
Markus Mattsson, New Haven	31	1701	110(1)	0	3.88
Vince Tremblay, Baltimore	28	1590	106(2)	0	4.00
Jim Ralph, Springfield	9	479	42(1)	0	5.26
Baltimore	25	1455	87	0	3.59
Totals	34	1934	129(1)	0	4.00
Sam St. Laurent, Maine	38	2158	145(6)	0	4.03
Wendell Young, Fredericton	11	569	39(1)	1	4.11
Michel Larocque, Springfield	5	301	21	0	4.19
Steve Baker, Binghamton	6	345	35(1)	0	6.09
Maine	13	744	41(2)	0	3.31
Totals	19	1089	76(3)	0	4.19
Greg Moffett, Nova Scotia	10	493	35(2)	0	4.26
Rollie Boutin, Binghamton	45	2623	188(1)	3	4.30
Gil Hudon, Springfield	27	1395	101(2)	0	4.34
Mike Blake, New Haven	16	864	64	0	4.44
Corrado Micalef, Adirondack	29	1769	132(1)	0	4.48
Mike Moffat, Hershey	30	1592	124	0	4.67
Nick Ricci, St. Catharines	15	597	47	0	4.72
Bob Parent, St. Catharines	18	900	73(2)	0	4.87
Darren Eliot, New Haven	7	365	30	0	4.93
Gary Laskoski, New Haven	22	1179	97(2)	0	4.94
Mark Laforest, Adirondack	7	351	29	0	4.96
Dave Parro, Hershey	42	2277	190(1)	1	5.01
Paul Pageau, Sherbrooke	45	2432	*205(2)	0	5.06
Paul Fricker, Binghamton	30	1731	149(3)	0	5.16
Warren Skorodenski, Sherbrooke	19	1048	88(1)	0	5.04
Springfield	14	756	67	0	5.32
Totals	33	1804	155(1)	0	5.16
Bob McNamara, Rochester	5	171	15	0	5.26
Brian Hayward, Sherbrooke	15	781	69	0	5.30
Dave Ross, New Haven	8	430	38(1)	0	5.30
Al Jensen, Hershey	3	180	16	0	5.33
Gray Weicker, Binghamton	2	120	11	0	5.50
Bob Mason, Hershey	5	282	26	0	5.53
Mike Veisor, Sherbrooke	5	259	24(1)	0	5.56
Mario Lessard, New Haven	5	281	27(1)	0	5.77
Bob O'Connor, Sherbrooke	5	299	29	0	5.82
Bruce Dowie, St. Catharines	9	410	41	0	6.00

( )—Empty Net Goals. Do not count against a goaltender's average.

Individual 1983-84 Leaders

Goals	Mal Davis, Rochester—	55
Assists	Ross Yates, Binghamton—	73
Points	Claude Larose, Sherbrooke—	120
Penalty Minutes	Mitch Wilson, Maine—	349
	Bennett Wolf, Baltimore—	349
Goaltending Average (25 Games)	Brian Ford, Fredericton—	2.94
Shutouts	Phil Myre, Rochester—	4

1984 Calder Cup Playoffs

Quarterfinals
(Best-of-seven series)

SERIES "A"

	W.	L.	Pts.	GF.	GA.
Nova Scotia	4	3	8	33	31
Fredericton	3	4	6	31	33

(Nova Scotia wins series, 4 games to 3)

SERIES "B"

	W.	L.	Pts.	GF.	GA.
Maine	4	3	8	25	22
Adirondack	3	4	6	22	25

(Maine wins series, 4 games to 3)

SERIES "C"

	W.	L.	Pts.	GF.	GA.
Baltimore	4	0	8	28	15
Springfield	0	4	0	15	28

(Baltimore wins series, 4 games to 0)

SERIES "D"

	W.	L.	Pts.	GF.	GA.
Rochester	4	3	8	29	23
St. Catharines	3	4	6	23	29

(Rochester wins series, 4 games to 3)

Semifinals
(Best-of-seven series)

SERIES "E"	W.	L.	Pts.	GF.	GA.
Maine	4	1	8	24	14
Nova Scotia	1	4	2	14	24

(Maine wins series, 4 games to 1)

SERIES "F"	W.	L.	Pts.	GF.	GA.
Rochester	4	2	8	27	21
Baltimore	2	4	4	21	27

(Rochester wins series, 4 games to 2)

Finals - For the Calder Cup
(Best-of-seven series)

SERIES "G"	W.	L.	Pts.	GF.	GA.
Maine	4	1	8	26	19
Rochester	1	4	2	19	26

(Maine wins series, and Calder Cup, 4 games to 1)

Top 10 Playoff Scorers

	Games	G.	A.	Pts.	Pen.
1. Paul Gardner, Baltimore	10	*12	10	*22	0
2. Bud Stefanski, Maine	17	*12	9	21	16
Glenn Merkosky, Maine	17	11	10	21	20
4. Bob Mongrain, Rochester	18	11	9	20	46
5. Yvon Lambert, Rochester	18	8	11	19	2
John Newberry, Nova Scotia	12	7	12	19	22
7. Geordie Robertson, Rochester	18	9	9	18	42
Al Hill, Maine	17	6	12	18	12
9. Larry Floyd, Maine	16	9	8	17	4
Tom Thornbury, Baltimore	10	2	*15	17	8

Team-by-Team Playoff Scoring

Adirondack Red Wings
(Lost quarterfinals to Maine, 4-3)

	Games	G.	A.	Pts.	Pen.
Andre St. Laurent	7	4	4	8	23
Jody Gage	6	3	4	7	2
Wayne Crawford	7	3	4	7	4
Rejean Cloutier	7	2	4	6	9
Ted Nolan	7	2	3	5	18
Kirt Bjork	7	2	3	5	4
Gerrard Gallant	7	1	3	4	34
Ted Speers	7	2	1	3	9
Larry Trader	6	1	1	2	4
Brad Smith	7	1	1	2	26
Ken Solheim	7	1	1	2	0
Ted Huesing	7	0	2	2	2
Rory Cava	7	0	1	1	30
Greg Joly	7	0	1	1	19
Derek Smith	1	0	0	0	0
C. Micalef (Goalie)	1	0	0	0	0
Randy MacGregor	2	0	0	0	2
Charlie Skjodt	2	0	0	0	0
Dave Korol	3	0	0	0	0
Mike Stern	4	0	0	0	2
Joe Kocur	5	0	0	0	28
Ken Holland (Goalie)	7	0	0	0	2
Brian Johnson	7	0	0	0	40
John Beukeboom	7	0	0	0	25

Baltimore Skipjacks
(Lost semifinals to Rochester, 4-2)

	Games	G.	A.	Pts.	Pen.
Paul Gardner	10	12	10	22	0
Tom Thornbury	10	2	*15	17	8
Bobby Simpson	10	7	5	12	8
Jim Hamilton	9	6	6	12	0
Steve Carlson	10	7	3	10	8
Dave Hannan	10	2	6	8	27
Warren Young	10	2	6	8	18
Ted Bulley	10	2	5	7	2
Greg Tebbutt	10	0	6	6	20
Rod Schutt	10	3	1	4	22
Dean Defazio	10	2	2	4	19
Mitch Lamoureux	9	1	3	4	2
Rod Buskas	10	1	3	4	22
Brian Lundberg	10	0	3	3	8
Tim Tookey	8	1	1	2	2
R. Romano (Goalie)	9	0	2	2	0
Bennett Wolf	10	0	2	2	24
Troy Loney	10	0	2	2	19
Bob Geale	7	1	0	1	2
Jim Ralph (Goalie)	2	0	0	0	0
Dave Goertz	6	0	0	0	0

Fredericton Express
(Lost quarterfinals to Nova Scotia, 4-3)

	Games	G.	A.	Pts.	Pen.
Mark Lanthier	7	4	6	10	0
Grant Martin	7	4	5	9	16
Jean Gaulin	7	2	5	7	0
John VanBoxmeer	7	2	5	7	8
Marc Crawford	7	4	2	6	23
Jim Dobson	7	3	2	5	2
Rejean Vignola	7	3	2	5	13
Mark Kirton	7	2	3	5	6
Gerry Minor	7	1	4	5	20
Wally Weir	7	2	2	4	14
Claude Julien	7	0	4	4	6
Gord Donnelly	7	1	1	2	43
Garth Butcher	6	0	2	2	19
David Mancuso	3	1	0	1	0
Michel Bolduc	7	0	1	1	19
Mike Hough	1	0	0	0	7
Steve Driscoll	1	0	0	0	0
Mark Kumpel	3	0	0	0	15
Mike Eagles	4	0	0	0	5
Michel Dufour (Goalie)	4	0	0	0	2
Brian Ford (Goalie)	4	0	0	0	0
Bruce Holloway	5	0	0	0	0
Stu Kulak	5	0	0	0	59

Maine Mariners
(Winners of 1984 Calder Cup Playoffs)

	Games	G.	A.	Pts.	Pen.
Bud Stefanski	17	*12	9	*21	16
Glenn Merkosky	17	11	10	21	20
Al Hill	17	6	12	18	12
Larry Floyd	16	9	8	17	4
Kevin Maxwell	17	5	11	16	36
Rob Palmer	17	3	10	13	8
Mike Antonovich	17	4	8	12	8
Garry Howatt	17	4	7	11	46
Paul Evans	17	3	7	10	4
Bruce Driver	16	0	10	10	8
Mitch Wilson	17	3	6	9	98
Mike Hordy	17	2	6	8	4
Roy Sommer	14	6	1	7	24
Grant Mulvey	16	5	2	7	39
Murray Brumwell	17	1	5	6	15
Yvon Joly	14	0	5	5	4
Mike Busniuk	16	1	1	2	*105
Rich Chernomaz	2	0	1	1	0
Mike Stothers	17	0	1	1	34
S. MacKenzie (Goalie)	1	0	0	0	0
Jeff Bandura	1	0	0	0	0
Alain Vigneault	1	0	0	0	4
Carmine Cirella	3	0	0	0	19
Allan Stewart	3	0	0	0	4
Steve Baker (Goalie)	6	0	0	0	0
Sam St. Laurent (Goalie)	13	0	0	0	25

Nova Scotia Voyageurs
(Lost semifinals to Maine, 4-1)

	Games	G.	A.	Pts.	Pen.
John Newberry	12	7	12	19	22
Wayne Thompson	12	5	8	13	4
Dan Bonar	12	4	7	11	38
Brian Skrudland	12	2	8	10	14
Larry Landon	12	7	2	9	2
Bill Riley	12	2	5	7	8

	Games	G.	A.	Pts.	Pen.
Blair Barnes	6	4	2	6	12
Alain Heroux	12	3	2	5	4
Remi Gagne	7	2	3	5	10
Michel Therrien	11	1	4	5	37
Whitney Richards	9	2	2	4	16
Dave Stoyanovich	11	2	1	3	17
Dave Allison	6	0	3	3	25
Stan Hennigar	12	0	3	3	19
Bill Kitchen	10	1	1	2	8
Jocelyn Gauvreau	3	1	1	2	0
Ted Fauss	7	0	2	2	28
Sergio Momesso	8	0	2	2	4
Steve Lalor	12	0	2	2	13
Claude Lemieux	2	1	0	1	6
Mike Jeffrey	7	1	0	1	7
Mark Holden (Goalie)	10	0	1	1	0
Greg Moffett (Goalie)	5	0	0	0	0
Stephan Lefebvre	8	0	0	0	25

Rochester Americans
(Lost finals to Maine, 4-1)

	Games	G.	A.	Pts.	Pen.
Bob Mongrain	18	11	9	20	46
Yvon Lambert	18	8	11	19	2
Geordie Robertson	18	9	9	18	42
Daniel Naud	18	4	12	16	4
Jim Wiemer	18	3	13	16	20
Mal Davis	15	6	9	15	33
Claude Verret	18	5	9	14	4
Gates Orlando	18	4	10	14	6
Randy Cunneyworth	17	5	5	10	55
Mark Renaud	15	2	8	10	39
Ron Fischer	15	4	3	7	19
Warren Harper	18	3	3	6	11
Lou Crawford	17	2	4	6	87
Chris Langevin	15	3	2	5	39
Dave Fenyves	16	1	4	5	22
Tom St. James	13	0	5	5	4
Steve Patrick	13	2	1	3	18
Jim Aldred	11	2	0	2	33
Dirk Rueter	18	1	1	2	39
Bob Bodak	3	0	2	2	0
Jacques Cloutier (G.)	18	0	1	1	10
Bob McNamara	1	0	0	0	25
Clint Fehr	2	0	0	0	5
Venci Sebek	4	0	0	0	5
Steve Dykstra	6	0	0	0	46

St. Catharines Saints
(Lost quarterfinals to Rochester, 4-3)

	Games	G.	A.	Pts.	Pen.
Norm Aubin	7	5	3	8	8
Gary Yaremchuk	7	5	1	6	2
Ken Strong	7	3	3	6	4
Frank Nigro	7	0	6	6	9
Ernie Godden	7	4	1	5	28
Lee Norwood	7	0	5	5	31
Bruce Boudreau	7	0	5	5	11
Pat Graham	7	1	2	3	9
Garry Lariviere	7	0	3	3	2
Mike Kaszycki	5	1	1	2	7
Fred Perlini	7	1	1	2	17
Rich Costello	4	1	0	1	0
Greg Britz	7	1	0	1	0
Fred Boimistruck	7	1	0	1	19
Dave Farrish	7	0	1	1	4

	Games	G.	A.	Pts.	Pen.
Craig Muni	7	0	1	1	0
Russ Adam	7	0	1	1	10
Rick St. Croix (Goalie)	3	0	0	0	0
Tim Bernhardt (Goalie)	5	0	0	0	0
Basil McRae	6	0	0	0	40
Bob McGill	6	0	0	0	26

	Games	G.	A.	Pts.	Pen.
Peter Marsh	4	2	0	2	0
Dan Wood	4	1	1	2	0
Randy Boyd	4	0	2	2	34
Steve Blyth	4	0	1	1	2
Darrel Anholt	4	0	1	1	2
Florent Robideux	4	0	1	1	6
Dan Frawley	4	0	1	1	12
Perry Pelensky	4	0	1	1	9
Taras Zytynsky	4	0	1	1	8
Bob Mormina	1	0	0	0	0
Gil Hudon (Goalie)	2	0	0	0	0
W. Skorodenski (Goalie)	2	0	0	0	0
Dennis Cyr	3	0	0	0	0
Marc Bergevin	4	0	0	0	0
Steve Smith	4	0	0	0	0
Dave Michayluk	4	0	0	0	2

Springfield Indians
(Lost quarterfinals to Baltimore, 4-0)

	Games	G.	A.	Pts.	Pen.
Steve Tsujiura	4	4	3	7	2
Ross Fitzpatrick	4	3	2	5	2
Tom McMurchy	4	4	0	4	0
John Ollson	4	1	2	3	12
Alain Lemieux	4	0	3	3	2

COMPLETE CALDER CUP GOALTENDING

	Games	Mins.	Goals	SO.	Avg.
Shawn MacKenzie, Maine	1	0	0	0	0.00
Corrado Micalef, Adirondack	1	1	0	0	0.00
Sam St. Laurent, Maine	12	708	32	*1	*2.71
Tim Bernhardt, St. Catharines	5	288	17(1)	0	3.54
Jacques Cloutier, Rochester	*18	*1145	*68(2)	0	3.56
Ken Holland, Adirondack	7	416	25	0	3.61
Greg Moffett, Nova Scotia	5	182	11(2)	0	3.63
Steve Baker, Maine	6	353	23	0	3.91
Roberto Romano, Baltimore	9	544	36	0	3.97
Michel Dufour, Fredericton	4	194	14	0	4.33
Jim Ralph, Baltimore	2	82	6	0	4.39
Mark Holden, Nova Scotia	10	534	40(2)	0	4.49
Rick St. Croix, St. Catharines	3	133	10(1)	0	4.51
Brian Ford, Fredericton	4	223	18(1)	0	4.84
Warren Skorodenski, Springfield	2	124	13	0	6.29
Gil Hudon, Springfield	2	119	15	0	7.56

( )—Empty Net Goals. Do not count against a goaltender's average.

★★★★★★★★★★★★★★★★★★★★★★★★★

AHL 1983-84 ALL-STARS

First Team	Position	Second Team
Brian Ford, Fredericton	Goal	Tim Bernhardt, St. Catharines
Garry Lariviere, St. Catharines	Defense	Tom Thornbury, Baltimore
Rick Lapointe, Fredericton	Defense	Greg Joly, Adirondack
Murray Eaves, Sherbrooke	Center	Mike Kaszycki, St. Catharines
Mal Davis, Rochester	Right Wing	Mark Lofthouse, New Haven
Claude Larose, Sherbrooke	Left Wing	Daryl Evans, New Haven

AHL 1983-84 TROPHY WINNERS

John B. Sollenberger Trophy (Leading Scorer) .... Claude Larose, Sherbrooke
Les Cunningham Plaque (Most Valuable Player) .... Mal Davis, Rochester
                                                                                         Garry Lariviere, St. Catharines
Harry (Hap) Holmes Memorial Trophy (Top Goalie) .... Brian Ford, Fredericton
Dudley (Red) Garrett Memorial Trophy (Top Rookie) .... Claude Verret, Rochester
Eddie Shore Plaque (Outstanding Defenseman) .... Garry Lariviere, St. Catharines
Fred Hunt Memorial Award (Sportsmanship, Determination, Dedication) .... Claude Larose, Sherbrooke
Louis A. R. Pieri Memorial Award (Top AHL Coach) .... Gene Ubriaco, Baltimore
Baz Bastien Trophy (Coaches pick as top AHL Goalie) .... Brian Ford, Fredericton
Jack Butterfield Trophy (Calder Cup Playoff MVP) .... Bud Stefanski, Maine

★★★★★★★★★★★★★★★★★★★★★★★★★

AHL All-Time Trophy Winners

John B. Sollenberger Trophy
Leading Scorer

(Originally called Wally Kilrea Trophy, later changed to Carl Liscombe Trophy and during summer of 1955 given current name)

Year	Player, Team	Games	G.	A.	Pts.	Pen.
1936-37	Jack Markle, Syracuse	48	21	39	60	2
1937-38	Jack Markle, Syracuse	48	22	32	54	8
1938-39	Don Deacon, Pittsburgh	46	24	41	65	41
1939-40	Norm Locking, Syracuse	55	31	32	63	12
1940-41	Les Cunningham, Cleveland	56	22	42	64	10
1941-42	Pete Kelly, Springfield	46	34	44	78	11
1942-43	Wally Kilrea, Hershey	56	31	68	99	8
1943-44	Tommy Burlington, Cleveland	52	33	49	82	17
1944-45	Bob Gracie, Pittsburgh	58	40	55	95	4
	Bob Walton, Pittsburgh	58	37	58	95	17
1945-46	Les Douglas, Indianapolis	62	44	46	90	35
1946-47	Phil Hergesheimer, Philadelphia	64	48	44	92	20
1947-48	Carl Liscombe, Providence	68	50	68	118	10
1948-49	Sid Smith, Pittsburgh	68	55	57	112	4
1949-50	Les Douglas, Cleveland	67	32	68	100	27
1950-51	Ab DeMarco, Buffalo	64	37	76	113	35
1951-52	Ray Powell, Providence	67	35	62	97	6
1952-53	Eddie Olson, Cleveland	61	32	54	86	33
1953-54	George Sullivan, Hershey	69	30	89	119	54
1954-55	Eddie Olson, Cleveland	60	41	47	88	48
1955-56	Zellio Toppazzini, Providence	64	42	71	113	44
1956-57	Fred Glover, Cleveland	64	42	57	99	111
1957-58	Willie Marshall, Hershey	68	40	64	104	56
1958-59	Bill Hicke, Rochester	69	41	56	97	41
1959-60	Fred Glover, Cleveland	72	38	69	107	143
1960-61	Bill Sweeney, Springfield	70	40	68	108	26
1961-62	Bill Sweeney, Springfield	70	40	61	101	14
1962-63	Bill Sweeney, Springfield	69	38	65	103	16
1963-64	Gerry Ehman, Rochester	66	36	49	85	26
1964-65	Art Stratton, Buffalo	71	25	84	109	32
1965-66	Dick Gamble, Rochester	71	47	51	98	22
1966-67	Gordon Labossiere, Quebec	72	40	55	95	71
1967-68	Simon Nolet, Quebec	70	44	52	96	45
1968-69	Jeannot Gilbert, Hershey	71	35	65	100	13
1969-70	Jude Drouin, Montreal	65	37	69	106	88
1970-71	Fred Speck, Baltimore	72	31	61	92	40
1971-72	Don Blackburn, Providence	76	34	65	99	12
1972-73	Yvon Lambert, Nova Scotia	76	52	52	104	84
1973-74	Steve West, New Haven	76	50	60	110	41
1974-75	Doug Gibson, Rochester	75	44	72	116	81
1975-76	Jean-Guy Gratton, Hershey	73	35	58	93	38
1976-77	Andre Peloffy, Springfield	79	42	57	99	106
1977-78	Gord Brooks, Philadelphia	81	42	56	98	40
	Rick Adduono, Rochester	76	38	60	98	34
1978-79	Bernie Johnston, Maine	70	29	66	95	40
1979-80	Norm Dube, Nova Scotia	77	40	61	101	51
1980-81	Mark Lofthouse, Hershey	74	48	55	103	131
1981-82	Mike Kasczyki, New Brunswick	80	36	82	118	67
1982-83	Ross Yates, Binghamton	77	41	84	125	28
1983-84	Claude Larose, Sherbrooke	80	53	67	120	6

Les Cunningham Plaque
Most Valuable Player

1947-48—Carl Liscombe, Providence
1948-49—Carl Liscombe, Providence
1949-50—Les Douglas, Cleveland
1950-51—Ab DeMarco, Buffalo
1951-52—Ray Powell, Providence
1952-53—Eddie Olson, Cleveland
1953-54—George "Red" Sullivan, Hershey
1954-55—Ross Lowe, Springfield
1955-56—Johnny Bower, Providence
1956-57—Johnny Bower, Providence
1957-58—Johnny Bower, Cleveland
1958-59—Bill Hicke, Rochester
        Rudy Migay, Rochester (tie)
1959-60—Fred Glover, Cleveland
1960-61—Phil Maloney, Buffalo
1961-62—Fred Glover, Cleveland

1962-63—Denis DeJordy, Buffalo
1963-64—Fred Glover, Cleveland
1964-65—Art Stratton, Buffalo
1965-66—Dick Gamble, Rochester
1966-67—Mike Nykoluk, Hershey
1967-68—Dave Creighton, Providence
1968-69—Gilles Villemure, Buffalo
1969-70—Gilles Villemure, Buffalo
1970-71—Fred Speck, Baltimore
1971-72—Garry Peters, Boston
1972-73—Billy Inglis, Cincinnati
1973-74—Art Stratton, Rochester

1974-75—Doug Gibson, Rochester
1975-76—Ron Andruff, Nova Scotia
1976-77—Doug Gibson, Rochester
1977-78—Blake Dunlop, Maine
1978-79—Rocky Saganiuk, New Brunswick
1979-80—Norm Dube, Nova Scotia
1980-81—Pelle Lindbergh, Maine
1981-82—Mike Kasczyki, New Brunswick
1982-83—Ross Yates, Binghamton
1983-84—Mal Davis, Rochester
Garry Lariviere, St. Catharines (tie)

Harry (Hap) Holmes Memorial Trophy
Outstanding Goaltender

	Games	Goals	SO.	Avg.
1936-37—Bert Gardiner, Philadelphia	47	108	4	2.29
1937-38—Frank Brimsek, Providence	48	86	5	1.79
1938-39—Alfie Moore, Hershey	53	105	7	1.98
1939-40—Moe Roberts, Cleveland	56	130	5	2.32
1940-41—Chuck Rayner, Springfield	36	87	6	2.42
1941-42—Bill Beveridge, Cleveland	31	73	8	2.35
1942-43—Gordie Bell, Buffalo	52	125	9	2.40
1943-44—Nick Damore, Hershey	54	133	4	2.46
1944-45—Yves Nadon, Buffalo	30	87	3	2.90
1945-46—Connie Dion, St. Louis-Buffalo	42	124	1	2.95
1946-47—Baz Bastien, Pittsburgh	40	140	7	2.60
1947-48—Baz Bastien, Pittsburgh	68	170	5	2.50
1948-49—Baz Bastien, Pittsburgh	68	175	6	2.57
1949-50—Gil Mayer, Pittsburgh	50	142	4	2.84
1950-51—Gil Mayer, Pittsburgh	71	174	6	2.45
1951-52—Johnny Bower, Cleveland	68	165	3	2.43
1952-53—Gil Mayer, Pittsburgh	62	146	6	2.35
1953-54—Jacques Plante, Buffalo	55	148	3	2.69
1954-55—Gil Mayer, Pittsburgh	64	179	3	2.80
1955-56—Gil Mayer, Pittsburgh	56	151	5	2.70
1956-57—Johnny Bower, Providence	57	138	4	2.42
1957-58—Johnny Bower, Cleveland	64	140	8	2.19
1958-59—Bob Perreault, Hershey	50	134	6	2.68
1959-60—Ed Chadwick, Rochester	67	184	4	2.75
1960-61—Marcel Paille, Springfield	67	188	8	2.81
1961-62—Marcel Paille, Springfield	45	115	2	2.56
1962-63—Denis DeJordy, Buffalo	67	187	6	2.79
1963-64—Roger Crozier, Pittsburgh	44	103	4	2.34
1964-65—Gerry Cheevers, Rochester	72	195	5	2.68
1965-66—Les Binkley, Cleveland	66	192	2	2.93
1966-67—Andre Gill, Hershey	56	161	4	2.90
1967-68—Bob Perreault, Rochester	57	149	6	2.88
1968-69—Gilles Villemure, Buffalo	62	148	6	2.41
1969-70—Gilles Villemure, Buffalo	65	156	8	2.52
1970-71—Gary Kurt, Cleveland	42	101	3	2.67
1971-72—Dan Bouchard, Boston	50	122	4	2.51
Ross Brooks, Boston	30	65	1	2.38
1972-73—Michel Larocque, Nova Scotia	47	114	1	2.50
1973-74—Jim Shaw, Nova Scotia	41	104	3	2.68
Dave Elenbaas, Nova Scotia	39	109	3	2.96
1974-75—Ed Walsh, Nova Scotia	46	128	2	2.77
Dave Elenbaas, Nova Scotia	30	93	1	3.15
1975-76—Dave Elenbaas, Nova Scotia	48	114	5	2.42
Ed Walsh, Nova Scotia	31	91	2	3.06
1976-77—Ed Walsh, Nova Scotia	40	115	3	2.86
Dave Elenbaas, Nova Scotia	31	81	5	2.61
1977-78—Bob Holland, Nova Scotia	38	120	1	3.17
Maurice Barrette, Nova Scotia	39	107	2	2.74
1978-79—Pete Peeters, Maine	35	100	2	2.90
Robbie Moore, Maine	26	84	1	3.38
1979-80—Rick St. Croix, Maine	46	132	1	2.90
Robbie Moore, Maine	32	106	1	3.48
1980-81—Pelle Lindbergh, Maine	51	165	1	3.26
Robbie Moore, Maine	25	92	1	3.86

	Games	Goals	SO.	Avg.
1981-82—Bob Janecyk, New Brunswick	53	153	2	2.85
Warren Skorodenski, New Brunswick	28	70	3	2.55
1982-83—Brian Ford, Fredericton	27	84	0	3.49
Clint Malarchuk, Fredericton	25	78	1	3.11
1983-84—Brian Ford, Fredericton	36	105	2	2.94

Dudley (Red) Garrett Memorial Trophy
Outstanding Rookie Player

1947-48—Bob Solinger, Cleveland Barons
1948-49—Terry Sawchuk, Indianapolis Caps
1949-50—Paul Meger, Buffalo Bisons
1950-51—Wally Hergesheimer, Cleveland Barons
1951-52—Earl "Dutch" Reibel, Indianapolis Caps
1952-53—Guyle Fielder, St. Louis Flyers
1953-54—Don Marshall, Buffalo Bisons
1954-55—Jimmy Anderson, Springfield Indians
1955-56—Bruce Cline, Providence Reds
1956-57—Boris "Bo" Elik, Cleveland Barons
1957-58—Bill Sweeney, Providence Reds
1958-59—Bill Hicke, Rochester Americans
1959-60—Stan Baluik, Providence Reds
1960-61—Ronald "Chico" Maki, Buffalo Bisons
1961-62—Les Binkley, Cleveland Barons
1962-63—Doug Robinson, Buffalo Bisons
1963-64—Roger Crozier, Pittsburgh Hornets
1964-65—Ray Cullen, Buffalo Bisons
1965-66—Mike Walton, Rochester Americans
1966-67—Bob Rivard, Quebec Aces
1967-68—Gerry Desjardins, Cleveland Barons
1968-69—Ron Ward, Rochester Americans
1969-70—Jude Drouin, Montreal Voyageurs
1970-71—Fred Speck, Baltimore Clippers
1971-72—Terry Caffery, Cleveland Barons
1972-73—Ron Anderson, Boston Braves
1973-74—Rick Middleton, Providence Reds
1974-75—Jerry Holland, Providence Reds
1975-76—Greg Holst, Providence (tie)
  Pierre Mondou, Nova Scotia
1976-77—Rod Schutt, Nova Scotia
1977-78—Norm Dupont, Nova Scotia
1978-79—Mike Meeker, Binghamton
1979-80—Daryl Sutter, New Brunswick
1980-81—Pelle Lindbergh, Maine
1981-82—Bob Sullivan, Binghamton
1982-83—Mitch Lamoureux, Baltimore
1983-84—Claude Verret, Rochester

Fred Hunt Memorial Award
AHL Coaches' MVP

1977-78—Blake Dunlop, Maine
1978-79—Bernie Johnston, Maine
1979-80—Norm Dube, Nova Scotia
1980-81—Tony Cassolato, Hershey
1981-82—Mike Kasczyki, New Brunswick
1982-83—Ross Yates, Binghamton
1983-84—Claude Larose, Sherbrooke

Eddie Shore Plaque
Outstanding Defenseman

1958-59—Steve Kraftcheck, Rochester
1959-60—Larry Hillman, Providence
1960-61—Bob McCord, Springfield
1961-62—Kent Douglas, Springfield
1962-63—Marc Reaume, Hershey
1963-64—Ted Harris, Cleveland
1964-65—Al Arbour, Rochester
1965-66—Jim Morrison, Quebec
1966-67—Bob McCord, Pittsburgh
1967-68—Bill Needham, Cleveland
1968-69—Bob Blackburn, Buffalo
1969-70—Noel Price, Springfield
1970-71—Marshall Johnston, Cleveland
1971-72—Noel Price, Nova Scotia
1972-73—Ray McKay, Cincinnati
1973-74—Gordon Smith, Springfield
1974-75—Joe Zanussi, Providence
1975-76—Noel Price, Nova Scotia
1976-77—Brian Engblom, Nova Scotia
1977-78—Terry Murray, Maine
1978-79—Terry Murray, Maine
1979-80—Rick Vasko, Adirondack
1980-81—Craig Levie, Nova Scotia
1981-82—Dave Farrish, New Brunswick
1982-83—Greg Tebbutt, Baltimore
1983-84—Garry Lariviere, St. Catharines

Louis A. R. Pieri Memorial Award
Outstanding Coach

1967-68—Vic Stasiuk, Quebec
1968-69—Frank Mathers, Hershey
1969-70—Fred Shero, Buffalo
1970-71—Terry Reardon, Baltimore
1971-72—Al MacNeil, Nova Scotia
1972-73—Floyd Smith, Cincinnati
1973-74—Don Cherry, Rochester
1974-75—John Muckler, Providence
1975-76—Chuck Hamilton, Hershey
1976-77—Al MacNeil, Nova Scotia
1977-78—Bob McCammon, Maine
1978-79—Parker MacDonald, New Haven
1979-80—Doug Gibson, Hershey
1980-81—Bob McCammon, Maine
1981-82—Orval Tessier, New Brunswick
1982-83—Jacques Demers, Fredericton
1983-84—Gene Ubriaco, Baltimore

AHL All-Time Championship Teams

REGULAR SEASON		PLAY-OFFS (Calder Cup)	
Div.	Championship Team (Coach)	Year	Championship Team (Coach)
E	Philadelphia (Herb Gardiner)	1936-37	Syracuse Stars (E. Powers)
W	Syracuse (Eddie Powers)		
E	Providence (Bun Cook)	1937-38	Providence Reds (Bun Cook)
W	Cleveland (Bill Cook)		
E	Philadelphia (Herb Gardiner)	1938-39	Cleveland Barons (Bill Cook)
W	Hershey (Herb Mitchell)		
E	Providence (Bun Cook)	1939-40	Providence Reds (Bun Cook)
W	Indianapolis (Herb Lewis)		
E	Providence (Bun Cook)	1940-41	Cleveland Barons (Bill Cook)
W	Cleveland (Bill Cook)		
E	Springfield (Johnny Mitchell)	1941-42	Indianapolis Caps (Herb Lewis)
W	Indianapolis (Herb Lewis)		
	Hershey (Cooney Weiland)	1942-43	Buffalo Bisons (Art Chapman)
E	Hershey (Cooney Weiland)	1943-44	Buffalo Bisons (Art Chapman)
W	Cleveland (Bun Cook)		
E	Buffalo (Art Chapman)	1944-45	Cleveland Barons (Bun Cook)
W	Cleveland (Bun Cook)		
E	Buffalo (Frank Beisler)	1945-46	Buffalo Bisons (Frank Beisler)
W	Indianapolis (Earl Seibert)		
E	Hershey (Don Penniston)	1946-47	Hershey Bears (Don Penniston)
W	Cleveland (Bun Cook)		
E	Providence (Terry Reardon)	1947-48	Cleveland Barons (Bun Cook)
W	Cleveland (Bun Cook)		
E	Providence (Terry Reardon)	1948-49	Providence Reds (Terry Reardon)
W	St. Louis (Ebbie Goodfellow)		
E	Buffalo (Roy Goldsworthy)	1949-50	Indianapolis Caps (Ott Heller)
W	Cleveland (Bun Cook)		
E	Buffalo (Roy Goldsworthy)	1950-51	Cleveland Barons (Bun Cook)
W	Cleveland (Bun Cook)		
E	Hershey (John Crawford)	1951-52	Pittsburgh Hornets (King Clancy)
W	Pittsburgh (King Clancy)		
	Cleveland (Bun Cook)	1952-53	Cleveland Barons (Bun Cook)
	Buffalo (Frank Eddolls)	1953-54	Cleveland Barons (Bun Cook)
	Pittsburgh (Howie Meeker)	1954-55	Pittsburgh Hornets (H. Meeker)
	Providence (John Crawford)	1955-56	Providence Reds (J. Crawford)
	Providence (John Crawford)	1956-57	Cleveland Barons (Jack Gordon)
	Hershey (Frank Mathers)	1957-58	Hershey Bears (Frank Mathers)
	Buffalo (Bobby Kirk)	1958-59	Hershey Bears (Frank Mathers)
	Springfield (Pat Egan)	1959-60	Springfield Indians (Pat Egan)
	Springfield (Pat Egan)	1960-61	Springfield Indians (Pat Egan)
E	Springfield (Pat Egan)	1961-62	Springfield Indians (Pat Egan)
W	Cleveland (Jack Gordon)		
E	Providence (Fern Flaman)	1962-63	Buffalo Bisons (Billy Reay)
W	Buffalo (Billy Reay)		
E	Quebec (Floyd Curry)	1963-64	Cleveland Barons (Fred Glover)
W	Pittsburgh (Vic Stasiuk)		
E	Quebec (Bernie Geoffrion)	1964-65	Rochester Americans (Joe Crozier)
W	Rochester (Joe Crozier)		
E	Quebec (Bernie Geoffrion)	1965-66	Rochester Americans (J. Crozier)
W	Rochester (Joe Crozier)		
E	Hershey (Frank Mathers)	1966-67	Pittsburgh Hornets (Baz Bastien)
W	Pittsburgh (Baz Bastien)		
E	Hershey (Frank Mathers)	1967-68	Rochester Americans (J. Crozier)
W	Rochester (Joe Crozier)		

REGULAR SEASON		PLAY-OFFS (Calder Cup)	
Div.	Championship Team (Coach)	Year	Championship Team (Coach)
E	Hershey (Frank Mathers)	1968-69	Hershey Bears (Frank Mathers)
W	Buffalo (Fred Shero)		
E	Montreal (Al MacNeil)	1969-70	Buffalo Bisons (Fred Shero)
W	Buffalo (Fred Shero)		
E	Providence (Larry Wilson)	1970-71	Springfield Kings (John Wilson)
W	Baltimore (Terry Reardon)		
E	Boston (Armond Guidolin)	1971-72	Nova Scotia Voyageurs (Al MacNeil)
W	Baltimore (Terry Reardon)		
E	Nova Scotia (Al MacNeil)	1972-73	Cincinnati Swords (Floyd Smith)
W	Cincinnati (Floyd Smith)		
N	Rochester (Don Cherry)	1973-74	Hershey Bears (Chuck Hamilton)
S	Baltimore (Terry Reardon)		
N	Providence (John Muckler)	1974-75	Springfield Indians (Ron Stewart)
S	Virginia (Doug Barkley)		
N	Nova Scotia (Al MacNeil)	1975-76	Nova Scotia Voyageurs (Al MacNeil)
S	Hershey (Chuck Hamilton)		
	Nova Scotia (Al MacNeil)	1976-77	Nova Scotia Voyageurs (Al MacNeil)
N	Maine (Bob McCammon)	1977-78	Maine Mariners (Bob McCammon)
S	Rochester (Duane Rupp)		
N	Maine (Bob McCammon)	1978-79	Maine Mariners (Bob McCammon)
S	New Haven (Parker MacDonald)		
N	New Brunswick (Crozier-Angotti)	1979-80	Hershey Bears (Doug Gibson)
S	New Haven (Parker MacDonald)		
N	Maine (Bob McCammon)	1980-81	Adirondack Red Wings (Tom Webster, J. P. LeBlanc)
S	Hershey (Bryan Murray)		
N	New Brunswick (Orval Tessier)	1981-82	New Brunswick (Orval Tessier)
S	Binghamton (Larry Kish)		
N	Fredericton (Jacques Demers)	1982-83	Rochester (Mike Keenan)
S	Rochester (Mike Keenan)		
N	Fredericton (Earl Jessiman)	1983-84	Maine (John Paddock)
S	Baltimore (Gene Ubriaco)		

1983-84 Final Central Hockey League Standings

	G.	W.	L.	T.	Pts.	GF.	GA.
Colorado Flames	76	48	25	3	99	343	287
(a)Tulsa Oilers	68	36	27	5	77	252	248
Salt Lake Golden Eagles	72	35	35	2	72	334	330
Indianapolis Checkers	72	34	36	2	70	308	289
Montana Magic	76	20	52	4	44	276	381
U.S. Olympic Team	10	6	4	0	12	48	31
Canadian Olympic Team	10	5	5	0	10	34	29

(a)—Tulsa Oilers played the final six weeks of the CHL as a road team after the franchise was suspended on February 16, 1984.

Top 20 Scorers for the Phil Esposito Trophy

	Games	G.	A.	Pts.	Pen.
1. Scott MacLeod, Salt Lake	68	43	*75	*118	30
2. Bruce Eakin, Colorado	67	33	69	102	18
3. Dirk Graham, Salt Lake	57	37	57	94	72
4. John Markell, Montana	69	*44	40	84	61
5. Pierre Rioux, Colorado	65	37	46	83	22
6. Bobby Francis, Colorado	68	32	50	82	53
7. Red Laurence, Indianapolis	69	41	37	78	42
8. Ron Handy, Indianapolis	66	29	46	75	40
9. Tim Harrer, Salt Lake	66	42	27	69	46
Alain Lemieux, Montana	38	28	41	69	36
11. Scott Howson, Indianapolis	71	34	34	68	40
12. Dave Simpson, Indianapolis	72	24	43	67	26
13. Garth MacGuigan, Indianapolis	68	25	41	66	109
14. Dave Barr, Tulsa	50	28	37	65	24
Stan Weir, Montana	73	21	44	65	20
16. Tim Coulis, Salt Lake	63	25	35	60	225
17. Jack Callander, Montana	72	27	32	59	69
18. Gary Burns, Tulsa	68	28	30	58	95
19. Craig Homola, Salt Lake	68	29	27	56	37
Richie Hansen, Salt Lake	63	24	32	56	22

Colorado Flames

	Games	G.	A.	Pts.	Pen.
Bruce Eakin	67	33	69	102	18
Pierre Rioux	65	37	46	83	22
Bobby Francis	68	32	50	82	53
Dan Bolduc	60	37	17	54	34
Gord Hampson	62	19	25	44	89
Charles Bourgeois	54	12	32	44	133
Greg Meredith	54	23	20	43	39
Todd Hooey	67	19	21	40	40
Mario Simioni	54	16	21	37	35
Mike Clayton	69	20	16	36	126
Jeff Brubaker	57	16	19	35	218
Jeff Vaive	67	13	21	34	39
Jim Jackson	25	5	27	32	4
Pat Ribble	53	4	27	31	60
Dale DeGray	67	16	14	30	67
Keith Hanson	39	5	21	26	64
Neil Sheehy	74	5	18	23	151
Tony Curtale	54	3	20	23	80
Tony Stiles	39	3	18	21	24
Allan MacInnis	19	5	14	19	22
Mickey Volcan	30	8	9	17	20
George White	36	5	12	17	28
John Harrington	10	5	5	10	4
Colin Patterson	6	2	3	5	9
Mike Vernon (Goalie)	46	0	3	3	3
Keith Knight	6	0	2	2	0
Marc D'Amour (Goalie)	36	0	2	2	6
Jeff Lastiwka (Goalie)	1	0	0	0	0
Kari Jalonen	1	0	0	0	0
Steve Mulholland	3	0	0	0	5

Indianapolis Checkers

	Games	G.	A.	Pts.	Pen.
Red Laurence	69	41	37	78	42
Ron Handy	66	29	46	75	40
Scott Howson	71	34	34	68	40
Dave Simpson	72	24	43	67	26
Garth MacGuigan	68	25	41	66	109
Mark Hamway	71	22	32	54	38
Kevin Devine	71	23	30	53	201
Bruce Affleck	54	13	40	53	18
Roger Kortko	64	16	27	43	48
Monty Trottier	69	18	23	41	135
Jacques Sylvestre	62	22	16	38	26
Ken Leiter	68	10	26	36	46
Paul Boutilier	50	6	17	23	56
Tim Lockridge	71	2	16	18	95
Neal Coulter	58	7	10	17	25
Gord Dineen	26	4	13	17	63
Darcy Regier	68	4	12	16	112
Bill Dowd	14	1	9	10	21
Bob Hess	9	2	6	8	10
Glen Fester	9	2	4	6	4
Lorne Stamler	15	3	2	5	0
Kelly Hrudey (Goalie)	6	0	1	1	0
Rob Holland (Goalie)	39	0	1	1	10
Dave Hanson	1	0	0	0	0
Kevin Beaton	1	0	0	0	7
Mike Greeder: Salt Lake	2	0	0	0	16
Indianapolis	1	0	0	0	2
Totals	3	0	0	0	18
Ron Kennedy	7	0	0	0	7
Todd Lumbard	25	0	0	0	6

Montana Magic

	Games	G.	A.	Pts.	Pen.
John Markell	69	*44	40	84	61
Alain Lemieux	38	28	41	69	36
Stan Weir	73	21	44	65	20
Jock Callander	72	27	32	59	69
Mike Forbes	76	13	38	51	83
Reg Leach	76	21	29	50	34
Perry Ganchar	59	23	22	45	77
Michel Galarneau	66	18	22	40	44
Pat Rabbitt	46	16	16	32	21
John Beukeboom	59	6	26	32	166
Blaine Peerless	73	6	18	24	80
Cary Eades	34	10	12	22	60
Don Murdoch	17	10	10	20	2
Jim Pavese	47	1	19	20	147
Jim McTaggert	70	5	13	18	104
John Smyth	65	5	11	16	30
Mike Seide	61	4	12	16	99
Alain Vigneault	47	2	14	16	139
Perry Anderson	8	7	3	10	34
Doug McGrath	11	3	6	9	8
Dan Wood	14	2	7	9	14
Richard Zemlak	14	2	2	4	17
Dean McArthur	8	0	4	4	0
Tim Bothwell	4	0	3	3	0
Rik Wilson	6	0	3	3	2
Paul Polin	6	1	1	2	0
Brad Hammett	8	0	2	2	2
Blair MacDonald	4	1	0	1	0
Daryl MacLeod	6	0	1	1	2
Marty Ruff	1	0	0	0	2
Paul Skidmore (Goalie)	1	0	0	0	0
Mark Botell	2	0	0	0	2
Mike Kouwenhoven	2	0	0	0	0
Reg Thomas	3	0	0	0	0
L. Middlebrook (Goalie)	36	0	0	0	6
Ken Ellacott (Goalie)	41	0	0	0	0

Salt Lake Golden Eagles

	Games	G.	A.	Pts.	Pen.
Scott MacLeod	68	43	*75	*118	30
Dirk Graham	57	37	57	94	72
Tim Harrer	66	42	27	69	46
Tim Coulis	63	25	35	60	225
Craig Homola	68	29	27	56	37
Richie Hansen	63	24	32	56	22
Bill Stewart	68	23	27	50	31
Tim Trimper	35	18	27	45	26
Walt McKechnie	69	9	32	41	36
Tony Feltrin	65	8	22	30	94
Glenn Hicks	62	4	26	30	87
Craig Levie	37	8	20	28	101
Randy Velischek	43	7	21	28	54
Chris Pryor	72	7	21	28	215
Jean Francois Boutin	31	11	12	23	18
Rob Tudor	32	10	12	22	35
Bob Bergloff	44	4	17	21	78
Scott Bjugstad	15	10	8	18	6
Jali Wahlsten	35	7	9	16	8
Jeff Brownschidle	11	1	7	8	12
Terry Tait	36	1	7	8	7
David H. Jensen	13	0	7	7	6
Dave Richter	10	1	4	5	39
Dan Mandich	3	2	2	4	13
Brian Gualazzi	20	2	0	2	2
Jim Craig (Goalie)	27	0	2	2	18
Rick Hendricks	1	1	0	1	0
Dave Orleski	3	0	1	1	4
Wendell Young	20	0	1	1	2
Mike Sands (Goalie)	23	0	1	1	34
Dave Falkenberg	1	0	0	0	2
Len Frig	2	0	0	0	4
Bill Nichols	3	0	0	0	0
Chris Trinceri	6	0	0	0	0
Don Beaupre (Goalie)	7	0	0	0	0

Tulsa Oilers
(Played only road games during the final six weeks of the season)

	Games	G.	A.	Pts.	Pen.
Dave Barr	50	28	37	65	24
Gary Burns	68	28	30	58	95
Cam Connor	64	18	32	50	218
George McPhee	49	20	28	48	133
Mike Backman	50	12	28	40	103
Mikko Leinonen	33	15	23	38	38
Bob Scurfield	60	18	15	33	14
Bill Baker	59	11	22	33	47
Graeme Nicolson	62	7	24	31	61
Gary DeGrio	65	10	19	29	24
Jim Malone	57	16	11	27	58
Grant Ledyard	58	9	17	26	71
Robbie Ftorek	25	11	11	22	10
Chris Renaud	63	3	18	21	49
Mike Blaisdell	32	10	8	18	23
Chris Kontos	21	5	13	18	8
Steve Richmond	38	1	17	18	114
Rob McClanahan	10	4	10	14	10
Kurt Kleinendorst	24	4	9	13	10
Doug Baran	51	5	7	12	24
Steve Hakala	40	4	7	11	6
Scott Kleinendorst	10	4	5	9	4
Steve Martinson	42	3	6	9	*240
Mark Morrison	11	4	4	8	2
Rick Chartraw	28	1	4	5	25
Bjorn Skaare	2	1	1	2	5
Tim Leavins	1	0	0	0	0
Rick LaFerriere (Goalie)	2	0	0	0	0
Steve Weeks (Goalie)	3	0	0	0	0
Ron Scott (Goalie)	29	0	0	0	2
J. Vanbiesbrouck (G.)	36	0	0	0	6

Complete CHL Goaltending

	Games	Mins.	Goals	SO.	Avg.
Steve Weeks, Tulsa	3	180	7	0	2.33
Rick LaFerriere, Tulsa	2	79	4	0	3.04
Mike Vernon, Colorado	*46	*2648	148(3)	1	*3.35
Kelly Hrudey, Indianapolis	6	370	21	0	3.41
John Vanbiesbrouck, Tulsa	37	2153	124(3)	*3	3.46
Rob Holland, Indianapolis	39	2149	131(1)	0	3.66
Ron Scott, Tulsa	20	1717	109(1)	0	3.81
Chris Trinceri, Salt Lake	6	177	12	0	4.07
Marc D'Amour, Colorado	36	1917	131(2)	0	4.10
Jim Craig, Salt Lake	27	1532	108(1)	1	4.23
Todd Lumbard, Indianapolis	25	1491	106(1)	1	4.27
Don Beaupre, Salt Lake	7	419	30(1)	0	4.30
Wendell Young, Salt Lake	20	1094	80(1)	0	4.39
Lindsay Middlebrook, Montana	36	2104	162(1)	0	4.62
Lorne Molleken, Indianapolis	6	364	29	0	4.78
Mike Sands, Salt Lake	23	1145	93(4)	0	4.87
Ken Ellacott, Montana	41	2441	*208(2)	1	5.11
Jeff Lastiwka, Colorado	1	34	3	0	5.29
Paul Skidmore, Montana	1	60	8	0	8.00

( )—Empty Net Goals. Do not count against a Goaltender's average.

Individual Leaders (1983-84)

Goals	John Markell, Montana—	44
Assists	Scott MacLeod, Salt Lake—	75
Points	Scott MacLeod, Salt Lake—	118
Penalty Minutes	Steve Martinson, Tulsa—	240
Goaltender's Average (25 Games)	Mike Vernon, Colorado—	3.35
Shutouts	John Vanbiesbrouck, Tulsa—	3

CHL Playoffs for the Adams Cup

Semifinals
(Best-of-Seven Series)

SERIES "A"

	W.	L.	Pts.	GF.	GA.
Indianapolis	4	2	8	23	20
Colorado	2	4	4	20	23

(Indianapolis wins series, 4 games to 2)

SERIES "B"

	W.	L.	Pts.	GF.	GA.
Oilers (Tulsa)	4	1	8	23	21
Salt Lake City	1	4	2	21	23

(Oilers win series, 4 games to 1)

Finals—For the Adams Cup
(Best-of-seven series)

SERIES "C"

	W.	L.	Pts.	GF.	GA.
Tulsa	4	0	8	20	11
Indianapolis	0	4	0	11	20

(Tulsa wins Adams Cup, 4-0)

Top 10 Playoff Scorers

	Games	G.	A.	Pts.	Pen.
Red Laurence, Indianapolis	10	9	4	13	0
Mike Blaisdell, Tulsa	9	6	6	12	6
Gary Burns, Tulsa	9	3	9	12	2
Dirk Graham, Salt Lake	5	3	8	11	2
Bob Scurfield, Tulsa	9	6	4	10	4
Scott MacLeod, Salt Lake	5	3	7	10	8
Grant Ledyard, Tulsa	9	5	4	9	10
Robbie Ftorek, Tulsa	9	4	5	9	2
Pierre Rioux, Colorado	6	2	7	9	4
Bjorn Skaare, Tulsa	9	2	7	9	2
Mark Morrison, Tulsa	7	4	4	8	2
Monty Trottier, Indianapolis	10	1	7	8	2

Colorado Flames
(Lost semifinals to Indianapolis, 4-2)

	Games	G.	A.	Pts.	Pen.
Pierre Rioux	6	2	7	9	4
Bruce Eakin	6	4	2	6	0
John Harrington	6	2	3	5	2
Jeff Brubaker	6	3	1	4	15
Keith Hanson	6	2	2	4	16
Tony Curtale	6	0	4	4	2
Dan Bolduc	6	2	1	3	4
Greg Meredith	6	1	2	3	9
Mario Simioni	5	0	3	3	2
Brian Bradley	4	2	0	2	2
Dale DeGray	6	1	1	2	2
Pat Ribble	6	0	2	2	4
Jeff Vaive	6	0	2	2	2
Todd Hooey	6	1	0	1	2
Mike Clayton	6	0	1	1	4
Mike Vernon (Goalie)	6	0	1	1	0
Bobby Francis	1	0	1	1	0
Mickey Volcan	5	0	0	0	11
Keith Knight	2	0	0	0	0
Marc D'Amour (Goalie)	1	0	0	0	0
Tony Stiles	1	0	0	0	0

Salt Lake Golden Eagles
(Lost semifinals to Tulsa, 4-1)

	Games	G.	A.	Pts.	Pen.
Dirk Graham	5	3	8	11	2
Scott MacLeod	5	3	7	10	8
Tim Trimper	5	4	3	7	9
Scott Bjugstad	5	3	4	7	0
Bob Rouse	4	2	2	4	2
Tim Coulis	4	1	2	3	35
Rob Tudor	5	1	2	3	21
Chris Pryor	5	1	2	3	11
Tim Harrer	5	1	2	3	5
Randy Velischek	5	0	3	3	2
Tony Feltrin	5	2	0	2	5
Craig Homola	5	0	2	2	0
Glenn Hicks	5	0	1	1	16
David H. Jensen	5	0	1	1	5
Jim Craig (Goalie)	3	0	0	0	14
Bob Bergloff	2	0	0	0	4
Richie Hansen	5	0	0	0	2
Don Biggs	3	0	0	0	2
Wendell Young (Goalie)	4	0	0	0	0
Bill Stewart	2	0	0	0	0

Indianapolis Checkers
(Lost finals to Tulsa, 4-0)

	Games	G.	A.	Pts.	Pen.
Red Laurence	10	9	4	13	0
Monty Trottier	10	1	7	8	2
Kevin Devine	10	4	3	7	8
Ken Leiter	10	3	4	7	0
Ron Handy	10	2	5	7	0
Gerald Diduck	10	1	6	7	19
Garth MacGuigan	10	3	3	6	2
Bob Hess	9	2	4	6	6
Roger Kortko	9	1	5	6	9
Dave Simpson	10	1	5	6	2
Scott Howson	7	1	3	4	2
Jacques Slyvestre	10	2	1	3	2
Neal Coulter	4	2	0	2	0
Darcy Regier	10	1	1	2	13
Mark Hamway	9	1	1	2	0
Tim Lockridge	4	0	1	1	16
Bill Dowd	7	0	1	1	2
Dale Henry	2	0	0	0	7
Vern Smith	7	0	0	0	4
Todd Lumbard (Goalie)	4	0	0	0	2
Rob Holland (Goalie)	7	0	0	0	0
Bruce Affleck	2	0	0	0	0
Lorne Molleken (Goalie)	1	0	0	0	0

Tulsa Oilers
(Winners of 1984 Adams Cup, CHL Playoffs)

	Games	G.	A.	Pts.	Pen.
Mike Blaisdell	9	6	6	12	6
Gary Burns	9	3	9	12	2
Bob Scurfield	9	6	4	10	4
Grant Ledyard	9	5	4	9	10
Robbie Ftorek	9	4	5	9	2
Bjorn Skaare	9	2	7	9	2
Mark Morrison	7	4	4	8	2
Graeme Nicolson	9	1	6	7	12
Mike Backman	9	4	2	6	22
Doug Baran	9	2	4	6	14
Chris Renaud	9	0	5	5	7
Kurt Kleinendorst	9	2	2	4	7
Gary DeGrio	9	2	0	2	2
Cam Connor	6	1	1	2	34
Jim Malone	7	1	1	2	0
Jim Leavins	5	0	1	1	2
J. Vanbiesbrouck (G.)	4	0	1	1	2
Steve Hakala	5	0	1	1	0
Ron Scott (Goalie)	5	0	1	1	0
Steve Martinson	6	0	0	0	43
Rick LaFerriere (Goalie)	1	0	0	0	0

Complete Adams Cup Goaltending

	Games	Mins.	Goals	SO.	Avg.
Marc D'Amour, Colorado	1	20	0	0	0.00
John Vanbiesbrouck, Tulsa	4	240	10	0	2.50
Rob Holland, Indianapolis	7	379	22	0	3.48
Mike Vernon, Colorado	6	347	21	0	3.63
Jim Craig, Salt Lake	3	177	12	0	4.07
Ron Scott, Tulsa	5	280	20	0	4.29
Todd Lumbard, Indianapolis	4	167	12	0	4.31
Lorne Molleken, Indianapolis	1	59	5	0	5.08
Wendell Young, Salt Lake	4	122	11	0	5.41
Rick LaFerriere, Tulsa	1	20	2	0	6.00

Individual Adams Cup Leaders

Goals	Red Laurence, Indianapolis—	9
Assists	Gary Burns, Tulsa—	9
Points	Red Laurence, Indianapolis—	13
Penalty Minutes	Steve Martinson, Tulsa—	43
Goaltender's Average	John Vanbiesbrouck, Tulsa—	2.50
Shutouts	None	

★★★★★★★★★★★★★★★★★★★★★★★★★★★★★

1983-84 CHL All-Stars

First Team	Position	Second Team
John Vanbiesbrouck, Tulsa	Goal	Mike Vernon, Colorado
Bruce Affleck, Indianapolis	Defense	Graeme Nicolson, Tulsa
Charles Bourgeois, Colorado	Defense	Pat Ribble, Colorado
Scott MacLeod, Salt Lake	Center	Bruce Eakin, Colorado
Dirk Graham, Salt Lake	Right Wing	Pierre Rioux, Colorado
John Markell, Montana	Left Wing	Ron Handy, Indianapolis

1983-84 CHL Trophy Winners

Phil Esposito Trophy (Leading Scorer) .... Scott MacLeod, Salt Lake
Tommy Ivan Trophy (Most Valuable Player) .... (tie) Bruce Affleck, Indianapolis
and John Vanbiesbrouck, Tulsa
Ken McKenzie Trophy (Rookie of Year) .... Scott MacLeod, Salt Lake
Terry Sawchuk Trophy (Top Goaltending Average) . John Vanbiesbrouck and Ron Scott, Tulsa
Bobby Orr Trophy (Best Defenseman) .... Bruce Affleck, Indianapolis
Bob Gassoff Award (Most Improved Defenseman) .... Grant Ledyard, Tulsa
Don Ashby Memorial Trophy (Ironman Award) .... Chris Pryor, Salt Lake
Max McNab Trophy (Playoff MVP) .... Bruce Affleck, Indianapolis
Jake Milford Trophy (Coach of the Year) .... Tom Webster, Tulsa

★★★★★★★★★★★★★★★★★★★★★★★★★★★★★

Championship Teams

Regular Season		Play-Offs
Omaha Knights	1963-64	Tulsa Oilers
St. Paul Rangers	1964-65	Omaha Knights
Minnesota Rangers	1965-66	St. Paul Rangers
Oklahoma City Blazers	1966-67	Oklahoma City Blazers
Tulsa Oilers (Northern Division) Oklahoma City Blazers (Southern Division)	1967-68	Oklahoma City Blazers
Tulsa Oilers (Northern Division) Oklahoma City Blazers (Southern Division)	1968-69	Dallas Black Hawks
Omaha Knights	1969-70	Omaha Knights
Omaha Knights	1970-71	Omaha Knights
Dallas Black Hawks	1971-72	Dallas Black Hawks
Dallas Black Hawks	1972-73	Omaha Knights
Oklahoma City Blazers	1973-74	Dallas Black Hawks
Salt Lake Golden Eagles (North) Dallas Black Hawks (South)	1974-75	Salt Lake Golden Eagles
Tulsa Oilers	1975-76	Tulsa Oilers
Kansas City Blues	1976-77	Kansas City Blues
Fort Worth Texans	1977-78	Fort Worth Texans
Salt Lake Golden Eagles	1978-79	Dallas Black Hawks
Salt Lake Golden Eagles	1979-80	Salt Lake Golden Eagles
Dallas Black Hawks	1980-81	Salt Lake Golden Eagles
Salt Lake Golden Eagles	1981-82	Indianapolis Checkers
Indianapolis Checkers	1982-83	Indianapolis Checkers
Colorado Flames	1983-84	Tulsa Oilers

Individual Awards

Phil Esposito Trophy
(Leading Scorers)

	Games	G.	A.	Pts.	Pen.
1963-64—Alain Caron, St. Louis	71	77	48	125	22
1964-65—Tom McCarthy, Tulsa	68	53	44	97	110
1965-66—Art Stratton, St. Louis	66	28	66	94	14
1966-67—Art Stratton, St. Louis	67	34	56	90	46
1967-68—Ron Ward, Tulsa	67	31	54	85	30
1968-69—Jim Lorentz, Oklahoma City	56	33	68	101	67
1969-70—Jack Egers, Omaha	70	42	48	90	83
1970-71—Pierre Jarry, Omaha	71	46	46	92	94
1971-72—Ross Perkins, Forth Worth	68	41	56	97	47
Jean Payette, Tulsa	72	33	64	97	44
1972-73—Lyle Moffat, Tulsa	71	40	40	80	108
Danny Gruen, Forth Worth	68	35	45	80	194
1973-74—Wayne Schaab, Omaha	72	31	58	89	41
1974-75—Wayne Schaab, Omaha	78	36	49	85	51
1975-76—Jim Wiley, Tulsa	76	33	63	96	21
1976-77—Steve West, Oklahoma City	76	33	63	96	42
1977-78—Doug Palazzari, Salt Lake City	70	45	56	101	82
1978-79—Rick Shinske, Salt Lake City	66	22	66	88	31
1979-80—Doug Palazzari, Salt Lake City	74	48	61	109	62
1980-81—Joe Mullen, Salt Lake City	80	59	58	117	8
1981-82—Bobby Francis, Oklahoma City	80	48	66	114	76
1982-83—Wes Jarvis, Birmingham	75	40	68	108	36
1983-84—Scott MacLeod, Salt Lake City	68	43	75	118	30

Tommy Ivan Award
(Most Valuable Player)

1963-64— Jeannot Gilbert, Minneapolis
1964-65— Cesare Maniago, Minneapolis
1965-66— Art Stratton, St. Louis
1966-67— Art Stratton, St. Louis
1967-68— Bryan Watson, Houston
1968-69— Jim Lorentz, Oklahoma City
1969-70— Dan Johnson, Tulsa
1970-71— Joe Zanussi, Forth Worth and Gerry Ouellette, Peter McDuffe and Andre Dupont, Omaha (tied)
1971-72— Gregg Sheppard, Oklahoma City
1972-73— Mike Cormier, Forth Worth
1973-74— Glenn Resch, Fort Worth
1974-75— Wayne Schaab, Omaha
1975-76— Ian McKegney, Dallas
1976-77— Barclay Plager, Kansas City
1977-78— Doug Palazzari, Salt Lake City
1978-79— Ron Low, Kansas City
1979-80— Doug Palazzari, Salt Lake City
1980-81— Joe Mullen, Salt Lake City
1981-82— Bobby Francis, Oklahoma City
1982-83— Kelly Hrudey, Indianapolis
1983-84— Bruce Affleck, Indianapolis and John Vanbiesbrouck, Tulsa (tied)

Bobby Orr Trophy
(Most Valuable Defenseman)

1963-64— Barclay Plager, Omaha
1964-65— Mike McMahon, St. Paul
1965-66— Al Labrun, Minnesota
1966-67— Mike McMahon, Houston
1967-68— Bryan Watson, Houston
1968-69— Barry Gibbs, Oklahoma City
1969-70— Mike Robitaille, Omaha
1970-71— Andre Dupont, Omaha
1971-72— Bart Crashley, Dallas
1972-73— Len Frig, Dallas
1973-74— Clare Alexander, Oklahoma City
1974-75— Ian McKegney, Dallas
1975-76— Ian McKegney, Dallas
1976-77— Mike O'Connell, Dallas
1977-78— Larry Giroux, Kansas City
1978-79— Greg Hubick, Dallas
1979-80— Bruce Affleck, Dallas
1980-81— Bruce Affleck, Indianapolis
1981-82— Dan Poulin, Nashville
1982-83— Gord Dineen, Indianapolis
1983-84— Bruce Affleck, Indianapolis

Terry Sawchuk Award
(Leading Goalies)

1963-64— Ernie Wakely, Omaha
1964-65— Cesare Maniago, Minneapolis
1965-66— Wayne Rutledge, Minnesota
1966-67— Gerry Cheevers, Oklahoma City
1967-68— Russ Gillow, Oklahoma City
1968-69— Phil Myre, Houston
1967-68— Serge Aubry, Tulsa
1970-71— Peter McDuffe, Omaha
1971-72— John Adams, Oklahoma City
1972-73— Mike Veisor, Dallas
1973-74— John Voss, Omaha
1974-75— Ray Martyniuk, Salt Lake
1975-76— Mike Veisor, Dallas
1976-77— Gord McRae, Dallas, and Yves Belanger, Kansas City (tied)
1977-78— Doug Grant and Ed Staniowski, Salt Lake City
1978-79— Terry Richardson and Doug Grant, Salt Lake City
1979-80— Richard Brodeur and Jim Park, Ind.
1980-81— Paul Harrison and Ken Ellacott, Dallas
1981-82— Kelly Hrudey and Rob Holland, Ind.
1982-83— Kelly Hrudey and Rob Holland, Ind.
1983-84— John Vanbiesbrouck and Ron Scott, Tulsa

Ken McKenzie
(Rookie-of-the-Year)

1963-64— Poul Popiel, St. Louis and Garry Peters, Omaha (tie)
1964-65— Mike Walton, Tulsa
1965-66— Doug Roberts, Memphis
1966-67— Serge Savard, Houston
1967-68— Jim Lorentz, Oklahoma City
1968-69— Steve Atkinson, Oklahoma City
1969-70— Andre Dupont, Omaha
1970-71— Mike Murphy, Omaha
1971-72— Tom Williams, Omaha
1972-73— Mike Veisor, Dallas
1973-74— Clare Alexander, Oklahoma City
1974-75— Guy Chouinard, Omaha
1975-76— Brad Gassoff, Tulsa
1976-77— Bernie Federko, Kansas City
1977-78— Glen Hanlon, Tulsa
1978-79— Mike Eaves, Oklahoma City
1979-80— Joe Mullen, Salt Lake City
1980-81— Roland Melanson, Indianapolis
1981-82— Bobby Francis, Oklahoma City
1982-83— Larry Floyd, Wichita
1983-84— Scott MacLeod, Salt Lake City

Don Ashby Memorial Trophy
(Iron Man Award)

1976-77— Glen Surbey, Tulsa
1977-78— Duane Wylie, Dallas
1978-79— Floyd Thomson, Salt Lake City
1979-80— Darcy Reigier, Indianapolis
1980-81— Kevin Devine, Indianapolis
1981-82— Reg Thomas, Cincinnati
1982-83— Red Laurence, Indianapolis
1983-84— Chris Pryor, Salt Lake City

Penalty Leaders

Season	Player	Penalty Minutes
1963-64	Barclay Plager, Omaha Knights	208
1964-65	Larry Johnston, Tulsa Oilers	262
1965-66	Tracy Pratt, St. Louis Braves	206
1966-67	Real Lemieux, Memphis Wings	211
1967-68	Bryan Watson, Houston Apollos	293
1968-69	Barry Gibbs, Oklahoma City Blazers	194
1969-70	Dennis O'Brien, Iowa Stars	331
1970-71	Andre Dupont, Omaha Knights	308
1971-72	Steve Durbano, Omaha Knights	402
1972-73	Danny Gruen, Fort Worth Wings	194
1973-74	Alf Handrahan, Tulsa Oilers	240
1974-75	Randy Holt, Dallas Black Hawks	411
1975-76	Paul Tantardini, Salt Lake Golden Eagles	325
1976-77	Gary Holt, Salt Lake City Golden Eagles	226
1977-78	Alain Belanger, Dallas Black Hawks	262
1978-79	Steve Short, Kansas City Red Wings	216
1979-80	Brad Gassoff, Dallas Black Hawks	353
1980-81	Tim Hunter, Birmingham Bulls	236
1981-82	Archie Henderson, Nashville	320
1982-83	Mike Seide, Tulsa	337
1983-84	Steve Martinson, Tulsa	240

Bob Gassoff Trophy
(Most Improved Defenseman)

1977-78— Mike Hordy, Fort Worth
1978-79— Jeff Bandura, Dallas
1979-80— Gord Wappel, Birmingham
1980-81— Dave Feamster, Dallas
1981-82— Dan Poulin, Nashville
1982-83— Gord Dineen, Indianapolis
1983-84— Grant Ledyard, Tulsa

Jake Milford Trophy
Coach-of-the-Year Award

1968-69—John McLellan, Tulsa Oilers
1969-70—Marcel Pronovost, Tulsa Oilers
1970-71—Fred Shero, Omaha Knights
1971-72—Bobby Kromm, Dallas Black Hawks
1972-73—Fred Creighton, Omaha Knights
1973-74—Gerry Moore, Oklahoma City Blazers
1974-75—Jack Evans, Salt Lake City Golden Eagles
1975-76—Orland Kurtenbach, Tulsa Oilers
1976-77—John Choyce, Fort Worth Texans
1977-78—Billy MacMillan, Fort Worth Texans
1978-79—Jack Evans, Salt Lake City Golden Eagles and John Muckler, Dallas Black Hawks (tie)
1979-80—Jack Evans, Salt Lake City
1980-81—Dan Belisle, Dallas
1981-82—Fred Creighton, Indianapolis
1982-83—Fred Creighton, Indianapolis
1983-84—Tom Webster, Tulsa

International Hockey League
(Organized, December 21, 1945)

Commissioner—Bud Poile
Suite 538
8900 Key Stone Crossing
Indianapolis, Ind.
(317) 848-9950

Fred Blackburn—Referee-in-Chief
Sam Sisco—Supervisor of Officials

Flint Generals
President—Eugene Chardoul, M.D.
Treasurer—Jack Magee
General Manager/Coach—Dennis Desrosiers
Director of Public Relations—Bob Sack
Director of Communications—Doug Pettit
Home Ice—I.M.A. Sports Arena (4,021)
Address—3501 Lapeer Road,
 Flint, Mich. 48503
Affiliations—Montreal Canadiens and Buffalo Sabres
Phone—(313) 744-0072

Fort Wayne Komets
Chairman of the Board—Kenneth D. Ullyot
President/Majority Owner—Colin Lister
General Manager and Coach—Ron Ullyot
Director of Public Relations, Sales and Marketing—
 Jerry Clark
Home Ice—Allen County Memorial (8,022)
Address—4000 Parnell Ave.,
 Fort Wayne, Ind. 46805
Affiliations—Washington Capitals, Los Angeles Kings,
 New Jersey Devils and Winnipeg Jets
 and Vancouver Canucks
Phone—(219) 484-2581

Indianapolis Checkers
Owner—Al Sabill
General Manager—Fred Creighton
Coach—Fred Creighton
Media Relations—Rick Burns
Home Ice—Skate Fair Coliseum (8,364)
Address—1202 E. 38th Street
 Indianapolis, Ind. 46205
Affiliations—New York Islanders, Minnesota North
 Stars and Boston Bruins
Phone—(317) 545-2326

Kalamazoo Wings
Chairman of the Board—Ted Parfet
President—Jim Gilmore, Jr.
Director—Martha G. Parfet
Gen. Manager/Coach—Bill Inglis
Director of Public Relations—Stephen Doherty
Director of Communications—Terry Ficorelli
Home Ice—Wings Stadium (5,121)
Address—3620 Van Rick Dr.,
 Kalamazoo, Mich. 49002
Affiliations—Detroit Red Wings and Philadelphia
 Flyers
Phone—(616) 349-9772

Milwaukee Admirals
Owner/President—Lloyd Pettit and Jane B. Pettit
Governor/Legal Counsel—Joseph E. Tierney Jr.
Exec. V.P.—Phil Wittliff
Coach—Cliff Koroll
Director of Public Relations and Marketing—Mike
 Wojciechowski
Home Ice—Milwaukee Arena (8,946)
Address—710 N. Plankington, Suite 310,
 Milwaukee, Wis. 53203
Affiliation—Chicago Black Hawks
Phone—(414) 278-7711

Muskegon Pro Hockey Club
Governor—I. John Snider II
Owner/General Manager—Larry Gordon
Coach—To be announced
Public Relations Dir.—Bob Heethuis
Marketing Dir.—Leo Hunstiger
Home Ice—L. C. Walker Sports Arena (5,061)
Address—470 W. Western Ave.
 Muskegon, Mich. 49440
Affiliation—To be announced
Phone—(616) 726-5058

Peoria Rivermen
Governor—Harold Hansen
Coach/General Manager—Pat Kelly
Director of Public Relations, Marketing and Sales—
 Don Clasen
Home Ice—Peoria Civic Center—(9,000)
Address—P.O. Box 3581, 201 S. W.
 Jefferson, Peoria, Ill. 61614
Affiliation—St. Louis Blues
Phone—(309) 673-8900

Salt Lake City Golden Eagles
Owner/General Manager—Art Teece
Owners—Bill Acord, Dean Acord
Asst. G.M./Public Relations Dir.—Chuck Schell
Coach—Tom Webster
Home Ice—The Salt Palace (10,594)
Address—100 S.W. Temple
 Salt Lake City, Utah 84101
Affiliations—Hartford Whalers, New York Rangers
 and Calgary Flames
Phone—(801) 521-6120

Toledo Goaldiggers
Managing Partner/G.M.—Jerry Francis
Coach—To be announced
Media Information and Communications—Mike
 Miller
Sale Manager—Jim Donnelly
Director of Marketing and Public Relations—To be
 announced
Home Ice—Sports Arena (5,286)
Address—One Main Street,
 Toledo, O. 43605
Affiliation—Los Angeles Kings
Phone—(419) 698-1800

1983-84 Final IHL Standings

	G.	W.	L.	T.	Pts.	GF.	GA.
Fort Wayne	82	52	23	7	112	371	273
Milwaukee	82	46	30	6	101	403	335
Flint	82	41	32	9	93	375	319
Toledo	82	41	36	5	91	326	318
Kalamazoo	82	37	38	7	83	333	316
Peoria	82	29	48	5	66	298	392
Muskegon	82	19	58	5	46	282	435

IHL teams were awarded one point for going into an overtime, and a second point if they won the overtime game.

Top 20 Scorers for the Leo P. Lamoureux Memorial Trophy

	Games	G.	A.	Pts.	Pen.
1. Wally Schreiber, Fort Wayne	82	47	66	*113	44
2. Doug Rigler, Fort Wayne	75	42	62	104	30
Dale Yakiwchuk, Milwaukee	74	35	*69	104	67
4. Bernie Gallant, Flint	81	50	53	103	22
Jeff Pyle, Flint	80	44	59	103	20
6. Daniel LeCours, Milwaukee	70	48	49	97	28
7. Scott Gruhl, Muskegon	56	40	56	96	49
Fred Berry, Milwaukee	82	38	58	96	50
9. Christian Tanguay, Milwaukee	74	44	50	94	23
Ron Leef, Fort Wayne	65	37	57	94	57
Rob Davies, Kalamazoo	69	31	63	94	52
12. Rob Motz, Fort Wayne	81	*54	35	89	43
13. John Flesch, Milwaukee	81	43	44	87	27
Neil Meadmore, Kalamazoo	82	39	48	67	267
15. Jim Bissett, Toledo	79	37	49	86	73
Pete Horachek, Flint	82	34	52	86	34
17. Yves Preston, Milwaukee	82	36	49	85	37
18. Kevin Beaton, Toledo	75	29	55	84	49
19. Robbie Laird, Fort Wayne	77	37	46	83	137
20. Ian Macinnis, Peoria	79	38	44	82	31
Grant Rezansoff, Peoria	82	36	46	82	11
Brent Jarrett, Kalamazoo	70	18	64	82	84

Flint Generals

	Games	G.	A.	Pts.	Pen.
Bernie Gallant	81	50	53	103	22
Jeff Pyle	80	44	59	103	20
Pete Horachek	82	34	52	86	34
Lawrie Nisker	57	28	44	72	78
Steve Stockman	49	43	27	70	14
Mel Hewitt, Peoria	24	6	6	12	80
Flint	45	18	34	52	86
Totals	69	24	40	64	166
Pierre Giroux	56	24	37	61	274
Mike Klassen	79	20	38	58	*321
Tony Fiore	38	24	26	50	24
Greg Lynott	79	11	36	47	147
Pierre Thibault	79	7	37	44	44
Wade Dawson, Peoria	29	2	5	7	53
Flint	51	9	26	35	105
Totals	80	11	31	42	158
Mike Martin	82	10	31	41	192
Mike Brown, Kalamazoo	12	0	1	1	21
Flint	63	9	29	38	176
Totals	75	9	30	39	197
George Kotsopoulos	24	3	19	22	34
Dave Nichols	12	12	9	21	57
Terry McDougall	23	4	13	17	8
Tom Thomson	32	4	4	8	10

	Games	G.	A.	Pts.	Pen.
Bill Dowd, Toledo	21	1	3	4	8
Flint	7	1	1	2	4
Totals	28	2	4	6	12
Larry Power	14	1	5	6	2
Rick Knickle (Goalie)	60	0	6	6	16
Jeff Eatough	5	4	1	5	6
Chris Delabbio	9	1	2	3	7
Lance Breault	14	0	3	3	71
John Hawkins	2	0	1	1	0
Steve Haniger	1	0	0	0	0
Dan St. Jean	1	0	0	0	2
Dave Westner	1	0	0	0	0
Don Delabbio	2	0	0	0	0
Bill Maguire	3	0	0	0	0
Dan Burrows (Goalie)	5	0	0	0	0
Rick Wilson (Goalie)	23	0	0	0	2

Fort Wayne Komets

	Games	G.	A.	Pts.	Pen.
Wally Schreiber	82	47	66	*113	44
Doug Rigler	75	42	62	104	30
Ron Leef	65	37	57	94	57
Rob Motz	81	*54	35	89	43
Robbie Laird	77	37	46	83	137
Dale Baldwin	80	20	54	74	209

	Games	G.	A.	Pts.	Pen.
Vic Morin	80	15	49	64	94
Bob Attwell	70	25	35	60	22
Steve Salvucci	77	31	27	58	271
Mike Boland	81	8	49	57	161
Bill Nichols	74	14	31	45	87
John Hilworth	75	10	20	30	124
Craig Steensen	57	3	19	22	58
Wayne Bishop	79	3	19	22	130
Bob Hehir	6	4	1	5	0
Kim Collins	7	1	2	3	2
Bill McNaught	7	2	0	2	0
John Baldassari	10	1	1	2	14
Eric Calder	3	0	2	2	0
Craig Hurley	13	0	2	2	12
Darren Jensen (Goalie)	56	0	2	2	6
Paul Lohnes	4	0	1	1	2
Dan Sanscartier (Goalie)	19	0	1	1	2
Alain Bouchard	1	0	0	0	2
Bob O'Connor (Goalie)	1	0	0	0	0
Bill Oleschuk (Goalie)	1	0	0	0	0
Dan Lempe	4	0	0	0	2

Kalamazoo Wings

	Games	G.	A.	Pts.	Pen.
Rob Davies	69	31	63	94	52
Neil Meadmore	82	39	48	87	267
Brent Jarrett	70	18	64	82	84
Jim MacRae	71	40	37	77	25
Steve Banonis	81	42	31	73	49
Kevin Schamehorn	76	37	31	68	154
Ray Markham, Flint	12	2	3	5	39
Kalamazoo	69	23	28	51	172
Totals	81	25	31	56	211
Scott McGeowen	64	14	40	54	32
Jeff Johnston	82	7	36	43	52
Lee MacKenzie	79	23	18	41	36
Mike Corrigan	68	17	23	40	128
Mike Clarke, F. Wayne	19	5	8	13	10
Kalamazoo	39	11	15	26	20
Totals	58	16	23	39	30
Floyd LaHache	69	8	24	32	165
Dan Poliziani, F. Wayne	11	4	6	10	2
Kalamazoo	25	9	6	15	2
Totals	36	13	12	25	4
John Baby	46	2	14	16	35
Rick Dorman, Muskegon	12	3	3	6	15
Milwaukee	17	0	7	7	20
Kalamazoo	10	0	1	1	33
Totals	39	3	11	14	68
Mike O'Connor	39	0	12	12	67
Bruce Howes	26	2	9	11	30
Alf Beasley	12	3	2	5	13
Georges Gagnon (G.)	67	0	5	5	27
John Capel	8	2	2	4	0
Bill MacNaught	12	0	3	3	0
D. Ross, F. Wayne (G.)	7	0	0	0	6
Kalamazoo (G.)	10	0	2	2	14
Totals	17	0	2	2	20
Bernie Saunders	1	0	0	0	0
Glen Johannesen	3	0	0	0	0
George Harrison	4	0	0	0	4
Brian McDavid	6	0	0	0	15
Joe Paniccia	6	0	0	0	2
Mark LaForest (Goalie)	13	0	0	0	11

Milwaukee Admirals

	Games	G.	A.	Pts.	Pen.
Dale Yakiwchuk	74	35	*69	104	67
Daniel LeCours	70	48	49	97	28
Fred Berry	82	38	58	96	50
Christian Tanguay	74	44	50	94	23
John Flesch	81	43	44	87	27
Yves Preston	82	36	49	85	37
Gord Stafford	79	36	45	81	35
Kevin Willison	82	21	52	73	73
Bill McCreary	81	28	35	63	44
Jay McFarlane	80	16	44	60	53
Bruce McKay	82	10	41	51	146
Cal Roadhouse	59	19	24	43	45
Derek Davis	62	11	27	38	287
Barry Scully, Muskegon	19	11	6	17	2
Fort Wayne	18	8	7	15	8
Milwaukee	4	2	1	3	0
Totals	41	21	14	35	10
Jeff Hiltz	53	4	24	28	37
Richard Turmel	43	2	14	16	50
Mike Waghorne, Peoria	13	2	2	4	15
Milwaukee	4	2	1	3	0
Totals	17	4	3	7	15
Paul Miller	3	1	3	4	2
Robbie Moore (Goalie)	49	0	4	4	22
Doug Derkson	9	1	2	3	6
Claude Julien	5	0	3	3	2
Daryl Henry	4	1	1	2	0
Jim Bannatyne	7	0	1	1	0
Sheldon Currie	1	0	0	0	0
Randy Wilson (Goalie)	2	0	0	0	0
Alex Belcourt, Muskegon	2	0	0	0	0
Milwaukee	2	0	0	0	2
Totals	4	0	0	0	2
Wendell Young (Goalie)	6	0	0	0	0
R. McNamara, Peo. (G.)	2	0	0	0	2
Milwaukee (Goalie)	5	0	0	0	0
Totals	7	0	0	0	2
Michel Dufour (Goalie)	21	0	0	0	4

Muskegon Mohawks

	Games	G.	A.	Pts.	Pen.
Scott Gruhl	56	40	56	96	49
Mike Krensing, Milw.	12	3	2	5	0
Muskegon	63	46	28	74	24
Totals	75	49	30	79	24
Kevin Reeves	82	26	41	67	8
Neil Hawryliw	66	25	37	62	36
Paul Fulcher	80	24	37	61	112
Doug Derkson	67	21	38	59	53
Norm LeFrancois	65	16	21	37	108
Brian Rorabeck, Kal.	35	5	20	25	10
Muskegon	7	4	5	9	4
Totals	42	9	25	34	14
Brent Shaw	51	17	16	33	52
Bruce McDonough	41	14	17	31	0
Erle Switzer	47	2	20	22	96
Tony Gilliard	65	5	16	21	174
Jim Turner	60	2	19	21	67
Marty Ruff, Toledo	2	0	1	1	0
Muskegon	44	3	15	18	44
Totals	46	3	16	19	44
Mike Rusin	73	3	14	17	202
Roger Lemelin	57	3	13	16	65
Brian Lundberg	34	3	12	15	46

	Games	G.	A.	Pts	Pen.
Marc Magnan	19	3	10	13	30
Leigh Verstraete	19	5	5	10	123
Jim Egerton	12	2	8	10	15
Joe Ward	9	3	2	5	2
Ed Cooper	5	1	3	4	0
Bob Parent (Goalie)	35	0	2	2	2
Paul Miller	4	0	1	1	0
Norm McCauley	11	0	1	1	29
Keith Wright	2	0	0	0	0
Nick Ricci (Goalie)	13	0	0	0	0
Rick LaFerriere (Goalie)	16	0	0	0	2
Bruce Dowie (Goalie)	25	0	0	0	19

	Games	G.	A.	Pts	Pen.
Scott Lauder	5	0	1	1	2
Gilles Heroux (Goalie)	13	0	1	1	0
Jeff Lastiwka (Goalie)	39	0	1	1	4
Tim Mouser (Goalie)	1	0	0	0	0
Troy Nelson	1	0	0	0	0
Todd Sheppard	1	0	0	0	0
Tony Curtale	2	0	0	0	2
Mark Evans (Goalie)	2	0	0	0	0
Terry Jensen	2	0	0	0	0
Kevin Knight	2	0	0	0	2

Peoria Prancers

	Games	G.	A.	Pts	Pen.
Ian MacInnis	79	38	44	82	31
Grant Rezanoff	82	36	46	82	11
Mike Prestidge	68	40	40	80	4
Brad Kempthorne	80	15	47	62	47
Brian Shaw	54	27	27	54	49
Steve Harrison	82	11	40	51	52
Keith Knight	65	28	15	43	18
Glenn Oliver	54	12	30	42	19
Marc Roy	45	19	22	41	144
Jerry August	71	12	22	34	56
Ron Megan	67	7	26	33	61
Doug Poirier, Flint	18	3	4	7	41
Peoria	42	3	18	21	66
Totals	60	6	22	28	107
Don Keller, Flint	29	6	8	14	93
Peoria	13	4	7	11	56
Totals	42	10	15	25	149
Randy Turnbull	73	3	18	21	213
Marcel Frere	34	5	11	16	97
Andre Cote, Milwaukee	13	2	7	9	2
Peoria	11	2	5	7	2
Totals	24	4	12	16	4
Clint Fehr, Flint	21	3	5	8	16
Peoria	7	1	7	8	2
Totals	28	4	12	16	18
Don Walker	23	6	6	12	7
Alan Graves, Milwaukee	3	0	0	0	2
Peoria	28	6	4	10	75
Totals	31	6	4	10	77
Ed Kurpieski	23	3	5	8	0
Bob Fleming	21	2	6	8	36
John Multan	6	3	1	4	2
Joe Netti	4	1	2	3	0
George White	7	2	0	2	7
Tom Ward	4	1	1	2	0
Frank Loconsole	2	0	2	2	0
Rich Sirois, Milw. (G.)	4	0	0	0	2
Peoria (Goalie)	34	0	2	2	14
Totals	38	0	2	2	16
Peter Crawford	2	1	0	1	0
Kent Jackson	2	0	1	1	2

Toledo Goaldiggers

	Games	G.	A.	Pts	Pen.
Jim Bissett	79	37	49	86	73
Kevin Beaton	75	29	55	84	49
Dave Falkenberg	82	39	39	78	122
Bill Joyce	63	26	35	61	97
Kevin Cameron	63	33	23	56	35
Rick Hendricks	80	13	42	55	154
Rob Flockhart	54	33	20	53	33
Brian Tutt	82	7	44	51	79
Mark Botell	78	16	27	43	164
Brian Kinsella	41	18	19	37	27
Dave Hanson	68	11	26	37	120
Blake Stephen	62	14	18	32	175
Mike Greeder	75	10	22	32	250
Mike Shea	75	5	25	30	156
Richard Zemlak	45	8	19	27	101
Jali Walhsten	31	11	12	23	7
Tim Salmon	10	5	5	10	2
Kevin Conway	10	3	7	10	5
Paul Tantardini	11	1	6	7	52
William Terry	3	2	2	4	4
Neal Coulter	5	1	3	4	0
Lorne Molleken (Goalie)	56	0	4	4	22
Scott McLellan	5	1	2	3	0
Gordie Brooks	5	0	3	3	0
Mike Hartman	3	1	1	2	0
Ken Latta	3	1	0	1	6
Bernie Chiverelli	1	0	1	1	0
Dave Dziedzic	2	0	1	1	5
T. Lumbard, Peo. (G.)	1	0	0	0	0
Toledo (Goalie)	11	0	1	1	2
Totals	12	0	1	1	2
Paul Mercier	1	0	0	0	5
Jim Mollard	1	0	0	0	0
Paul Adey	2	0	0	0	0
Jock Callander	2	0	0	0	0
Larry Ell	2	0	0	0	2
John Giftopoulous	2	0	0	0	2
Jay Miller	2	0	0	0	4
Chris Trinceri (Goalie)	2	0	0	0	0
Jim Cunningham	3	0	0	0	4
Scott Varga	3	0	0	0	0
Terry Tait	5	0	0	0	2
Paul Billing (Goalie)	15	0	0	0	2

Individual Department Leaders

Goals	Rob Motz, Fort Wayne—	54
Assists	Dale Yakiwchuk, Milwaukee—	69
Points	Wally Schreiber, Fort Wayne—	113
Penalty Minutes	Mike Klassen, Flint—	321
Goaltender's Average (25 games)	Darren Jensen, Fort Wayne—	2.92
Shutouts	Darren Jensen, Fort Wayne—	4

Individual IHL Goaltending

	Games	Mins.	Goals	SO.	Avg.
Darren Jensen, Fort Wayne	56	3325	162(1)	*4	*2.92
Wendell Young, Milwaukee	6	339	17	0	3.01
Rick Knickle, Flint	60	3518	203(2)	3	3.46
Georges Gagnon, Kalamazoo	*67	*3889	*225(6)	1	3.47
Lorne Molleken, Toledo	56	3345	196(3)	1	3.52
Dan Sanscartier, Fort Wayne	19	1101	67(2)	1	3.65
Todd Lumbard, Peoria	1	60	7	0	7.00
Toledo	11	664	38(1)	0	3.43
Totals	12	724	45(1)	0	3.73
Michel Dufour, Milwaukee	21	1255	79	0	3.78
Mark LaForest, Kalamazoo	13	718	48	1	4.01
Robbie Moore, Milwaukee	49	2788	195(3)	0	4.20
Jeff Lastiwka, Peoria	39	2110	154(2)	1	4.38
Gilles Heroux, Peoria	13	698	51	0	4.38
Bob McNamara, Peoria	2	43	6	0	8.37
Milwaukee	5	230	14	0	3.65
Totals	7	273	20	0	4.40
Bruce Dowie, Muskegon	25	1306	100	2	4.59
Rick Wilson, Flint	23	1218	94(1)	0	4.63
Nick Ricci, Muskegon	13	764	59(5)	0	4.63
Rich Sirois, Milwaukee	4	239	13(1)	1	3.26
Peoria	34	1932	155(5)	0	4.81
Totals	38	2171	168(6)	1	4.64
Dan Burrows, Flint	5	238	19	0	4.79
Paul Billing, Toledo	15	823	68(1)	0	4.96
Dave Ross, Fort Wayne	7	423	27(1)	0	3.83
Kalamazoo	10	348	37	0	6.38
Totals	17	771	64(1)	0	4.98
Bob Parent, Muskegon	35	2063	185(1)	0	5.38
Chris Trinceri, Toledo	2	120	11	0	5.50
Mark Evans, Peoria	2	90	9	0	6.00
Bob O'Connor, Fort Wayne	1	60	6	0	6.00
Rick LaFerriere, Muskegon	16	817	83(2)	0	6.10
Tim Mouser, Peoria	1	27	3	0	6.67
Bill Oleschuk, Fort Wayne	1	60	7	0	7.00
Randy Wilson, Milwaukee	2	104	13	0	7.50

( )—Empty Net Goals. Do not count against a Goaltender's average.

1983-84 Turner Cup Playoffs

SERIES "A"
(Best-of-three series)

	W.	L.	Pts.	GF.	GA.
Toledo	2	1	4	14	7
Kalamazoo	1	2	2	7	14

(Toledo wins series, 2 games to 1)

SERIES "B"
(Best-of-seven series)

	W.	L.	Pts.	GF.	GA.
Flint	4	0	8	17	11
Milwaukee	0	4	0	11	17

(Flint wins series, 4 games to 0)

SERIES "C"
(Best-of-seven series)

	W.	L.	Pts.	GF.	GA.
Toledo	4	2	8	21	20
Ft. Wayne	2	4	4	20	21

(Toledo wins series, 4 games to 2)

SERIES "D"
(Best-of-seven series)

	W.	L.	Pts.	GF.	GA.
Flint	4	0	8	22	13
Toledo	0	4	0	13	22

(Flint wins 1984 Turner Cup Playoffs, 4 games to 0)

Top Ten Playoff Scorers

	Games	G.	A.	Pts.	Pen.
1. Jeff Pyle, Flint	8	*7	8	*15	11
Lawrie Nisker, Flint	8	5	*10	*15	37
Kevin Conway, Toledo	13	5	*10	*15	12
Jim Bissett, Toledo	13	5	*10	*15	12
5. Tim Salmon, Toledo	13	6	6	12	8
Rick Hendricks, Toledo	13	4	8	12	29
7. Dave Falkenberg, Toledo	13	4	7	11	18
8. Bernie Gallant, Flint	8	3	7	10	7
9. Bill Joyce, Toledo	12	4	5	9	26
Mike Shea, Toledo	13	2	7	9	32

Flint Generals
(Won 1984 IHL Turner Cup Playoffs)

	Games	G.	A.	Pts.	Pen.
Jeff Pyle	8	*7	8	*15	11
Lawrie Nisker	8	5	*10	*15	37
Bernie Gallant	8	3	7	10	7
Mel Hewitt	8	4	4	8	12
Mike Brown	8	1	6	7	16
Mike Klassen	8	4	2	6	19
Dave Nichols	8	4	2	6	15
Steve Stockman	8	4	2	6	6
George Kotsopoulos	8	2	4	6	8
Peter Horachek	8	2	3	5	12
Pierre Thibault	8	2	2	4	8
Wade Dawson	8	0	4	4	10
Greg Lynott	8	0	4	4	12
Mike Martin	8	1	2	3	6
Rick Knickle (Goalie)	8	0	1	1	2

Fort Wayne Komets
(Lost semifinals to Toledo, 4-2)

	Games	G.	A.	Pts.	Pen.
Doug Rigler	5	3	5	8	4
Vic Morin	6	4	3	7	2
Ron Leef	6	2	5	7	18
Wally Schreiber	6	3	3	6	6
Steve Salvucci	6	2	4	6	24
Rob Motz	6	4	0	4	13
Dale Baldwin	5	0	3	3	36
Mike Boland	6	0	3	3	35
Craig Steensen	6	0	3	3	4
Bob Attwell	6	1	1	2	0
Bill Nichols	4	1	0	1	6
Robbie Laird	4	0	1	1	17
Wayne Bishop	6	0	1	1	8
Paul Adey	3	0	0	0	0
John Hilworth	6	0	0	0	11
Darren Jensen (Goalie)	6	0	0	0	0

Kalamazoo Wings
(Lost quarterfinals to Toledo, 2-1)

	Games	G.	A.	Pts.	Pen.
Mike Clarke	3	2	1	3	2
Ray Markham	3	1	2	3	9
Steve Banonis	3	1	1	2	0
Jeff Johnston	3	1	1	2	0
Scott McGeown	3	1	1	2	6
Kevin Schamehorn	3	0	2	2	9

	Games	G.	A.	Pts.	Pen.
Jim MacRae	3	1	0	1	2
Brent Jarrett	3	0	1	1	6
John Baby	3	0	0	0	4
Mike Corrigan	3	0	0	0	14
G. Gagnon (Goalie)	3	0	0	0	0
Floyd LaHache	3	0	0	0	20
Lee MacKenzie	3	0	0	0	2
Neil Meadmore	3	0	0	0	26
Mike O'Connor	3	0	0	0	0

Milwaukee Admirals
(Lost semifinals to Flint, 4-0)

	Games	G.	A.	Pts.	Pen.
Fred Berry	4	3	1	4	2
Dale Yakiwchuk	4	2	2	4	12
Cal Roadhouse	4	2	1	3	0
Derek Davis	4	1	1	2	13
Daniel LeCours	4	1	1	2	0
Jay McFarlane	4	1	1	2	2
Gord Stafford	4	1	1	2	2
John Flesch	4	0	2	2	0
Bill McCreary	4	0	2	2	2
Bruce McKay	4	0	2	2	0
Yves Preston	4	0	2	2	0
Christian Tanguay	4	0	2	2	0
Kevin Willison	4	0	2	2	0
Jeff Lastiwka (Goalie)	1	0	0	0	0
Richard Turmel	3	0	0	0	5
Robbie Moore (Goalie)	4	0	0	0	10

Toledo Goaldiggers
(Lost finals to Flint, 4-0)

	Games	G.	A.	Pts.	Pen.
Jim Bissett	13	5	*10	*15	12
Kevin Conway	13	5	*10	*15	12
Tim Salmon	13	6	6	12	8
Rick Hendricks	13	4	8	12	29
Dave Falkenberg	13	4	7	11	18
Bill Joyce	12	4	5	9	26
Mike Shea	13	2	7	9	32
Kevin Beaton	13	5	3	8	17
Kevin Cameron	9	4	4	8	9
Mike Greeder	13	4	3	7	*85
Blake Stephen	11	1	6	7	63
Brian Tutt	13	0	6	6	16
Dave Hanson	9	1	3	4	33
Mark Botell	9	2	1	3	6
Jali Walhsten	2	1	1	2	0
Lorne Molleken (Goalie)	13	0	0	0	4

Complete Turner Cup Goaltending

	Games	Mins.	Goals	SO.	Avg.
Rick Knickle, Flint	8	480	24	0	*3.00
Darren Jensen, Fort Wayne	6	358	21	0	3.52
Lorne Molleken, Toledo	13	778	47(2)	*1	3.62
Robbie Moore, Milwaukee	4	206	13	0	3.79
Georges Gagnon, Kalamazoo	3	180	14	0	4.67
Jeff Lastiwka, Milwaukee	1	35	4	0	6.86

( )—Empty Net Goals. Do not count against a Goaltender's average.

Individual Department Leaders

Goals	Jeff Pyle, Flint—	7
Assists	Jim Bissett, Toledo—	10
	Kevin Conway, Toledo—	10
	Lawrie Nisker, Flint—	10
Points	Jeff Pyle, Flint—	15
	Lawrie Nisker, Flint—	15
	Kevin Conway, Toledo—	15
	Jim Bissett, Toledo—	15
Penalty Minutes	Mike Greeder, Toledo—	85
Goaltender's Average	Rick Knickle, Flint—	3.00
Shutouts	Lorne Molleken, Toledo—	1

★★★★★★★★★★★★★★★★★★★★★★★★★

1983-84 IHL All-Stars

First Team	Position	Second Team
Darren Jensen, Fort Wayne	Goal	Rick Knickle, Flint
Kevin Willison, Milwaukee	Defense	Brian Tutt, Toledo
Vic Morin, Fort Wayne	Defense	Mike Greeder, Toledo
Bernie Gallant, Flint	Center	Rob Davies, Kalamazoo
Scott Gruhl, Muskegon	Left Wing	Rob Motz, Fort Wayne
Wally Schreiber, Fort Wayne	Right Wing	Ian MacInnis, Peoria
		Christian Tanguay, Milwaukee

1983-84 IHL Trophy Winners

James Gatschene Memorial Trophy (Most Valuable Player)	Darren Jensen, Fort Wayne
Leo P. Lamoureux Trophy (Leading Scorer)	Wally Schreiber, Fort Wayne
James Norris Memorial Trophy (Top Goalie)	Darren Jensen, Fort Wayne
Governors Trophy (Top defenseman)	Kevin Willison, Milwaukee
Garry F. Longman Memorial Trophy (Top rookie)	Darren Jensen, Fort Wayne
Ken McKenzie Trophy (Top U.S.-Born rookie)	Mike Krensing, Muskegon
Coach of the Year	Phil Witliff, Milwaukee

★★★★★★★★★★★★★★★★★★★★★★★★★

1983-84 Final Atlantic Coast Hockey League Standings

	G.	W.	L.	T.	Pts.	GF.	GA.
Carolina Thunderbirds	72	43	24	5	92	381	300
Erie Golden Blades	72	42	26	4	91	377	310
Virginia Lancers	73	34	37	2	71	384	400
Mohawk Valley Stars	74	28	39	7	68	322	370
Pinebridge Bucks	72	25	47	0	52	329	422
*Birmingham Bulls	3	2	1	0	4	17	8

*Birmingham ceased operations after three games.
ACHL teams were awarded one point for going into an overtime, and a second point if they won the overtime game.

Final Scoring

	Games	G.	A.	Pts.	Pen.
Rob Clavette, Pinebridge/Erie	72	53	*78	*131	78
Kim Elliott, Carolina	71	48	76	124	92
Paul O'Neill, Virginia/Birmingham	70	51	72	123	8
Michel Cote, Erie	63	54	67	121	150
Stan Gulutzan, Virginia	73	41	75	116	19
Dave Lair, Mohawk Valley	73	60	54	114	21
Paul Mancini, Erie	60	56	57	113	18
Ron Carter, Virginia	62	51	59	110	20
Lee Blossom, Virginia	69	*61	47	108	56
Dave MacQueen, Mohawk Valley	63	54	54	108	22
Ben LaPorte, Carolina	52	54	48	102	86
Brian Carroll, Carolina	68	37	65	102	174
Ernie Boutin, Erie/Birmingham	66	34	63	97	91
Jim Cowell, Erie	70	30	61	91	126
Dave Burke, Pinebridge	70	34	55	89	76
Peter Dunkley, Carolina	72	29	60	89	39
Dave Herbst, Erie	50	39	49	88	187
Rich Suwek, Mohawk Valley	68	40	47	87	69
Ken Latta, Pinebridge	60	43	43	86	71
Steve Lyons, Virginia/Mohawk Valley	72	34	50	84	32
Larry Ell, Mohawk Valley	69	19	59	78	26
Todd Scott, Carolina/Pinebridge	63	29	36	75	26
Mike Brisebois, Pinebridge/Carolina	72	40	33	73	45
Bob Hehir, Virginia	52	30	43	73	47
John Liprando, Virginia	73	28	44	72	37
John Giftopolous, Virginia/Birmingham	67	18	53	71	74
Jerry Ingram, Carolina	48	17	53	70	131
Kelly Barnet, Virginia	63	14	56	70	68
Dave Dziedzic, P.B./Caro./Erie/Birm.	65	22	46	68	173
Kim Collins, Pinebridge	58	32	35	67	38
Dick Popeil, Erie	72	18	49	67	127
Larry Power, Mohawk Valley	57	28	36	64	46
John Tortorella, Virginia/Erie	64	25	37	62	77
Lynn Jorgenson, Carolina	51	20	40	60	150
Tony Circelli, Virginia/Birmingham	67	12	48	60	179
Brian Gustafson, Carolina/Mohawk Valley	66	22	33	55	*354
Mark Salvucci, Mohawk Valley	68	24	29	53	235
Kelly Rissling, Pinebridge	57	20	31	51	101
Jay Miller, Mohawk Valley	48	15	36	51	167
Randy Irving, Carolina	55	15	35	50	163
Bill Smith, Pinebridge	43	16	32	48	21
Larry Mollard, Pinebridge	60	10	38	48	121
Pat Ethier, Carolina	68	19	27	46	67
Jay Fraser, Carolina	29	16	29	45	85
Scott Higgins, P.B./Caro./Vir./M.V./Birm.	64	13	32	45	98
Sylvain Cote, Erie	32	14	29	43	252
Robert Dore, Carolina	68	9	34	43	245
Barry Tabobondung, Erie	70	6	37	43	57
Michel Lanouette, Carolina	30	19	20	39	76
Ron Hansis, Erie	37	17	22	39	44
Ed Smith, Mohawk Valley	23	16	23	39	6

	Games	G.	A.	Pts.	Pen.
Bruce Aikens, Pinebridge	40	22	16	38	33
Wayne Van Dorp, Erie	45	19	18	37	202
Frank Perkins, Pinebridge	26	10	27	37	131
Greg Squires, Carolina	37	15	31	36	25
Dave Watson, Carolina	29	17	16	33	56
Alan Bouchard, Virginia	15	12	20	32	26
Darren Yankovsky, Carolina/Erie/Pinebridge	47	7	25	32	87
Bob Fleming, Pinebridge	27	12	16	28	39
Andre Chartrain, Erie	20	9	19	28	16
Bill Maguire, Mohawk Valley	56	7	18	25	45
Joe Bilodeau, Mohawk Valley	48	4	21	25	40
Bruce Grieg, M.V./Caro./Vir./P.B.	37	12	12	24	206
Dave Miles, Mohawk Valley	23	12	11	23	16
Nelson Burton, Erie	65	10	12	22	156
Dwayne Venema, Erie/Birmingham	39	7	15	22	73
Larry Meads, Virginia/Carolina	33	4	18	22	72
Norm Stefan, Pinebridge	24	10	11	21	10
Rick Harris, Pinebridge	44	4	17	21	56
Tom Madson, Pinebridge/Carolina	55	2	19	21	48
Jeff Wylie, Pinebridge	17	9	10	19	15
Bo Tucker, Mohawk Valley	45	2	16	18	85
Jim Beaton, Mohawk Valley	65	2	16	18	277
Trent Graham, Erie/Virginia	67	4	13	17	113
Wayne Cameron, Virginia	15	5	10	15	6
Joe Panick, Pinebridge	13	9	4	13	12
Pierre Legace, Erie	11	5	7	12	2
Keith Wright, Pinebridge/Mohawk Valley	16	2	10	12	21
Dan Barber, Pinebridge	16	3	8	11	29
Tony Trase, Mohawk Valley	17	2	9	11	8
Bob O'Brien, Erie	8	5	5	10	25
Paul Mercier, Erie	19	3	7	10	8
Ari Vudri, Virginia	14	2	8	10	2
Craig Steenson, Virginia/Pinebridge	15	2	8	10	17
Sean Coady, Mohawk Valley	23	1	9	10	46
Dick Barber, Pinebridge	11	5	4	9	4
Luc Bachand, Virginia	10	2	7	9	16
John Higgins, Carolina	11	2	7	9	10
Alf Beasley, Erie	13	1	8	9	8
Steve Arnold, Virginia/Birmingham	6	5	3	8	11
Dar Switzer, Carolina/Birmingham	9	4	4	8	12
Mark Pettygrove, Pinebridge	23	0	8	8	8
Keith Hosken, Mohawk Valley	19	3	4	7	57
Bob Smith, Virginia	19	3	4	7	36
Mark Fidler, Pinebridge	6	3	3	6	5
Brent Sapergla, Erie	4	2	4	6	0
Chris Tomlin, Pinebridge	7	2	4	6	0
Darrell Ulrich, Pinebridge	16	2	4	6	10
Glen Abrahamson, Pinebridge	16	1	5	6	41
Pierre Hamel, Carolina (Goalie)	38	0	6	6	58
Darrell May, Erie (Goalie)	43	0	6	6	38
Greg McPhee, Virginia	8	2	3	5	7
Steve Heittola, Pinebridge (Goalie)	53	0	5	5	14
Paul Skidmore, Carolina (Goalie)	29	0	5	5	0
Cam Botting, Erie	13	2	2	4	22
Tom Mullen, Virginia	4	2	2	4	0
Tim Jacobs, Mohawk Valley/Virginia	8	1	3	4	26
Steve Stockman, Erie	3	1	3	4	0
Zlato Dopud, Pinebridge	10	0	4	4	6
Mike Lay, Birmingham	3	0	4	4	2
Gilles Heroux, Virginia (Goalie)	35	0	4	4	13
Carey Walker, Erie (Goalie)	34	0	4	4	4
Mike Bloski, Mohawk Valley (Goalie)	44	0	4	4	30
Dan Burrows, Pinebridge (Goalie)	20	0	4	4	4
Allan Luciw, Virginia	14	1	2	3	43
Gilles Bilodeau, Birmingham	2	1	2	3	16
John Hawkins, Mohawk Valley	8	0	3	3	8
Gray Weicker, Mohawk Valley (Goalie)	38	0	3	3	35

	Games	G.	A.	Pts.	Pen.
Tom Anderson, Erie	5	1	1	2	7
Dennis Smith, Erie	2	1	1	2	2
Jim Turkiewicz, Birmingham	2	1	1	2	0
Bob Breen, Virginia	11	0	2	2	66
Doug Ellithorpe, Mohawk Valley	5	0	2	2	6
Dennis Auclair, Virginia (Goalie)	14	0	2	2	2
Mark Vinet, Erie	4	1	0	1	11
Mike McGuiness, Carolina	2	1	0	1	0
Ward Gleason, Mohawk Valley	3	1	0	1	4
Ron Turkiewicz, Birmingham	3	1	0	1	0
Reg Aubert, Birmingham	1	1	0	1	0
Todd Pearson, Pinebridge (Goalie)	2	0	1	1	6
Mike Deegan, Carolina	2	0	1	1	2
Paul Higgins, Carolina	4	0	1	1	18
Dan Olson, Virginia/Carolina (Goalies)	34	0	1	1	8
Jim Warden, Carolina (Goalie)	6	0	1	1	2
Ron Scales, Mohawk Valley	5	0	0	0	16
Marc Marchand, Mohawk Valley	2	0	0	0	8
Joe Pannicia, Virginia	13	0	0	0	45
George Swift, Virginia	1	0	0	0	0
Scott Ashburn, Carolina	2	0	0	0	0
Mark Emerson, Carolina	1	0	0	0	0
Paul Stanger, Erie	6	0	0	0	15
Frank Laconsole, Erie	4	0	0	0	2
Reynald Cyr, Virginia	5	0	0	0	8
Bill Morris, Carolina	2	0	0	0	0
Andy Whitby, Mohawk Valley	1	0	0	0	0
Paul Joswiak, Virginia/Birmingham (Goalie)	3	0	0	0	0
Mark Walton, Pinebridge (Goalie)	3	0	0	0	0
Ron Petronella, Virginia (Goalie)	4	0	0	0	0
Dave Jaimison, Pinebridge/Virginia (Goalie)	7	0	0	0	0
Paul Evans, Birmingham	1	0	0	0	0

Complete ACHL Individual Goaltending

	Games	Mins.	Goals	SO.	Avg.
Jim Warden, Carolina	6	299	14	1	2.81
Darrell May, Erie	43	2404	163(7)	1	*4.07
Pierre Hamel, Carolina	38	2192	151(1)	*2	4.13
Paul Skidmore, Carolina	29	1621	112(3)	0	4.15
Dennis Auclair, Virginia	14	700	48(1)	1	4.19
Carey Walker, Erie	34	1938	139(1)	0	4.30
Paul Joswiak, Virginia/Birmingham	3	180	13	0	4.33
Mike Bloski, Mohawk Valley	44	2453	192(4)	1	4.70
Dan Olson, Carolina/Virginia	34	1826	147(3)	0	4.83
Gray Weicker, Mohawk Valley	38	2045	172(2)	0	5.05
Dave Jaimison, Pinebridge/Birmingham	7	329	28(1)	1	5.11
Steve Heittola, Pinebridge	*53	*2764	*254(1)	0	5.51
Dan Burrows, Pinebridge	20	1083	101(1)	0	5.63
Gilles Heroux, Virginia	35	1909	189	0	5.94
Mark Walton, Pinebridge	3	115	19	0	9.91
Todd Pearson, Pinebridge	2	100	17	0	10.20
Ron Petronella, Virginia	4	139	26	0	11.22

( )—Empty Net Goals. Do not count against a Goaltender's average.

Individual ACHL Departmental Leaders

Goals	Lee Blossom, Virginia—	61
Assists	Rob Clavette, Pinebridge/Erie—	78
Points	Rob Clavette, Pinebridge/Erie—	131
Penalty Minutes	Brian Gustafson, Carolina/Mohawk Valley—	354
Goaltender's Average (25 games)	Darrell May, Erie—	4.07
Shutouts	Pierre Hamel, Carolina—	2

1984 ACHL Playoffs
Semifinals
(Best-of-seven series)

SERIES "A"	W.	L.	Pts.	GF.	GA.
Carolina	4	1	8	23	15
Mohawk Valley	1	4	2	15	23

(Carolina wins series, 4 games to 1)

SERIES "B"	W.	L.	Pts.	GF.	GA.
Erie	4	0	8	22	9
Virginia	0	4	0	9	22

(Erie wins series, 4 games to 0)

Finals
(Best-of-seven series)

	W.	L.	Pts.	GF.	GA.
Erie	4	1	8	21	10
Carolina	1	4	2	10	21

(Erie wins Championship, 4 games to 1)

Playoff Scoring

	Games	G.	A.	Pts.	Pen.
Ernie Boutin, Erie	9	7	*10	*17	6
Paul Mancini, Erie	9	5	*10	15	2
Dave Herbst, Erie	9	*9	4	13	28
Jim Cowell, Erie	9	3	*10	13	4
Michel Cote, Erie	9	5	5	10	20
Kim Elliott, Carolina	10	3	7	10	6
Dick Popeil, Erie	9	2	8	10	6
Ben LaPorte, Carolina	6	5	4	9	0
Pat Ethier, Carolina	10	4	5	9	11
Ron Hansis, Erie	9	4	5	9	8
Andre Chartrain, Erie	9	3	6	9	2
Dave Watson, Carolina	10	4	4	8	13
Randy Irving, Carolina	10	3	5	8	50
Dave MacQueen, Mohawk Valley	5	2	6	8	2
Jerry Ingram, Carolina	10	1	7	8	59
Ed Smith, Mohawk Valley	5	6	1	7	12
Greg Squires, Carolina	10	3	3	6	4
Brian Carroll, Carolina	10	2	4	6	17
Dennis Smith, Erie	9	2	4	6	8
Sylvain Cote, Erie	9	2	3	5	*82
Dave Lair, Mohawk Valley	5	2	3	5	2
Lee Blossom, Virginia	4	3	1	4	0
Brian Gustafson, Carolina	10	2	2	4	40
Peter Dunkley, Carolina	10	2	2	4	12
Lynn Jorgenson, Carolina	9	1	3	4	4
Pierre Hamel, Carolina (Goalie)	8	0	4	4	4
Robert Dore, Carolina	10	0	4	4	36
Bo Tucker, Mohawk Valley	5	0	4	4	12
Mark Salvucci, Mohawk Valley	5	3	0	3	15
Michel Lanouette, Carolina	7	2	1	3	22
Wayne Van Dorp, Erie	8	1	2	3	46
Ron Carter, Virginia	4	1	2	3	10
Barry Tabobondung, Erie	9	0	3	3	33
Todd Scott, Carolina	10	1	1	2	0
Stan Gulutzan, Virginia	4	1	1	2	0
Joe Bilodeau, Mohawk Valley	5	1	1	2	14
Keith Hosken, Mohawk Valley	5	1	1	2	26
Kelly Barnet, Virginia	4	1	1	2	0
John Tortorella, Virginia	4	1	1	2	18
Sean Cody, Mohawk Valley	5	0	2	2	27
Bruce Greig, Mohawk Valley	5	0	2	2	49
Larry Ell, Mohawk Valley	5	0	2	2	2
Paul O'Neill, Virginia	4	1	0	1	0
John Liprando, Virginia	4	1	0	1	4
Nelson Burton, Erie	9	0	1	1	79
Jim Beaton, Mohawk Valley	5	0	1	1	4
Jay Miller, Mohawk Valley	5	0	1	1	2
Tony Trace, Mohawk Valley	5	0	1	1	0

	Games	G.	A.	Pts.	Pen.
Rich Suwek, Mohawk Valley	5	0	1	1	0
Mike Bloski, Mohawk Valley (Goalie)	5	0	1	1	0
Trent Graham, Virginia	4	0	1	1	0
Bob Hehir, Virginia	4	0	1	1	15
John Giftopolous, Virginia	4	0	1	1	2
Bob Smith, Virginia	2	0	1	1	39
Steve Lyons, Virginia	3	0	0	0	5
Tony Circelli, Virginia	4	0	0	0	0
Greg McPhee, Virginia	2	0	0	0	5
Gray Weicker, Mohawk Valley (Goalie)	2	0	0	0	2
Darren Yankovsky, Erie	9	0	0	0	22
Gilles Heroux, Virginia (Goalie)	2	0	0	0	0
Darrell May, Erie (Goalie)	7	0	0	0	16
Carey Walker, Erie (Goalie)	2	0	0	0	0
Jim Warden, Carolina (Goalie)	2	0	0	0	0
Dan Olson, Virginia (Goalie)	2	0	0	0	0

Complete ACHL Playoff Goaltending

	Games	Mins.	Goals	SO.	Avg.
Carey Walker, Erie	2	120	3	0	*1.50
Darrell May, Erie	7	461	16	*1	2.08
Pierre Hamel, Carolina	*8	*500	*26(1)	0	3.12
Dan Olson, Virginia	2	134	7	0	3.13
Mike Bloski, Mohawk Valley	5	233	14(1)	0	3.61
Jim Warden, Carolina	2	119	9	0	4.54
Gray Weicker, Mohawk Valley	2	71	8	0	6.76
Gilles Heroux, Virginia	2	131	15	0	6.87

( )—Empty Net Goals. Do not count against a Goaldenter's average.

Individual ACHL Playoff Leaders

Goals	Dave Herbst, Erie—	9
Assists	Ernie Boutin, Erie—	10
	Jim Cowell, Erie—	10
	Paul Mancini, Erie—	10
Points	Ernie Boutin, Erie—	17
Penalty Minutes	Sylvain Cote, Erie—	82
Goaltender's Average (60 minutes)	Carey Walker, Erie—	1.50
Shutouts	Darrell May, Erie—	1

★ ★ ★ ★ ★ ★ ★ ★ ★ ★ ★ ★ ★ ★

ACHL 1983-84 All-Star Team

First Team	Position	Second Team
Pierre Hamel, Carolina	Goal	Darrell May, Erie
Randy Irving, Carolina	Defense	Barry Tabobondung, Erie
John Giftopolous, Virginia	Defense	Kelly Barnet, Virginia
Michel Cote, Erie	Center	Paul O'Neill, Virginia
Kim Elliott, Carolina	Left Wing	Lee Blossom, Virginia
Rob Clavette, Pinebridge	Right Wing	Ben LaPorte, Carolina

ACHL Most Valuable Player	Paul O'Neill, Virginia
ACHL Coach of the Year	Paul O'Neill, Virginia

★ ★ ★ ★ ★ ★ ★ ★ ★ ★ ★ ★ ★ ★

MEMORIAL CUP WINNERS

Season	Team	Season	Team
1918-19	University of Toronto Schools	1951-52	Guelph Biltmores
1919-20	Toronto Canoe Club	1952-53	Barrie Flyers
1920-21	Winnipeg Falcons	1953-54	St. Catharines Tee Pees
1921-22	Fort William War Veterans	1954-55	Toronto Marlboros
1922-23	Univ. of Manitoba-Winnipeg	1955-56	Toronto Marlboros
1923-24	Owen Sound Greys	1956-57	Flin Flon Bombers
1924-25	Regina Pats	1957-58	Ottawa-Hull Jr. Canadiens
1925-26	Calgary Canadians	1958-59	Winnipeg Braves
1926-27	Owen Sound Greys	1959-60	St. Catharines Tee Pees
1927-28	Regina Monarchs	1960-61	Toronto St. Michael's Majors
1928-29	Toronto Marlboros	1961-62	Hamilton Red Wings
1929-30	Regina Pats	1962-63	Edmonton Oil Kings
1930-31	Winnipeg Elmwoods	1963-64	Toronto Marlboros
1931-32	Sudbury Wolves	1964-65	Niagara Falls Flyers
1932-33	Newmarket	1965-66	Edmonton Oil Kings
1933-34	Toronto St. Michael's	1966-67	Toronto Marlboros
1934-35	Winnipeg Monarchs	1967-68	Niagara Falls Flyers
1935-36	West Toronto Redmen	1968-69	Montreal Jr. Canadiens
1936-37	Winnipeg Monarchs	1969-70	Montreal Jr. Canadiens
1937-38	St. Boniface Seals	1970-71	Quebec Remparts
1938-39	Oshawa Generals	1971-72	Cornwall Royals
1939-40	Oshawa Generals	1972-73	Toronto Marlboros
1940-41	Winnipeg Rangers	1973-74	Regina Pats
1941-42	Portage la Prairie	1974-75	Toronto Marlboros
1942-43	Winnipeg Rangers	1975-76	Hamilton Fincups
1943-44	Oshawa Generals	1976-77	New Westminster Bruins
1944-45	Toronto St. Michael's	1977-78	New Westminster Bruins
1945-46	Winnipeg Monarchs	1978-79	Peterborough Petes
1946-47	Toronto St. Michael's	1979-80	Cornwall Royals
1947-48	Port Arthur West End Bruins	1980-81	Cornwall Royals
1948-49	Montreal Royals	1981-82	Kitchener Rangers
1949-50	Montreal Jr. Canadiens	1982-83	Portland Winter Hawks
1950-51	Barrie Flyers	1983-84	Ottawa 67's

Ontario Hockey League

Commissioner—David Branch
Chairman of the Board—Dr. Robert Vaughan
655 Dixon Rd., Rexdale, Ontario M9W 1J4
Phone—(416) 243-3100
Director of Information and Statistics—Herb Morrell
Director of Officiating—Ken Bodendistel
Director of Central Scouting—Jack Ferguson

1983-84 Ontario Hockey League Final Standings

Hap Emms Division

	G.	W.	L.	T.	Pts.	GF.	GA.
Kitchener Rangers	70	82	16	2	106	418	276
Brantford Alexanders	70	39	28	3	81	303	235
Sault Ste. Marie Greyhounds	70	38	28	4	80	373	321
London Knights	70	32	37	1	65	288	319
North Bay Centennials	70	22	43	5	49	236	327
Windsor Spitfires	70	22	46	2	46	280	379
Guelph Platers	70	20	46	4	44	252	366
Sudbury Wolves	70	19	50	1	39	287	427

Matt Leyden Division

	G.	W.	L.	T.	Pts.	GF.	GA.
Ottawa 67's	70	50	18	2	102	347	223
Toronto Marlboros	70	45	24	1	91	392	317
Peterborough Petes	70	43	23	4	90	380	307
Oshawa Generals	70	37	32	1	75	315	297
Belleville Bulls	70	33	37	0	66	319	304
Cornwall Royals	70	33	37	0	66	348	375
Kingston Canadians	70	25	45	0	50	313	378

Top 10 Scorers for the Eddie Powers Memorial Trophy

	Games	G.	A.	Pts.	Pen.
1. Tim Salmon, Kingston	69	45	*100	*145	35
2. Wayne Presley, Kitchener	70	63	76	139	156
3. Wayne Groulx, Sault Ste. Marie	70	59	78	137	48
4. Peter Zezel, Toronto	68	47	86	133	31
5. David Gans, Oshawa	62	56	76	132	89
6. Kevin Conway, Kingston	63	*65	65	130	20
7. Doug Evans, Peterborough	61	45	79	124	98
8. Scott Morrison, London	70	47	73	120	30
9. Don McLaren, Ottawa	70	53	60	113	20
10. Scott Tottle, Peterborough	70	63	47	110	24

Belleville Bulls

	Games	G.	A.	Pts.	Pen.
Dave MacLean	70	58	51	109	47
Dunc MacIntyre	70	34	53	87	52
Mike Savage, Sudbury	11	1	2	3	10
Belleville	57	32	28	60	45
Totals	68	33	30	63	55
Brian Martin, Guelph	19	3	9	12	7
Belleville	50	18	32	50	25
Totals	69	21	41	62	32
Dan Quinn	24	23	36	59	12
Darren Gani	67	16	40	56	22
Scott Gardiner	55	26	29	55	12
Craig Coxe	45	17	28	45	90
Rob Crocock	70	6	35	41	49
Brian Small	66	18	19	37	65
Mario Martini, Guelph	18	1	3	4	14
Belleville	51	17	15	32	27
Totals	69	18	18	36	41
Jim Andonoff	68	7	24	31	55
Charlie Moore	63	11	16	27	117
Scott McMichael	58	8	19	27	164
Tim Bean	63	12	13	25	131
Mike Vellucci	67	2	20	22	83
Kent Brimmer, Ottawa	14	1	1	2	9
Belleville	42	2	13	15	18
Totals	56	3	14	17	27
Ali Butorac	11	0	7	7	9
Al Iafrate	10	2	4	6	2
Grant Robertson, Sud.	6	0	0	0	6
Belleville	57	2	4	6	37
Totals	63	2	4	6	43

	Games	G.	A.	Pts.	Pen.
Bruce Fry	21	2	2	4	36
Craig Billington (Goalie)	44	0	2	2	7
Gord Greer	3	0	1	1	0
Larry Stevens, Sudbury..	11	0	1	1	11
Belleville	7	0	0	0	12
Totals	18	0	1	1	23
Joe Mantione, Kitch. (G.)	7	0	0	0	0
Belleville (Goalie)	30	0	1	1	0
Totals	37	0	1	1	0
Ken Dunlop (Goalie)	1	0	0	0	0
Keith Van Rooyen	1	0	0	0	0
Joe Shunock (Goalie)	2	0	0	0	0
Darcy Huber	4	0	0	0	0
Randy Plumb	4	0	0	0	11

Brantford Alexanders

	Games	G.	A.	Pts.	Pen.
Mike Millar	69	50	45	95	48
Jason LaFreniere	70	24	57	81	4
Bob Probert	65	35	38	73	189
Shayne Corson	66	25	46	71	165
Jeff Jackson	58	27	42	69	78
Steve Linseman	55	16	32	48	16
Bruce Bell	63	7	41	48	55
Todd Francis	55	13	33	46	109
Ken Gagner	67	11	26	37	57
Grant Anderson	50	10	27	37	79
John Meulenbroeks	68	7	25	32	39
Bob Pierson, London	13	2	6	8	22
Brantford	47	12	11	23	46
Totals	60	14	17	31	68
Brian MacDonald	69	13	13	26	50
Rob Moffat	57	8	18	26	26
Dave Gagner	12	7	13	20	4
Wray Brimmer, Ottawa	32	1	5	6	20
Brantford	27	4	9	13	17
Totals	59	5	14	19	37
Marc West	50	8	9	17	4
Phil Priddle, Oshawa	4	0	0	0	0
Brantford	49	4	12	16	33
Totals	53	4	12	16	33
Steve Short	17	3	10	13	8
Larry Van Herzele	53	2	6	8	29
Chris Glover	35	3	3	6	4
Tom Searle	9	1	4	5	19
Gary Corbiere	21	0	3	3	27
Keith Ransome	5	1	1	2	0
Steve Smith	7	1	1	2	0
Mike Maurice	8	1	1	2	0
Allan Bester (Goalie)	23	0	1	1	4
Doug Brown	1	0	0	0	0
Joe Stefan	2	0	0	0	0
Peter Richards (Goalie)	3	0	0	0	2
Mark Seymour	3	0	0	0	5
Scott Rex	5	0	0	0	0
Scott Hoag	8	0	0	0	6
John Thornton	14	0	0	0	2
Chris Pusey (Goalie)	50	0	0	0	21

Cornwall Royals

	Games	G.	A.	Pts.	Pen.
Steve Driscoll	63	38	51	89	13
Mike Tomlak	64	24	64	88	21
Ray Sheppard	68	44	36	80	69
Rob Norman	65	43	37	80	72
Mark Hegarty, Belleville	2	1	0	1	2
London	8	5	4	9	2
Cornwall	55	30	40	70	54
Totals	65	36	44	80	58
Mike Bukowski	64	29	47	76	57
Mike Stapleton	70	24	45	69	94
Brent Loney	62	24	38	62	56
Dave Shellington	57	22	25	47	72
Bob Mantha	66	9	33	42	76
Dave Waldie	50	16	22	38	21
Tim Ferguson	69	12	26	38	50
Joe Reekie, North Bay	9	1	0	1	18
Cornwall	53	6	27	33	166
Totals	62	7	27	34	184
Pierre Baril	61	2	26	28	133
Neil Sandilands, Kit.	32	2	13	15	59
Cornwall	30	4	6	10	59
Totals	62	6	19	25	118
Kevin Skilliter	65	7	10	17	57
John Copple	67	4	13	17	68
Doug Archie	60	2	14	16	127
Tyler Sunday	54	3	8	11	36
Tony Vial	13	2	7	9	4
Paul Kenny (Goalie)	41	0	2	2	25
Mike Patrick (Goalie)	2	0	0	0	0
Mike Arthur	5	0	0	0	2
Dennis Schrapp (Goalie)	41	0	0	0	12

Guelph Platers

	Games	G.	A.	Pts.	Pen.
Kirk Muller	49	31	63	94	27
Mike Webb	62	31	35	66	16
Jim Mayne	56	27	36	63	43
Trevor Stienburg	65	33	18	51	104
Greg Royce, Belleville	15	2	7	9	25
Guelph	50	11	31	42	45
Totals	65	13	38	51	70
Paul Brydges	68	27	23	50	37
Kevin Hopkins	63	11	31	42	141
Mark Cupolo	60	28	13	41	61
Jay Barwell	64	15	24	39	53
Grant Sanders, Sudbury	11	3	1	4	4
Belleville	7	1	1	2	7
Guelph	35	4	25	29	15
Totals	53	8	27	35	26
Luc Sabourin	67	5	19	24	35
Dave Andreoli	70	3	16	19	134
Tom Nickolau	61	5	13	18	98
Bill Fordy	53	3	15	18	25
Tony Kolic	59	5	12	17	67
Tim Kaiser, Ottawa	31	1	3	4	26
Guelph	28	5	5	10	16
Totals	59	6	8	14	42
Neil Jones	61	2	8	10	47
Steve Chiasson	55	1	9	10	112
Rob MacInnis, Kitchener	12	3	3	6	9
Guelph	5	0	3	3	20
Totals	17	3	6	9	29
Dave Sikorski, Cornwall	14	0	6	6	14
Ottawa	21	0	2	2	6
Guelph	15	0	1	1	2
Totals	50	0	9	9	22
Denis Larocque	65	1	5	6	74
Darren MacIvor	32	0	2	2	47
Marvin MacNeil	19	0	1	1	14
Steve Guenette (Goalie)	38	0	1	1	2

	Games	G.	A.	Pts.	Pen.
Scott Mosey (Goalie)	45	0	1	1	6
Paul Currie	1	0	0	0	0
Dave Nicholls	1	0	0	0	2
Darren Wright	2	0	0	0	5
Darren McLaughlin	4	0	0	0	2
Norm Fennell	9	0	0	0	7
Rich Jukosky	11	0	0	0	36

Kingston Canadians

	Games	G.	A.	Pts.	Pen.
Tim Salmon	69	45	*100	*145	35
Kevin Conway, S.S.M.	2	3	0	3	0
Kingston	61	62	65	127	20
Totals	63	*65	65	130	20
Roger Belanger	67	44	46	90	66
Scott Metcalfe	68	25	49	74	154
Dennis Smith	62	10	40	50	136
Allen Bishop, North Bay	14	0	8	8	8
Kingston	48	8	34	42	103
Totals	62	8	42	50	111
Barry Burkholder	67	19	26	45	51
Ted Linseman	64	14	19	33	38
Mike King	68	15	17	32	9
David Simurda	59	13	15	28	81
Craig Kales	45	12	13	25	28
D. R. Wright, Kitchener	37	5	8	13	28
Kingston	31	4	6	10	31
Totals	68	9	14	23	59
David James	61	14	8	22	21
Joel Brown	61	5	16	21	152
Todd Elik	64	5	16	21	17
Mike Plesh	61	2	17	19	103
M. Chettleburgh, Brant.	38	2	7	9	30
Kingston	25	0	7	7	30
Totals	63	2	14	16	60
Jeff Chychrun	63	1	13	14	137
David Lundmark	65	2	9	11	66
Steve King	28	3	6	9	27
Chris Clifford (Goalie)	50	0	3	3	6
Mike Morrison	5	1	0	1	0
Ben Levesque	13	1	0	1	7
Clint Ellicott	5	0	1	1	0
Todd Smith	1	0	0	0	0
B. Whitehead (Goalie)	1	0	0	0	0
Marty Lipman (Goalie)	1	0	0	0	0
Kingston (Goalie)	1	0	0	0	0
Totals	2	0	0	0	0
Darren B. Wright	2	0	0	0	0
Jeff Carter	3	0	0	0	0
Tony Harris (Goalie)	5	0	0	0	2
David Hoover	14	0	0	0	12
J. Hogg, Oshawa (G.)	6	0	0	0	0
Kingston (Goalie)	22	0	0	0	0
Totals	28	0	0	0	0

Kitchener Rangers

	Games	G.	A.	Pts.	Pen.
Wayne Presley	70	63	76	139	156
John Tucker	39	40	60	100	25
Greg Puhalski	44	30	69	99	55
David Bruce	62	52	40	92	203
Shawn Burr	68	41	44	85	50
Garnet McKechney	68	31	45	76	107
Brian Wilks	64	21	54	75	36
Jim Quinn	70	9	40	49	71

	Games	G.	A.	Pts.	Pen.
Dave Shaw	58	14	34	48	73
Dave Latta	66	17	26	43	54
Lou Berardicurti	56	5	36	41	79
Carmine Vani, N. B.	17	14	3	17	58
Kitchener	24	15	8	23	75
Totals	41	29	11	40	133
Mike Stevens	66	19	21	40	109
Scott MacLellan	30	9	30	39	35
Kent Paynter	65	9	27	36	94
Scott Kerr	64	13	15	28	80
Bert Weir	49	3	16	19	18
Brian Ross	57	4	7	11	27
Tom Allen, Kingston	26	0	4	4	18
Kitchener	24	1	3	4	12
Totals	50	1	7	8	30
Matt Dajia, London	17	0	0	0	25
Kitchener	26	2	5	7	45
Totals	43	2	5	7	70
Jeff LeClair, Guelph	11	0	2	2	23
Kitchener	7	0	0	0	13
Totals	18	0	2	2	36
Ray LeBlanc (Goalie)	54	0	1	1	7
Tom Buchinski	1	0	0	0	0
Greg Sliz	1	0	0	0	0
David Whistle	1	0	0	0	0
Robert Forcier	2	0	0	0	0
D. Boudreau (G.)	3	0	0	0	0
Shane Beal (Goalie)	7	0	0	0	2
J. McDonald, Belle. (G.)	5	0	0	0	0
Kitchener (Goalie)	12	0	0	0	0
Totals	17	0	0	0	0

London Knights

	Games	G.	A.	Pts.	Pen.
Scott Morrison	70	47	73	120	30
Brian Bradley	49	40	60	100	24
Dave Lowry	66	29	47	76	125
Brian Dobbin	70	30	40	70	70
Rick Barkovich	67	25	29	54	83
Paul Louttit	66	7	39	46	48
Jim Sandlak	68	23	18	41	143
Peter McLeod	67	17	19	36	138
Ed Kastelic	68	17	16	33	218
Mike Murray	70	8	24	32	14
Bob Halkidis	51	9	22	31	123
Greg Smyth	64	4	21	25	*252
Bob Nicholson	48	5	18	23	30
Dan Ryder	61	3	18	21	49
Ed Kister	60	2	15	17	30
Sean Hastings, Sudbury	29	4	7	11	8
London	5	2	1	3	2
Totals	34	6	8	14	10
Doug Thiel	58	2	11	13	81
Bill Hill	26	3	6	9	34
Brad Balshin, Kitchener	17	1	3	4	16
London	38	2	3	5	14
Totals	45	3	6	9	30
Robert Dawe	49	3	6	9	18
Mark Eros	62	2	4	6	51
Wayne Vansevenant	14	1	5	6	4
Mike Bishop (Goalie)	37	0	2	2	4
Dale Gibbon	5	0	1	1	0
Jeff Reese (Goalie)	43	0	1	1	4
Rob Nixon (Goalie)	1	0	0	0	2

North Bay Centennials

	Games	G.	A.	Pts	Pen.
Rob Nichols, Kitchener...	12	5	8	13	46
North Bay...............	46	36	32	68	98
Totals	58	41	40	81	144
Curtis Collin................	49	30	30	60	159
Rob DeGagne	54	15	39	54	35
Ron Sanko, Kingston......	12	4	4	8	29
North Bay...............	46	16	27	43	65
Totals	58	20	31	51	94
Kevin Hatcher	67	10	39	49	61
John Capel	37	15	30	45	19
Mark LaVarre	41	19	22	41	15
Scot Birnie, Cornwall	5	2	1	3	12
North Bay...............	59	10	24	34	108
Totals	64	12	25	37	120
Jim Hunter, Kingston......	8	1	3	4	16
North Bay...............	40	16	15	31	33
Totals	48	17	18	35	49
Kevin Vescio.................	67	2	26	28	75
Brett MacDonald	70	8	18	26	83
Kevin Kerr...................	66	7	19	26	138
Nick Kypreos, Kitchener...	4	2	0	2	0
North Bay...............	47	10	11	21	36
Totals	51	12	11	23	36
Mike Webber	62	3	13	16	85
Peter Woodgate	24	4	9	13	6
Greg Larsen	55	4	9	13	25
Mark Hatcher	64	1	12	13	226
Wayne MacPhee	66	3	9	12	69
Mike Larouche	68	3	3	6	23
Peter McGrath...............	68	0	6	6	87
Tom Warden	28	3	2	5	16
Scott Hampel	21	0	2	2	8
Rob Mattucci	3	1	0	1	2
Don Edwardson	3	0	1	1	0
Dean Harvey	7	0	1	1	0
Dave Cook (Goalie).........	1	0	0	0	0
Joel Smith (Goalie)	1	0	0	0	0
Brian Harper	2	0	0	0	2
Don Young	5	0	0	0	0
R. Thompson (Goalie)	7	0	0	0	0
Richard Benoit (Goalie)..	25	0	0	0	0
Peter Abric (Goalie)........	47	0	0	0	2

Oshawa Generals

	Games	G.	A.	Pts	Pen.
David Gans	62	56	76	132	89
Don Biggs....................	58	31	60	91	149
John Hutchings	65	20	60	80	113
Mike Stern	56	38	38	76	118
Dan Gratton	63	40	34	74	55
John MacLean	30	23	36	59	58
Lee Giffin	70	23	27	50	88
Todd Charlesworth	57	11	35	46	54
Gary McColgan	66	11	28	39	14
Brad Walcot, Kingston.....	11	3	7	10	5
Oshawa.................	48	6	13	19	37
Totals	59	9	20	29	42
Scott Brydges	51	8	17	25	71
Joel Curtis	67	8	12	20	68
Jeff Steffen...................	63	8	10	18	39
C. Morrison, Windsor	8	0	1	1	9
Oshawa.................	51	6	11	17	69
Totals	59	6	12	18	77
Bruce Melanson	60	8	9	17	78
Mark Haarmann	70	6	9	15	68

Ottawa 67's

	Games	G.	A.	Pts	Pen.
Brent Maki...................	53	3	10	13	26
John Stevens.................	70	1	10	11	71
Ian Ferguson.................	65	2	7	9	30
Guy Jacob	22	2	5	7	40
Brian Gray	14	2	4	6	14
Steve Hedington	23	1	3	4	0
P. Sidorkiewicz (Goalie).	52	0	4	4	16
Mike Sutherland	2	0	3	3	0
Chip Crandall	13	0	0	0	6
Kirk McLean (Goalie).....	17	0	0	0	11

Ottawa 67's

	Games	G.	A.	Pts	Pen.
Don McLaren	70	53	60	113	20
Bruce Cassidy	67	27	68	95	58
Adam Creighton	56	42	49	91	79
Brad Shaw	68	11	71	82	75
John Hanna	63	34	37	71	13
Bill Bennett...................	70	29	38	67	31
Darcy Roy	70	21	41	62	98
Brian McKinnon	58	31	27	58	27
Gary Roberts	48	27	30	57	144
Phil Patterson	42	22	17	39	18
Bob Giffin	68	5	23	28	57
Mark Paterson	45	8	16	24	114
Mike James	55	7	13	20	59
Richard Adolfi, Belleville	21	1	3	4	37
Ottawa.................	33	2	14	16	81
Totals	54	3	17	20	118
Roy Myllari, Cornwall......	38	1	8	9	65
Ottawa.................	31	1	10	11	27
Totals	69	2	18	20	92
Steve Hrynewich	62	7	11	18	59
Steve Simoni	63	6	12	18	13
Tim Helmer, North Bay..	18	5	2	7	5
Ottawa.................	29	3	6	9	19
Totals	47	8	8	16	24
Frank Simoni, Belleville .	11	0	1	1	7
Ottawa.................	19	3	10	13	9
Totals	30	3	11	14	16
Todd Clarke	66	4	8	12	89
Scott Hammond.............	55	1	4	5	20
Darren Pang (Goalie).....	43	0	2	2	8
Howie Attenborough	13	0	1	1	16
Greg Coram (Goalie)....	40	0	1	1	9
Jacques Brault (Goalie) .	2	0	0	0	0
Luc Ouellette.................	2	0	0	0	2

Peterborough Petes

	Games	G.	A.	Pts	Pen.
Doug Evans	61	45	79	124	98
Scott Tottle	70	63	47	110	24
Shawn Evans	67	21	88	109	116
Steve Sequin	67	55	51	106	84
David Reid	60	33	64	97	12
Derrick Smith	70	30	36	66	31
Mark Teevens	70	27	37	64	70
John Vecchiarelli	67	19	40	59	133
Brad Ramsden	62	10	36	46	89
Dave Russell	58	20	22	42	105
Darren Treloar..............	51	12	23	35	16
Kris King	62	13	19	32	168
Mike Posavad	63	3	25	28	78
Terry Carkner	66	4	21	25	91
Ian Armstrong	67	1	23	24	66
Paul Bellamy.................	51	10	10	20	26

	Games	G.	A.	Pts.	Pen.
Randy Burridge	55	6	7	13	44
Larry Shaw	64	1	11	12	64
Angelo Catenaro	47	2	7	9	47
Kevin MacDonald, Belv.	4	0	0	0	4
Sudbury	1	0	0	0	0
Peterborough	32	3	3	6	78
Totals	37	3	3	6	82
John Johnson	7	1	4	5	0
Bruce Shoebottom	16	0	5	5	73
Kay Whitmore (Goalie)	29	0	2	2	2
Shawn Kilroy (Goalie)	49	0	2	2	21
Terry Crump	5	1	0	1	0
John Druce	1	0	0	0	0
John Sawyer	1	0	0	0	0
Jeff Stanton	1	0	0	0	0
Kevin Evans	2	0	0	0	0

Sault Ste. Marie Greyhounds

	Games	G.	A.	Pts.	Pen.
Wayne Groulx	70	59	78	137	48
Rick Tocchet	64	44	64	108	209
Chris Felix	70	32	61	93	77
Steve Graves	67	41	48	89	47
Pat Lahey	63	30	45	75	58
Rick Fera	70	30	33	63	49
Mike Lococo	57	13	44	57	41
Graeme Bonar, Windsor	21	5	9	14	37
Sault Ste. Marie	44	10	30	40	43
Totals	65	15	39	54	80
Gus Greco	48	17	30	47	84
Tim Hoover	70	8	34	42	50
Mike Oliverio	66	17	24	41	6
Alec Haidy	54	17	20	37	121
Jeff Beukeboom	61	6	30	36	178
Joe Rampton	68	14	15	29	99
Chris Brant, Kingston	7	0	4	4	14
Sault Ste. Marie	60	9	12	21	50
Totals	67	9	16	25	64
Ken Sabourin	63	7	13	20	157
John English	64	6	11	17	144
Jean-Marc MacKenzie	29	5	10	15	12
Brit Peer	34	1	9	10	45
Marc Tournier	41	1	9	10	40
Darren King	3	1	2	3	7
Lyle Murray	1	0	1	1	0
Ron Maurice (Goalie)	22	0	1	1	0
Jim Samec, Glph. (G.)	3	0	0	0	0
SSM. (Goalie)	28	0	1	1	0
Totals	31	0	1	1	0
Andre Dugas	1	0	0	0	0
Mike McColman	1	0	0	0	0
Dave Menard	1	0	0	0	0
Mike Rouleau	1	0	0	0	0
Ralph Tuck	1	0	0	0	0
Brian Kozak	2	0	0	0	0
Mike Barbeau	3	0	0	0	0
George Koval	3	0	0	0	0
Steve Tattersall (Goalie)	6	0	0	0	2
Jerry Iuliano (Goalie)	26	0	0	0	0

Sudbury Wolves

	Games	G.	A.	Pts.	Pen.
Jim Koudys	70	46	45	91	34
Jeff Brown	68	17	60	77	39
Craig Duncanson	62	38	38	76	178
Glenn Greenough	67	26	43	69	33

	Games	G.	A.	Pts.	Pen.
Ken Minello	49	32	34	66	37
Brian Verbeek	69	24	38	62	50
Todd Sepkowski, Belv.	10	1	0	1	0
Sudbury	57	23	36	59	10
Totals	67	24	36	60	10
Chris McRae, Belleville	9	0	0	0	19
Sudbury	53	14	31	45	120
Totals	62	14	31	45	139
Daran Moxam, Belleville	4	0	2	2	0
Sudbury	55	12	24	36	87
Totals	59	12	26	38	87
Dan Chiasson	60	15	17	32	75
Ed Smith	60	6	23	29	68
Mike Cassin, Belleville	10	0	1	1	8
Sudbury	55	5	17	22	35
Totals	65	5	18	23	43
Bob Clerke	55	8	14	22	24
John Landry	65	3	16	19	102
Jon Lawson	47	3	13	16	41
Dan Nowak	60	6	6	12	24
Steve McCharles	62	1	8	9	87
Rick Gladu	41	0	5	5	36
Paul Hawkins	12	0	2	2	5
Norm Reid	6	0	1	1	2
Mitch Denault	18	0	1	1	30
Sean Evoy (Goalie)	34	0	1	1	10
Dan Longe (Goalie)	44	0	1	1	20
Ben Levesque	1	0	0	0	0
Marc Pharand	1	0	0	0	2
Gord Murray	2	0	0	0	2
Roger Martelle	9	0	0	0	0
Mike Labelle (Goalie)	12	0	0	0	5

Toronto Marlboros

	Games	G.	A.	Pts.	Pen.
Peter Zezel	68	47	86	133	31
Steve Thomas	70	51	54	105	77
Garry Lacey	59	41	60	101	77
Kevin Robinson	65	40	45	85	55
Greg Johnston	57	38	35	73	67
John LaFontaine	65	25	44	69	44
Vito Cramarossa	66	18	40	58	63
Glen Murphy	53	24	30	54	30
George Spezza	65	14	35	49	78
John Del Col	67	22	24	46	94
Lou Kiriakou	68	10	35	45	74
Mike Rowe	59	9	36	45	208
Mike Richard	66	19	17	36	12
Gerry Peach	54	11	20	31	4
Jeff Triano	62	6	24	30	116
Jim Thomson	60	10	18	28	68
Scott Mohns	63	3	20	23	76
Jeff Cornelius	64	2	14	16	117
Kevin Hunter	53	1	10	11	26
Dave Meszaros (Goalie)	53	0	4	4	21
Dan Jackson	28	0	3	3	14
Rob Lane	1	1	0	1	0
Mike Dobrijevic	6	0	0	0	0
Bill Speed	9	0	0	0	6
Marty Abrams (Goalie)	20	0	0	0	2

Windsor Spitfires

	Games	G.	A.	Pts.	Pen.
Paul Lawless	55	31	49	80	26
Jamie Jefferson	68	24	47	71	72
Rick Pickersgill	69	33	32	65	42

	Games	G.	A.	Pts.	Pen.
Dan Mahon	64	31	28	59	79
Todd Gill	68	9	48	57	184
Keith Gretzky	70	15	38	53	8
Shaun Reagan	67	19	31	50	29
Doug Stewart, Brantford	26	8	16	24	45
Windsor	25	12	10	22	46
Totals	51	20	26	46	91
Peter Bakovic, Kitchener	28	2	6	8	87
Windsor	35	10	25	35	74
Totals	63	12	31	43	161
Alain Raymond	59	14	26	40	35
Mike Neill, SSM	20	2	6	8	42
Windsor	49	9	17	26	101
Totals	69	11	23	34	143
J. D. Urbanic	54	12	18	30	39
Wilf Payne	67	9	18	27	16
Pierre Dupuis	64	13	13	26	24
Tyler Verhaeghe	41	3	19	22	70
Rob Veccia	51	7	14	21	38
Brian MacDonald	67	4	17	21	58
Terry Maki	35	7	11	18	29
Mike Battista	52	4	5	9	33
Tim Burgess, Oshawa	11	1	4	5	7
Windsor	25	2	2	4	18
Totals	36	3	6	9	25
Jay Zeidel, Ottawa	1	0	0	0	2
Windsor	22	1	3	4	70
Totals	23	1	3	4	72
Rick Gosnell	20	0	4	4	35
George Finn	4	2	1	3	10
Brad Belland	2	0	3	3	0
Paul McKenzie	8	0	3	3	25
Steve Collins	1	2	0	2	2
Jim Olsson	4	1	1	2	7
Kevin Meyer	1	0	2	2	2
Paul Martin (Goalie)	37	0	2	2	4
Brian Rome	1	1	0	1	0
Mark Samoyloff	1	0	1	1	0
Glen Schofield	4	0	1	1	2
J. Armellin, SSM (G.)	15	0	1	1	2
Windsor (Goalie)	8	0	0	0	0
Totals	23	0	1	1	2
Kerry Kerch (Goalie)	35	0	1	1	0
John Tamer	39	0	1	1	10
Paul Beauparlant	1	0	0	0	0
Jamie Hofford	1	0	0	0	2
Paul Paliani	1	0	0	0	0
Richard Paliani (Goalie)	7	0	0	0	0

Complete 1983-84 OHL Goaltending

	Games	Mins.	Goals	SO.	Avg.
Peter Richards, Brantford	3	134	4	0	1.79
Ken Dunlop, Belleville	1	43	2	0	2.79
Darren Pang, Ottawa	43	2318	117	2	*3.03
Chris Pusey, Brantford	50	2858	158(1)	2	3.32
Greg Coram, Ottawa	40	1882	104	*3	3.32
Shane Beal, Kitchener	7	307	17	0	3.32
Allan Bester, Brantford	23	1271	71(1)	1	3.35
Jerry Iuliano, Sault Ste. Marie	26	1136	69(1)	*3	3.64
Ray LeBlanc, Kitchener	*54	2965	185	1	3.74
Peter Sidorkiewicz, Oshawa	52	2966	205(5)	1	4.15
Shawn Kilroy, Peterborough	49	2784	193(2)	0	4.16
Craig Billington, Belleville	44	2335	162(1)	1	4.16
Joe Mantione, Kitchener	7	328	23	0	4.21
Belleville	30	1576	110(1)	1	4.19
Totals	37	1903	133(1)	1	4.19
Richard Benoit, North Bay	25	1300	91(1)	1	4.20
Peter Abric, North Bay	47	2556	180(3)	0	4.23
Darryl Boudreau, Kitchener	3	170	12	0	4.24
Marty Abrams, Toronto	20	1137	81	0	4.27
Kirk McLean, Oshawa	17	940	67(1)	0	4.28
Mike Bishop, London	37	1909	139(2)	0	4.37
Dave Meszaros, Toronto	53	*3106	*232(4)	1	4.48
Kay Whitmore, Peterborough	29	1471	110(2)	0	4.49
Jeff Reese, London	43	2308	173(3)	0	4.50
Paul Martin, Windsor	37	1890	144(4)	0	4.57
Joe Shunock, Belleville	2	104	8	0	4.62
Paul Kenny, Cornwall	41	2101	163(4)	1	4.65
Ron Maurice, Sault Ste. Marie	22	920	73(1)	0	4.76
Scott Mosey, Guelph	45	2307	186(6)	0	4.84
Chris Clifford, Kingston	50	2808	229(4)	2	4.89
Jim Samec, Guelph	3	161	16	0	5.96
Sault Ste. Marie	28	1312	105(2)	0	4.80
Totals	31	1473	121(2)	0	4.93
Steve Tattersall, Sault Ste. Marie	6	293	25(1)	0	5.12
Steve Guenette, Guelph	38	1808	155(3)	0	5.14
Jeff Hogg, Oshawa	6	350	19	0	3.26
Kingston	22	1096	105(2)	0	5.75
Totals	28	1446	124(2)	0	5.15
Richard Paliani, Windsor	7	253	22	0	5.22
John Armellin, Sault Ste. Marie	15	589	43(1)	0	4.38
Windsor	8	321	38(1)	0	7.08
Totals	23	911	81(2)	0	5.33

	Games	Mins.	Goals	SO.	Avg.
Dan Longe, Sudbury	44	2378	216(4)	0	5.47
John McDonald, Belleville	5	176	20	0	6.82
Kitchener	12	463	39	0	5.05
Totals	17	639	59	0	5.54
Kerry Kerch, Windsor	35	1777	166(2)	1	5.60
Jacques Brault, Ottawa	2	21	2	0	5.71
Dennis Schrapp, Cornwall	41	2000	195(2)	0	5.85
Mike Patrick, Cornwall	2	112	11	0	5.89
Rob Nixon, London	1	20	2	0	6.00
Sean Evoy, Sudbury	34	1536	159(1)	1	6.21
Tony Harris, Kingston	5	201	22	0	6.57
Randall Thompson, North Bay	7	338	39	0	6.92
Brian Whitehead, Kingston	1	60	7	0	7.00
Mike Labelle, Sudbury	12	333	44(3)	0	8.17
Dave Cook, North Bay	1	55	8	0	8.73
Marty Lipman, Windsor	1	2	2	0	60.00
Kingston	1	60	8(1)	0	8.00
Totals	2	62	10(1)	0	9.68
Joel Smith, North Bay	1	15	5	0	20.00

( )—Empty Net Goals. Do not count against a Goaltender's average.

Individual 1983-84 OHL Leaders

Goals	Kevin Conway, Kingston—	65
Assists	Tim Salmon, Kingston—	100
Points	Tim Salmon, Kingston—	145
Penalty Minutes	Greg Smyth, London—	252
Goaltender's Average (25 games)	Darren Pang, Ottawa—	3.03
Shutouts	Greg Coram, Ottawa—	3
	Jerry Iuliano, Sault Ste. Marie—	3

1984 J. Ross Robertson Cup Playoffs
Division Quarterfinals
(Six point series)

Emms Division

Series "A"

	W.	L.	T.	Pts.	GF.	GA.
Sault Ste. Marie	3	0	0	6	23	7
Windsor	0	3	0	0	7	23

(Sault Ste. Marie wins series, 6 points to 0)

Series "B"

	W.	L.	T.	Pts.	GF.	GA.
London	3	1	0	6	20	16
North Bay	1	3	0	2	16	20

(London wins series, 6 points to 2)

Leyden Division

Series "A"

	W.	L.	T.	Pts.	GF.	GA.
Peterborough	3	0	0	6	19	10
Cornwall	0	3	0	0	10	19

(Peterborough wins series, 6 points to 0)

Series "B"

	W.	L.	T.	Pts.	GF.	GA.
Oshawa	3	0	0	6	13	6
Belleville	0	3	0	0	6	13

(Oshawa wins series, 6 points to 0)

Division Semifinals
(Eight point series)

Emms Division

Series "C"

	W.	L.	T.	Pts.	GF.	GA.
Kitchener	4	0	0	8	28	14
London	0	4	0	0	14	28

(Kitchener wins series, 8 points to 0)

Series "D"

	W.	L.	T.	Pts.	GF.	GA.
Sault Ste. Marie	2	0	4	8	23	16
Brantford	0	2	4	4	16	23

(Sault Ste. Marie wins series, 8 points to 4)

Leyden Division

Series "C"

	W.	L.	T.	Pts.	GF.	GA.
Ottawa	4	0	0	8	21	9
Oshawa	0	4	0	0	9	21

(Ottawa wins series, 8 points to 0)

Series "D"

	W.	L.	T.	Pts.	GF.	GA.
Toronto	4	1	0	8	25	28
Peterborough	1	4	0	2	28	25

(Toronto wins series, 8 points to 2)

Division Finals
(Eight point series)

Emms Division
Series "E"

	W.	L.	T.	Pts.	GF.	GA.
Kitchener	4	3	0	8	35	36
Sault Ste. Marie	3	4	0	6	36	35

(Kitchener wins series, 8 points to 6)

Leyden Division
Series "E"

	W.	L.	T.	Pts.	GF.	GA.
Ottawa	4	0	0	8	28	8
Toronto	0	4	0	0	8	28

(Ottawa wins series, 8 points to 0)

OHL Final Series For The J. Ross Robertson Cup
(Eight point series)

Series "F"

	W.	L.	T.	Pts.	GF.	GA.
Ottawa	3	0	2	8	38	26
Kitchener	0	3	2	2	26	38

(Ottawa wins Robertson Cup playoffs, 8 points to 2)

Top 10 OHL Playoff Scorers

	Games	G.	A.	Pts.	Pen.
1. Rick Tocchet, Sault Ste. Marie	16	*22	14	*36	41
Wayne Groulx, Sault Ste. Marie	16	14	22	*36	13
3. John Tucker, Kitchener	12	12	18	30	8
4. Brad Shaw, Ottawa	13	2	*27	29	9
5. Wayne Presley, Kitchener	16	12	16	28	38
6. Adam Creighton, Ottawa	13	16	11	27	28
7. Bill Bennett, Ottawa	13	9	14	23	0
Chris Felix, Sault Ste. Marie	16	3	20	23	16
9. Bruce Cassidy, Ottawa	13	6	16	22	6
10. Scott Kerr, Kitchener	16	7	13	20	12
Mike Lococo, Sault Ste. Marie	16	7	13	20	13
Brian Wilks, Kitchener	16	6	14	20	9

Team-by-Team Playoff Scoring

Belleville Bulls
(Lost division quarterfinals to Oshawa, 6 points to 0)

	Games	G.	A.	Pts.	Pen.
Scott McMichael	3	0	4	4	6
Dunc MacIntyre	3	2	1	3	2
Craig Coxe	3	2	0	2	4
Brian Martin	3	0	2	2	0
Jim Andonoff	3	1	0	1	0
Mike Vellucci	3	1	0	1	6
Kent Brimmer	3	0	1	1	0
Al Iafrate	3	0	1	1	5
Craig Billington (Goalie)	1	0	0	0	0
Tim Bean	3	0	0	0	0
Darren Gani	3	0	0	0	0
Scott Gardiner	3	0	0	0	0
Dave MacLean	3	0	0	0	0
Joe Mantione (Goalie)	3	0	0	0	0
Mario Martini	3	0	0	0	0
Charlie Moore	3	0	0	0	0
Grant Robertson	3	0	0	0	0
Mike Savage	3	0	0	0	0
Brian Small	3	0	0	0	4

Brantford Alexanders
(Lost division semifinals to Sault Ste. Marie, 8 points to 4)

	Games	G.	A.	Pts.	Pen.
Jason LaFreniere	6	2	4	6	2
Shayne Corson	6	4	1	5	26
Mike Millar	6	4	0	4	2
Steve Linseman	6	3	1	4	0

	Games	G.	A.	Pts.	Pen.
Dave Gagner	6	0	4	4	6
Bob Pierson	6	1	2	3	0
Bruce Bell	6	0	3	3	16
Bob Probert	6	0	3	3	16
Todd Francis	6	0	2	2	21
Phil Priddle	6	0	2	2	0
Grant Anderson	6	1	0	1	4
Brian MacDonald	6	1	0	1	7
Jeff Jackson	2	1	0	1	0
John Muelenbroeks	6	0	1	1	12
Steve Short	6	0	1	1	4
Allan Bester (Goalie)	1	0	0	0	0
Chris Glover	1	0	0	0	0
Larry Van Herzele	1	0	0	0	0
Gary Corbiere	4	0	0	0	10
Ken Gagner	5	0	0	0	2
Rob Moffat	5	0	0	0	2
Chris Pusey (Goalie)	5	0	0	0	0
Wray Brimmer	6	0	0	0	0

Cornwall Royals
(Lost division quarterfinals to Peterborough, 6 points to 0)

	Games	G.	A.	Pts.	Pen.
Ray Sheppard	3	2	4	6	0
Steve Driscoll	3	2	3	5	0
Mike Tomlak	3	1	3	4	2
Rob Norman	3	2	1	3	0
Mike Stapleton	3	1	2	3	4
Dave Shellington	3	2	0	2	0

	Games	G.	A.	Pts.	Pen.
Pierre Baril	3	0	2	2	2
Mike Bukowski	3	0	2	2	2
John Copple	3	0	1	1	0
Kevin Skilliter	3	0	1	1	0
Mike Arthur	1	0	0	0	0
Tyler Sunday	1	0	0	0	0
Doug Archie	2	0	0	0	0
Bob Mantha	2	0	0	0	0
Dennis Schrapp (Goalie)	2	0	0	0	0
Tim Ferguson	3	0	0	0	0
Mark Hegarty	3	0	0	0	2
Paul Kenny (Goalie)	3	0	0	0	2
Brent Loney	3	0	0	0	0
Joe Reekie	3	0	0	0	4
Neil Sandilands	3	0	0	0	2
Dave Waldie	3	0	0	0	0

Kitchener Rangers
(Lost league finals to Ottawa, 8 points to 2)

	Games	G.	A.	Pts.	Pen.
John Tucker	12	12	18	30	8
Wayne Presley	16	12	16	28	38
Scott Kerr	16	7	13	20	12
Brian Wilks	16	6	14	20	9
Scott MacLellan	16	3	15	18	14
Mike Stevens	16	10	7	17	40
Shawn Burr	16	5	12	17	22
David Bruce	10	5	8	13	20
Kent Paynter	16	4	9	13	18
Dave Shaw	16	4	9	13	12
Carmine Vani	10	6	6	12	17
Greg Puhalski	10	2	10	12	8
Garnet McKechney	16	6	4	10	8
Dave Latta	16	3	6	9	9
Lou Berardicurti	16	2	3	5	11
Tom Allen	10	1	2	3	15
Bert Weir	16	1	2	3	14
Jim Quinn	7	1	0	1	2
Darryl Boudreau (G.)	1	0	0	0	0
John McDonald (Goalie)	1	0	0	0	0
Jeff LeClair	8	0	0	0	14
Matt Dajia	11	0	0	0	0
Brian Ross	14	0	0	0	9
Ray LeBlanc (Goalie)	16	0	0	0	2

London Knights
(Lost division semifinals to Kitchener, 8 points to 0)

	Games	G.	A.	Pts.	Pen.
Scott Morrison	8	4	9	13	0
Dave Lowry	8	6	6	12	41
Jim Sandlak	8	1	11	12	13
Brian Dobbin	8	9	1	10	17
Peter McLeod	8	5	4	9	10
Rick Barkovich	8	2	5	7	11
Brian Bradley	4	2	4	6	0
Mike Murray	8	1	4	5	2
Paul Louttit	6	0	5	5	6
Bob Nicholson	3	0	3	3	2
Brad Balshin	8	1	1	2	0
Dan Ryder	8	1	1	2	10
Robert Dawe	7	0	2	2	2
Bob Halkidis	8	0	2	2	27
Ed Kastelic	8	0	2	2	41
Greg Smyth	6	1	0	1	24
Wayne Vansevenant	7	0	1	1	6
Ed Kister	8	0	1	1	2

	Games	G.	A.	Pts.	Pen.
Dale Gibbon	1	0	0	0	0
Mike Bishop (Goalie)	3	0	0	0	0
Mark Eros	6	0	0	0	15
Jeff Reese (Goalie)	6	0	0	0	9
Doug Thiel	8	0	0	0	6

North Bay Centennials
(Lost division quarterfinals to London, 6 points to 2)

	Games	G.	A.	Pts.	Pen.
Scot Birnie	4	2	5	7	9
Ron Sanko	4	3	3	6	11
Nick Kypreos	4	3	2	5	9
Rob Nichols	4	1	4	5	11
Kevin Hatcher	4	2	2	4	11
Rob DeGagne	1	1	2	3	0
Mark Hatcher	4	0	3	3	38
Wayne MacPhee	4	0	3	3	16
Kevin Kerr	4	1	1	2	18
Greg Larsen	4	1	1	2	2
Kevin Vescio	4	1	1	2	9
Mike Larouche	4	1	0	1	0
Bret MacDonald	4	0	1	1	0
Peter McGrath	4	0	1	1	14
Mike Webber	4	0	1	1	2
Richard Benoit (Goalie)	2	0	0	0	0
Peter Abric (Goalie)	3	0	0	0	0
Scott Hampel	4	0	0	0	0
Dean Harvey	4	0	0	0	0
Tom Warden	4	0	0	0	5

Oshawa Generals
(Lost division semifinals to Ottawa, 8 points to 0)

	Games	G.	A.	Pts.	Pen.
Don Biggs	7	4	4	8	18
David Gans	6	3	4	7	9
Dan Gratton	7	2	5	7	15
John MacLean	7	2	5	7	18
Craig Morrison	7	3	2	5	4
Lee Giffin	7	1	4	5	12
Mike Stern	7	3	1	4	8
John Hutchings	7	1	3	4	6
Todd Charlesworth	7	0	4	4	4
Jeff Steffen	7	2	0	2	4
Scott Brydges	7	1	1	2	13
Gary McColgan	5	0	2	2	4
Mark Haarmann	7	0	1	1	2
Brent Maki	7	0	1	1	2
Bruce Melanson	7	0	1	1	0
John Stevens	7	0	1	1	6
Brad Walcot	1	0	0	0	0
Joel Curtis	4	0	0	0	0
Ian Ferguson	5	0	0	0	0
Guy Jacob	7	0	0	0	9
P. Sidorkiewicz (Goalie)	7	0	0	0	0

Ottawa 67's
(Winners of 1984 J. Ross Robertson Cup Playoff)

	Games	G.	A.	Pts.	Pen.
Brad Shaw	13	2	*27	29	9
Adam Creighton	13	16	11	27	28
Bill Bennett	13	9	14	23	0
Bruce Cassidy	13	6	16	22	6
Darcy Roy	13	9	10	19	16
Brian McKinnon	13	10	7	17	12
Gary Roberts	13	10	7	17	*62

	Games	G.	A.	Pts.	Pen.
Don McLaren	13	5	8	13	6
John Hanna	13	6	5	11	7
Phil Patterson	13	6	5	11	9
Mark Paterson	13	2	7	9	16
Roy Myllari	13	1	6	7	25
Bob Giffin	13	2	4	6	13
Tim Helmer	12	2	3	5	4
Steve Hrynewich	13	0	5	5	5
Mike James	13	1	2	3	15
Richard Adolfi	6	0	2	2	11
Steve Simoni	9	0	1	1	2
Todd Clarke	10	0	1	1	6
Darren Pang (Goalie)	13	0	1	1	4
Greg Coram (Goalie)	2	0	0	0	0
Scott Hammond	2	0	0	0	0

Peterborough Petes
(Lost division semifinals to Toronto, 8 points to 2)

	Games	G.	A.	Pts.	Pen.
Shawn Evans	8	1	16	17	8
Steve Seguin	8	8	8	16	11
Doug Evans	8	4	12	16	26
Scott Tottle	8	10	5	15	5
David Reid	8	2	7	9	12
Derrick Smith	8	4	4	8	7
Mark Teevens	8	3	4	7	4
Kris King	8	3	3	6	14
Terry Carkner	8	0	6	6	13
Randy Burridge	8	3	2	5	7
Mike Posavad	8	3	2	5	8
Brad Ramsden	8	2	3	5	15
John Vecchiarelli	8	1	4	5	13
Darren Treloar	8	1	3	4	4
Paul Bellamy	7	2	0	2	0
Ian Armstrong	4	0	1	1	4
Kevin MacDonald	8	0	1	1	16
Angelo Catenaro	5	0	0	0	0
Larry Shaw	5	0	0	0	12
Shawn Kilroy (Goalie)	8	0	0	0	2

Sault Ste. Marie Greyhounds
(Lost division finals to Kitchener, 8 points to 6)

	Games	G.	A.	Pts.	Pen.
Rick Tocchet	16	*22	14	*36	41
Wayne Groulx	16	14	22	*36	13
Chris Felix	16	3	20	23	16
Mike Lococo	16	7	13	20	13
Gus Greco	15	5	14	19	21
Steve Graves	16	6	8	14	8
Pat Lahey	15	1	10	11	16
Graeme Bonar	16	6	4	10	15
Tim Hoover	16	2	6	8	10
Jeff Beukeboom	16	1	7	8	43
Rick Fera	16	5	2	7	20
Mike Oliverio	16	3	3	6	2
Alec Haidy	9	2	4	6	7
John English	16	0	6	6	45
Darren King	13	4	1	5	17
Chris Brant	15	1	2	3	30

	Games	G.	A.	Pts.	Pen.
Ken Sabourin	9	0	1	1	25
Joe Rampton	14	0	1	1	7
Jim Samec (Goalie)	16	0	1	1	0
Mike Rouleau	1	0	0	0	2
Marc Tournier	5	0	0	0	5
Brit Peer	7	0	0	0	0
Jean-Marc MacKenzie	9	0	0	0	0

Toronto Marlboros
(Lost division finals to Ottawa, 8 points to 0)

	Games	G.	A.	Pts.	Pen.
Peter Zezel	9	7	5	12	4
Lou Kiriakou	9	3	7	10	11
George Spezza	9	3	6	9	17
Steve Thomas	9	2	6	8	26
Garry Lacey	6	4	3	7	22
Greg Johnston	9	4	2	6	13
John LaFontaine	9	3	2	5	4
Mike Rowe	9	0	5	5	45
John Del Col	9	1	3	4	14
Glen Murphy	9	1	3	4	0
Mike Richard	9	2	1	3	0
Kevin Robinson	9	1	2	3	7
Jeff Triano	9	0	3	3	31
Jeff Cornelius	9	0	2	2	28
Vito Cramarossa	9	1	0	1	13
Jim Thompson	9	1	0	1	26
Marty Abrams (Goalie)	1	0	0	0	0
Bill Speed	1	0	0	0	0
Scott Mohns	5	0	0	0	0
Kevin Hunter	7	0	0	0	2
Dave Meszaros (Goalie)	9	0	0	0	4
Gerry Peach	9	0	0	0	0

Windsor Spitfires
(Lost division quarterfinals to S.S. Marie, 6 points to 0)

	Games	G.	A.	Pts.	Pen.
Doug Stewart	3	3	0	3	12
Shaun Reagan	3	0	3	3	0
Steve Collins	3	2	0	2	19
Todd Gill	3	1	1	2	10
Peter Bakovic	3	0	2	2	14
Mike Neill	3	1	0	1	2
Brad Belland	2	0	1	1	0
Paul Lawless	2	0	1	1	0
Dan Mahon	2	0	1	1	0
J. D. Urbanic	2	0	1	1	0
Keith Gretzky	3	0	1	1	2
Jamie Jefferson	3	0	1	1	7
Rick Pickersgill	3	0	1	1	2
Alain Raymond	2	0	0	0	0
John Tamer	2	0	0	0	0
Paul Martin (Goalie)	3	0	0	0	2
Brian McDonald	3	0	0	0	0
Kevin Meyer	3	0	0	0	0
Richard Paliani (Goalie)	3	0	0	0	0
Wilf Payne	3	0	0	0	0
Glen Schofield	3	0	0	0	0
Bob Veccia	3	0	0	0	9

Complete Robertson Cup Goaltending

	Games	Mins.	Goals	SO.	Avg.
Darren Pang, Ottawa	13	726	40	*1	*3.31
Greg Coram, Ottawa	2	54	3	0	3.33
Jim Samec, Sault Ste. Marie	*16	*960	57(2)	0	3.56
Chris Pusey, Brantford	5	300	17	0	3.60
Joe Mantione, Belleville	3	150	9(1)	0	3.60
Peter Sidorkiewicz, Oshawa	7	420	27	*1	3.86
Shawn Kilroy, Peterborough	8	480	33(2)	0	4.13
Peter Abric, North Bay	3	159	11	0	4.15
Jeff Reese, London	6	327	27	0	4.95
Allan Bester, Brantford	1	60	5	0	5.00
Ray LeBlanc, Kitchener	*16	914	*79(1)	0	5.19
Mike Bishop, London	3	153	15(2)	0	5.88
Dave Meszaros, Toronto	9	517	51	0	5.92
Craig Billington, Belleville	1	30	3	0	6.00
Paul Kenny, Cornwall	3	136	14	0	6.18
Richard Benoit, North Bay	2	81	9	0	6.67
John McDonald, Kitchener	1	27	3	0	6.67
Dennis Schrapp, Cornwall	2	44	5	0	6.82
Richard Paliani, Windsor	3	59	7	0	7.12
Paul Martin, Windsor	3	121	16	0	7.93
Marty Abrams, Toronto	1	23	5	0	13.04
Darryl Boudreau, Kitchener	1	19	5	0	15.79

( )—Empty Net Goals. Do not count against a Goaltender's average.

Individual Robertson Cup Leaders

Goals	Rick Tocchet, Sault Ste. Marie—	22
Assists	Brad Shaw, Ottawa—	27
Points	Rick Tocchet, Sault Ste. Marie—	36
	Wayne Groulx, Sault Ste. Marie—	36
Penalty Minutes	Gary Roberts, Ottawa—	62
Goaltender's average (3 games)	Darren Pang, Ottawa—	3.31
Shutouts	Darren Pang, Ottawa—	1
	Peter Sidorkiewicz, Oshawa—	1

★ ★ ★ ★ ★ ★ ★ ★ ★ ★ ★ ★ ★ ★ ★ ★ ★

1983-84 OHL All-Star Teams

First Team	Position	Second Team
Darren Pang, Ottawa	Goal	Chris Pusey, Brantford
Brad Shaw, Ottawa	Defense	Shawn Evans, Peterborough
Dave Shaw, Kitchener	Defense	Bruce Cassidy, Ottawa
John Tucker, Kitchener	Center	W. Groulx, Sault Ste. Marie
Wayne Presley, Kitchener	Right Wing	Don McLaren, Ottawa
Garry Lacey, Toronto	Left Wing	Paul Lawless, Windsor

1983-84 OHL Trophy Winners

Red Tilson Trophy (Outstanding Player)	John Tucker, Kitchener
Max Kaminsky Trophy (Outstanding Defenseman)	Brad Shaw, Ottawa
William Hanley Trophy (Most Gentlemanly)	Kevin Conway, Kingston
Emms Family Award (Rookie of the Year)	Shawn Burr, Kitchener
Matt Leyden Trophy (Coach of the Year)	Tom Barrett, Kitchener
Eddie Powers Memorial Trophy (Scoring Champion)	Tim Salmon, Kingston
Jim Mahon Memorial Trophy (Top scoring Right Wing)	Wayne Presley, Kitchener
Dave Pinkney Trophy (Lowest Goaltender Average)	Darren Pang, Ottawa
	Greg Coram, Ottawa
F.W. Dinty Moore Trophy (Lowest avg. by a rookie goalie)	Jerry Iuliano, Sault Ste. Marie

Historical OHL Trophy Winners

Red Tilson MVP Trophy

Season	Player	Club
1944-45	Doug McMurdy	St. Catharines
1945-46	Tod Sloan	St. Michael's
1946-47	Ed Sanford	St. Michael's
1947-48	George Armstrong	Stratford
1948-49	Gil Mayer	Barrie
1949-50	George Armstrong	Marlboros
1950-51	Glenn Hall	Windsor
1951-52	Bill Harrington	Kitchener
1952-53	Bob Attersley	Oshawa
1953-54	Brian Cullen	St. Catharines
1954-55	Hank Ciesla	St. Catharines
1955-56	Ron Howell	Guelph
1956-57	Frank Mahovlich	St. Michael's
1957-58	Murray Oliver	Hamilton
1958-59	Stan Mikita	St. Catharines
1959-60	Wayne Connelly	Peterborough
1960-61	Rod Gilbert	Guelph
1961-62	Pit Martin	Hamilton
1962-63	Wayne Maxner	Niagara Falls
1963-64	Yvan Cournoyer	Montreal
1964-65	Andre Lacroix	Peterborough
1965-66	Andre Lacroix	Peterborough
1966-67	Mickey Redmond	Peterborough
1967-68	Walt Tkaczuk	Kitchener
1968-69	Rejean Houle	Montreal
1969-70	Gilbert Perreault	Montreal
1970-71	Dave Gardner	Marlboros
1971-72	Don Lever	Niagara Falls
1972-73	Rick Middleton	Oshawa
1973-74	Jack Valiquette	Sault Ste. Marie
1974-75	Dennis Maruk	London
1975-76	Peter Lee	Ottawa
1976-77	Dale McCourt	St. Catharines
1977-78	Bobby Smith	Ottawa
1978-79	Mike Foligno	Sudbury
1979-80	Jim Fox	Ottawa
1980-81	Ernie Godden	Windsor
1981-82	Dave Simpson	London
1982-83	Doug Gilmour	Cornwall
1983-84	John Tucker	Kitchener

Eddie Powers Scoring Trophy

Season	Player	Club
1933-34	J. Groboski	Oshawa
1934-35	J. Good	Toronto Lions
1935-36	John O'Flaherty	West Toronto
1936-37	Billy Taylor	Oshawa
1937-38	Hank Goldup	Tor. Marlboros
1938-39	Billy Taylor	Oshawa
1939-40	Jud McAtee	Oshawa
1940-41	Gaye Stewart	Tor. Marlboros
1941-42	Bob Wiest	Brantford
1942-43	Norman "Red" Tilson	Oshawa
1943-44	Ken Smith	Oshawa
1944-45	Leo Gravelle	St. Michael's
1945-46	Tod Sloan	St. Michael's
1946-47	Fleming Mackell	St. Michael's
1947-48	George Armstrong	Stratford
1948-49	Bert Giesebrecht	Windsor
1949-50	Earl Reibel	Windsor
1950-51	Lou Jankowski	Oshawa
1951-52	Ken Laufman	Guelph
1952-53	Jim McBurney	Galt
1953-54	Brian Cullen	St. Catharines
1954-55	Hank Ciesla	St. Catharines
1955-56	Stan Baliuk	Kitchener
1956-57	Bill Sweeney	Guelph
1957-58	John McKenzie	St. Catharines
1958-59	Stan Mikita	St. Catharines
1959-60	Chico Maki	St. Catharines
1960-61	Rod Gilbert	Guelph
1961-62	Andre Boudrias	Montreal
1962-63	Wayne Maxner	Niagara Falls
1963-64	Andre Boudrias	Montreal
1964-65	Ken Hodge	St. Catharines
1965-66	Andre Lacroix	Peterborough
1966-67	Derek Sanderson	Niagara Falls
1967-68	Tom Webster	Niagara Falls
1968-69	Rejean Houle	Montreal
1969-70	Marcel Dionne	St. Catharines
1970-71	Marcel Dionne	St. Catharines
1971-72	Bill Harris	Toronto
1972-73	Blake Dunlop	Ottawa
1973-74	Jack Valiquette	Sault Ste. Marie
	Rick Adduono	St. Catharines
1974-75	Bruce Boudreau	Toronto
1975-76	Mike Kaszycki	Sault Ste. Marie
1976-77	Dwight Foster	Kitchener
1977-78	Bobby Smith	Ottawa
1978-79	Mike Foligno	Sudbury
1979-80	Jim Fox	Ottawa
1980-81	John Goodwin	Sault Ste. Marie
1981-82	Dave Simpson	London
1982-83	Doug Gilmour	Cornwall
1983-84	Tim Salmon	Kingston

Dave Pinkney Goaltending Trophy

Season	Player	Club
1948-49	Gil Mayer	Barrie
1949-50	Don Lockhart	Marlboros
1950-51	Don Lockhart	Marlboros
	Lorne Howes	Barrie
1951-52	Don Head	Marlboros
1952-53	John Henderson	Marlboros
1953-54	Dennis Riggin	Hamilton
1954-55	John Albani	Marlboros
1955-56	Jim Crockett	Marlboros
1956-57	Len Broderick	Marlboros
1957-58	Len Broderick	Marlboros
1958-59	Jacques Carron	Peterborough
1959-60	Gerry Cheevers	St. Michael's
1960-61	Bud Blom	Hamilton
1961-62	George Holmes	Montreal
1962-63	Chuck Goddard	Peterborough
1963-64	Bernie Parent	Niagara Falls
1964-65	Bernie Parent	Niagara Falls
1965-66	Ted Quimet	Montreal
1966-67	Peter MacDuffe	St. Catharines
1967-68	Bruce Mullet	Montreal
1968-69	Wayne Wood	Montreal
1969-70	John Garrett	Peterborough
1970-71	John Garrett	Peterborough
1971-72	Michel Lacroque	Ottawa
1972-73	Mike Palmateer	Toronto
1973-74	Don Edwards	Kitchener
1974-75	Greg Millen	Peterborough
1975-76	Jim Bedard	Sudbury
1976-77	Pat Riggin	London
1977-78	Al Jensen	Hamilton
1978-79	Nick Ricci	Niagara Falls
1979-80	Rick LaFerriere	Peterborough
1980-81	Jim Ralph	Ottawa
1981-82	Marc D'Amour	Sault Ste. Marie
1982-83	Peter Sidorkiewicz	Oshawa
	Jeff Hogg	Oshawa
1983-84	Darren Pang	Ottawa
	Greg Coram	Ottawa

Max Kaminsky Defenseman Award

Season   Player   Club
1969-70—Ron Plumb, Peterborough
1970-71—Jocelyn Guevremont, Montreal
1971-72—Denis Potvin, Ottawa
1972-73—Denis Potvin, Ottawa
1973-74—Jim Turkiewicz, Peterborough
1974-75—Mike O'Connell, Kingston
1975-76—Rick Green, London
1976-77—Craig Hartsburg, S. Ste. Marie
1977-78—Brad Marsh, London
           Rob Ramage, London
1978-79—Greg Theberge, Peterborough
1979-80—Larry Murphy, Peterborough
1980-81—Steve Smith, Sault Ste. Marie
1981-82—Ron Meighan, Niagara Falls
1982-83—Allan MacInnis, Kitchener
1983-84—Brad Shaw, Ottawa

William Hanley Trophy
(Awarded annually for gentlemanly play.)

Season   Player   Club
1960-61—Bruce Draper, St. Michael's
1961-62—Lowell MacDonald, Hamilton
1962-63—Paul Henderson, Hamilton
1963-64—Fred Stanfield, St. Catharines
1964-65—Jimmy Peters, Hamilton
1965-66—Andre Lacroix, Peterborough

Season   Player   Club
1966-67—Mickey Redmond, Peterborough
1967-68—Tom Webster, Niagara Falls
1968-69—Rejean Houle, Montreal
1969-74—No award presented
1974-75—Doug Jarvis, Peterborough
1975-76—Dale McCourt, Hamilton
1976-77—Dale McCourt, St. Catharines
1977-78—Wayne Gretzky, S.S. Marie
1978-79—Sean Simpson, Ottawa
1979-80—Sean Simpson, Ottawa
1980-81—John Goodwin, Sault Ste. Marie
1981-82—Dave Simpson, London
1982-83—Kirk Muller, Guelph
1983-84—Kevin Conway, Kingston

Hap Emms Rookie Award

Season   Player   Club
1972-73—Dennis Maruk, London
1973-74—Jack Valiquette, Sault Ste. Marie
1974-75—Danny Shearer, Hamilton
1975-76—John Travella, Sault Ste. Marie
1976-77—Yvan Joly, Ottawa
1977-78—Wayne Gretzky, S. S. Marie
1978-79—John Goodwin, Sault Ste. Marie
1979-80—Bruce Dowie, Toronto
1980-81—Tony Tanti, Oshawa
1981-82—Pat Verbeek, Sudbury
1982-83—Bruce Cassidy, Ottawa
1983-84—Shawn Burr, Kitchener

Western Hockey League

(Known as Western Canada Hockey League prior to 1978-79)

President—Ed Chynoweth
Executive Assistant—Richard Doerksen
Statistician—Norman Dueck
616-5920 MacLeod Trail S., Calgary, Alberta T2H OK2
Phone—(403) 253-8113

Final 1983-84 WHL Standings

East Division

	G.	W.	L.	T.	Pts.	GF.	GA.
Regina Pats	72	48	23	1	97	426	284
Medicine Hat Tigers	72	45	26	1	91	404	288
Brandon Wheat Kings	72	44	26	2	90	463	346
Lethbridge Broncos	72	44	28	0	88	271	256
Prince Albert Raiders	72	41	29	2	84	411	357
Calgary Wranglers	72	36	36	0	72	353	345
Saskatoon Blades	72	36	36	0	72	347	350
Winnipeg Warriors	72	9	63	0	18	239	580

West Division

	G.	W.	L.	T.	Pts.	GF.	GA.
Kamloops Junior Oilers	72	50	22	0	100	467	332
New Westminster Bruins	72	34	36	2	70	304	348
Portland Winter Hawks	72	33	39	0	66	430	449
Seattle Breakers	72	32	39	1	65	350	379
Victoria Cougars	72	32	40	0	64	340	338
Kelowna Wings	72	15	56	1	31	295	448

Top 20 Scorers for the Bob Brownridge Memorial Trophy

	Games	G.	A.	Pts.	Pen.
1. Ray Ferraro, Brandon	72	*108	84	*192	84
2. Dan Hodgson, Prince Albert	66	62	*119	181	65
3. Dale Derkatch, Regina	62	72	87	159	92
4. Taylor Hall, Regina	69	63	79	142	42
5. Cam Plante, Brandon	72	22	118	140	96
6. Dean Evason, Kamloops	57	49	88	137	89
7. Cliff Ronning, New Westminster	71	69	67	136	10
Mark Lamb, Medicine Hat	72	59	77	136	30
9. Fabian Joseph, Victoria	72	52	75	127	27
10. Dave Pasin, Prince Albert	71	68	54	122	68
11. Ken Quinney, Calgary	71	64	54	118	38
Jack MacKeigan, Victoria	71	55	63	118	112
13. Doug Kyle, Lethbridge/Saskatoon	62	56	59	115	71
14. Grant Sasser, Portland	66	44	69	113	24
15. Alan Kerr, Seattle	66	46	66	112	141
Allen Conroy, Medicine Hat	69	38	74	112	89
17. Mike Lay, Medicine Hat	61	54	56	110	32
18. Emanuel Viveiros, Prince Albert	67	15	94	109	48
19. Terry Sargent, Seattle	70	41	60	101	54
Byron Lomow, Brandon	71	44	57	101	44

Team-by-Team Breakdown of WHL Scoring

Brandon Wheat Kings

	Games	G.	A.	Pts.	Pen.
Ray Ferraro	72	*108	84	*192	84
Cam Plante	72	22	118	140	96
Byron Lomow	71	44	57	101	44
Stacy Pratt	55	34	64	98	19
David Curry, Seattle	33	13	17	30	14
Brandon	33	32	31	63	2
Totals	66	45	48	93	16
Brad Wells	68	25	40	65	142
Allen Tarasuk	65	27	32	59	134
Gord Paddock	72	14	37	51	151
Bryan Wells	53	22	23	45	259
Derek Laxdal	70	23	20	43	86
Brent Jessiman	60	20	13	33	89
Pat Loyer	63	4	28	32	69
Dave Thomlinson	41	17	12	29	62
Brad Duggan	18	3	25	28	6
John Dzikowski	47	12	11	23	99
Jim Agnew	71	6	17	23	107
Boyd Lomow, Kelowna	4	0	0	0	7
Brandon	35	10	12	22	27
Totals	39	10	12	22	34
Kelly Glowa	7	7	14	21	10
Paul More	34	9	11	20	23
Roy Caswell	29	7	5	12	8
Kelly Kozak	71	4	7	11	125
Rob Ordman, N. W.M.	1	1	0	1	0
Brandon	28	3	5	8	9
Totals	29	4	5	9	9
Randy Cameron, Winn.	26	1	2	3	88
Brandon	35	0	6	6	87
Totals	61	1	8	9	175
Ron Hextall (Goalie)	46	0	8	8	117
Jay Palmer (Goalie)	30	0	3	3	17
Darwin Penny	7	1	0	1	0
Lee Davis	1	0	1	1	0
Kevin Baumgartner (G.)	2	0	1	1	0
Tim Bzowey	1	0	0	0	0
Bernie Legault (Goalie)	1	0	0	0	0
Brent Mireau	1	0	0	0	0
Dean Sexsmith	1	0	0	0	0
Ken Therrien	1	0	0	0	0
Murray Rice	2	0	0	0	0
T. Brown, Kamloops (G.)	1	0	0	0	0
Brandon (Goalie)	2	0	0	0	0
Totals	3	0	0	0	0
Kevin Scott	3	0	0	0	11
Darin Jorgenson	6	0	0	0	11

Calgary Wranglers

	Games	G.	A.	Pts.	Pen.
Ken Quinney	71	64	54	118	38
Doug Moffat	72	32	68	100	42
Barry Bracko	46	22	49	71	48
Scott Machej	54	36	34	70	47
Scott Makin	56	27	42	69	56
Garth Hildebrand	54	28	28	56	33
Allen Measures	69	17	36	53	96
Landis Chaulk	72	21	28	49	123
Rod Matechuk	64	29	18	47	55
Rob McKechney	72	6	31	37	104
Doug Houda	69	6	30	36	195
Dana Murzyn	65	11	20	31	135
Pat Mangold	69	18	11	29	107
Jim Playfair, Portland	16	5	6	11	38
Calgary	46	6	9	15	96
Totals	60	11	15	26	134
Darrel Daignault	66	11	10	21	43
Mitch Cornett	64	3	15	18	92
Ken Spangler	71	1	12	13	119
Mike Zimmel	44	2	9	11	8
Ted Materi	12	3	2	5	16
Ross McKay (Goalie)	42	0	4	4	19
Chris Churchill (Goalie)	29	0	2	2	6
Mike Mansfield	2	0	1	1	0
Rod Taylor	3	0	1	1	2
Bob Cooper (Goalie)	8	0	1	1	12
Rob Nealon, P. Albert	8	0	1	1	25
Calgary	12	0	0	0	7
Totals	20	0	1	1	32
Chad Fleck	1	0	0	0	0
Mike Kardash	1	0	0	0	0
Darren Taylor	2	0	0	0	0
Mike Hall	3	0	0	0	0
Shannon Krusky	7	0	0	0	0
Darcy Money	10	0	0	0	12
Mike Bukta	11	0	0	0	5

Kamloops Junior Oilers

	Games	G.	A.	Pts.	Pen.
Dean Evason	57	49	88	137	89
Doug Bodger	70	21	77	98	90
Mike Nottingham	71	48	43	91	60
Tony Vogel	65	41	48	89	44
Stacey Wakabayashi	72	32	38	70	34
Greg Evtushevski	64	27	43	70	176
Ryan Stewart	69	31	38	69	88
Doug Saunders	48	35	25	60	94
Rob Brown	50	16	42	58	80
Jim Camazzola, Seattle	3	1	1	2	0
Kamloops	29	26	24	50	25
Totals	32	27	25	52	25
Brian Bertuzzi	69	29	21	50	99
Dean Clark	54	18	28	46	64
Robin Bawa	64	16	28	44	40
Gord Mark	67	12	30	42	202
Mark Ferner	72	9	30	39	162
Ken Daneyko	19	6	28	34	52
Greg Hawgood	49	10	23	33	39
Todd Carnelley	70	7	23	30	66
Mark Kachowsky	57	6	9	15	156
Rudy Poeschuk	47	3	9	12	93
Daryl Reaugh (Goalie)	55	0	5	5	18
Neil Pilon	9	0	2	2	0
Rex Grant, Seattle (G.)	9	0	0	0	4
Kamloops (Goalie)	40	0	1	1	12
Totals	49	0	1	1	16
Will Anderson	1	0	0	0	0
Dean Gladue	1	0	0	0	0
Brian Powell	1	0	0	0	2
Russ Goglin	3	0	0	0	0
Mike Goodwin	3	0	0	0	0
Martin Hood (Goalie)	3	0	0	0	0
Ron Viglasi	3	0	0	0	9

Kelowna Wings

	Games	G.	A.	Pts.	Pen.
Terry Zaporzan	72	36	60	96	10
Jeff Fenton	67	32	58	90	105
Grant Delcourt	72	22	53	75	55
Dave McLay	71	34	34	68	112
Darren Cota	66	30	31	61	152
Mark Fioretti, Calgary	24	1	11	12	58
Kelowna	47	11	35	46	45
Totals	71	12	46	58	103
Shawn Vincent	58	17	22	39	44
Rocky Dundas	72	15	24	39	57
Dave MacDonald, M.H.	12	2	4	6	5
Kelowna	32	15	16	31	22
Totals	44	17	20	37	27
Jeff Sharples	72	9	24	33	51
Cam Lazoruk	70	14	16	30	100
Brent Gilchrist	69	16	11	27	16
Kodie Nelson, Med. Hat	15	1	2	3	14
Saskatoon	36	5	9	14	47
Kelowna	0	1	4	5	8
Totals	51	7	15	22	69
Ed Palichuk	71	2	10	12	47
Bob Shaw	23	4	5	9	26
Chad Walker	49	2	7	9	33
Dean Tambellini, Leth	40	2	4	6	13
Kelowna	20	1	1	2	6
Totals	60	3	5	8	19
Greg Zuk	53	2	6	8	36
Darwin Moeller	34	3	2	5	2
Todd Voshell	14	0	5	5	18
Richard Lindstrom	33	1	2	3	45
Doug Wilson	9	0	2	2	4
Mikael Jonnson	21	0	2	2	8
Glen Barre	1	0	0	0	0
Greg Hollomay (Goalie)	1	0	0	0	0
Scott Young	1	0	0	0	0
Peter Martin (Goalie)	2	0	0	0	0
Paul Mottishaw	2	0	0	0	0
Greg Moberg, Seattle	3	0	0	0	8
Kelowna	2	0	0	0	0
Totals	5	0	0	0	8
Mike Wegleitner	8	0	0	0	0
Darcy Wakulak (Goalie)	31	0	0	0	16
Bruno Campese (Goalie)	48	0	0	0	6

Lethbridge Broncos

	Games	G.	A.	Pts.	Pen.
Rick Gal	72	40	49	89	16
J.C. McEwan	68	32	55	87	167
Darin Sceviour	71	37	28	65	28
Bob Rouse	71	18	42	60	101
Jim Odland	72	21	27	48	90
Dwight Mullins	70	20	23	43	101
Steve Nemeth	68	22	20	42	33
Cam Douglas, Winnipeg	39	21	14	35	40
Lethbridge	3	1	1	2	0
Totals	42	22	15	37	40
Todd Stokowski	72	11	25	36	30
Gerald Diduck	65	10	24	34	133
Rich Wiest	71	17	16	33	138
Grant Couture	70	9	23	32	149
Stu Wenaas, Winnipeg	2	0	0	0	0
Kelowna	33	14	16	30	53
Lethbridge	1	0	0	0	0
Totals	36	14	16	30	53
Darcy Kaminski	71	5	15	20	96

	Games	G.	A.	Pts.	Pen.
Mark Tinordi	72	5	14	19	53
Todd Sceviour	72	6	10	16	46
Trent Kaese	64	6	6	12	33
Mike Berger	41	2	9	11	60
Ward Carlson, Seattle	10	2	5	7	9
Lethbridge	1	0	0	0	5
Totals	11	2	5	7	14
Kevin Pylypow	27	3	3	6	37
Stuart Sage	23	1	3	4	9
Ken Williston	59	1	1	2	45
Ken Wregget (Goalie)	53	0	1	1	26
Ray Guenther	1	0	0	0	0
Darren Mazutinec	1	0	0	0	0
Mike Morin	2	0	0	0	7
Rod Williams	2	0	0	0	0
Jamie Bowman (Goalie)	13	0	0	0	0
Shawn Oswald (Goalie)	16	0	0	0	0

Medicine Hat Tigers

	Games	G.	A.	Pts.	Pen.
Mark Lamb	72	59	77	136	30
Allen Conroy	69	38	74	112	89
Mike Lay	61	54	56	110	32
Murray Craven	48	38	56	94	53
Rocky Trottier	65	34	50	84	41
Brent Meckling	67	10	53	63	71
Matt Kabayama	72	21	41	62	29
Bob Bassen	72	29	29	58	93
Kevan Guy	72	15	42	57	117
Darrel Henry	58	24	22	46	98
Gord Shmyrko	72	23	16	39	46
Dan Turner	72	17	22	39	181
Terry Knight	68	12	15	27	39
Brent Steblyk	48	2	22	24	47
Gord Hynes	72	5	14	19	39
Al Pedersen	44	0	11	11	47
Shane Churla	48	3	7	10	115
Trevor Semeniuk	71	1	6	7	79
Jim Kambeitz	34	2	3	5	41
Dean McArthur	3	2	1	3	0
Carey Bracko	8	0	2	2	13
G. Johnson, Winn. (G.)	2	0	0	0	7
Med. Hat (G.)	37	0	1	1	25
Totals	39	0	1	1	32
Blair MacGregor (G.)	39	0	1	1	31
Craig Penner	1	0	0	0	2
Kelly Schacher	1	0	0	0	0
Jeff Wenaas	1	0	0	0	0
Randy Wong	1	0	0	0	0
Cory Brown (Goalie)	2	0	0	0	0
Todd Pederson	2	0	0	0	0
Steve Risling	2	0	0	0	0
Brent Kisillvich (Goalie)	3	0	0	0	0
Mark Pederson	3	0	0	0	0

New Westminster Bruins

	Games	G.	A.	Pts.	Pen.
Cliff Ronning	71	69	67	136	10
Roger Mulvenna	72	25	35	60	48
Vern Smith	69	13	44	57	94
Randy Maxwell	33	14	34	48	30
Brent Hughes	67	21	18	39	133
Shawn Nagurny, M.H.	9	5	0	5	10
New Westminster	34	7	27	34	16
Totals	43	12	27	39	26
Kent Hayes	70	20	18	38	32

	Games	G.	A.	Pts.	Pen.
Craig Berube	70	11	20	31	104
Troy Farkvam	36	13	17	30	43
Al Chatlain, P. Albert	31	0	6	6	29
New Westminster	34	9	15	24	20
Totals	65	9	21	30	49
Doug Quinn	68	8	22	30	122
Shawn Green, Leth.	1	1	1	2	0
New Westminster	58	12	14	26	115
Totals	59	13	15	28	115
Rob Benjamin	66	15	10	25	39
Todd Ewen	68	11	13	24	176
Dave Johnston	62	9	10	19	152
Mark Zeitlin	70	3	16	19	38
Brad Hammett	22	6	8	14	18
Dale Thompson, Calg.	38	7	6	13	41
New Westminster	4	0	0	0	7
Totals	42	7	6	13	48
Lee Trimm	68	1	10	11	43
Kevin Griffin	9	5	5	10	33
Mark McLeary	8	4	5	9	2
Laine Jeannotte	20	2	7	9	21
Dale Briscoe, Seattle	3	1	2	3	4
New Westminster	8	3	2	5	0
Totals	11	4	4	8	4
Jamie Cayford	28	3	5	8	21
Dwight Boss, Seattle	6	0	1	1	35
New Westminster	11	4	1	5	20
Totals	17	4	2	6	55
Chris Crossman	9	1	2	3	7
Darin Choquette	8	0	2	2	14
Bill Ranford (Goalie)	27	0	2	2	0
Dean Kolstad	4	1	0	1	0
Pokey Reddick (Goalie)	50	0	1	1	6
Robert Foglietta, Kam.	1	0	0	0	0
New Westminster	1	0	0	0	0
Totals	2	0	0	0	0
Mike O'Brien	2	0	0	0	0
Scott Harlow	4	0	0	0	0
Pat Seely	4	0	0	0	0

Portland Winter Hawks

	Games	G.	A.	Pts.	Pen.
Grant Sasser	60	44	69	113	24
Jeff Rohlicek	71	44	53	97	22
Ray Podloski	66	46	50	96	44
Randy Heath	60	44	46	90	107
Sean Harder, Seattle	25	5	14	19	8
Portland	53	24	30	54	10
Totals	*78	29	44	73	18
Gord Walker	58	28	41	69	65
Terry Perkins	68	35	30	65	75
Alfie Turcotte	32	22	41	63	39
John Kordic	67	9	50	59	232
Curt Brandolini	42	22	26	48	91
Brian Benning	38	6	41	47	108
John Bekkers, Regina	32	8	1	9	25
Portland	22	21	14	35	17
Totals	54	29	15	44	42
Tim Lorenz	64	19	14	33	112
Bryan Walker	67	6	25	31	182
Cam Neely	19	8	18	26	29
Rick Davidson	72	3	22	25	47
Terry Jones	28	6	18	24	25
Craig Butz, Kelowna	20	3	7	10	59
Portland	54	2	10	12	214
Totals	74	5	17	22	*273

	Games	G.	A.	Pts.	Pen.
Dave MacKenzie, Kam.	23	11	9	20	12
Portland	3	0	0	0	0
Totals	26	11	9	20	12
Jamie Nicolls	44	7	12	19	14
Rich Kromm	10	10	4	14	13
Trevor Hendry, Seattle	18	2	3	5	12
Portland	33	2	4	6	39
Totals	51	4	7	11	51
Blaine Chrest	12	5	4	9	2
Marty Ruff	10	4	2	6	30
Glen Wesley	3	1	2	3	0
Dan Woodley	6	1	2	3	2
Ian Wood (Goalie)	40	0	3	3	10
Troy Arndt	3	1	1	2	4
Benton Hadley	1	1	0	1	0
Ali Butorac	2	0	1	1	0
David Archibald	7	0	1	1	2
Peter Fry (Goalie)	39	0	1	1	27
Jeff Finley	5	0	0	0	0
M. Mais'euve, Sea. (G.)	8	0	0	0	2
Portland (Goalie)	16	0	0	0	2
Totals	24	0	0	0	4

Prince Albert Raiders

	Games	G.	A.	Pts.	Pen.
Dan Hodgson	66	62	*119	181	65
Dave Pasin	71	68	54	122	68
Emanuel Viveiros	67	15	94	109	48
Todd Bergen	43	57	39	96	15
Al Stewart	67	44	39	83	216
Ken Morrison	71	30	37	67	20
Dale McFee	70	24	40	64	142
Dave Goertz	60	13	47	60	111
Derek Karolat	58	16	41	57	26
Brad Bennett, Winnipeg	30	14	8	22	38
Prince Albert	28	5	15	20	49
Totals	58	19	23	42	87
Mitch Poulin, New W.M.	29	8	7	15	22
Prince Albert	32	7	11	18	15
Totals	61	15	18	33	37
Steve Gotaas	65	10	22	32	47
Colin Feser	71	17	13	30	90
Wally Niewchas	71	4	23	27	116
Steve Brunner	70	5	21	26	123
John Davis	58	8	17	25	98
Kim Issel	31	9	9	18	24
Warren Yadlowski, Cal.	11	2	2	4	2
Prince Albert	23	6	6	12	8
Totals	34	8	8	16	10
Dave Manson	70	2	7	9	233
Tim Weiss	34	0	9	9	37
Cy Laflamme	16	3	4	7	44
Ken Baumgartner	57	1	6	7	203
Ward Komonosky (G.)	45	0	4	4	42
John Lamb	25	2	1	3	47
Dan Moberg (Goalie)	31	0	3	3	4
Pat Elyniuk	2	1	0	1	0
Brent Wahpoosyan	2	1	0	1	0
Marc Casavant	3	1	0	1	2
Mel Marshall	4	0	1	1	8
Dan Baker	1	0	0	0	0
Sheldon Brost	1	0	0	0	0
Dave Kendall	1	0	0	0	2
Dale Kushner	1	0	0	0	5
Lee Pederson	3	0	0	0	0
Roy Gunn (Goalie)	6	0	0	0	0

Regina Pats

	Games	G.	A.	Pts.	Pen.
Dale Derkatch	62	72	87	159	92
Taylor Hall	69	63	79	142	42
Doug Trapp	59	43	50	93	44
Lyndon Byers	58	32	57	89	154
Jason Meyer	70	16	67	83	39
Kurt Wickenheiser	69	38	31	69	60
John Miner	70	27	42	69	132
Tim Iannone	69	30	34	64	26
Selmar Odelein	71	9	42	51	45
Bob Lowes	71	21	27	48	118
Brent Fedyk	63	15	28	43	30
Jeff Lawson, Winnipeg	10	5	4	9	21
Regina	57	9	9	18	109
Totals	67	14	13	27	130
Allan Acton, Saskatoon	14	3	3	6	19
Regina	54	7	11	18	56
Totals	68	10	14	24	75
Len Nielsen	57	9	15	24	20
Rick Herbert	58	3	18	21	78
Stu Grimson	63	8	8	16	131
Kevin Clemens	47	5	8	13	14
Brad Lauer	60	5	7	12	51
Robert Dirk	62	2	10	12	64
Frank Joo	50	2	7	9	90
Jim Appleby (Goalie)	4	0	1	1	0
Gerald Bzdel	1	0	0	0	0
Ken Karius	1	0	0	0	0
Tim Logan	1	0	0	0	0
Kenton Rein (Goalie)	1	0	0	0	0
Dean Shaw	1	0	0	0	0
Troy Edwards	2	0	0	0	0
Bob MacKenzie	2	0	0	0	0
Larry Dyck (Goalie)	26	0	0	0	17
Jamie Reeve (Goalie)	47	0	0	0	22

Saskatoon Blades

	Games	G.	A.	Pts.	Pen.
Doug Kyle, Lethbridge	3	1	1	2	0
Saskatoon	59	55	58	113	71
Totals	62	56	59	115	71
Joey Kocur	69	40	41	81	258
Dale Henry	71	41	36	77	162
Dan Leier	72	23	46	69	99
Wendel Clark	72	23	45	68	225
Ron Dreger	71	29	37	66	56
Trent Yawney	72	13	46	59	81
Larry Korchinski	62	26	21	47	29
Dwaine Hutton, Regina	14	2	2	4	2
Saskatoon	35	13	30	43	16
Totals	49	15	32	47	18
R.J. Dundas, Kelowna	48	9	25	34	62
Saskatoon	19	4	7	11	24
Totals	67	13	32	45	86
Randy Smith	69	19	21	40	53
Dave Chartier	59	9	21	30	136
Mark Thietke	70	10	13	23	40
Todd McLellan	50	8	14	22	15
Kerry Laviolette	70	8	10	18	100
Grant Jennings	64	5	13	18	102
Rick Smith	21	10	7	17	6
Duncan McPherson	45	0	14	14	74
Kevin Kowalchuk	56	1	7	8	4
Curtis Chamberlin	69	2	5	7	73
Al Larochelle (Goalie)	56	0	4	4	27
Greg Lebsack	25	1	2	3	11

	Games	G.	A.	Pts.	Pen.
Greg Holtby (Goalie)	30	0	3	3	6
Adrian Sakundiak	5	0	1	1	5
Tim Hildebrandt	1	0	0	0	0
Lubo Dzurilla	2	0	0	0	0
Ward Edwards	3	0	0	0	0
Steve Balas	5	0	0	0	10
Bryan Larkin	6	0	0	0	0
Robin Harper	7	0	0	0	0

Seattle Breakers

	Games	G.	A.	Pts.	Pen.
Alan Kerr	66	46	66	112	141
Terry Sargent	70	41	60	101	54
Gary Stewart	71	24	63	87	170
Darren Schmidt, Bran.	39	9	18	27	48
Seattle	36	21	26	47	59
Totals	75	30	44	74	107
Derek Ruppel, Kamloops	6	1	4	5	17
Seattle	56	29	28	57	105
Totals	62	30	32	62	122
John Bacso	63	22	39	61	133
Tim Ziola	72	17	39	56	124
Ken Jorgenson, M.H.	3	0	0	0	7
Seattle	67	23	31	54	99
Totals	70	23	31	54	106
Kelly Para, Kamloops	37	12	10	22	42
Seattle	32	16	6	22	49
Totals	69	28	16	44	91
Brent Severyn	72	14	22	36	49
Scott Robinson	44	17	18	35	105
Jim Bechtold	70	16	19	35	140
Bob Ginnetti, New W.M.	21	4	13	17	11
Seattle	29	0	6	6	22
Totals	50	4	19	23	33
Craig Endean	67	16	6	22	14
Brad Melin	27	4	13	17	4
Brian McFarlane	65	6	10	16	12
Scott Shaw, Lethbridge	1	0	0	0	9
Seattle	51	2	12	14	133
Totals	52	2	12	14	142
Jamie Huscroft, Portland	18	0	5	5	15
Seattle	45	0	7	7	62
Totals	63	0	12	12	77
Ray Savard	67	5	6	11	68
Jim Dokter	33	3	8	11	61
Chris Tarnowski	37	3	4	7	40
Kelly Argotow	16	2	1	3	20
Brian Pascal, Lethbridge	13	0	2	2	6
Seattle	3	0	1	1	2
Totals	16	0	3	3	8
Theo Van Gervan	6	2	0	2	13
Ben Pernosky	6	0	1	1	27
Mark Centrone	1	0	0	0	0
Marcel Raby	2	0	0	0	0
Dino Vulpitta	6	0	0	0	7
Greg Hubert (Goalie)	21	0	0	0	0
Dwayne Murray (G.)	48	0	0	0	31

Victoria Cougars

	Games	G.	A.	Pts.	Pen.
Fabian Joseph	72	52	75	127	27
Jack MacKeigan	71	55	63	118	112
Tom Martin	60	30	45	75	261
Eric Thurston	65	17	51	68	37
Russ Courtnall	32	29	37	66	63
Rob Kivell	52	16	33	49	145

	Games	G.	A.	Pts.	Pen.
Paul Bifano	66	22	23	45	25
Simon Wheeldon	56	14	24	38	43
Dave Mackey	69	15	15	30	97
Steve Bayliss	40	12	16	28	74
Ken Priestly	55	10	18	28	31
Richard Hajdu	42	17	10	27	106
Leroy Remple	22	10	15	25	17
Matt Hervey	67	4	19	23	89
Dean Drozdiak	70	4	18	22	44
Brenn Leach	70	3	19	22	89
Adam Morrison	38	9	10	19	6
Misko Antisin	47	7	12	19	129
Greg Davies	69	7	3	10	34
Randy Siska	57	3	4	7	4
Jim Gunn	54	1	5	6	69
Dan Sexton	25	3	2	5	8
Darren Moren (Goalie)	45	0	3	3	35
Ed Jones (Goalie)	1	0	0	0	2
Kent Lewis	3	0	0	0	0
Richard Moreau	4	0	0	0	9
Randy Hansch (Goalie)	36	0	0	0	4

Winnipeg Warriors

	Games	G.	A.	Pts.	Pen.
Tony Grenier	60	42	31	73	28
Dave Koral	57	15	48	63	49
Rick Strachan	72	14	47	61	59
Troy Vollhoffer	66	22	37	59	92
Joe Van Ness	59	17	21	38	125
Fred Ledlin, Portland	3	2	1	3	2
Medicine Hat	11	7	3	10	12
Winnipeg	16	5	19	24	6

	Games	G.	A.	Pts.	Pen.
Totals	30	14	23	37	20
Ross McGowan	56	12	23	35	34
Peter Derksen	34	9	21	30	40
Dean Braham	72	12	17	29	122
Corey Picknicki	68	7	16	23	48
Jeff Frank, Kelowna	1	1	1	2	5
Winnipeg	29	10	10	20	23
Totals	30	11	11	22	28
Mark Howery	58	10	8	18	33
Walter Shutter, Regina	2	0	0	0	0
Winnipeg	34	7	9	16	49
Totals	36	7	9	16	49
Dan Hart	35	4	12	16	38
Don Herczeg	54	4	11	15	122
Ian Spencer	51	2	11	13	194
Scott McGregor	53	2	4	6	54
Brian Martens	61	1	5	6	66
Cliff Keller, Prince Alb.	11	0	0	0	26
Winnipeg	20	1	3	4	18
Totals	31	1	3	4	44
Glenn Madden	7	2	0	2	0
Mick Vukota	3	1	1	2	10
Dennis Cann	3	0	1	1	5
Curtis Fayant	3	0	1	1	0
Troy Kennedy	3	0	1	1	0
Gilles Savard	4	0	1	1	0
Jamie Dubberly (Goalie)	36	0	1	1	0
Mike Kean	1	0	0	0	0
Ken Mayer	1	0	0	0	0
Barry Pitz	1	0	0	0	0
Selby McFarlane	30	0	0	0	0
Doug Lunney (Goalie)	50	0	0	0	2

Complete WHL Individual Goaltending

	Games	Mins.	Goals	SO.	Avg.
Ed Jones, Victoria	1	28	0	0	0.00
Bernie Legault, Brandon	1	13	0	0	0.00
Kenton Rein, Regina	1	7	0	0	0.00
Ken Wregget, Lethbridge	53	*3053	161	0	*3.16
Jamie Reeve, Regina	47	2663	168(1)	*3	3.79
Blair MacGregor, Medicine Hat	39	2119	134	1	3.79
Larry Dyck, Regina	26	1436	95	0	3.97
Shawn Oswald, Lethbridge	16	666	45(1)	0	4.05
Ron Hextall, Brandon	46	2670	190	0	4.27
Daryl Reaugh, Kamloops	55	2748	199	1	4.34
Pokey Reddick, New Westminster	50	2930	215(1)	0	4.40
Ross McKay, Calgary	42	2342	175(2)	0	4.48
Cory Brown, Medicine Hat	2	120	9	0	4.50
Peter Martin, Kelowna	2	80	6	0	4.50
Gary Johnson, Winnipeg	2	119	17(1)	0	8.57
Medicine Hat	37	2047	146(1)	0	4.28
Totals	39	2166	163(2)	0	4.52
Randy Hansch, Victoria	36	1894	144(2)	0	4.56
Jamie Bowman, Lethbridge	13	637	49	0	4.62
Greg Holtby, Saskatoon	30	1319	104	1	4.73
Darren Moren, Victoria	45	2419	191(1)	2	4.74
Chris Churchill, Calgary	29	1582	126(3)	0	4.78
Dan Moberg, Prince Albert	31	1589	127	0	4.80
Al Larochelle, Saskatoon	*56	3033	244(2)	0	4.83
Rex Grant, Seattle	9	430	37	0	5.16
Kamloops	40	1857	147(1)	0	4.75
Totals	49	2287	184(1)	0	4.83
Greg Hubert, Seattle	21	920	75	0	4.89
Ward Komonosky, Prince Albert	45	2521	207	1	4.93
Jim Appleby, Regina	4	240	20	0	5.00
Dwayne Murray, Seattle	48	2630	222(2)	0	5.06
Bill Ranford, New Westminster	27	1450	130(2)	0	5.38
Roy Gunn, Prince Albert	6	254	23	0	5.43
Jay Palmer, Brandon	30	1594	146	0	5.50
Brent Kisilivich, Medicine Hat	3	172	16	0	5.58

	Games	Mins.	Goals	SO.	Avg.
Bob Cooper, Calgary	8	413	39	0	5.67
Peter Fry, Portland	39	1930	186(2)	0	5.78
Ian Wood, Portland	40	2049	207(1)	0	6.06
Bruno Campese, Kelowna	48	2696	274(1)	0	6.10
Darcy Wakulak, Kelowna	31	1555	163(1)	0	6.29
Doug Lunney, Winnipeg	50	2641	*304(3)	0	6.91
Mike Maissoneuve, Seattle	8	373	43	0	6.92
Portland	16	746	96	0	7.72
Totals	24	1119	139	0	7.45
Kevin Baumgartner, Brandon	2	64	8	0	7.50
Martin Wood, Kamloops	3	110	15	0	8.18
Tim Brown, Kamloops	1	49	7	0	8.57
Brandon	2	65	9	0	8.31
Totals	3	114	16	0	8.42
Grey Hollomay, Kelowna	1	20	3	0	9.00
Jamie Dubberly, Winnipeg	36	1575	254(1)	0	9.68

( )—Empty Net Goals. Do not count against a Goaltender's average.

Individual WHL Regular Season Leaders

Goals	Ray Ferraro, Brandon—	108
Assists	Dan Hodgson, Prince Albert—	119
Points	Ray Ferraro, Brandon—	192
Penalty Minutes	Craig Butz, Kelowna/Portland—	273
Goaltender's Average	Ken Wregget, Lethbridge—	3.16
Shutouts	Jamie Reeve, Regina—	3

1984 WHL Playoff

East Division Quarterfinals
(Best-of-seven series)

SERIES "A"
	W.	L.	Pts.	GF.	GA.
Regina	4	0	8	28	13
Calgary	0	4	0	13	28

(Regina wins series, 4 games to 0)

SERIES "B"
	W.	L.	Pts.	GF.	GA.
Medicine Hat	4	1	8	32	21
Prince Albert	1	4	2	21	32

(Medicine Hat wins series, 4 games to 1)

SERIES "C"
	W.	L.	Pts.	GF.	GA.
Brandon	4	1	8	30	13
Lethbridge	1	4	2	13	30

(Brandon wins series, 4 games to 1)

East Division Semifinals
(Best-of-three series)

SERIES "D"
	W.	L.	Pts.	GF.	GA.
Regina	2	1	4	16	12
Brandon	1	2	2	12	16

(Regina wins series, 2 games to 1)

West Division Semifinals
(Best-of-nine series)

SERIES "E"
	W.	L.	Pts.	GF.	GA.
Kamloops	5	0	10	31	13
Seattle	0	5	0	13	31

(Kamloops wins series, 5 games to 0)

SERIES "F"
	W.	L.	Pts.	GF.	GA.
Portland	5	4	10	55	48
New Westminster	4	5	8	48	55

(Portland wins series, 5 games to 4)

East Division Finals
(Best-of-seven series)

SERIES "G"
	W.	L.	Pts.	GF.	GA.
Regina	4	1	8	24	18
Medicine Hat	1	4	2	18	24

(Regina wins series, 4 games to 1)

West Division Finals
(Best-of-nine series)

SERIES "H"
	W.	L.	Pts.	GF.	GA.
Kamloops	5	0	10	39	22
Portland	0	5	0	22	39

(Kamloops wins series, 5 games to 0)

Western Hockey League Playoff Finals
(Best-of-seven series)

SERIES "I"
	W.	L.	Pts.	GF.	GA.
Kamloops	4	3	8	30	27
Regina	3	4	6	27	30

(Kamloops wins WHL Playoffs, 4 games to 3)

Top 10 WHL Playoff Scorers

	Games	G.	A.	Pts.	Pen.
1. Dale Derkatch, Regina	23	12	*41	**53	54
2. Dean Evason, Kamloops	17	*21	20	41	33
Taylor Hall, Regina	23	*21	20	41	26
4. Lyndon Byers, Regina	23	17	18	35	78
5. John Miner, Regina	23	9	25	34	54
6. Jim Camazzola, Kamloops	17	12	19	31	44
7. Ray Ferraro, Brandon	11	13	15	28	20
8. Kelly Glowa, Brandon	12	11	16	27	13
9. Doug Saunders, Kamloops	15	13	13	26	21
10. Doug Trapp, Regina	23	12	12	24	38

**Established new points record, breaking old record of 45 set in 1975-76 season by Bernie Federko of Saskatoon.

Team-by-Team Playoff Scoring

Brandon Wheat Kings
(Lost East Division semifinals to Regina, 2-1)

	Games	G.	A.	Pts.	Pen.
Ray Ferraro	11	13	15	28	20
Kelly Glowa	12	11	16	27	13
Cam Plante	11	4	16	20	14
Stacy Pratt	12	3	12	15	2
David Curry	12	9	2	11	2
Bryan Wells	12	3	4	7	*86
Byron Lomow	12	1	5	6	16
Gord Paddock	12	1	5	6	23
John Dzikowski	12	5	0	5	7
Dave Thomlinson	12	3	2	5	24
Randy Cameron	10	1	4	5	33
Brad Wells	10	1	3	4	18
Derek Laxdal	12	0	4	4	10
Brent Jessiman	12	1	1	2	18
Pat Loyer	11	0	2	2	19
Allan Tarasuk	9	1	0	1	13
Boyd Lomow	5	0	1	1	13
Ron Hextall (Goalie)	10	0	1	1	8
Jim Agnew	12	0	1	1	39
Rob Ordman	1	0	0	0	0
Paul More	3	0	0	0	4
Jay Palmer (Goalie)	3	0	0	0	4
Murray Rice	5	0	0	0	4
Kelly Kozak	8	0	0	0	10

Calgary Wranglers
(Lost East Division quarterfinals to Regina, 4-0)

	Games	G.	A.	Pts.	Pen.
Doug Moffat	4	0	9	9	0
Ken Quinney	4	5	2	7	0
Allan Measures	4	3	4	7	0
Landis Chaulk	4	3	1	4	0
Barry Bracko	4	1	2	3	8
Rod Matechuk	4	1	0	1	0
Mike Zimmel	2	0	1	1	0
Ron Bonora	4	0	1	1	0
Jim Playfair	4	0	1	1	2
Chris Churchill (Goalie)	3	0	0	0	0
Shannon Krusky	2	0	0	0	0
Dana Murzyn	2	0	0	0	10
Rod Taylor	2	0	0	0	0
Ross McKay (Goalie)	1	0	0	0	4
Mike Bukta	4	0	0	0	2
Mitch Cornett	4	0	0	0	2
Darrel Daignault	4	0	0	0	4
Doug Houda	4	0	0	0	7
Scott Makin	4	0	0	0	0

	Games	G.	A.	Pts.	Pen.
Pat Mangold	4	0	0	0	2
Rob McKechney	4	0	0	0	4
Ken Spangler	4	0	0	0	6

Kamloops Junior Oilers
(Winners of 1984 WHL Playoffs)

	Games	G.	A.	Pts.	Pen.
Dean Evason	17	*21	20	41	33
Jim Camazzola	17	12	19	31	44
Doug Saunders	15	13	13	26	21
Tony Vogel	17	9	12	21	15
Greg Evtushevski	17	9	9	18	64
Doug Bodger	17	2	15	17	12
Ryan Stewart	16	7	7	14	19
Ken Daneyko	17	4	9	13	28
Mike Nottingham	17	5	5	10	28
Stacey Wakabayaashi	17	5	5	10	7
Mark Ferner	14	1	8	9	20
Gord Mark	17	2	6	8	27
Robin Bawa	13	4	2	6	4
Mark Kachowsky	16	4	2	6	29
Brian Bertuzzi	16	1	5	6	17
Todd Carnelley	17	0	6	6	4
Rob Brown	15	1	2	3	17
Dean Clark	13	0	3	3	12
Greg Hawgood	6	0	2	2	2
Rudy Poeschuk	8	0	2	2	7
Daryl Reaugh (Goalie)	17	0	1	1	0
Wil Anderson	2	0	0	0	2
Neil Pilon	2	0	0	0	2
Rex Grant (Goalie)	3	0	0	0	0

Lethbridge Broncos
(Lost East Division quarterfinals to Brandon, 4-1)

	Games	G.	A.	Pts.	Pen.
Rick Gal	5	3	2	5	0
Gerald Diduck	5	1	4	5	27
Darin Sceviour	5	2	2	4	0
Jim Odland	5	2	1	3	0
Rich Wiest	5	1	2	3	19
Grant Couture	5	0	3	3	39
J.C. McEwan	5	1	1	2	20
Steve Nemeth	5	1	1	2	2
Todd Stokowski	5	1	1	2	4
Mark Tinordi	5	1	0	1	7
Mike Berger	5	0	1	1	7
Cam Douglas	4	0	1	1	2
Bob Rouse	5	0	1	1	28

	Games	G.	A.	Pts.	Pen.
Todd Seviour	5	0	1	1	4
Trent Kaese	1	0	0	0	0
Shawn Oswald (Goalie)	2	0	0	0	0
Ken Williston	2	0	0	0	0
Stu Wenaas	3	0	0	0	6
Stuart Sage	4	0	0	0	2
Ken Wregget (Goalie)	4	0	0	0	6
Darcy Kaminski	5	0	0	0	4
Dwight Mullins	5	0	0	0	9

Medicine Hat Tigers
(Lost East Division finals to Regina, 4-1)

	Games	G.	A.	Pts.	Pen.
Mark Lamb	14	12	11	23	6
Allen Conroy	14	10	13	23	39
Bob Bassen	14	5	11	16	12
Rocky Trottier	14	5	10	15	13
Mike Lay	14	5	8	13	9
Dan Turner	14	6	6	12	44
Brent Meckling	14	2	8	10	20
Matt Kabayama	14	2	7	9	17
Murray Craven	4	5	3	8	4
Darrel Henry	14	5	3	8	21
Brent Steblyk	14	1	7	8	20
Kevan Guy	14	3	4	7	14
Shane Churla	14	1	5	6	41
Gord Shmyrko	14	3	0	3	13
Terry Knight	13	2	1	3	5
Gary Johnson (Goalie)	12	0	2	2	4
Al Pedersen	14	0	2	2	24
Steve Rissling	1	0	0	0	0
Blair MacGregor (G.)	3	0	0	0	0
Jim Kambeitz	10	0	0	0	5
Gord Hynes	14	0	0	0	0
Trevor Semeniuk	14	0	0	0	2

New Westminster Bruins
(Lost West Division semifinals to Portland, 5-4)

	Games	G.	A.	Pts.	Pen.
Cliff Ronning	9	8	13	21	10
Randy Maxwell	9	6	6	12	27
Vern Smith	9	6	6	12	12
Kevin Griffin	9	7	2	9	4
Roger Mulvenna	9	4	3	7	2
Kent Hayes	9	3	3	6	2
Doug Quinn	9	1	4	5	14
Brent Hughes	9	2	2	4	27
Al Chatlain	9	1	3	4	12
Dave Johnston	9	1	3	4	34
Todd Ewen	7	2	1	3	15
Rob Benjamin	8	2	1	3	4
Craig Berube	8	1	2	3	5
Shawn Green	9	1	2	3	19
Marc Zeitlen	9	0	3	3	8
Shawn Nagurny	6	0	2	2	2
Mark McLeary	9	2	0	2	6
Bill Ranford (Goalie)	1	0	0	0	0
Dean Kolstad	2	0	0	0	0
Dale Brisco	6	0	0	0	2
Lee Trimm	8	0	0	0	0
Pokey Reddick (Goalie)	9	0	0	0	0

Portland Winter Hawks
(Lost West Division finals to Kamloops, 5-0)

	Games	G.	A.	Pts.	Pen.
Ray Podloski	14	8	14	22	14

	Games	G.	A.	Pts.	Pen.
Jeff Rohlicek	14	13	8	21	10
Randy Heath	14	9	12	21	10
Gord Walker	14	8	11	19	18
Blaine Chrest	14	6	9	15	0
John Bekkers	14	5	10	15	6
Curt Brandolini	14	9	4	13	16
Grant Sasser	14	5	8	13	2
John Kordic	14	0	13	13	56
Terry Perkins	14	8	4	12	2
Sean Harder	14	3	7	10	10
Bryan Walker	14	0	8	8	41
Tim Lorenz	14	1	5	6	18
Craig Butz	14	0	5	5	41
Dan Woodley	8	1	3	4	4
Rick Davidson	14	1	3	4	2
Jamie Nicolls	14	1	0	1	8
Jeff Finley	5	0	1	1	4
Ian Wood (Goalie)	12	0	1	1	0
Mike Maissoneuve (G.)	2	0	0	0	0
Peter Fry (Goalie)	4	0	0	0	7
Trevor Hendry	5	0	0	0	2

Prince Albert Raiders
(Lost East Division quarterfinals to Medicine Hat, 4-1)

	Games	G.	A.	Pts.	Pen.
Dan Hodgson	5	5	3	8	7
Todd Bergen	5	2	5	7	4
Derek Karolat	5	2	5	7	2
Dave Goertz	5	2	3	5	0
Dave Pasin	5	1	4	5	0
Kim Issel	5	4	0	4	9
Brad Bennett	5	1	3	4	5
Dale McFee	5	1	2	3	22
Al Stewart	5	1	2	3	29
Emanuel Viveiros	2	0	3	3	0
Ken Morrison	5	0	2	2	0
Wally Niewchas	5	0	2	2	4
John Davis	2	0	1	1	2
Tim Weiss	4	0	1	1	0
Steve Brunner	5	1	0	1	2
Colin Feser	5	1	0	1	13
Steve Gotaas	5	0	1	1	0
Dan Moberg (Goalie)	1	0	0	0	0
Mitch Poulin	3	0	0	0	5
Ken Baumgartner	4	0	0	0	23
Ward Komonosky (G.)	5	0	0	0	0
Dave Manson	5	0	0	0	4

Regina Pats
(Lost WHL finals to Kamloops, 4-3)

	Games	G.	A.	Pts.	Pen.
Dale Derkatch	23	12	*41	*53	54
Taylor Hall	23	*21	20	41	26
Lyndon Byers	23	17	18	35	78
John Miner	23	9	25	34	54
Doug Trapp	23	12	12	24	38
Kurt Wickenheiser	23	10	7	17	18
Brent Fedyk	23	8	7	15	6
Selmar Odelein	23	4	11	15	45
Tim Iannone	23	8	5	13	17
Robert Dirk	23	1	12	13	24
Bob Lowes	23	1	8	9	41
Jeff Lawson	23	4	3	7	39
Allan Acton	22	3	4	7	22
Jayson Meyer	6	1	3	4	10
Len Nielsen	23	0	2	2	4

	Games	G.	A.	Pts.	Pen.		Games	G.	A.	Pts.	Pen.
Jamie Reeve (Goalie)	23	0	2	2	0	Brent Severyn	5	2	1	3	2
Rick Herbert	23	1	0	1	23	Jim Bechtold	5	1	2	3	4
Brad Lauer	16	0	1	1	24	Derrick Ruppel	5	1	2	3	10
Frank Joo	17	0	1	1	15	Darren Schmidt	3	1	1	2	0
Stu Grimson	21	0	1	1	29	Ken Jorgenson	5	0	1	1	13
Kevin Clemens	10	0	0	0	2	Scott Robinson	5	0	1	1	25
						Greg Hubert (Goalie)	3	0	0	0	0
						Dwayne Murray (G.)	3	0	0	0	0

Seattle Breakers

(Lost West Division semifinals to Kamloops, 5-0)

	Games	G.	A.	Pts.	Pen.
Alan Kerr	5	1	4	5	12
Craig Endean	5	2	2	4	2
Gary Stewart	5	2	2	4	33
John Bacso	5	1	3	4	12
Terry Sargent	5	2	1	3	2
Scott Shaw	3	0	0	0	21
Jim Dokter	5	0	0	0	4
Jamie Huscroft	5	0	0	0	15
Brian McFarlane	5	0	0	0	0
Kelly Para	5	0	0	0	7
Ray Savard	5	0	0	0	7
Tim Ziola	5	0	0	0	9

Complete WHL Playoff Goaltending

	Games	Mins.	Goals	SO.	Avg.
Blair MacGregor, Medicine Hat	3	160	8	0	*3.00
Daryl Reaugh, Kamloops	17	972	57	0	3.52
Gary Johnson, Medicine Hat	12	721	45(1)	*1	3.74
Ron Hextall, Brandon	10	592	37(1)	0	3.75
Jamie Reeve, Regina	*23	*1393	*90	0	3.88
Bill Ranford, New Westminster	1	27	2	0	4.44
Rex Grant, Kamloops	3	63	5	0	4.76
Ward Komonosky, Prince Albert	5	283	23	0	4.88
Greg Hubert, Seattle	3	160	13	0	4.88
Peter Fry, Portland	4	145	12	0	4.97
Ken Wregget, Lethbridge	4	210	18	0	5.14
Ian Wood, Portland	12	604	59(2)	*1	5.86
Pokey Reddick, New Westminster	9	542	53	0	5.87
Chris Churchill, Calgary	3	179	18(1)	0	6.03
Jay Palmer, Brandon	3	146	15	0	6.16
Mike Maissoneuve, Portland	2	120	13	0	6.50
Dwayne Murray, Seattle	3	140	18	0	7.71
Shawn Oswald, Lethbridge	2	90	12	0	8.00
Ross McKay, Calgary	1	60	9	0	9.00
Dan Moberg, Prince Albert	1	40	9	0	13.50

( ) Empty Net Goals. Do not count against a Goaltender's average.

Individual WHL Playoff Leaders

Goals	Dean Evason, Kamloops—	21
	Taylor Hall, Regina—	21
Assists	Dale Derkatch, Regina—	41
Points	Dale Derkatch, Regina—	53
Penalty Minutes	Bryan Wells, Brandon—	86
Goaltender's Average (60 minutes)	Blair MacGregor, Medicine Hat—	3.00
Shutouts	Gary Johnson, Medicine Hat—	1
	Ian Wood, Portland—	1

1983-84 WHL All-Star Teams

First Team—East Division	Position	First Team—West Division
Ken Wregget, Lethbridge	Goal	Pokey Reddick, N. Westminster
Bob Rouse, Lethbridge	Defense	Doug Bodger, Kamloops
Cam Plante, Brandon	Defense	Gary Stewart, Seattle
Ray Ferraro, Brandon	Center	Dean Evason, Kamloops
Taylor Hall, Regina	Right Wing	Allan Kerr, Seattle
Mark Lamb, Medicine Hat	Left Wing	Randy Heath, Portland

1984 WHL Trophy Winners

Most Valuable Player	Ray Ferraro, Brandon
Frank Boucher Memorial Trophy (Most Gentlemanly)	Mark Lamb, Medicine Hat
Bob Brownridge Memorial Trophy (Top Scorer)	Ray Ferraro, Brandon
Top Defenseman	Bob Rouse, Lethbridge
Top Goaltender	Ken Wregget, Lethbridge
Stuart "Butch" Paul Memorial Trophy (Top Rookie)	Cliff Ronning, New Westminster
Coach of the Year	Terry Simpson, Prince Albert

Historical WHL Trophy Winners

(Canadian Major Junior Hockey League in 1966-67, renamed the Western Canadian Hockey League from 1967-68 to 1976-77. Has been named the Western Hockey League since 1977-78 season).

Most Valuable Player Trophy

Player	Season	Bob Brownridge Mem. Trophy (Leading Scorer)
Gerry Pinder, Saskatoon	1966-67	Gerry Pinder, Saskatoon (140 pts)
Jim Harrison Estevan	1967-68	Bobby Clarke, Flin Flon (168 pts)
Bobby Clarke, Flin Flon	1968-69	Bobby Clarke, Flin Flon (137 pts)
Reg Leach, Flin Flon	1969-70	Reg Leach, Flin Flon (111 pts)
Ed Dyck, Calgary	1970-71	Chuck Arnason, Flin Flon (163 pts)
John Davidson, Calgary	1971-72	Tom Lysiak, Medicine Hat (143 pts)
Dennis Sobchuk, Regina	1972-73	Tom Lysiak, Medicine Hat (154 pts)
Ron Chipperfield, Brandon	1973-74	Ron Chipperfield, Brandon (162 pts)
Bryan Trottier, Lethbridge	1974-75	Mel Bridgman, Victoria (157 pts)
Bernie Federko, Saskatoon	1975-76	Bernie Federko, Saskatoon (187 pts)
Berry Beck, New Westminster	1976-77	Bill Derlago, Brandon (178 pts)
Ryan Walter, Seattle	1977-78	Brian Propp, Brandon (182 pts)
Perry Turnbull, Portland	1978-79	Brian Propp, Brandon (194 pts)
Doug Wickenheiser, Regina	1979-80	Doug Wickenheiser, Regina (170 pts)
Steve Tsujiura, Medicine Hat	1980-81	Brian Varga, Regina (187 pts)
Mike Vernon, Calgary	1981-82	Jock Callander, Regina (190 pts)
Mike Vernon, Calgary	1982-83	Dale Derkatch, Regina (179 pts)
Ray Ferraro, Brandon	1983-84	Ray Ferraro, Brandon (192 pts)

Stewart Paul Memorial Trophy (Rookie of the Year)

Player	Season	Frank Boucher Memorial Trophy (Most Gentlemanly Player)
Ron Garwasiuk, Regina	1966-67	Morris Stefaniw, Estevan
Ron Fairbrother, Saskatoon	1967-68	Bernie Blanchette, Saskatoon
Ron Williams, Edmonton	1968-69	Bob Liddington, Calgary
Gene Carr, Flin Flon	1969-70	Randy Rota, Calgary
Stan Weir, Medicine Hat	1970-71	Lorne Henning, Estevan
Dennis Sobchuk, Regina	1971-72	Ron Chipperfield, Brandon
Rick Blight, Brandon	1972-73	Ron Chipperfield, Brandon
Cam Connor, Flin Flon	1973-74	Mike Rogers, Calgary
Don Murdoch, Medicine Hat	1974-75	Danny Arndt, Saskatoon
Steve Tambellini, Lethbridge	1975-76	Blair Chapman, Saskatoon
Brian Propp, Brandon	1976-77	Steve Tambellini, Lethbridge
J. Ogrodnick, N.W.-K. Brown, Port.	1977-78	Steve Tambellini, Lethbridge
Kelly Kisio, Calgary	1978-79	Errol Rausse, Seattle
Grant Fuhr, Victoria	1979-80	Steve Tsujiura, Medicine Hat
Dave Michayluk, Regina	1980-81	Steve Tsujiura, Medicine Hat
Dale Derkatch, Regina	1981-82	Mike Moller, Lethbridge
Dan Hodgson, Prince Albert	1982-83	Darren Boyko, Winnipeg
Cliff Ronning, New Westminster	1983-84	Mark Lamb, Medicine Hat

Top Defenseman Trophy

Player	Season	Top Goaltender Trophy
Barry Gibbs, Estevan	1966-67	Ken Brown, Moose Jaw
Gerry Hart, Flin Flon	1967-68	Chris Worthy, Flin Flon
Dale Hoganson, Estevan	1968-69	Ray Martyniuk, Flin Flon
Jim Hargreaves, Winnipeg	1969-70	Ray Martyniuk, Flin Flon
Ron James, Edmonton	1970-71	Ed Dyck, Calgary
Jim Watson, Calgary	1971-72	John Davidson, Calgary
George Pesut, Saskatoon	1972-73	Ed Humphreys, Saskatoon
Pat Price, Saskatoon	1973-74	Garth Malarchuk, Calgary
Rick LaPointe, Victoria	1974-75	Bill Oleschuk, Saskatoon
Kevin McCarthy, Winnipeg	1975-76	Carey Walker, New Westminster
Barry Beck, New Westminster	1976-77	Glen Hanlon, Brandon
Brad McCrimmon, Brandon	1977-78	Bart Hunter, Portland
Keith Brown, Portland	1978-79	Rick Knickle, Brandon
David Babych, Portland	1979-80	Kevin Eastman, Victoria
Jim Benning, Portland	1980-81	Grant Fuhr, Victoria
Gary Nylund, Portland	1981-82	Mike Vernon, Calgary
Gary Leeman, Regina	1982-83	Mike Vernon, Calgary
Bob Rouse, Lethbridge	1983-84	Ken Wregget, Lethbridge

Quebec Hockey League
(Formerly the Quebec Major Junior Hockey League)

Vice President—John Horman
Executive Director—Paul Dumont
Statistician—Jacques Dion
4635 1st Avenue, Room 240
Charlesbourg, Quebec G1H 2T1
Phone—(418) 623-1508

Final 1983-84 QHL Standings

Robert LeBel Division

	G.	W.	L.	T.	Pts.	GF.	GA.
Laval Voisons	70	54	16	0	108	527	289
Verdun Juniors	70	40	27	3	83	359	309
Longueuil Chevaliers	70	37	33	0	74	371	358
St. Jean Beavers	70	30	36	4	64	366	363
Cranby Bisons	70	31	38	1	63	308	348
Hull Olympics	70	25	45	0	50	301	411

Frank Dilio Division

	G.	W.	L.	T.	Pts.	GF.	GA.
Shawinigan Cataracts	70	37	33	0	74	329	287
Quebec Remparts	70	36	32	2	74	338	372
Drummondville Voltigeurs	70	35	35	0	70	355	351
Chicoutimi Sagueneens	70	30	38	2	62	303	382
Trois-Riviers Draveurs	70	23	45	2	48	301	388

Top 20 Scorers for the Jean Beliveau Trophy

	Games	G.	A.	Pts.	Pen.
1. Mario Lemieux, Laval	70	*133	*149	*282	92
2. Jacques Goyette, Laval	62	76	94	170	64
3. Claude Gosselin, Quebec	65	56	64	140	55
4. Claude Lefebvre, Quebec	70	62	73	135	110
5. Guy Rouleau, Longueuil	70	60	73	133	28
6. Francois Sills, Laval	70	56	74	130	39
Sergio Momesso, Shawinigan	68	42	88	130	235
8. Santino Pellegrino, Longueuil	70	52	72	124	62
Paul Gagne, Chicoutimi	62	51	73	124	8
10. Yves Courteau, Laval	62	45	75	120	52
11. Guy Pigeon, Drummondville	59	45	71	116	79
12. Hilton Ruggles, Longueuil	59	63	50	113	82
Luc Marengere, St. Jean	71	56	57	113	41
Alain Bisson, Laval	59	31	82	113	95
15. Steve Pepin, Drummondville	64	54	58	112	173
16. Jean-Maurice Cool, Verdun	61	43	65	108	201
17. Dave Kasper, Shawinigan	69	44	62	106	141
18. Marc Chamard, St. Jean	66	44	59	103	104
19. Francis Lapointe, Granby	70	41	62	102	29
20. Yves Lapointe, St. Jean	66	51	47	98	127
Claude Gagnon, Trois-Rivieres	65	38	60	98	16
Patrick Emond, Chicoutimi	68	33	65	98	24

Team-by-Team Regular Season QHL Scoring

Chicoutimi Sagueneens

	Games	G.	A.	Pts.	Pen.
Paul Gagne	62	51	73	124	8
Patrick Emond	68	33	65	98	24
Joel Haillargeon	60	48	35	83	184
Alain Heroux	58	31	42	73	53
Sylvain Simard	57	31	33	64	54
Yves Heroux	56	28	25	53	67
Marc Fortier	67	16	30	46	51
Marc Bergevin	70	10	35	45	125
Stephane Roy	67	12	26	38	25
Daniel Crassoski	48	8	25	33	226
Mike Marcinkiewicz	46	14	18	32	52
Jean-Guy Chenier	55	12	12	24	298
Rene L'Ecuyer	66	4	20	24	131
Marc Bureau	56	6	16	22	14
Jean-Marc Richard	61	1	20	21	41
Steve Girard	37	9	10	19	13

	Games	G.	A.	Pts.	Pen.
Christian Duperron	62	3	13	16	115
Gilbert Paiement	49	1	15	16	35
Martin Guay (Goalie)	56	0	3	3	8
Christian Marcotte	1	0	1	1	0
Marc Simard	1	0	1	1	7
Andre Lapensee (Goalie)	23	0	1	1	25
Carol Gravel	1	0	0	0	0
Sylvain Hudon	2	0	0	0	0
Daniel Legare (Goalie)	4	0	0	0	0

Drummondville Voltigeurs

	Games	G.	A.	Pts.	Pen.
Guy Pigeon	59	45	71	116	79
Steve Pepin	64	54	58	112	173
Jose Charbonneau	65	31	59	90	110
Michel Couvrette	67	34	54	88	46
Guy Benoit	61	26	56	82	25
Rock Jutras	68	30	38	68	48
Patrice Brisson	61	24	44	68	70
Andre Desy	67	38	29	67	75
Tom Karalis	67	16	37	53	306
J.-Guy Charbonneau	64	17	19	36	22
Daniel Poudrier	64	7	28	35	15
Steve Duchesne	67	1	34	35	79
James Gasseau	68	6	25	31	72
Craig Jenkins	33	11	18	29	11
Mario Carrier	69	2	26	28	91
Robert Brine	56	5	10	15	112
Denis Gosselin	50	6	5	11	23
Serge Roberge	58	1	7	8	287
Doug Bailey	46	0	2	2	2
Jude Labillois (Goalie)	46	0	2	2	8
Francois Martel	9	0	1	1	11
D. Berthiaume (G.)	28	0	1	1	0
S. Bergeron (G.)	1	0	0	0	0
Jocelyn Perreault (G.)	12	0	0	0	8

Granby Bisons

	Games	G.	A.	Pts.	Pen.
Francis Lapointe	70	41	62	102	29
Chyslain Provencher	68	30	65	95	55
Martin Bouliane	62	41	41	82	6
Stephane Richer	67	39	37	76	58
Rene Breton	59	23	47	70	23
Jocelyn Gauvreau	58	19	39	58	55
Guy Charbonneau	68	17	34	51	68
Denis Lapointe	63	23	23	46	267
Gregory Choules	55	19	23	42	43
Denis Gaudreau	67	5	23	28	104
Luc Chenier	62	10	15	25	36
Marc Lemay	70	5	20	25	169
Mario Canuel	68	3	19	22	188
Sylvain Cote	45	8	11	19	28
Francis Lapierre	53	5	8	13	96
Andre Charbonneau	62	2	7	9	27
Claude Lajoie	45	1	7	8	31
Darryl Paris	25	0	6	6	39
Patrick Roy (Goalie)	61	0	6	6	15
Daniel Hebert	12	0	2	2	4
Michel Nadeau	10	0	1	1	10
Francois Chartrand	15	0	1	1	7
Pierre Ruyssen (Goalie)	3	0	0	0	0
Bruno Guillemette (G.)	5	0	0	0	2

Hull Olympics

	Games	G.	A.	Pts.	Pen.
David Purcell	67	48	43	91	40
Luc Robitaille	70	32	53	85	48
John Leblanc	69	39	35	74	32
Mario Ouellet	66	22	34	56	116
Joe Foglietta	66	16	37	53	2
Sylvain Beauchamps	56	17	33	50	62
J. Francois Vezina	67	21	28	49	37
Stephane Richer	70	8	38	46	42
Tony Vourantonis	52	14	30	44	60
Rodolphe Turgeon	65	4	31	35	118
Sam Lang	46	13	19	32	4
Alain Latreille	62	7	19	26	31
Armel Parisee	64	4	22	26	165
Rick Hayward	67	6	17	23	220
Pierre Schinck	51	5	18	23	30
Michel Larose	33	10	10	20	95
Gilles Proulx	62	12	6	18	99
Michel Charbonneau	55	2	9	11	244
Claude Beauregard	46	4	5	9	75
Todd Smith	49	1	1	2	18
Steve Averill (Goalie)	23	0	1	1	6
Stephane Fortin (Goalie)	56	0	1	1	32
Christian Belanger	2	0	0	0	0

Laval Voisins

	Games	G.	A.	Pts.	Pen.
Mario Lemieux	70	*133	*149	*282	92
Jacques Goyette	62	76	94	170	64
Francois Sills	70	56	73	129	39
Yves Courteau	62	45	75	120	52
Alain Bisson	59	31	82	113	95
Michel Mongeau	60	45	49	94	30
Vincent Damphousse	66	29	36	65	25
Sylvain Boutin	68	16	40	56	15
Rene Badeau	64	13	40	53	279
Steve Finn	68	7	39	46	159
Bob Dollas	54	12	33	45	80
Raynald Gagne	50	16	25	41	30
Steve Woodburn	52	7	28	35	160
Steven Latour	46	15	17	32	51
Michel Caron	63	3	28	31	201
Joe Cerone	36	9	16	25	103
Rich Kokila	62	2	18	20	35
Ian O'Rear	28	3	14	17	9
Tom Paradis	45	6	10	16	104
Eddie Smith	45	4	10	14	34
Tony Haladuick (Goalie)	53	0	4	4	17
Michel Bourque	10	1	0	1	58
Stephane Bellerose	1	0	0	0	2
Benoit Picard	5	0	0	0	0
Eric Petigrew (Goalie)	20	0	0	0	4
Carl Parker (Goalie)	25	0	0	0	15

Longueuil Chevaliers

	Games	G.	A.	Pts.	Pen.
Guy Rouleau	70	60	73	133	28
Santino Pellegrino	70	52	72	124	62
Hilton Ruggles	59	63	50	113	82
Jean Bourgeois	*72	44	49	93	65
Alain Tousignant	65	24	47	71	199
Joe Mercuri	66	24	39	63	146
Luc Gauthier	70	8	54	62	207
Franco Iammateo	64	27	32	59	48
Graham Herring	68	9	44	53	101

	Games	G.	A.	Pts.	Pen.
J. Philippe Lemoine	66	11	26	37	228
Raymond Beauchamps	66	9	23	32	97
Gilbert Poulin	68	7	18	25	237
Denis Paquet	57	7	16	23	180
Peter Kasper	53	10	11	21	4
Sylvain Harvey	61	2	13	15	17
Jean-Jac. Daigneault	10	2	11	13	6
Michel Carbonneau	35	6	6	12	25
Richard Bourdeau	28	1	4	5	40
Chris Smith	50	2	2	4	64
Daniel Savoie (Goalie)	30	0	3	3	18
Normand Plasse	2	0	0	0	0
Danny Wall	7	0	0	0	6
Daniel Brazeau (G.)	11	0	0	0	0
Yves Turenne	21	0	0	0	101
Martin Plante (Goalie)	44	0	0	0	10

Quebec Remparts

	Games	G.	A.	Pts.	Pen.
Claude Gosselin	65	56	84	140	55
Claude Lefebvre	70	62	73	135	110
Daniel Letendre	67	25	41	66	35
Sylvain Cote	66	15	50	65	89
Roger Dube	64	31	25	56	112
Ron Choules	37	24	31	55	145
Joel Guimont	59	22	22	44	71
Mario Roberge	60	12	28	40	253
Alain Varennes	68	12	23	35	31
Guy Ouellette	51	9	24	33	18
Normand Nellis	64	9	22	31	153
MacIntyre Stephen	68	6	16	22	36
Blair MacIsaac	42	3	18	21	71
Alain Cote	60	3	17	20	40
Guy Belisle	59	13	5	18	4
Donald Deschesnes	33	6	10	16	23
Martin Simard	59	6	10	16	26
Robert Spencer	53	1	14	15	59
Simon Dube	17	0	6	6	0
Yvan Deblois	44	1	4	5	42
Kelvin Fraser	30	0	5	5	32
Luc Cuenette (Goalie)	67	0	3	3	6
Guy Coupal	3	0	0	0	0
Andre Couture	3	0	0	0	5
Claude Landry (Goalie)	4	0	0	0	0
Louis Gravel (Goalie)	8	0	0	0	0

St. Jean Beavers

	Games	G.	A.	Pts.	Pen.
Luc Marengere	71	56	57	113	41
Marc Chamard	66	44	59	103	104
Yves Lapointe	66	51	47	98	127
Denis Dore	58	32	59	91	65
Stephane Thivierge	70	35	34	69	167
Carl Vermette	60	28	38	66	110
Guay Eric	68	11	43	54	89
Luc Dagenais	55	16	25	43	19
Jean-Guy Bergeron	71	9	34	43	126
Carl Cleary	64	11	22	33	45
Steve Pinard	54	3	30	33	168
Benoit Hogue	59	14	11	25	42
Eric Germain	57	2	15	17	60
Eric Collin	53	12	4	16	86
Francois Olivier	22	2	11	13	15
Ken New	42	2	8	10	13
Eric Boisvert	50	0	10	10	57
Jean-Pierre Lessard	60	0	10	10	93

	Games	G.	A.	Pts.	Pen.
Claude Larocque	16	1	2	3	0
Francois Dupuis	1	0	1	1	0
Daniel Marcotte (Goalie)	29	0	1	1	2
Marc Bolduc (Goalie)	2	0	0	0	0
Michel Campeau (G.)	58	0	0	0	23

Shawinigan Cataracts

	Games	G.	A.	Pts.	Pen.
Sergio Momesso	68	42	88	130	235
Dave Kasper	69	44	62	106	141
Robert Lebrun	58	32	61	93	79
Paul Adey	56	37	52	89	78
Eric Leveille	66	32	52	84	94
Marc Damphousse	54	25	40	65	60
Yves Beaudoin	68	14	43	57	93
Mario Belanger	45	26	20	46	53
Jean Houde Jr.	68	13	25	38	227
Patrick Murray	56	14	22	36	83
Denis Paul	60	13	20	33	42
Sylvain Falardeau	60	14	15	29	26
Ralf DiFiore	65	6	22	28	38
Charles Doucet	59	7	20	27	63
Sylvain Laroche	65	3	18	21	102
Eric Demers	65	5	13	18	153
Victor Cowen	27	5	3	8	10
Steve Masse	46	3	4	7	174
Benoit Richard	20	4	2	6	60
Michel Fortin	23	2	3	5	37
Barry Maguire	25	2	3	5	2
Jasmin Naud	47	1	3	4	0
Sylvain Ledu	2	1	0	1	0
Dave Quigley Jr. (G.)	47	0	1	1	8
Benoit Beaudoin (G.)	3	0	0	0	0
Marc Desbiens (Goalie)	26	0	0	0	0

Trois-Rivieres Draveurs

	Games	G.	A.	Pts.	Pen.
Claude Gagnon	65	38	60	98	16
Mario Paradis	70	24	60	84	46
Michel Boucher	65	28	51	79	81
Luc Duval	64	32	44	76	35
Serge Poudrier	66	14	39	53	41
Derrick Ivall	68	27	16	43	135
Luc Boucher	67	23	20	43	134
Sylvain Nantel	53	21	20	41	*564
Benoit Gosselin	40	17	17	34	59
Alain Guerette	60	15	15	30	74
Steven Gauthier	63	9	15	24	205
Sylvain Boyer	68	4	20	24	104
Yves Neault	36	11	11	22	11
Gontran Gilbert	36	8	12	20	4
Donald Dufresne	67	7	12	19	97
Alex Daviault	44	3	13	16	128
Richard Paquette	37	3	10	13	96
Max Daviault	28	4	6	10	41
Richard Soucy	49	0	10	10	64
Denis Fortin	31	6	3	9	78
Peter DiRinaldo	52	2	7	9	104
G. Eymard (G.)	2	0	0	0	0
Donald Soucy	3	0	0	0	7
Rene Paquin	6	0	0	0	4
Serge Gauthier (Goalie)	13	0	0	0	7
Yvan Theriault	20	0	0	0	41
Alain Raymond (Goalie)	53	0	0	0	6

Verdun Juniors

	Games	G.	A.	Pts.	Pen.
Jean-Maurice Cool	61	43	65	108	201
Ronald Fillion	68	35	56	91	56
Billy Campbell	65	24	66	90	59
Claude Lemieux	51	41	45	86	225
Muttart Randy	61	36	37	73	61
Martin Thibeault	68	33	36	69	30
Jeff Hamilton	30	19	39	58	6
Jerome Carrier	69	14	38	52	42
Jim Nesish	70	22	24	46	35
Sylvain Venne	68	18	28	46	18
Shane MacEachern	65	13	27	40	62
Alain Paquette	60	11	24	35	48
Franco DeSantis	69	9	26	35	76
Tom Kolioupoulos	39	16	15	31	26
Henri Marcoux	52	6	17	23	4
Richard Little	55	9	12	21	29
Gerry Fleming	52	4	11	15	270
Peter Karmanos	40	1	9	10	16
Wray Quigley	51	2	3	5	154
Alain Bedard	52	0	2	2	114
Don Gallant	11	0	1	1	61
Vincent Riendeau (G.)	41	0	1	1	8
Marc Delorme (Goalie)	8	0	0	0	2
Troy Crosby (Goalie)	34	0	0	0	13

Complete QHL Regular Season Goaltending

	Games	Mins.	Goals	SO.	Avg.
Benoit Beaudoin, Shawinigan	3	135	8	0	3.56
Tony Haladuick, Laval	53	2925	185(2)	0	*3.79
Dave Quigley, Shawinigan	47	2432	160(2)	1	3.95
Troy Crosby, Verdun	34	1863	125(1)	1	4.03
Vincent Riendeau, Verdun	41	2133	147(2)	*2	4.14
Eric Petigrew, Laval	20	734	52(1)	0	4.25
Patrick Roy, Granby	61	3585	265(4)	0	4.44
Jude Labillois, Drummondville	46	2563	196(5)	0	4.59
Martin Plante, Longueuil	44	2328	180(2)	1	4.64
Michel Campeau, St. Jean	58	3397	264(6)	0	4.66
Marc Desbiens, Shawinigan	26	1310	104(3)	0	4.76
Martin Guay, Chicoutimi	56	2894	231(4)	0	4.79
Alain Raymond, Trois-Rivieres	53	2725	223(3)	*2	4.91
Daniel Berthiaume, Drummondville	28	1562	131(3)	0	5.03
Daniel Marcotte, St. Jean	29	1336	112(3)	0	5.03
Luc Guenette, Quebec	*67	*3729	*314(5)	0	5.05
Daniel Savoie, Longueuil	30	1454	126	1	5.20
Louis Gravel, Quebec	8	340	30	0	5.29
Bruno Guillemette, Granby	5	232	22	0	5.69
Stephane Fortin, Hull	56	2946	284(2)	1	5.78
Carl Parker, Laval	25	1383	141	0	6.12
Steve Averill, Hull	23	1019	105(1)	0	6.18
Andre Lapensee, Chicoutimi	23	1186	124	0	6.27
Serge Gauthier, Trois-Rivieres	13	539	59	0	6.57
Marc Delorme, Verdun	7	307	34	0	6.64
Daniel Brazeau, Longueuil	11	443	50	0	6.77
Guillaume Eymard, Trois-Rivieres	2	97	11	0	6.80
Daniel Legare, Chicoutimi	4	187	22(1)	0	7.06
Jocelyn Perreault, Drummondville	12	371	45(2)	0	7.28
Stephane Bergeron, Drummondville	1	42	6	0	8.57
Claude Landry, Quebec	4	160	23	0	8.63
Pierre Ruyssen, Granby	3	127	20	0	9.45
Marc Bolduc, St. Jean	2	39	8	0	12.31

( )—Empty Net Goals. Do not count against a Goaltender's average.

Individual 1983-84 Department Leaders

Goals	Mario Lemieux, Laval—	133
Assists	Mario Lemieux, Laval—	149
Points	Mario Lemieux, Laval—	282
Penalty Minutes	Sylvain Nantel, Trois-Rivieres—	564
Goaltender's Average	Tony Haladuick, Laval—	3.79
Shutouts	Alain Raymond, Trois-Rivieres—	2
	Vincent Riendeau, Verdun—	2

1984 QHL President Cup Playoffs

Quarterfinals

	W.	L.	Pts.	GF.	GA.
Verdun	4	0	8	38	21
St. Jean	0	4	0	21	38

(Verdun wins series, 4 games to 0)

	W.	L.	Pts.	GF.	GA.
Laval	4	0	8	22	10
Granby	0	4	0	10	22

(Laval wins series, 4 games to 0)

	W.	L.	Pts.	GF.	GA.		W.	L.	Pts.	GF.	GA.
Longueuil	4	1	8	25	15	Drummondville	4	2	8	31	24
Quebec	1	4	2	15	25	Shawinigan	2	4	4	24	31

(Longueuil wins series, 4 games to 1)   (Drummondville wins series, 4 games to 2)

Semifinals

	W.	L.	Pts.	GF.	GA.		W.	L.	Pts.	GF.	GA.
Longueuil	4	2	8	33	31	Laval	4	0	8	24	13
Verdun	2	4	4	31	33	Drummondville	0	4	0	13	24

(Longueuil wins series, 4 games to 2)   (Laval wins series, 4 games to 0)

Finals

	W.	L.	Pts.	GF.	GA.
Laval	4	2	8	40	19
Longueuil	2	4	4	19	40

(Laval wins series, and President Cup, 4 games to 2)

Top 10 Playoff Scorers

	Games	G.	A.	Pts.	Pen.
1. Mario Lemieux, Laval	14	*29	*23	*52	29
2. Guy Rouleau, Longueuil	17	9	20	29	42
3. Hilton Ruggles, Longueuil	17	12	16	28	22
Jacques Goyette, Laval	13	11	17	28	8
5. Yves Courteau, Laval	14	11	16	27	6
Santino Pellegrino, Longueuil	17	11	16	27	18
7. Jean Bourgeois, Longueuil	17	13	10	23	20
8. Jeff Hamilton, Verdun	10	12	9	21	0
Franco Iammateo, Longueuil	17	8	13	21	8
10. Claude Lemieux, Verdun	9	8	12	20	63
Joe Mercuri, Longueuil	17	7	13	20	27

Team-by-Team QHL Playoff Scoring

Drummondville Voltigeurs
(Lost semifinals to Laval, 4-0)

	Games	G.	A.	Pts.	Pen.
Michel Couvrette	10	3	9	12	8
Guy Pigeon	10	5	6	11	6
Jose Charbonneau	10	5	5	10	9
Steve Pepin	10	5	5	10	19
Steve Duchesne	10	3	7	10	17
Rock Jutras	10	3	6	9	8
Mario Carrier	10	1	8	9	6
Patrice Brisson	10	5	3	8	17
Guy Benoit	10	4	4	8	2
Tom Karalis	10	2	6	8	28
J. Guy Charbonneau	9	2	4	6	4
Daniel Poudrier	10	2	3	5	4
James Gasseau	10	0	4	4	12
Andre Desy	7	2	1	3	2
Robert Brine	6	1	1	2	0
Serge Roberge	10	0	2	2	*105
Denis Gosselin	10	0	1	1	31
Jude Labillois (Goalie)	10	0	1	1	2
Francois Martel	2	0	0	0	0
D. Berthiaume (G.)	3	0	0	0	0
Doug Bailey	6	0	0	0	0

Granby Bisons
(Lost quarterfinals to Laval, 4-0)

	Games	G.	A.	Pts.	Pen.
Martin Bouliane	4	3	3	6	2
Jocelyn Gauvreau	4	2	3	5	0
Denis Lapointe	4	2	2	4	12
Rene Breton	4	1	3	4	7

	Games	G.	A.	Pts.	Pen.
Stephane Richer	3	1	1	2	4
Denis Gaudreau	4	0	2	2	8
Francis Lapierre	4	0	2	2	11
Francis Lapointe	3	1	0	1	2
Mario Canuel	4	0	1	1	13
Ghyslain Provencher	4	0	1	1	2
Bruno Guillemette (G.)	1	0	0	0	0
Daniel Hebert	1	0	0	0	0
Sylvain Cote	2	0	0	0	0
Andre Charbonneau	3	0	0	0	0
Marc Lemay	3	0	0	0	2
Guy Charbonneau	4	0	0	0	2
Luc Chenier	4	0	0	0	6
Gregory Choules	4	0	0	0	2
Daniel Jomphe	4	0	0	0	4
Michel Nadeau	4	0	0	0	2
Patrick Roy (Goalie)	4	0	0	0	0

Laval Voisins
(Winners of 1984 President Cup Playoffs)

	Games	G.	A.	Pts.	Pen.
Mario Lemieux	14	*29	*23	*52	29
Jacques Goyette	13	11	17	28	8
Yves Courteau	14	11	16	27	6
Alain Bisson	14	5	10	15	20
Francois Sills	14	2	11	13	0
Joe Cerone	14	7	5	12	22
Michel Mongeau	10	4	5	9	2
Bob Dollas	14	1	8	9	23
Vincent Damphousse	12	5	3	8	4
Sylvain Boutin	14	2	5	7	0
Steve Latour	14	2	5	7	14

	Games	G.	A.	Pts.	Pen.
Steve Finn	14	1	6	7	27
Rene Badeau	10	3	3	6	49
Steve Woodburn	14	0	6	6	31
Tom Paradis	14	2	3	5	14
Rich Kokila	14	0	4	4	0
Michel Caroi	14	1	1	2	59
Tony Haladuick (Goalie)	14	0	1	1	4
Eddie Smith	2	0	0	0	19
Raynald Gagne	3	0	0	0	2
Carl Parker (Goalie)	3	0	0	0	0
Michel Bourque	8	0	0	0	36

Longueuil Chevaliers
(Lost finals to Laval, 4-2)

	Games	G.	A.	Pts.	Pen.
Guy Rouleau	17	9	20	29	42
Hilton Ruggles	17	12	16	28	22
Santino Pellegrino	17	11	16	27	18
Jean Bourgeois	17	13	10	23	20
Franco Iammateo	17	8	13	21	8
Joe Mercuri	17	7	13	20	27
Jean-J. Daigneault	14	3	13	16	30
Luc Gauthier	17	4	9	13	24
Alain Tousignant	17	4	3	7	34
Sylvain Harvey	17	2	4	6	12
Jean-Phil. Lemoine	16	2	1	3	64
Daniel Savoie (Goalie)	13	0	1	1	0
Raymond Beauchamps	14	0	1	1	12
Richard Bourdeau	17	0	1	1	31
Dimitris Kritikos	1	0	0	0	0
Mario De Benedictis	3	0	0	0	0
Daniel Brazeau	5	0	0	0	0
Denis Paquet	5	0	0	0	26
Martin Plante (Goalie)	10	0	0	0	14
Peter Kasper	13	0	0	0	2
Gilbert Poulin	14	0	0	0	4
Chris Smith	15	0	0	0	2

Quebec Remparts
(Lost quarterfinals to Longueuil, 4-1)

	Games	G.	A.	Pts.	Pen.
Claude Lefebvre	5	4	4	8	6
Ron Choules	5	1	5	6	6
Daniel Letendre	5	2	3	5	4
Alain Varennes	5	2	3	5	2
Alain Cote	5	1	3	4	8
Roger Dube	5	1	2	3	4
Joel Guimont	5	1	2	3	10
Sylvain Cote	5	1	1	2	0
Guy Belisle	5	1	0	1	0
Yvan Deblois	5	1	0	1	2
Blair MacIsaac	5	0	1	1	2
Mario Roberge	5	0	1	1	22
Martin Simard	4	0	0	0	0
Kelvin Fraser	5	0	0	0	2
Luc Guenette (Goalie)	5	0	0	0	4
Stephen MacIntyre	5	0	0	0	0
Normand Nellis	5	0	0	0	13
Robert Spencer	5	0	0	0	4

Shawinigan Cataracts
(Lost quarterfinals to Drummondville, 4-2)

	Games	G.	A.	Pts.	Pen.
Dave Kasper	6	7	7	14	11
Paul Adey	6	6	3	9	13
Sergio Momesso	6	4	4	8	13
Yves Beaudoin	6	1	6	7	2

	Games	G.	A.	Pts.	Pen.
Marc Damphousse	6	1	5	6	8
Robert Lebrun	6	1	4	5	7
Paul Denis	6	1	1	2	4
Sylvain Falardeau	6	1	1	2	0
Sylvain Laroche	6	1	1	2	8
Eric Leveille	6	1	1	2	6
Steve Masse	6	0	2	2	18
Charles Doucet	6	0	1	1	16
Patrick Murray	6	0	1	1	10
D. Quigley Jr. (Goalie)	3	0	0	0	0
Marc Desbiens (Goalie)	4	0	0	0	2
Richard Benoit	5	0	0	0	2
Eric Demers	6	0	0	0	2
Ralf DiFiore	6	0	0	0	10
Jean Houde Jr.	6	0	0	0	32

St. Jean Beavers
(Lost quarterfinals to Verdun, 4-0)

	Games	G.	A.	Pts.	Pen.
Denis Daze	4	3	4	7	4
Luc Dagenais	4	2	4	6	2
Yves Lapointe	4	2	3	5	4
Luc Marengere	4	2	3	5	0
J-Guy Bergeron	4	1	4	5	0
Marc Chamard	4	1	4	5	2
Benoit Lafleur	4	1	4	5	13
Carl Vermette	4	1	2	3	11
J-Pierre Lessard	4	0	3	3	0
Eric Guay	4	2	0	2	4
Stephane Thivierge	4	2	0	2	13
Eric Collin	4	0	2	2	7
Eric Germain	4	1	0	1	6
Michel Grenier	3	0	1	1	0
Benoit Hogue	4	0	1	1	0
Carl Cleary	1	0	0	0	2
M. Campeau (Goalie)	2	0	0	0	0
Daniel Marcotte (Goalie)	2	0	0	0	0
Francois Olivier	2	0	0	0	0
Eric Boisvert	3	0	0	0	0
Marc Bolduc (Goalie)	3	0	0	0	0
Ken New	3	0	0	0	2

Verdun Juniors
(Lost semifinals to Longueuil, 4-2)

	Games	G.	A.	Pts.	Pen.
Jeff Hamilton	10	12	9	21	0
Claude Lemieux	9	8	12	20	63
Randy Muttart	10	9	9	18	10
Jean-Maurice Cool	10	7	10	17	24
Jim Nesish	10	11	5	16	2
Jerome Carrier	10	1	14	15	4
Ronald Filion	10	4	7	11	10
Richard Little	8	0	9	9	13
Martin Thibault	10	4	4	8	12
Shane MacEachern	10	3	5	8	30
Billy Campbell	10	2	5	7	4
Alain Paquette	9	4	2	6	15
Franco De Santis	10	1	4	5	12
Gerry Fleming	3	0	4	4	2
Henri Marcoux	9	0	4	4	2
Peter Karmanos	6	1	2	3	0
Wray Quigley	7	1	2	3	14
Sylvain Venne	8	2	0	2	4
Don Gallant	7	0	1	1	9
Alain Bedard	4	0	0	0	4
Troy Crosby (Goalie)	4	0	0	0	2
V. Riendeau (Goalie)	7	0	0	0	2

Complete 1984 President Cup Goaltending

	Games	Mins.	Goals	SO.	Avg.
Bruno Guillemette, Granby	1	8	0	0	0.00
Tony Haladuick, Laval	*14	*696	39	0	*2.94
Carl Parker, Laval	3	56	3	0	3.21
Troy Crosby, Verdun	4	204	11	0	3.24
Daniel Savoie, Longueuil	13	673	*46	0	4.10
Judes Labillois, Drummondville	10	446	32	0	4.30
Luc Guenette, Quebec	5	299	24(1)	0	4.82
Marc Desbiens, Shawinigan	4	217	18	0	4.98
Dave Quigley Jr., Shawinigan	3	143	12	0	5.03
Patrick Roy, Granby	4	244	22	0	5.41
Vincent Riendeau, Verdun	7	404	39(1)	0	5.79
Daniel Berthiaume, Drummondville	3	154	16	0	6.23
Martin Plante, Longueuil	10	355	41	0	6.93
Daniel Marcotte, St. Jean	2	40	5	0	7.50
Marc Bolduc, St. Jean	3	149	20	0	8.05
Michel Campeau, St. Jean	2	49	11	0	13.47

( )—Empty Net Goals. Do not count against a Goaltender's average.

1983-84 QHL Trophy Winners

Frank Selke Trophy (Most Gentlemanly)	Jerome Carrier, Verdun
Des Instructeurs Trophy (Top Rookie Forward)	Stephane Richer, Granby
Raymond Lagace Trophy (Top Rookie Defenseman)	James Gasseau, Drummondville
Michel Briere Trophy (Regular Season MVP)	Mario Lemieux, Laval
Jean Beliveau Trophy (Leading Scorer)	Mario Lemieux, Laval
Marcel Robert Trophy (Top Scholastic/Athletic Performer)	Gilbert Paiement, Chicoutimi
Mike Bossy Trophy (Top Pro Prospect)	Mario Lemieux, Laval
Emile "Butch" Bouchard Trophy (Top Defenseman)	Billy Campbell, Verdun
Jacques Plante Trophy (Best Goalie)	Tony Haladuick, Laval
Guy Lafleur Trophy (Playoff MVP)	Mario Lemieux, Laval
Robert LeBel Trophy (Best Team Defensive Average)	Shawinigan
John Rougeau Trophy (Regular Season Champions)	Laval Voisins
President Cup (Playoff Champions)	Laval Voisins

Individual President Cup Playoff Leaders

Goals	Mario Lemieux, Laval—	29
Assists	Mario Lemieux, Laval—	23
Points	Mario Lemieux, Laval—	52
Penalty Minutes	Serge Roberge, Drummondville—	105
Goaltender's Average	Tony Haladuick, Laval—	2.94

1983-84 QHL All-Star Teams

First Team	Position	Second Team
Alain Raymond, Trois-Rivieres	Goal	Luc Guenette, Quebec
Steve Finn, Laval	Defense	Jerome Carrier, Verdun
Billy Campbell, Verdun	Defense	Sylvain Cote, Quebec
Mario Lemieux, Laval	Center	Claude Levebvre, Quebec
Jacques Goyette, Laval	Right Wing	Claude Lemieux, Verdun
Claude Gosselin, Quebec	Left Wing	Yves Courteau, Laval
Pierre Creamer, Verdun	Coach	Jean Begin, Laval

Historical QHL Trophy Winners
Frank Selke Trophy
(Most Gentlemanly Player)

1970-71—Norm Dube, Sherbrooke
1971-72—Gerry Teeple, Cornwall
1972-73—Claude Larose, Drummondville
1973-74—Gary MacGregor, Cornwall
1974-75—Jean-Luc Phaneuf, Montreal
1975-76—Norm Dupont, Montreal
1976-77—Michael Bossy, Laval
1977-78—Kevin Reeves, Montreal
1978-79—Ray Bourque, Verdun
          Jean Francois Sauve, Trois Rivieres
1979-80—Jean Francois Sauve, Trois Rivieres
1980-81—Claude Verret, Trois Rivieres
1981-82—Claude Verret, Trois Rivieres
1982-83—Pat LaFontaine, Verdun
1983-84—Jerome Carrier, Verdun

Des Instructeurs Trophy*
(Top Rookie Forward)
1969-70—Serge Martel, Verdun
1970-71—Bob Murray, Cornwall
1971-72—Bob Murray, Cornwall
1972-73—Pierre Larouche, Sorel
1973-74—Michael Bossy, Laval
1974-75—Dennis Pomerleau, Hull
1975-76—Jean-Marc Bonamie, Shawinigan
1976-77—Rick Vaive, Sherbrooke
1977-78—Norm Rochefort, Trois Rivieres
         Denis Savard, Montreal
1978-79—Alan Grenier, Laval
1979-80—Dale Hawerchuk, Cornwall
1980-81—Claude Verret, Trois Rivieres
1981-82—Sylvain Turgeon, Hull
1982-83—Pat LaFontaine, Verdun
1983-84—Stephane Richer, Granby

Raymond Lagace Trophy
(Top Rookie Defenseman)
1980-81—Billy Campbell, Montreal
1981-82—Michel Petit, Sherbrooke
1982-83—Bob Dollas, Laval
1983-84—James Gasseau, Drummondville

Jean Beliveau Trophy
(Leading Point Scorer)
1969-70—Luc Simard, Trois Rivieres
1970-71—Guy Lafleur, Quebec
1971-72—Jacques Richard, Quebec
1972-73—Andre Savard, Quebec
1973-74—Pierre Larouche, Sorel
1974-75—Norm Dupont, Montreal
1975-76—Richard Dalpe, Trois Rivieres
         Sylvain Locas, Chicoutimi
1976-77—Jean Savard, Quebec
1977-78—Ron Carter, Sherbrooke
1978-79—Jean-Francois Sauve, Trois Rivieres
1979-80—Jean-Francois Sauve, Trois Rivieres
1980-81—Dale Hawerchuk, Cornwall
1981-82—Claude Verret, Trois Rivieres
1982-83—Pat LaFontaine, Verdun
1983-84—Mario Lemieux, Laval

Michael Briere Trophy
(Regular Season Most Valuable Player)
1972-73—Andre Savard, Quebec
1973-74—Gary MacGregor, Cornwall
1974-75—Mario Viens, Cornwall
1975-76—Peter Marsh, Sherbrooke
1976-77—Lucien DeBlois, Sorel
1977-78—Kevin Reeves, Montreal
1978-79—Pierre Lacroix, Trois Rivieres
1979-80—Denis Savard, Montreal
1980-81—Dale Hawerchuk, Cornwall
1981-82—John Chabot, Sherbrooke
1982-83—Pat LaFontaine, Verdun
1983-84—Mario Lemieux, Laval

Emile "Butch" Bouchard Trophy
(Top QHL Defenseman)
1975-76—Jean Gagnon, Quebec
1976-77—Robert Picard, Montreal
1977-78—Mark Hardy, Montreal
1978-79—Raymond Bourque, Verdun
1979-80—Gaston Therrien, Quebec
1980-81—Fred Boimistruck, Cornwall
1981-82—Paul Andre Boutilier, Sherbrooke
1982-83—Jean-Jacques Daigneault, Longueuil
1983-84—Billy Campbell, Verdun

Jacques Plante Trophy
(Best Goalie)
1969-70—Michael Deguise, Sorel
1970-71—Reynald Fortier, Quebec
1971-72—Richard Brodeur, Cornwall
1972-73—Pierre Perusse, Quebec
1973-74—Claude Legris, Sorel
1974-75—Nick Sanza, Sherbrooke
1975-76—Tim Bernhardt, Cornwall
1976-77—Tim Bernhardt, Cornwall
1977-78—Tim Bernhardt, Cornwall
1978-79—Jacques Cloutier, Trois Rivieres
1979-80—Corrado Micalef, Sherbrooke
1980-81—Michel Dufour, Sorel
1981-82—Jeff Barratt, Montreal
1982-83—Tony Haladuick, Laval
1983-84—Tony Haladuick, Laval

Guy Lafleur Trophy
(Most Valuable Player During Playoffs)
1977-78—Richard David, Trois Rivieres
1978-79—Jean-Francois Sauve, Trois Rivieres
1979-80—Dale Hawerchuk, Cornwall
1980-81—Alain Lemieux, Trois Rivieres
1981-82—Michel Morissette, Sherbrooke
1982-83—Pat LaFontaine, Verdun
1983-84—Mario Lemieux, Laval

The Governors Trophy
(Team that collects most points in regular season)
1969-70—Quebec Remparts
1970-71—Quebec Remparts
1971-72—Cornwall Royals
1972-73—Quebec Remparts
1973-74—Sorel Black Hawks
1974-75—Sherbrooke Beavers
1975-76—Sherbrooke Beavers
1976-77—Quebec Remparts
1977-78—Trois Rivieres Draveurs
1978-79—Trois Rivieres Draveurs
1979-80—Sherbrooke Beavers
1980-81—Cornwall Royals
1981-82—Sherbrooke Beavers
1982-83—Laval Voisins
1983-84—Laval Voisins

The President's Cup
(Playoff Champions)
1969-70—Quebec Remparts
1970-71—Quebec Remparts
1971-72—Cornwall Royals
1972-73—Quebec Remparts
1973-74—Quebec Remparts
1974-75—Sherbrooke Beavers
1975-76—Quebec Remparts
1976-77—Sherbrooke Beavers
1977-78—Trois Rivieres Draveurs
1978-79—Trois Rivieres Draveurs
1979-80—Cornwall Royals
1980-81—Cornwall Royals
1981-82—Sherbrooke Beavers
1982-83—Verdun Juniors
1983-84—Laval Voisins

* Prior to 1980-81 season, award was given to QMJHL Rookie-of-the-Year.

National Collegiate Athletic Association

Year	Champion	Coach	Runner-Up
1948	Michigan	Vic Heyliger	Dartmouth
1949	Boston College	John Kelley	Dartmouth
1950	Colorado College	Cheddy Thompson	Boston University
1951	Michigan	Vic Heyliger	Brown
1952	Michigan	Vic Heyliger	Colorado College
1953	Michigan	Vic Heyliger	Minnesota
1954	Rensselaer Poly	Ned Harkness	Minnesota
1955	Michigan	Vic Heyliger	Colorado College
1956	Michigan	Vic Heyliger	Michigan Tech
1957	Colorado College	Thomas Bedecki	Michigan
1958	Denver	Murray Armstrong	North Dakota
1959	North Dakota	Bob May	Michigan State
1960	Denver	Murray Armstrong	Michigan Tech
1961	Denver	Murray Armstrong	St. Lawrence
1962	Michigan Tech	John MacInnes	Clarkson
1963	North Dakota	Barry Thorndycraft	Denver
1964	Michigan	Al Renfrew	Denver
1965	Michigan Tech	John MacInnes	Boston College
1966	Michigan State	Amo Bessone	Clarkson
1967	Cornell	Ned Harkness	Boston University
1968	Denver	Murray Armstrong	North Dakota
1969	Denver	Murray Armstrong	Cornell
1970	Cornell	Ned Harkness	Clarkson
1971	Boston University	Jack Kelley	Minnesota
1972	Boston University	Jack Kelley	Cornell
1973	Wisconsin	Bob Johnson	Denver
1974	Minnesota	Herb Brooks	Michigan Tech
1975	Michigan Tech	John MacInnes	Minnesota
1976	Minnesota	Herb Brooks	Michigan Tech
1977	Wisconsin	Bob Johnson	Michigan
1978	Boston University	Jack Parker	Boston College
1979	Minnesota	Herb Brooks	North Dakota
1980	North Dakota	John Gasparini	Northern Michigan
1981	Wisconsin	Bob Johnson	Minnesota
1982	North Dakota	John Gasparini	Wisconsin
1983	Wisconsin	Jeff Sauer	Harvard
1984	Bowling Green	Jerry York	Minnesota-Duluth

Western Collegiate Hockey Association

	W.	L.	T.	GF.	GA.	Pct.
Minnesota-Duluth (29-12-2)	19	5	2	138	85	.769
North Dakota (31-12-2)	16	8	2	117	82	.654
Minnesota (27-11-2)	16	9	1	106	97	.635
Wisconsin (21-17-1)	11	14	1	105	107	.442
Denver (14-25-0)	8	18	0	119	152	.308
Colorado College (9-25-1)	5	21	0	77	139	.192

Overall record in parentheses.

1983-84 WCHA All-Stars

First Team	Position	Second Team
John Casey, North Dakota	Goalie	Rick Kosti, Minnesota-Duluth
Tom Kurvers, Minnesota-Duluth	Defenseman	Rick Zombo, North Dakota
Jim Leavins, Denver	Defenseman	Tony Kellin, Minnesota
Bill Watson, Minnesota-Duluth	Forward	Norm Maciver, Minn.-Duluth
Dan Brennan, North Dakota	Forward	Matt Christiansen, Minn.-Du.
Tom Rothstein, Minnesota	Forward	Bob Lakso, Minnesota-Duluth
	Forward	Tom Herzig, Minnesota-Duluth

COACH OF THE YEAR: Mike Sertich, Minnesota-Duluth
MOST VALUABLE PLAYER: Tom Kurvers, Minnesota-Duluth
FRESHMAN OF THE YEAR: Rick Kosti, Minnesota-Duluth

Central Collegiate Hockey Association

	W.	L.	T.	GF.	GA.	Pct.
Bowling Green (34-8-2)	22	4	2	146	96	.821
Michigan State (34-12-0)	21	9	0	162	90	.700
Ohio State (30-10-1)	21	9	0	155	96	.700
Northern Michigan (17-22-1)	16	14	0	126	118	.535
Western Michigan (22-18-2)	13	14	1	125	114	.482
Michigan Tech (19-21-1)	14	16	0	123	128	.467
Ferris State (18-20-3)	13	15	2	128	138	.467
Lake Superior St. (18-20-2)	12	17	1	103	127	.417
Michigan (14-22-1)	11	18	1	105	148	.383
Miami (O.) (13-23-1)	10	20	0	116	156	.333
Illinois-Chicago (5-29-1)	5	22	1	83	163	.193

Overall record in parentheses.

1983-84 CCHA All-Stars

First Team	Position	Second Team
John Dougan, Ohio State	Goalie	Norm Foster, Michigan State
Garry Galley, Bowling Green	Defenseman	Dave Ellett, Bowling Green
Dan McFall, Michigan State	Defenseman	Jim File, Ferris State
Paul Pooley, Ohio State	Forward	Perry Pooley, Ohio State
Dan Dorian, Western Michigan	Forward	Randy Merrifield, Ferris State
Dan Kane, Bowling Green	Forward	John Samanski, Bowling Green

COACH OF THE YEAR: Bill Wilkinson, Western Michigan
PLAYER OF THE YEAR: Paul Pooley, Ohio State
ROOKIE OF THE YEAR: Gary Emmons, Northern Michigan and Bill Shibicky, Michigan State

Eastern Collegiate Athletic Association

East Region

	W.	L.	T.	GF.	GA.	Pct.
Boston College (26-9-0)	15	6	0	88	74	.714
Boston University (26-9-0)	15	6	0	75	60	.714
New Hampshire (20-17-1)	13	8	0	94	73	.619
Providence (21-12-2)	12	7	2	84	78	.619
Northeastern (16-12-1)	10	10	1	104	97	.500
Maine (14-20-0)	7	14	0	75	109	.333

West Region

	W.	L.	T.	GF.	GA.	Pct.
Rensselaer Poly. Inst. (28-4-0)	17	3	0	117	54	.850
Clarkson (19-9-2)	14	6	0	95	63	.700
Colgate (20-14-1)	10	9	1	83	89	.525
St. Lawrence (19-13-0)	10	10	0	107	81	.500
Vermont (10-18-1)	6	13	1	89	97	.325

Ivy League

	W.	L.	T.	GF.	GA.	Pct.
Harvard (10-14-3)	10	9	2	68	61	.524
Yale (12-13-1)	10	10	1	76	73	.500
Cornell (11-15-0)	9	12	0	83	94	.429
Princeton (6-18-1)	5	15	1	80	103	.220
Brown (6-19-1)	5	15	1	59	109	.220
Dartmouth (3-23-0)	3	18	0	58	119	.142

Overall record in parentheses.

1983-84 ECAC All-Stars

First Team	Position	Second Team
Cleon Daskalakis, Boston University	Goalie	Bruce Gillies, New Hampshire
Bob Armstrong, Clarkson	Defenseman	Peter Taglianetti, Providence
T.J. Connolly, Boston University	Defenseman	Brian Byrnes, New Hampshire
Jim Chisholm, Boston College	Forward	Adam Oates, Rensselaer P.I.
Kevin Foster, Vermont	Forward	John Carter, Rensselaer P.I.
Steve Smith, Colgate	Forward	Marty Dallman, Rensselaer P.I.
Gates Orlando, Providence	Forward	

PLAYER OF THE YEAR: Cleon Daskalakis, Boston University
ROOKIE OF THE YEAR: John Cullen, Boston University

1984 NCAA TOURNAMENT

Quarterfinal Series
(Two-Game, Total Goal Series)

Boston College at Michigan State
Michigan State 6, Boston College 2
Michigan State 7, Boston College 6
(Michigan State wins series, 13-8)

Bowling Green State at Boston University
Boston U. 6, Bowling Green St. 3
Bowling Green St. 5, Boston U. 1 (OT)
(Bowling Green St. wins series, 8-7)

Clarkson at Minnesota-Duluth
Minnesota-Duluth 6, Clarkson 2
Clarkson 6, Minnesota-Duluth 3
(Minnesota-Duluth wins series, 9-8)

North Dakota at Rensselaer Poly. Inst.
North Dakota 5, Rensselaer Poly. Inst. 4
North Dakota 4, Rensselaer Poly. Inst. 2
(North Dakota wins series, 9-6)

Semifinal Series
Played at Lake Placid, New York
Minnesota-Duluth 2, North Dakota 1 (OT)
Bowling Green State 2, Michigan State 1

Consolation Game
North Dakota 6, Michigan State 5 (OT)

Championship Game
Bowling Green State 5, Minnesota-Duluth 4 (4 OT)
1984 NCAA Champion: Bowling Green State University

1984 NCAA All-Tournament Team

Position	Player	Team
Goalie	Rick Kosti	Minnesota-Duluth
Defenseman	Dave Ellett	Bowling Green St.
Defenseman	Garry Galley	Bowling Green St.
Forward	Dean Barne Barsness	North Dakota
Forward	Bob Lakso	Minnesota-Duluth
Forward	Lyle Phair	Michigan State

NCAA Tournament MVP—GARY KRUZICH, Bowling Green State University

1983-84 Final Collegiate Hockey Polls

Media Poll	Rank	Coaches Poll
Minnesota-Duluth	1.	Minnesota-Duluth
Rensselaer Poly. Inst.	2.	Rensselaer Poly. Inst.
Michigan State	3.	Bowling Green State
Bowling Green State	4.	Boston University
Boston University	5.	Minnesota
North Dakota	6.	Michigan State
Boston College	7.	North Dakota
Ohio State, Clarkson	8.	Ohio State
	9.	Boston College
Western Michigan	10.	Clarkson

All-Time NCAA Tournament Records and Finishes

	Visits	Tournament W.	L.	GF	GA	Pct.	Finished 1st	2nd
University of Michigan	13	21	6	173	91	.778	7	2
University of Wisconsin	8	15	5	90	52	.750	4	1
University of Denver	10	16	6	108	56	.727	5	2
University of North Dakota	11	17	9	102	78	.654	4	3
University of Minnesota	10	15	8	109	89	.652	3	5
*Bowling Green State	5	6	4	38	42	.600	1	0
Michigan Tech University	10	13	9	118	85	.591	3	4
Boston University	14	16	14	129	140	.533	3	2
Cornell University	7	7	7	48	45	.500	2	2
Yale University	1	1	1	7	5	.500	0	0
†Michigan State University	6	6	7	54	48	.461	1	1
Clarkson College	8	7	9	48	67	.438	0	3
R.P.I.	5	4	6	34	38	.400	1	0
Dartmouth College	5	4	5	38	37	.444	0	2
Colorado College	9	6	10	76	84	.375	2	2
Brown University	3	2	4	28	38	.333	0	1
University of Minnesota-Duluth	2	2	4	20	24	.333	0	1
Boston College	13	6	18	83	148	.250	1	2
Northern Michigan University	2	1	3	10	19	.250	0	1
†Harvard University	9	4	15	65	106	.211	0	1
Providence College	3	3	4	20	20	.429	0	0
University of New Hampshire	4	2	8	35	56	.200	0	0
St. Lawrence University	8	3	14	51	92	.176	0	1
*Northeastern University	1	2	1	17	14	.625	0	0

(Denver also participated in 1973 tournament but its record was voided by the NCAA in 1977 upon discovery of violations by the University. The team had finished second in '73.)

*Bowling Green and Northeastern played to a 2-2 tie in 1981-82.
†Harvard and Michigan State played to a 3-3 tie in 1982-83.

HOBEY BAKER MEMORIAL TROPHY (Top College hockey player in U.S.): Tom Kurvers, Minnesota-Duluth.

Air Force Academy
(Overall: 8-16-2)

	Pos.	Class	Games	G.	A.	Pts.	Pen.
Frank Daldine	F	So.	26	17	14	31	12
Bruce Umland	C	Sr.	26	15	14	29	22
Bob Sullivan	F	Sr.	26	9	12	21	54
Tim Hartje	F	So.	26	10	10	20	2
Dan Johnson	F	Jr.	25	13	6	19	40
Joe Chapman	C	Fr.	23	5	13	18	10
Jim Mackey	F	Sr.	26	3	12	15	25
Charlie Morrison	F	Jr.	25	7	5	12	18
John Klimek	F	Fr.	22	3	10	13	2
Jim Andersen	F	So.	26	4	8	12	6
Jay Mosley	F	So.	21	5	4	9	14
Bill Andersen	D	Jr.	26	5	6	11	10
Russ Quinn	C	Jr.	25	1	8	9	18
Don Kochanski	D	Jr.	25	3	5	8	6
James Brunkow	D	Fr.	26	1	7	8	6
Keith Nightingale	D	Fr.	21	2	1	3	26
Brian Lloyd	F	So.	19	3	0	3	2
Mark Bucki	D	So.	25	0	1	1	4
Tom Zuccaro	D	Jr.	9	0	1	1	2
John Bailey	F	So.	3	0	1	1	0
Rich Curtis	D	Fr.	8	0	0	0	4
Paul Greenhaw	F	Fr.	7	0	0	0	0
Rob LaVigne	D	So.	4	0	0	0	0
Neil Sauve	F	So.	8	0	0	0	2
Neil Schubert	D	So.	4	0	0	0	6
Matt Crandall	G	Fr.	19	0	0	0	8

Boston College
(Overall: 26-13-0) (ECAC: 15-6-0)

	Pos.	Class	Games	G.	A.	Pts.	Pen.
Scott Harlow	F	So.	39	27	20	47	17
Ed Rauseo	F	Sr.	38	13	26	39	32
Billy McDonough	F	Sr.	39	11	25	36	30
Jim Herlihy	F	Jr.	38	12	20	32	20
Dominic Campedelli	D	So.	37	10	19	29	24
Tim Mitchell	F	Jr.	34	12	16	28	30
Bob Sweeney	F	So.	23	14	7	21	10
Doug Brown	F	So.	38	11	10	21	6
Neil Shea	F	So.	31	8	13	21	16
Kevin Stevens	F	Fr.	37	6	14	20	36
Jim Chisholm	D	Sr.	38	0	20	20	28
Robin Monleon	F	Sr.	38	9	10	19	36
Dan Griffin	D	Sr.	34	2	16	18	32
David Livingston	F	Jr.	38	10	7	17	18
Kevin Houle	F	So.	28	5	12	17	8
Chris Delaney	F	Jr.	30	9	7	16	44
John McNamara	D	So.	35	3	10	13	20
Bruce Milton	D	Jr.	18	7	4	11	14
Bob Emery	D	So.	35	2	7	9	32
John McLean	D	Fr.	16	1	4	5	4
George Boudreau	D	Jr.	20	0	3	3	12
John Orr	F	Sr.	4	0	3	3	2
David Whyte	F	Fr.	8	0	2	2	2
Jack McNeill	D	Fr.	2	1	0	1	0
Scott Gordon	G	So.	35	0	0	0	6
Michael Barron	D	So.	4	0	0	0	6

Boston University
(Overall: 28-11-1) (ECAC: 15-6-0)

	Pos.	Class	Games	G.	A.	Pts.	Pen.
John Cullen	C	Fr.	40	23	33	56	28
Mark Pierog	LW	Sr.	40	17	17	34	32
Joe Cappellano	RW	So.	37	10	24	34	26
Ed Lowney	RW	Fr.	40	21	12	33	26
Denis LaGarde	C	Sr.	39	13	18	31	32
Kevin Mutch	LW	Jr.	38	17	12	29	16
Scott Shaunessy	D	Fr.	40	6	22	28	48
Paul Gerlitz	RW	So.	40	14	13	27	46

	Pos.	Class	Games	G.	A.	Pts.	Pen.
Peter Marshall	C	So.	39	6	19	25	42
T.J. Connolly	D	Sr.	40	3	20	23	34
Chuck Sullivan	LW	So.	33	11	11	22	10
Brad MacGregor	LW	So.	38	5	16	21	28
Joe Delorey	D	Jr.	39	4	15	19	20
Cesare Carlacci	RW	Sr.	31	6	10	16	18
Dale Dunbar	D	Jr.	34	0	15	15	49
Chris Mays	LW	Sr.	22	1	9	10	24
Chris Matchett	D	So.	39	2	7	9	48
Tony Majkozak	LW	So.	23	3	5	8	14
John Tiano	C	So.	14	3	4	7	4
Jay Octeau	D	Fr.	27	1	6	7	20
David Thiesing	D	Fr.	19	1	2	3	10
Steve Crozier	C	Fr.	5	0	0	0	2
Cleon Daskalakis	G	Sr.	35	0	0	0	4

Bowling Green State University
(Overall: 34-8-2)   (CCHA: 22-4-2)

	Pos.	Class	Games	G.	A.	Pts.	Pen.
Dan Kane	C	Jr.	43	24	48	72	61
Garry Galley	D	Jr.	44	15	52	67	61
John Samanski	C	Sr.	42	25	35	60	52
Dave Ellett	D	So.	43	15	39	54	96
Jamie Wansbrough	W	So.	40	34	16	50	18
Gino Cavallini	W	So.	43	25	23	48	16
Dave O'Brian	W	Sr.	44	12	27	39	62
George Roll	W	Jr.	44	13	25	38	32
Mike Pikul	D	Sr.	41	7	30	37	36
Dave Randerson	W	Jr.	43	12	19	31	6
Perry Braun	W	Sr.	38	12	18	30	26
Wayne Wilson	D	Sr.	44	2	24	26	60
Tim Hack	C	Sr.	44	7	16	23	28
Iain Duncan	D	Fr.	44	9	11	20	65
Peter Wilson	W	Sr.	43	6	12	18	40
Nick Bandescu	C	Sr.	44	9	8	17	12
Todd Flichel	D	Fr.	44	1	3	4	12
Rob Urban	C	Fr.	14	0	3	3	4
Gary Kruzich	G	Fr.	28	0	0	0	14
Eddie Powers	G	So.	7	0	1	1	0

Brown University
(Overall: 6-19-1)   (ECAC: 5-15-1)

	Pos.	Class	Games	G.	A.	Pts.	Pen.
Dan Allen	C	Fr.	25	11	10	21	4
Bobby Jones	C	So.	22	9	7	16	14
Tom Wallack	RW	So.	25	5	9	14	36
Jim White	LW	Jr.	22	6	8	14	14
Steve Climo	LW	Fr.	25	5	8	13	6
Paul Salem	RW	Jr.	26	6	6	12	12
Tim O'Connor	RW	Jr.	19	2	8	10	10
Brian Driscoll	D	Sr.	25	3	6	9	10
Scott Staff	LW	Jr.	15	4	5	9	18
Scott Whittemore	D	Jr.	26	1	7	8	32
Al Randaccio	W	So.	17	3	3	6	4
Tom Roberts	D	Sr.	20	1	5	6	8
Pat Davis	D	So.	19	0	5	5	18
John McEvoy	RW	So.	26	2	3	5	10
Ed Pizzo	D	Jr.	21	1	4	5	16
Mark Rechan	RW	Fr.	21	2	3	5	2
Mike Girouard	D	Fr.	26	1	3	4	54
Mike Rechan	C	Fr.	13	2	2	4	17
Greg Diffley	C	Fr.	11	2	1	3	2
Dave Andreychuk	LW	Fr.	11	1	1	2	4
Joe Kuzneski	RW	So.	7	1	1	2	0
Rob McDonald	LW	Jr.	8	2	0	2	2
Bruce Prenda	RW	Fr.	6	0	2	2	0
Mark Janigan	C	So.	5	0	1	1	0
Greg Murphy	D	Fr.	23	0	1	1	46
Jens Gjerset	C	Fr.	2	0	0	0	2
Paul McCarthy	G	Sr.	14	0	0	0	2

Clarkson University
(Overall: 21-11-2) (ECAC: 14-6-0)

	Pos.	Class	Games	G.	A.	Pts.	Pen.
Michael Harvey	F	So.	34	18	26	44	50
Gord Sharpe	F	Jr.	32	16	21	37	30
James O'Meara	F	Sr.	34	13	24	37	10
Pat Haramis	F	Sr.	32	16	20	36	50
Bob Armstrong	D	Sr.	34	9	20	29	72
Derek Ray	F	So.	33	12	16	28	102
Andrew Otto	D	So.	34	8	19	27	16
Al Hill	F	Fr.	33	16	11	27	28
Dave Fretz	D	Jr.	34	10	17	27	54
Charles Meitner	F	So.	34	9	15	24	10
Ted Cline	F	Jr.	33	7	15	22	55
Pat O'Brien	F	Jr.	32	8	8	16	10
Bob Lenney	F	So.	29	5	8	13	14
Sheldon Camp	F	Jr.	34	3	10	13	30
Tom Hargrave	D	Jr.	20	1	8	9	14
James Lang	D	Jr.	34	2	7	9	34
Jeff Korchinski	D	Fr.	34	1	5	6	12
Greg Wiese	F	Jr.	20	1	2	3	2
Jim Carrigan	F	Jr.	4	0	2	2	0
Ross Bartell	D	Jr.	27	1	1	2	32
Moorie Moore	F	Fr.	13	0	1	1	4
Tom Sanders	F	Fr.	1	0	0	0	2
Jamie Falle	G	So.	27	0	0	0	12
Don Sylvestri	G	Sr.	16	0	0	0	2

Colgate University
(Overall: 20-14-1) (ECAC: 10-9-1)

	Pos.	Class	Games	G.	A.	Pts.	Pen.
Gerard Waslen	RW	So.	35	28	33	61	64
Steve Smith	C	Sr.	35	29	31	60	12
Jim Wallace	C	Sr.	34	26	31	57	6
Walt Dubas	RW	Sr.	35	14	20	34	32
Mike Walsh	RW	Sr.	35	16	17	33	94
Paul Silvio	LW	Jr.	31	11	17	28	24
Mike Leblanc	D	Jr.	34	8	19	27	44
Dan Maillet	D	Jr.	35	2	19	21	28
Paul McKinnon	D	So.	33	2	17	19	22
Scott Reston	RW	Fr.	33	7	10	17	40
Rod Powell	D	Sr.	27	4	11	15	39
Pete Ens	D	Sr.	33	3	12	15	10
Lou Wagar	RW	So.	33	6	6	12	14
Gerry Brockman	LW	So.	35	4	6	10	14
Harold Duvall	LW	Fr.	26	1	9	10	37
Doug Davis	C	Fr.	20	5	2	7	2
Rick Russell	D	Fr.	30	3	4	7	16
Lowell MacDonald	C	Fr.	20	1	4	5	8
Joe Tetzlaff	RW	So.	11	0	5	5	10
Paul Jenkins	D	Fr.	32	1	4	5	22
Dan Taylor	D	Fr.	2	0	0	0	2

Colorado College
(Overall: 9-25-1) (WCHA: 5-23-0)

	Pos.	Class	Games	G.	A.	Pts.	Pen.
Ken Filbey	C	So.	35	20	21	41	62
Rob Doyle	D	Fr.	34	5	29	34	112
Scott Schneider	C	Fr.	35	19	14	33	24
Brent Gropp	W	So.	34	10	22	32	82
Doug Clarke	D	Fr.	35	6	26	32	70
Dan Dolan	W	Jr.	35	12	12	24	24
Gord Whitaker	W	Fr.	33	10	10	20	44
Dan Brennan	W	So.	34	9	8	17	46
Tim Turner	W	Sr.	35	5	12	17	14
Dan Burns	C	Jr.	35	4	9	13	16
Peter Lindgren	W	Sr.	29	3	6	9	8
Scott Campbell	D	Fr.	34	2	6	8	34
Mark Krois	C	Fr.	33	5	2	7	14
Marty Ketola	W	Fr.	34	3	4	7	48

	Pos.	Class	Games	G.	A.	Pts.	Pen.
Dave Hardie	D	So.	34	2	5	7	26
Rick Boh	W	Fr.	27	1	5	6	12
Jim Gile	W	So.	16	0	2	2	4
Dave Baker	D	So.	29	0	1	1	18
Marty Wakelyn	G	So.	30	0	1	1	0
Kyle King	W	Fr.	1	0	0	0	4

Cornell University
(Overall: 11-15-0) (ECAC: 9-12-0)

	Pos.	Class	Games	G.	A.	Pts.	Pen.
Duane Moeser	W	So.	26	19	31	50	14
Geoff Dervin	C	Sr.	26	20	18	38	30
Gary Cullen	C	Jr.	22	13	25	38	4
Pete Marcov	W	Fr.	26	11	11	22	6
Mike Schafer	D	So.	25	4	16	20	42
Mark Canduro	C	So.	26	6	10	16	12
Mark Major	C	Fr.	25	5	9	14	2
Mark Henderson	W	Jr.	26	5	6	11	14
Dave Hunter	W	So.	21	4	7	11	22
Peter Natyshak	W	So.	25	4	6	10	36
Steve Inglehart	D	So.	25	1	9	10	12
Mike Foley	W	So.	21	1	9	10	22
Terry Gage	D	Sr.	26	2	5	7	55
Randy MacFarlane	C	Jr.	14	3	3	6	6
Dave Grbich	D	Jr.	22	2	3	5	14
Andy Craig	D	Fr.	18	1	4	5	2
John Wilson	W	Jr.	20	1	4	5	12
Mike LaFerle	D	Jr.	17	0	5	5	34
Keith Howie	W	Fr.	16	2	0	2	8
Larry Wasylishyn	C	So.	16	2	0	2	12
John Parry	D	Fr.	25	0	0	0	14
R.J. Farnworth	D	Fr.	1	0	0	0	0
Gary Matura	W	Jr.	1	0	0	0	0
Warren Fields	W	Jr.	1	0	0	0	0
Jim Edmands	G	Fr.	17	0	0	0	4
Don Fawcett	G	Fr.	15	0	0	0	2

Dartmouth College
(Overall: 3-23-0) (ECAC: 3-18-0)

	Pos.	Class	Games	G.	A.	Pts.	Pen.
Bruce Cullen	W	Sr.	26	10	15	25	20
Doug Hirsch	W	Jr.	26	9	13	22	12
Mark Lamoureux	C	Sr.	24	10	8	18	0
Allen Taber	C	Sr.	24	6	12	18	8
Kevin McCann	W	Fr.	26	4	10	14	10
Bob Cronin	D	Sr.	25	4	10	14	75
Bob Jangro	W	Jr.	26	5	8	13	16
Brien Jacobson	D/C	So.	23	4	6	10	34
John Sedgewick	W	Sr.	25	4	5	9	45
Todd Soutor	D	Jr.	26	3	6	9	36
Tom Norton	C	Jr.	8	2	4	6	10
John Earley	W/D	Jr.	22	2	3	5	35
Dan Nugent	W	So.	25	1	3	4	57
Mike Palmer	D	Sr.	20	1	3	4	32
Jeff Leonard	D	Jr.	16	1	3	4	4
David Foster	W	So.	12	2	1	3	6
Paul Dion	D	So.	25	1	2	3	47
Marty Sims	C	So.	25	1	1	2	16
Sam Lardner	W	So.	8	0	2	2	2
Dan Bourque	D	Jr.	14	1	0	1	10
Jack Bohn	D	Fr.	22	0	0	0	16
Jeff Bower	G	Fr.	18	0	0	0	6
Chris Hinkle	C	Jr.	6	0	0	0	2
Doug Vierthaler	W	So.	5	0	0	0	4
Philip Hebert	W	Fr.	4	0	0	0	2
Mike Roberts	D	Fr.	3	0	0	0	2
Jim Thomas	C	Fr.	2	0	0	0	2

University of Denver
(Overall: 14-25-0) (WCHA: 8-18-0)

	Pos.	Class	Games	G.	A.	Pts.	Pen.
John McMillan	C	Fr.	37	22	35	57	48
Dwight Mathiasen	W	Fr.	36	24	27	51	48
Ian Ramsay	W	Jr.	39	12	39	51	40
Dave Anderson	W	Jr.	38	23	27	50	75
Dave Berry	W	Sr.	38	18	28	46	39
Dallas Gaume	C	So.	32	12	25	38	22
Jim Leavins	D	Sr.	39	13	24	37	38
Grant Dion	D	So.	35	11	20	31	36
Deane Hansen	D	Sr.	39	7	17	24	70
Derik Sheers	W	So.	37	11	11	22	20
Jim Smith	D	So.	36	5	15	20	24
Tom Weiss	W	Fr.	38	12	7	19	34
Kermit Ecklebatger	W	Fr.	31	5	12	17	44
Don Mercier	D	Fr.	35	2	10	12	44
Jim Onstad	W	Fr.	39	4	7	11	6
Tom Xavier	C	Jr.	36	1	3	4	0
Peter Godfrey	D	So.	13	0	2	2	18
Jeff Perpich	D	Fr.	30	0	2	2	16
Jeff Lamb	C	Fr.	15	0	2	2	8
Eric Johnson	D	Fr.	29	0	2	2	10
Bobby Larscheid	C	So.	16	0	1	1	8

Ferris State College
(Overall: 18-20-3) (CCHA: 13-15-2)

	Pos.	Class	Games	G.	A.	Pts.	Pen.
Randy Merrifield	C	Sr.	41	20	53	73	14
Graham Craig	C	Jr.	30	25	26	51	62
Jim File	D	Sr.	39	11	38	49	74
Paul Couture	RW	So.	40	23	31	44	38
Peter Lowden	C	Fr.	41	9	22	31	22
Tim Wendt	RW	Jr.	36	11	19	30	30
Paul Lowden	RW	Fr.	40	16	13	29	30
Scott Seaver	LW	So.	30	11	16	27	48
Paul Podger	LW	Fr.	37	8	19	27	70
Jim Clement	LW	Fr.	36	9	5	14	36
Jean Landry	C/LW	So.	37	5	8	13	16
Ray Zabel	D	Fr.	36	3	10	13	56
Ken Stelmach	RW	So.	37	8	4	12	32
Judd Green	D	Fr.	30	6	5	11	18
Tony Byers	LW	Fr.	36	8	2	10	0
Brad Hildestad	D	Jr.	38	1	9	10	22
Scott Syring	D	Fr.	22	3	5	8	18
Brent Weller	D	So.	19	3	3	6	12
Dennis Garbarz	D	So.	39	1	5	6	54
Nick Manych	D	Jr.	11	0	5	5	22
Rob Brownlie	D	Jr.	21	1	2	3	30
Bill Shopovick	RW	Fr.	10	1	1	2	4
Terry Cyr	C	Fr.	5	1	1	2	8
Frank Damico	RW	So.	7	0	2	2	8
Kirk Aldridge	F	Fr.	9	0	2	2	6
Rob Hughston	G	Jr.	34	0	2	2	8
Norm Young	G	So.	20	0	1	1	4
Steve Jeremy	LW	Jr.	6	0	1	1	12

Harvard University
(Overall: 10-14-3) (ECAC: 10-9-2)

	Pos.	Class	Games	G.	A.	Pts.	Pen.
Brian Busconi	F	Jr.	25	12	6	18	12
Tony Visone	F	Sr.	24	8	9	17	41
Gary Martin	F	Sr.	26	8	8	16	22
Rob Wheeler	F	Sr.	27	8	8	16	10
Dave Connors	F	Sr.	26	5	11	16	22
Shayne Kukulowicz	F	Sr.	27	5	9	14	56
Rob Ohno	F	So.	27	4	9	13	4
Butch Cutone	D	Fr.	27	3	10	13	4

	Pos.	Class	Games	G.	A.	Pts.	Pen.
Phil Falcone	F	Sr.	14	7	5	12	4
Tim Barakett	F	Fr.	27	4	8	12	10
Peter Chiarelli	F	Fr.	27	4	8	12	18
Jay North	F	Sr.	20	4	5	9	2
Ken Code	D	Sr.	25	2	7	9	24
Brad Kwong	D	Jr.	25	1	7	8	14
Bill Cleary	D	Jr.	27	2	4	6	4
Peter Follows	F	So.	13	2	4	6	0
Tim Smith	F-D	So.	23	2	3	5	12
Tim McMahon	F	So.	11	1	3	4	6
Randy Taylor	D	Fr.	23	0	3	3	4
Grant Blair	G	So.	23	0	1	1	8
Brad Dorman	D	Sr.	21	0	1	1	16
Dickie McEvoy	G	So.	4	0	0	0	0
Ralph Hartmann	F	So.	7	0	0	0	0
Rick Haney	F	Fr.	1	0	0	0	0
Tim Hart	F	So.	2	0	0	0	0

University of Illinois-Chicago
(Overall: 5-29-1)   (CCHA: 5-22-1)

	Pos.	Class	Games	G.	A.	Pts.	Pen.
Mike Rucinski	W	Fr.	33	17	26	43	12
Colin Chin	C	Jr.	35	11	25	36	14
Ray Staszak	W	Fr.	31	15	17	32	42
Jamie Husgen	D	Fr.	35	6	17	23	76
Tom Palkowski	C	Fr.	35	7	13	20	14
Daryl Seltenreich	W	Fr.	35	9	10	19	30
Jeff McIntyre	W	Sr.	35	9	9	18	59
Harry Armstrong	D	Fr.	25	4	11	15	21
Greg Hooper	W	So.	34	7	6	13	21
Chad Johnson	C	Fr.	35	7	5	12	32
Terry Majich	C	So.	24	3	9	12	26
Joe Patzin	W	Sr.	32	3	7	10	22
Gary Hooper	W	Fr.	20	3	3	6	12
Tom Almquist	W	Fr.	29	3	3	6	18
Mike Mersch	D	Fr.	29	0	5	5	18
Shawn Cronin	D	So.	32	0	4	4	41
Steve Huglen	D	Fr.	35	0	3	3	26
Paul Pulis	W	Fr.	25	1	2	3	12
John Mynatt	D	Fr.	34	1	1	2	40
Frank Provenzano	W	Fr.	24	1	0	1	12
Jim Hickey	G	Fr.	25	0	0	0	4
John Whelan	G	Sr.	10	0	0	0	2

Lake Superior State College
(Overall: 18-20-2)   (CCHA: 12-18-1)

	Pos.	Class	Games	G.	A.	Pts.	Pen.
Allan Butler	C	Jr.	39	28	26	54	10
Monty Beauchamp	LW	Sr.	36	15	25	40	44
Chris Guy	D	Jr.	39	12	28	40	16
Kevin Collar	RW	Sr.	40	13	22	35	26
Paul Jerrard	D	Fr.	40	8	18	26	48
Jim Roque	C	Fr.	40	9	17	26	16
Nick Palumbo	LW	So.	36	8	18	26	14
Keith Martin	LW	So.	40	11	13	24	66
Chris Dahlquist	D	Jr.	40	4	19	23	76
Scott Johnson	RW	So.	39	9	13	22	32
Dean Dixon	C	Fr.	37	6	14	20	57
Nick Bumbacco	LW	So.	22	9	4	13	20
Mark Vichorek	D	So.	40	3	8	11	14
Mike Warus	RW	Fr.	35	6	4	10	33
Matt Cote	D	Fr.	40	0	9	9	30
Fred DeVuono	LW	So.	32	6	1	7	26
Grant Clark	D	Fr.	40	0	6	6	22
Pat Lizotte	LW	Fr.	20	1	3	4	6
Scott Stephens	RW	Jr.	12	1	3	4	6
Lawrence Dyck	G	Sr.	22	0	1	1	2
Joe Shawhan	G	So.	9	0	1	1	0
Gary Kiser	D	Jr.	12	0	0	0	14

University of Lowell
(Overall: 15-16-3)

	Pos.	Class	Games	G.	A.	Pts.	Pen.
Don McCoy	W	Sr.	34	27	25	52	14
Danny Craig	C	Jr.	24	16	25	41	27
Mike Opre	C	Jr.	32	11	14	25	25
Mike Hodson	D	So.	33	7	17	24	30
Jack Fahey	W	Sr.	25	6	10	16	42
Jim O'Brien	W	So.	34	4	12	16	38
Rob Spath	D	Sr.	15	3	13	16	44
Don McDonough	W	Fr.	33	7	8	15	12
Scott Wiebolt	D	Jr.	34	5	10	15	82
Dennis McCarroll	W	Fr.	21	8	6	14	48
Mike O'Neill	D	Jr.	32	6	8	14	49
Paul Mahan	C	Fr.	34	5	9	14	14
Paul Ames	D	Fr.	31	1	13	14	16
Tom Fahey	W	Fr.	30	8	5	13	28
John Bernie	D	Fr.	29	2	11	13	35
Tom Evangelista	W	Fr.	20	4	8	12	28
Mike Rawnsley	C	So.	25	2	9	11	8
Rob Silc	C	Fr.	23	5	4	9	19
Chris Wright	W	Sr.	12	1	7	8	2
Bob Braccia	W	Fr.	16	4	3	7	22
Bob Devereaux	W	Fr.	18	3	2	5	4
Chris Hillick	W	So.	10	1	2	3	6
Tom McComb	D	Fr.	18	1	1	2	8
Vinny Sica	W	Fr.	12	1	1	2	16
Scott McKee	W	Fr.	6	0	1	1	4
Dana Demole	G	So.	31	0	1	1	6
Bill Gravell	W	Fr.	1	0	0	0	2
Jim Pickens	D	Fr.	4	0	0	0	6

University of Maine
(Overall: 14-20-0) (ECAC: 7-14-0)

	Pos.	Class	Games	G.	A.	Pts.	Pen.
Todd Bjorkstrand	F	Sr.	32	15	37	52	18
Ray Jacques	F	Jr.	28	11	27	38	14
Paul Giacalone	F	Sr.	32	11	18	29	16
Rene Comeault	D	Jr.	21	6	21	27	12
Kevin Mann	F	Fr.	34	9	16	25	4
Jay Mazur	F	Fr.	34	14	9	23	14
Bruce Hegland	F	Jr.	34	10	12	22	35
John McDonald	F	So.	33	9	11	20	20
Steve Santini	F	Fr.	31	7	7	14	10
Joe Jirele	F	Jr.	34	7	6	13	8
Scott Boretti	F	Jr.	32	5	8	13	16
Jim Purcell	F	Fr.	32	5	7	12	26
Scott Smith	D	So.	32	1	9	10	62
Joel Steensen	D	Jr.	20	3	6	9	14
Duncan MacIntyre	D	So.	32	4	4	8	10
Neil Johnson	D	Sr.	18	3	5	8	18
Ron Hellen	F	Jr.	3	3	4	7	6
Mike Hernon	F	Fr.	17	3	4	7	6
Peter Maher	F	Jr.	9	0	7	7	0
Roger Grillo	D	So.	34	2	4	6	12
Brad Odegaard	F	Fr.	9	0	5	5	2
Jeff Kloewer	D	Jr.	33	1	2	3	18
John Baker	D	Fr.	19	1	1	2	12
Jim Bolger	F	Jr.	3	0	1	1	0
Dave Hunt	F-D	Sr.	1	0	0	0	2
Jean Lacoste	G	Fr.	17	0	0	0	4
Ray Roy	G	Jr.	8	0	0	0	2

Miami O. University
(Overall: 13-23-1) (CCHA: 10-20-0)

	Pos.	Class	Games	G.	A.	Pts.	Pen.
Greg Lukas	F	Sr.	37	15	35	50	32
John Ciotti	F	Jr.	34	21	21	42	26

	Pos.	Class	Games	G.	A.	Pts.	Pen.
Andy Cozzi	F	Jr.	37	15	26	41	6
Dave Wheeldon	F	Sr.	36	11	22	33	42
Bill Easdale	F	So.	34	13	16	29	6
Todd Channell	F	So.	34	14	14	28	4
Andy McMillin	D	Sr.	37	4	21	25	52
Jim Buettgen	F	Sr.	27	12	5	17	14
Paul Beirnes	F	So.	26	5	11	16	32
Shawn Lynes	F	Sr.	36	8	7	15	50
Bill Christie	F	So.	27	4	11	15	8
John O'Connor	F	Fr.	37	7	6	13	2
Tim Moore	D	So.	37	1	13	14	58
Dan Sojka	F	Fr.	21	8	3	11	18
Ron Renner	D	So.	34	0	11	11	24
Mark Dean	D	Jr.	25	4	6	10	14
Mike Martinec	F	Fr.	23	2	8	10	12
Jay Lees	D	Jr.	31	1	8	9	22
Tim Huettl	F	Fr.	19	3	2	5	24
Keith Bertrim	D	Fr.	27	1	4	5	8
Mike Macoun	F	Fr.	23	0	3	3	50
Greg Turner	F	So.	6	0	2	2	4
K.C. Chermak	F	Fr.	4	0	1	1	2
Al Chevrier	G	Sr.	32	0	1	1	0
Tim Hall	G	Fr.	18	0	1	1	2
Marty Pirjevec	D	Fr.	13	0	0	0	14
Mike Sroczyinski	D	Jr.	1	0	0	0	0

University of Michigan
(Overall: 14-22-1) (CCHA: 11-18-1)

	Pos.	Class	Games	G.	A.	Pts.	Pen.
Jim McCauley	RW	Sr.	36	17	26	43	12
Chris Seychel	LW	So.	31	16	20	36	34
Brad Jones	C	Fr.	37	8	26	34	32
Todd Carlile	D	So.	33	11	20	31	70
Ray Dries	C	Sr.	36	16	12	28	34
Tom Stiles	C/RW	So.	37	10	12	22	30
John Bjorkman	C	Fr.	36	9	12	21	33
Pat Goff	D	So.	37	4	17	21	38
John DeMartino	D	Sr.	28	4	12	16	42
Doug May	D/LW	Jr.	37	5	10	15	54
Frank Downing	RW	So.	27	6	8	14	18
Bill Brauer	D	So.	37	1	13	14	24
Kelly McCrimmon	RW	Sr.	30	8	5	13	34
Paul Spring	LW	Jr.	37	5	8	13	16
Bruce Macnab	LW	Fr.	34	5	7	12	30
Paul Kobylarz	RW	Jr.	25	3	5	8	14
Mike Neff	D	Jr.	22	2	6	8	26
Dan Goff	C/RW	So.	29	2	5	7	10
Dave McIntyre	D/RW	Jr.	22	1	4	5	6
Greg Hudas	D	So.	17	1	1	2	18
Jim Mans	LW	So.	4	0	0	0	10
Mark Chiamp	G	Jr.	33	0	0	0	2
Jim Switzer	LW	So.	11	0	0	0	0
Tom Dolan	D	So.	10	0	0	0	0
Jon Elliott	G	Jr.	7	0	0	0	0
Joe Grusser	D	Fr.	1	0	0	0	0

Michigan State University
(Overall: 34-12-0) (CCHA: 21-9-0)

	Pos.	Class	Games	G.	A.	Pts.	Pen.
Craig Simpson	C	Fr.	46	14	43	57	38
Bill Shibicky	C	Fr.	43	18	37	55	59
Jeff Eisley	D	Sr	45	13	41	54	57
Newell Brown	RW	Sr.	42	20	33	53	30
Kelly Miller	LW	Jr.	46	28	21	49	12
Gord Flegel	C	Jr.	46	23	21	44	26
Tom Anastos	RW	Sr.	46	22	16	38	35
Don McSween	D	Fr.	46	10	26	36	30

	Pos.	Class	Games	G.	A.	Pts.	Pen.
Dan McFall	D	Jr.	46	14	20	34	56
Mike Donnelly	LW	So.	44	18	14	32	40
Dale Krentz	LW	So.	44	12	20	32	34
Lyle Phair	LW	Jr.	45	15	16	31	58
Harvey Smyl	RW	So.	43	11	15	26	92
Jeff Parker	RW	Fr.	44	8	13	21	82
Mitch Messier	C	Fr.	37	6	15	21	22
David Taylor	D	Sr.	46	2	18	20	34
Brad Beck	D	So.	42	2	7	9	67
Dan Beaty	RW	Jr.	10	2	4	6	4
Neil Davey	D	Fr.	33	1	5	6	50
Dave Arkeilpane	RW	Fr.	7	1	2	3	4
Bob Essensa	G	Fr.	17	0	2	2	0
Dee Rizzo	RW	Jr.	11	0	2	2	8
Andre Lamarche	D	Sr.	9	1	1	2	12
Norm Foster	G	Fr.	32	0	1	1	4
Rick Fernandez	LW	Sr.	3	0	0	0	0

Michigan Technological University
(Overall: 19-21-1)   (CCHA: 14-16-0)

	Pos.	Class	Games	G.	A.	Pts.	Pen.
Chris Cichocki	RW	So.	40	25	20	45	36
Bill Terry	RW	Sr.	40	23	17	40	40
Geordie Hamilton	C	So.	39	13	26	39	22
Brian Hannon	RW	Fr.	40	17	16	33	16
Steve Murphy	RW	Sr.	33	12	20	32	32
Mark Maroste	C	Jr.	41	11	19	30	34
Doug Harris	LW	So.	39	13	12	25	27
Mike Nepi	D	Jr.	38	8	15	23	80
Kurt Pearson	LW	Jr.	36	8	15	23	86
Dave Reierson	D	So.	38	4	15	19	63
Brian Clark	D	Jr.	34	1	17	18	74
Al Radke	RW	Sr.	37	11	5	16	20
Ron Zuke	LW	Sr.	25	4	8	12	10
Paul Stone	RW	Jr.	23	2	7	9	16
Scott Campton	D	Jr.	41	0	9	9	76
Donnie Porter	RW	Fr.	31	4	4	8	8
Ally Cook	C	Fr.	31	2	5	7	6
Kevin Fritz	C	Fr.	13	2	3	5	16
Dave Wilson	LW	Fr.	21	0	5	5	16
Conrad Vachon	D	So.	17	0	3	3	18
Jim Husted	D	So.	6	0	2	2	8
Barry Riutta	D	Jr.	26	0	2	2	42
Randy Oswald	D	Fr.	41	0	2	2	44
Darryl Pierce	G	So.	15	0	1	1	2
Jim De Genaro	D	Fr.	2	0	1	1	0
Dave Roach	G	Fr.	27	0	0	0	0
Bart Tompsett	G	Jr.	7	0	0	0	2

University of Minnesota
(Overall: 27-11-2)   (WCHA: 16-9-1)

	Pos.	Class	Games	G.	A.	Pts.	Pen.
Tom Rothstein	W	Jr.	39	30	34	64	70
Pat Micheletti	C/W	So.	39	26	34	60	62
Jeff Larson	C	Sr.	39	12	26	38	63
Tony Kellin	D/W	So.	38	12	21	33	66
Todd Okerlund	W	Fr.	34	11	20	31	18
Roger Bowe	W	Jr.	34	11	16	27	8
Eric Lempe	C	So.	28	10	14	24	28
Mike Guentzel	D	So.	34	4	17	21	26
Gary Shopek	D	Fr.	39	4	15	19	34
Steve MacSwain	W	Fr.	28	8	10	18	12
Kurt Larson	D	Jr.	34	3	15	18	16
Jim Malwitz	W	Jr.	38	6	11	17	44
Wally Chapman	W/C	So.	30	10	6	16	20
Tom Parenteau	D	Jr.	35	3	13	16	40
Tim Bergland	C	Fr.	24	4	11	15	4
Billy Yon	W	Jr.	39	8	5	13	30

	Pos.	Class	Games	G.	A.	Pts.	Pen.
Rick Erdall	C	Jr.	9	5	7	12	8
Scott Knutson	C	So.	17	5	4	9	20
Steve Orth	C	Fr.	8	4	4	8	2
Dave Preuss	W	Jr.	19	4	4	8	36
Mike Anderson	W	So.	23	1	7	8	4
Tom Ward	D	So.	35	1	4	5	38
John Labatt	C	Fr.	11	2	2	4	2
Rich Geist	W	Fr.	5	2	1	3	2
Nick Holmes	W	So.	1	1	2	3	2
Craig Mack	D	Fr.	21	0	3	3	14
Bob Alexander	D/W	Fr.	3	0	2	2	2
Frank Pietrangelo	G	So.	20	0	2	2	0
Leo Hanna	W	So.	1	1	0	1	0
Sean Regan	D	Jr.	6	0	1	1	4
Larry Housley	D	So.	4	0	1	1	2
Mike Brodzinski	C	Fr.	1	0	1	1	0
Mike Vacanti	G	Sr.	20	0	0	0	12

University of Minnesota-Duluth
(Overall: 29-12-2)   (WCHA: 19-5-2)

	Pos.	Class	Games	G.	A.	Pts.	Pen.
Bill Watson	RW	So.	40	35	51	86	12
Tom Kurvers	D	Sr.	43	18	58	76	46
Bob Lakso	LW	Sr.	43	32	34	66	12
Matt Christensen	C	So.	42	24	39	63	16
Tom Herzig	LW	Jr.	43	24	22	46	20
Norm Maciver	D	So.	31	13	28	41	28
Mark Baron	W	Sr.	43	15	15	30	12
Bill Mason	RW	Sr.	33	10	15	25	20
Jim Johnson	D	Jr.	43	3	13	16	116
Mark Odnokon	LW	So.	43	7	9	16	66
Danny May	C	Jr.	43	7	8	15	46
Bill Grillo	D	Sr.	43	3	11	14	42
Brian Johnson	C/D	Fr.	39	4	9	13	30
Skeeter Moore	LW	Fr.	28	3	8	11	10
Jim Sprenger	D	Fr.	42	2	7	9	22
Sean Toomey	W	Fr.	29	3	5	8	8
Brian Durand	C	Fr.	24	2	5	7	4
Brian Glynn	C	Fr.	17	2	5	7	0
Guy Gosselin	D	So.	37	3	3	6	26
Jim Toninato	C/W	So.	32	3	2	5	18
Bruce Fishback	C/W	Fr.	13	2	2	4	4
Dave Cowan	C	Fr.	12	1	2	3	8
Kevin Smalley	C	Jr.	4	0	2	2	2
Jim Plankers	D	Fr.	4	0	1	1	0
Anders Andersson	C	Jr.	2	0	0	0	0
Brad Johnson	C	So.	1	0	0	0	0
Rick Kosti	G	Fr.	38	0	0	0	6
Jon Downing	G	Jr.	6	0	0	0	0

University of New Hampshire
(Overall: 20-17-1)   (ECAC: 13-8-0)

	Pos.	Class	Games	G.	A.	Pts.	Pen.
Dan Potter	F	Sr.	38	16	28	44	50
Dan Muse	F	Jr.	32	14	22	36	16
James Richmond	F	Fr.	34	10	24	34	18
Paul Barton	F	Sr.	37	9	25	34	10
Peter Douris	F	Fr.	38	19	15	34	14
Ken Chisholm	F	Sr.	38	15	15	30	18
Scott Ellison	F	Sr.	36	17	12	29	8
Mark Doherty	F	Sr.	38	9	17	26	20
David Lee	D	Jr.	34	7	18	25	38
Shane Skidmore	D	So.	36	8	16	24	24
Peter Herms	F	So.	38	6	18	24	22
Brian Byrnes	D	Sr.	37	6	16	22	50
Ralph Robinson	F	Jr.	19	9	12	21	20
Kirk Lussier	D	So.	38	9	5	14	26

	Pos.	Class	Games	G.	A.	Pts.	Pen.
Dwayne Robinson	D	Jr.	37	4	9	13	26
Chris Laganas	F	Fr.	27	5	5	10	2
Dave McAllister	F	Jr.	25	4	4	8	2
Allister Brown	D	Fr.	36	1	7	8	12
Michael Golden	F	Fr.	7	1	1	2	2
Peter Wotton	D	Fr.	6	0	1	1	0
Bruce Gillies	G	Jr.	34	0	0	0	4

University of North Dakota
(Overall: 31-12-2)   (WCHA: 16-8-2)

	Pos.	Class	Games	G.	A.	Pts.	Pen.
Dan Brennan	LW	Sr.	45	28	37	65	36
Perry Berezan	C	Fr.	44	28	24	52	29
Chris Jensen	RW	So.	44	24	25	49	100
Brian Williams	C	So.	45	17	31	48	62
Jim Archibald	RW	Jr.	44	21	15	36	156
Rick Zombo	D	Jr.	34	7	24	31	40
Dean Barsness	LW	Sr.	45	11	18	29	10
Scott Sandelin	D	So.	41	4	23	27	24
Malcolm Parks	LW	Fr.	33	11	10	21	42
Glen Klotz	D	So.	26	3	16	19	14
Steve Palmiscno	RW	Sr.	25	9	9	18	18
Mickey Kram	F	Fr.	36	9	9	18	12
Bill Whitsitt	D	Sr.	45	5	13	18	38
Eddie Christian	LW	Sr.	42	5	12	17	53
Perry Nakonechny	W	Fr.	29	6	7	13	12
Randy Maxwell	W/C	So.	20	3	10	13	14
Gord Sherven	C	Jr.	10	5	5	10	4
Jim Meuwissen	D	So.	27	2	8	10	20
Brad Berry	D	Fr.	32	2	7	9	8
Mark Huglen	LW	Jr.	29	1	7	8	10
Bill Claviter	C	Fr.	18	2	5	7	4
Tim Loven	D	So.	35	0	7	7	14
Jeff Bredahl	RW	So.	20	1	4	5	10
Tarek Howard	D	Fr.	24	0	1	1	14
Craig Perry	G	Fr.	2	0	1	1	0
Jon Casey	G	Sr.	37	0	1	1	20
Greg Strome	G	Fr.	7	0	0	0	2

Northeastern University
(Overall: 16-12-1)   (ECAC: 10-10-1)

	Pos.	Class	Games	G.	A.	Pts.	Pen.
Ken Manchurek	F	Sr.	29	27	24	51	24
Rod Isbister	F	So.	28	19	25	44	36
Stewart Emerson	F	So.	29	16	26	42	48
Jay Heinbuck	F	So.	29	9	26	35	26
Jim Averill	D	Jr.	28	4	27	31	26
Randy Bucyk	F	Sr.	29	16	13	29	11
Roman Kinal	F	Fr.	28	8	19	27	14
Bob Averill	F	Sr.	28	12	14	26	18
Mark Lori	F	Fr.	24	5	12	17	20
Craig Frank	D	Sr.	29	3	12	15	54
Greg Pratt	F	Fr.	29	10	4	14	18
Brian Fahringer	F	Sr.	27	3	9	12	30
Jim Madigan	F	Jr.	21	4	6	10	34
Maurizio Pasinato	D	Sr.	26	1	6	7	33
Bill Kessler	D	Sr.	29	0	7	7	26
Paul Fitzsimmons	D	So.	24	2	3	5	56
Jim Milewski	F	So.	13	2	3	5	4
Gerry Kiley	D	Fr.	20	1	3	4	18
Milan Mader	F	Fr.	10	1	2	3	4
Greg Neary	F	So.	14	1	2	3	4
Mike O'Brien	F	Jr.	9	0	2	2	4
Scott Marshall	F	So.	1	1	0	1	..
Bob Kimura	D	So.	15	0	1	1	2
Bill Whitfield	F	Fr.	3	0	1	1	..
Tim Marshall	G	Jr.	26	0	0	0	18

Northern Arizona University
(Overall: 20-6-0)

	Pos.	Class	Games	G.	A.	Pts.	Pen.
Greg Adams	C	So.	26	44	29	73	34
Rick O'Brien	RW	Sr.	26	17	28	45	48
Greg Stoike	C	Sr.	26	16	25	41	28
Scott Rupp	C	Jr.	27	19	13	32	12
Darryl Moise	D	Sr.	24	7	22	29	54
Bill Swarbrick	LW	Sr.	26	10	18	28	16
Steve Selva	D	Jr.	26	5	21	26	28
Dave Dupas	D	So.	26	8	16	24	46
Greg McCauley	LW	Sr.	15	3	20	23	34
Chico Baldwin	RW	So.	27	11	11	22	4
Dave Branting	D	Jr.	26	7	15	22	32
Tyler Johnson	RW	Sr.	24	4	17	21	37
Blair Larson	LW	Sr.	25	9	8	17	30
Garry Matson	D	So.	26	2	9	11	31
Wes Olsen	C	Sr.	22	4	7	11	35
Dave Coburn	RW	Sr.	25	3	6	9	36
Dave Kenney	D	Jr.	26	0	9	9	54
Mark Jaraczewski	RW	So.	12	1	5	6	0
Kris Kjolberg	LW	Jr.	26	1	4	5	34
Tony Cullen	RW	Jr.	12	1	2	3	10
Todd Brown	D	Fr.	13	0	2	2	10
Kreg Korinek	G	Sr.	18	0	1	1	12
Gary Shepherd	G	So.	10	0	0	0	4

Northern Michigan University
(Overall: 17-22-1) (CCHA: 16-14-0)

	Pos.	Class	Games	G.	A.	Pts.	Pen.
Gary Emmons	C	Fr.	40	28	21	49	42
Bob Curtis	F	So.	36	11	28	39	38
Ralph Vos	F	Fr.	39	7	28	35	26
Dave Randall	D	So.	40	8	24	32	52
Bill Schafhauser	D	Sr.	39	6	21	27	34
Kevin Trach	F	So.	39	11	16	27	18
Morey Gare	F	Jr.	40	14	12	26	71
Ron Chyzowski	C	Fr.	40	16	10	26	12
Dave Smith	D	Sr.	40	5	19	24	30
Dave Mogush	F	Sr.	40	14	7	21	22
Charlie Lundeen	C	Jr.	34	9	11	20	28
Leroy Rempel	F	So.	26	3	11	14	14
Phil Degaetano	D	Jr.	35	2	9	11	45
Dave Moree	D	Fr.	37	2	9	11	24
Kory Wright	F	Fr.	39	7	4	11	19
Colin Lundrigan	F	Fr.	20	5	6	11	52
Glen Hartley	F	Fr.	24	2	8	10	8
Al Chancellor	C	So.	19	1	4	5	6
Ron Brodeur	F	So.	27	3	1	4	17
Todd Morrissette	D	So.	24	1	2	3	65
Tom Strelow	F	Jr.	6	0	2	2	10
Jeff Poeschl	G	Sr.	34	0	0	0	0
Dennis Jiannaras	G	Fr.	8	0	0	0	0
Rick Osburn	D	Fr.	16	0	0	0	8

Princeton University
(Overall: 6-18-1) (ECAC: 5-15-1)

	Pos.	Class	Games	G.	A.	Pts.	Pen.
Bill Brady	F	So.	25	7	14	21	14
Paul Brodeur	F	So.	21	10	10	20	20
Ed Lee	F	Sr.	11	10	10	20	22
Cliff Abrecht	D	So.	23	9	9	18	62
Tim Oshier	F	So.	25	9	9	18	16
John Rocco	F	So.	25	4	14	18	8
Allan Gray	F	Fr.	20	9	7	16	50
Steve Biss	F	Fr.	25	6	10	16	26

	Pos.	Class	Games	G.	A.	Pts.	Pen.
Todd Ladda	F	Sr.	25	6	9	15	0
Jaimie MacPherson	F	Sr.	25	2	13	15	24
Tim Cole	D	Fr.	25	7	7	14	4
Steve MacDonald	F	Fr.	14	4	8	12	8
Danni Titus	F	Jr.	16	5	4	9	8
Tom Daccord	F	Fr.	18	3	6	9	6
Jeff York	D	So.	25	0	9	9	10
Scott Howe	D	Fr.	21	4	4	8	44
Norman Ross	F	Fr.	21	4	3	7	20
Rob Scheuer	D	Jr.	7	1	6	7	12
David Downing	F	Fr.	12	1	3	4	2
Fred Hnat	D	So.	25	0	3	3	10
Tim Driscoll	F	Fr.	16	0	2	2	6
Rick Valdarchi	D	Sr.	13	0	2	2	10
Wally McDonough	G	Sr.	21	0	1	1	6
Wes Johnston	D	Fr.	6	..	..	..	2

Providence College
(Overall: 21-11-2)   (ECAC: 12-7-2)

	Pos.	Class	Games	G.	A.	Pts.	Pen.
Gates Orlando	F	Sr.	34	23	30	53	52
Tim Army	F	Jr.	34	20	26	46	40
Steve Bianchi	F	So.	34	9	22	31	36
Artie Yeomelakis	F	So.	34	14	16	30	48
Peter Taglianetti	D	Jr.	30	4	25	29	68
Steve Rooney	F	Jr.	33	11	16	27	46
Steve Taylor	F	Sr.	34	11	16	27	36
John Deasey	F	Jr.	34	7	14	21	34
Jacques Delorme	D	Sr.	34	2	19	21	16
John DeVoe	F	So.	28	14	6	20	18
Nowel Catterall	D	So.	34	5	12	17	38
Jim Robbins	F	So.	32	10	6	16	8
Tim Sullivan	F	So.	34	3	8	11	16
Rene Boudreault	F	So.	22	4	4	8	12
Brian Till	F	Jr.	24	2	5	7	4
Mark Ostendorf	D	Sr.	25	1	5	6	8
Dave Wilkie	F	Jr.	26	1	4	5	10
Dan Wurst	D	Fr.	33	1	1	2	57
Mike Brill	D	So.	27	0	2	2	12
Mike Flanagan	D	Fr.	19	1	0	1	2
Mario Proulx	G	Sr.	28	0	0	0	2
Chris Terreri	G	So.	10	0	0	0	2

Rensselaer Polytechnic Institute
(Overall: 32-6-0)   (ECAC: 17-3-0)

	Pos.	Class	Games	G.	A.	Pts.	Pen.
Adam Oates	F	So.	38	26	57	83	15
John Carter	F	So.	38	35	39	74	52
Marty Dallman	F	Sr.	38	30	24	54	32
Mike Sadeghpour	F	Jr.	38	25	14	39	32
Bob DiPronio	F	Fr.	31	19	19	38	10
Terry Butryn	F	Fr.	38	9	19	28	12
Eric Magnuson	F	Sr.	38	6	21	27	40
Neil Hernberg	F	Fr.	36	13	13	26	20
Kraig Nienhuis	F	So.	35	10	12	22	26
Mark Jooris	F	So.	23	10	10	20	4
George Servinis	F	So.	12	5	13	18	14
Tim Friday	D	Jr.	32	4	14	18	22
Randy Koudys	F	Sr.	26	3	15	18	10
Ken Hammond	D	Jr.	34	5	11	16	72
Mike Robinson	D	Fr.	38	5	10	15	38
Mike Dark	D	So.	38	2	12	14	60
Trini Iturralde	F	Fr.	36	6	6	12	10
Marc Foland	D	Fr.	25	1	6	7	4
Frank Ferrara	F	Sr.	18	3	3	6	6
Pierre Langevin	D	Jr.	25	0	6	6	22
Jeff Prendergast	D	Jr.	15	0	3	3	6
Jeff Whiteside	D	So.	22	0	3	3	14
Mike Kappel	F	Fr.	5	1	0	1	0
Brian Jopling	G	Fr.	15	0	1	1	2

St. Lawrence University
(Overall: 19-13-0)   (ECAC: 10-10-0)

	Pos.	Class	Games	G.	A.	Pts.	Pen.
Ray Shero	F	Sr.	32	15	27	42	46
Mark Bonneau	F	Sr.	32	18	23	41	16
Benoit Quesnel	F	Jr.	32	17	22	39	18
Mike Gerrie	F	Fr.	32	15	24	39	17
Paul Castron	F	Jr.	32	13	23	36	38
Dave Saunders	F	Fr.	32	10	21	31	26
Steve Tuite	D	Jr.	32	10	18	28	24
Don Vaughan	F	Sr.	29	15	11	26	20
Steve Rhodes	F	Sr.	30	7	19	26	26
Steve Smith	D	Sr.	32	7	18	25	48
Bill Gerrie	F	Fr.	18	9	11	20	16
Chris Gunnarson	F	So.	30	9	9	18	26
Mark Leach	D	Sr.	32	1	17	18	18
Rick Rafter	D	Sr.	30	3	12	15	26
Scott Nickerson	F	So.	30	8	6	14	20
Len Thornbury	D	Sr.	32	4	9	13	2
Tom Pratt	D	Fr.	32	4	8	12	70
Rick Mulligan	F	Fr.	11	5	4	9	8
Mike Hynes	F	Sr.	8	2	7	9	0
Steve Rich	F	Sr.	12	2	6	8	2
Bob Rankin	F	So.	7	1	1	2	2
Todd Petkovich	F	Fr.	7	1	0	1	4
J.K. Trimble	G	So.	17	0	1	1	2
Rob Morrow	D	So.	7	0	0	0	2

United States International University
(Overall: 4-31-2)

	Pos.	Class	Games	G.	A.	Pts.	Pen.
Mark Genz	W	Sr.	33	10	18	28	35
Gary Bernard	W	Fr.	36	11	16	27	33
Mickey McCarthy	W	Sr.	37	18	8	26	40
Mark Schelde	C	Sr.	36	10	12	22	37
Kevin Poirier	C	Fr.	32	7	15	22	20
Don Yewchin	C	So.	33	12	8	20	34
Gordie Stewart	W	So.	36	10	8	18	49
Doug Hannesson	W	So.	37	7	11	18	38
Pat Mayer	D	Jr.	35	1	15	16	89
Tom Irving	D	Jr.	30	2	12	14	8
Lawrence Duke	W	Jr.	27	5	6	11	33
Rick Lundgren	D	Jr.	32	2	9	11	52
George Litzinger	C	Fr.	37	3	7	10	2
Ron Annear	D	Fr.	33	2	6	8	48
Joe Cunningham	D	Sr.	31	1	7	8	36
Darryl Finnell	D	Jr.	23	2	4	6	19
Darren Clarkin	D	Fr.	35	0	5	5	16
Matt Lundgren	W	Fr.	19	2	2	4	12
Peter Sorenson	C	Fr.	12	0	4	4	4
Paul Dawson	W	Fr.	28	1	2	3	12
Doug Fomenko	W	So.	22	1	2	3	10
Tom Johansson	D	Fr.	16	0	0	0	0
Terry Zaferakis	D	Fr.	4	0	0	0	2
Doug Spedding	G	So.	30	0	0	0	4

University of Vermont
(Overall: 10-18-1)   (ECAC: 6-13-1)

	Pos.	Class	Games	G.	A.	Pts.	Pen.
Kevin Foster	F	Jr.	29	21	36	57	18
Matt Winnicki	F	Sr.	29	15	24	39	14
Mark Litton	F	Sr.	27	14	19	33	6
Don Crowley	F	Sr.	29	15	16	31	12
Tony Messina	F	Sr.	29	7	24	31	24
Jeff Capello	F	Fr.	27	6	15	21	20
Rob McConnell	F	Sr.	26	9	11	20	8
Norris Jordan	F	Sr.	14	5	11	16	10
Mike O'Connor	F	Jr.	29	7	9	15	8

	Pos.	Class	Games	G.	A.	Pts.	Pen.
Sylvain Brosseau	D	Sr.	29	5	9	14	26
Craig Staff	F	Fr.	20	4	8	12	8
Steve Kayser	D	So.	28	3	7	10	28
Shannon Deegan	F	Fr.	28	5	5	10	14
John Leavitt	D	Sr.	29	2	5	7	16
Henry Owen	D	Jr.	29	0	7	7	6
Mike Hanley	D	Sr.	25	2	4	6	0
Chris DeLorey	F	Jr.	7	2	1	3	4
Mike Maher	F	So.	27	4	0	4	12
Jukka Vartola	D	So.	22	0	3	3	4
Todd Clark	D	So.	8	0	2	2	4
Tom Maher	D	So.	4	0	2	2	0
Rick Hubbart	F	Fr.	1	1	0	1	2
Bill McCormack	F	Fr.	22	0	1	1	10
Tom McDonough	F	Fr.	4	0	0	0	4

Western Michigan
(Overall: 22-18-2)   (CCHA: 13-14-1)

	Pos.	Class	Games	G.	A.	Pts.	Pen.
Dan Dorion	RW	So.	42	41	50	91	42
Troy Thrun	C	So.	40	23	29	52	26
Lance Johnston	LW	Jr.	42	18	34	52	26
Wayne Gagne	D	Fr.	41	8	35	43	32
Stuart Burnie	RW	So.	42	26	13	38	73
Rob Bryden	RW	Fr.	36	17	12	29	60
Pat Ryan	LW	Fr.	41	10	14	24	18
Jeff Crossman	C	So.	39	9	12	21	91
Glenn Johannesen	D	Sr.	41	4	16	20	80
Henry Fung	LW	Fr.	38	4	14	18	41
Jim Culhane	D	Fr.	42	1	14	15	88
Chris MacDonald	D	So.	32	0	15	15	38
Ron Pesetti	D	So.	33	3	11	14	44
Chuck Chiatto	F	Fr.	23	4	9	13	4
Rob Adams	C	So.	40	5	7	12	16
Gary Orhn	D	Jr.	38	3	9	12	107
Tom Fletcher	LW	So.	27	2	7	9	10
Jim Grillo	C	Jr.	36	1	8	9	16
Kevin Donoghue	RW	Fr.	27	4	1	5	37
Andy Atkinson	F	So.	13	1	2	3	4
David Cromer	F	So.	5	2	0	2	0
David Bina	D/F	So.	15	0	2	2	2
Todd Rosa	D	Fr.	1	1	0	1	0
Mike Hanson	G	Jr.	8	0	1	1	2
Glenn Healy	G	Jr.	38	0	1	1	13
Dan Newkirk	D	Fr.	4	0	0	0	4

University of Wisconsin
(Overall: 21-17-1)   (WCHA: 11-14-1)

	Pos.	Class	Games	G.	A.	Pts.	Pen.
Paul Houston	C	Jr.	38	25	23	48	18
John Johannson	C	Sr.	39	21	25	46	32
Jan-Ake Danielson	D	Jr.	38	5	36	41	16
Paul Houck	W	Jr.	37	20	20	40	29
Jim Johannson	W	So.	35	17	21	38	52
Dave Maley	W	So.	38	10	28	38	56
Ted Pearson	W	Sr.	35	13	20	33	60
Tony Granato	W	Fr.	35	14	17	31	48
Marty Wiitala	W	So.	33	11	19	30	4
Gary Suter	D	Fr.	35	4	18	22	68
Ernie Vargas	W	So.	36	5	15	20	32
Matt Walsh	D	So.	38	2	17	19	62
Tim Sager	C/W	Sr.	29	4	9	13	20
Mike McGrath	D	Fr.	39	3	9	12	36
Scott Sabo	W	Sr.	23	4	7	11	24
Lexi Doner	W	Sr.	34	3	7	10	4
Paul Graveline	W	Fr.	21	3	3	6	8
Steve Tschipper	W	So.	17	2	3	5	2
Tom Ryan	W	Jr.	13	4	0	4	0

	Pos.	Class	Games	G.	A.	Pts.	Pen.
Rick Heppner	D	Jr.	12	1	2	3	4
Jeff White	D	Jr.	39	1	2	3	26
Dennis Will	D	Fr.	7	0	2	2	4
Jeff Nate	W	Sr.	2	1	0	1	0
Eric Faust	D	So.	27	0	0	0	28
Terry Kleisinger	G	Sr.	24	0	0	0	16
Gary Baxter	G	So.	17	0	0	0	11

Yale University
(Overall: 12-13-1) (ECAC: 10-10-1)

	Pos.	Class	Games	G.	A.	Pts.	Pen.
Bob Kudelski	F	Fr.	21	14	12	26	12
Sean Neely	F	So.	26	13	12	25	16
Bob Logan	F	So.	22	9	13	22	25
Dave Williams	F	Sr.	21	8	11	19	12
Kevin Conley	F	Jr.	23	3	16	19	10
Darren Acheson	F	So.	26	11	7	18	16
Morrie Tobin	F	Jr.	26	4	12	16	22
Peter Sawkins	D	Jr.	25	2	14	16	24
Randy Wood	F	So.	18	7	7	14	10
Tom Rzeszut	D	So.	26	3	8	11	16
Eric Borg	F	So.	22	2	9	11	9
Matt Baab	D	Sr.	22	4	4	8	24
Scott Logie	F	Jr.	22	4	4	8	2
Ed McManus	F	Sr.	19	3	5	8	23
Gary Davidson	D	Fr.	25	1	5	6	12
Paul Marcotte	F	Fr.	18	1	5	6	6
Phil Edgar	D	Fr.	18	1	3	4	10
Scott Webster	D	So.	26	0	4	4	16
Dave Farnfield	F	Sr.	13	0	3	3	6
Scott Bradford	F	Fr.	8	1	1	2	6
Andy Deiss	F	So.	4	0	2	2	0
Ralph Russo	D	Fr.	8	0	2	2	4
Michael Schwalb	G	Fr.	11	0	1	1	2
Clay Yonce	D	Fr.	14	0	1	1	2

COLLEGIATE GOALTENDING RECORDS

	G.	W.	L.	T.	Min.	Goals	Avg.
AIR FORCE ACADEMY							
Mike McNeal	1	...	...	...	20	1	3.00
T.J. O'Shaughnessy	5	...	...	...	180	12	4.00
John Ducharme	8	...	...	...	380	28	4.42
Matt Crandall	19	...	...	...	1010	89	5.29
BOSTON COLLEGE	G.	W.	L.	T.	Min.	Goals	Avg.
Shaun Real	5	3	0	0	197	7	2.13
Joe Kelly	3	2	0	0	120	5	2.50
Scott Gordon	35	21	13	0	2034	127	3.75
BOSTON UNIVERSITY	G.	W.	L.	T.	Min.	Goals	Avg.
Terry Taillefer	10	3	1	1	412	20	2.91
Cleon Daskalakis	35	25	10	1	1972	96	2.92
BOWLING GREEN STATE UNIVERSITY	G.	W.	L.	T.	Min.	Goals	Avg.
Gary Kruzich	28	21	5	2	1725	83	2.89
Eddie Powers	7	4	1	0	305	18	3.54
Wayne Collins	12	9	2	0	703	43	3.67
Randy Johnson	2	0	0	0	15	2	8.00
BROWN UNIVERSITY	G.	W.	L.	T.	Min.	Goals	Avg.
John Franzosa	12	4	5	1	752	54	4.31
Paul McCarthy	14	2	12	0	828	78	5.65
Tim Nelson	1	0	0	0	20	2	6.00
CLARKSON COLLEGE	G.	W.	L.	T.	Min.	Goals	Avg.
Don Sylvestri	16	5	4	0	610	31	3.05
James Falle	27	16	7	2	1494	77	3.09
COLGATE UNIVERSITY	G.	W.	L.	T.	Min.	Goals	Avg.
Jeff Cooper	32	18	12	1	1874	121	3.87
Dan Delianedis	6	2	2	0	260	28	6.46

	G.	W.	L.	T.	Min.	Goals	Avg.
COLORADO COLLEGE							
Marty Wakelyn	30	6	22	1	1743	140	4.82
Dale Peterson	10	3	3	0	376	31	4.95
CORNELL UNIVERSITY	G.	W.	L.	T.	Min.	Goals	Avg.
Jim Edmands	17	6	8	0	920	63	4.04
Don Fawcett	15	5	7	0	656	50	4.48
DARTMOUTH COLLEGE	G.	W.	L.	T.	Min.	Goals	Avg.
Mark Hoppe	4	1	3	0	239	19	4.77
Jeff Bower	18	2	16	0	1035	96	5.57
Jay Samek	5	0	4	0	280	30	6.43
DENVER UNIVERSITY	G.	W.	L.	T.	Min.	Goals	Avg.
Jim Dalrymple	3	1	1	0	160	12	4.50
Chris Olson	15	7	6	0	871	74	5.10
Pat Tierney	23	6	18	0	1345	117	5.22
FERRIS STATE UNIVERSITY	G.	W.	L.	T.	Min.	Goals	Avg.
Mike Harden	3	0	0	0	35	1	1.71
Rob Hughston	34	15	13	1	1699	123	4.34
Norm Young	20	3	7	2	748	57	4.57
HARVARD UNIVERSITY	G.	W.	L.	T.	Min.	Goals	Avg.
Grant Blair	23	10	11	2	1391	71	3.06
Dickie McEvoy	4	0	3	1	258	19	4.42
UNIVERSITY OF ILLINOIS-CHICAGO	G.	W.	L.	T.	Min.	Goals	Avg.
Mike Rotter	2	0	0	0	60	4	4.00
John Whelan	14	2	9	0	706	71	6.03
Jim Hickey	25	3	20	1	1337	139	6.24
LAKE SUPERIOR STATE	G.	W.	L.	T.	Min.	Goals	Avg.
Lawrence Dyck	22	9	9	1	1165	71	3.66
Joe Shawhan	9	1	3	1	378	29	4.60
Randy Exelby	21	8	8	0	905	75	4.97
UNIVERSITY OF LOWELL	G.	W.	L.	T.	Min.	Goals	Avg.
Kip Manseau	5	2	1	0	199	13	3.92
Dana Demole	31	13	15	3	1878	148	4.73
UNIVERSITY OF MAINE	G.	W.	L.	T.	Min.	Goals	Avg.
Pete Smith	3	2	0	0	130	5	2.31
Jean Lacoste	17	7	9	0	854	61	4.29
Mike Silengo	14	4	8	0	748	59	4.73
Ray Roy	8	1	3	0	325	32	5.91
MIAMI (O.) UNIVERSITY	G.	W.	L.	T.	Min.	Goals	Avg.
Brent Smith	2	1	0	0	80	3	2.25
Al Chevrier	32	9	19	1	1509	123	4.89
Tim Hall	18	3	4	0	616	58	5.65
John Davis	1	0	0	0	40	4	6.00
UNIVERSITY OF MICHIGAN	G.	W.	L.	T.	Min.	Goals	Avg.
Mark Chiamp	33	12	22	1	1904	142	4.47
Jon Elliott	7	2	2	0	365	33	5.42
MICHIGAN STATE UNIVERSITY	G.	W.	L.	T.	Min.	Goals	Avg.
Norm Foster	32	23	8	0	1814	83	2.75
Bob Essensa	17	11	4	0	947	44	2.79
Tom Nowland	1	0	0	0	20	2	6.00
MICHIGAN TECH UNIVERSITY	G.	W.	L.	T.	Min.	Goals	Avg.
Dave Roach	27	12	12	0	1407	79	3.37
Darryl Pierce	15	5	5	1	722	54	4.49
Bart Tompsett	7	2	4	0	356	31	5.22
UNIVERSITY OF MINNESOTA	G.	W.	L.	T.	Min.	Goals	Avg.
Steve Kudebeh	1	1	0	0	60	2	2.00
Mike Sauer	1	1	0	0	60	3	3.00
Mike Vacanti	20	12	4	2	1133	63	3.34
Frank Pietrangelo	20	13	7	0	1141	66	3.47
UNIVERSITY OF MINNESOTA-DULUTH	G.	W.	L.	T.	Min.	Goals	Avg.
Rick Kosti	38	27	9	2	2347	119	3.04
Jon Downing	6	2	3	0	310	21	4.06
UNIVERSITY OF NEW HAMPSHIRE	G.	W.	L.	T.	Min.	Goals	Avg.
Bruce Gillies	34	19	15	0	1945	113	3.49
Greg Rota	5	1	1	1	251	19	4.54
..... DiBiase	1	0	1	0	61	4	3.93
UNIVERSITY OF NORTH DAKOTA	G.	W.	L.	T.	Min.	Goals	Avg.
Craig Perry	2	2	0	0	120	5	2.50
Jon Casey	37	25	10	2	2180	115	3.17
Greg Strome	7	4	2	0	385	24	3.74

	G.	W.	L.	T.	Min.	Goals	Avg.
NORTHEASTERN UNIVERSITY							
Shaun O'Sullivan	3	1	0	0	172	10	3.49
Chris Payette	3	1	1	0	121	8	3.97
Tim Marshall	26	14	11	1	1457	100	4.12
NORTHERN ARIZONA UNIVERSITY	G.	W.	L.	T.	Min.	Goals	Avg.
Kreg Korinek	18	15	2	0	1039	60	3.46
Gary Shepherd	10	5	4	0	580	36	3.72
NORTHERN MICHIGAN UNIVERSITY	G.	W.	L.	T.	Min.	Goals	Avg.
Jeff Poeschl	34	14	18	1	2029	132	3.90
Dennis Jiannaras	8	3	4	0	391	27	4.14
PRINCETON UNIVERSITY	G.	W.	L.	T.	Min.	Goals	Avg.
David Shea	2	1	0	0	80	4	3.00
Wally McDonough	21	4	16	1	1178	94	4.79
David Marotta	8	0	2	0	156	13	5.00
Tony Manory	3	1	0	0	101	11	6.53
PROVIDENCE COLLEGE	G.	W.	L.	T.	Min.	Goals	Avg.
Mario Proulx	28	17	9	2	1673	101	3.62
Chris Terreri	10	4	2	0	391	20	3.07
RENSSELAER POLYTECHNIC INST.	G.	W.	L.	T.	Min.	Goals	Avg.
Brian Jopling	15	8	0	0	458	22	2.88
Daren Puppa	32	24	6	0	1816	89	2.94
Mike Poisson	3	0	0	0	8	1	7.50
ST. LAWRENCE UNIVERSITY	G.	W.	L.	T.	Min.	Goals	Avg.
J.K. Trimble	17	10	5	0	888	49	3.31
Dave Kervick	10	4	4	0	561	40	4.28
Adolph Brink	11	5	4	0	444	31	4.19
Tim Flanigan	2	0	0	0	43	5	6.98
U.S. INTERNATIONAL UNIVERSITY	G.	W.	L.	T.	Min.	Goals	Avg.
Doug Spedding	30	3	21	2	1625	144	5.32
Mike Schwietz	13	1	10	0	614	70	6.84
UNIVERSITY OF VERMONT	G.	W.	L.	T.	Min.	Goals	Avg.
Tom Draper	20	8	12	0	1205	82	4.08
Gregg Thygesen	9	2	5	1	554	46	4.98
WESTERN MICHIGAN UNIVERSITY	G.	W.	L.	T.	Min.	Goals	Avg.
Lance Valentine	1	0	0	0	3	0	0.00
Glenn Healy	38	19	16	2	2242	146	3.91
Mike Hanson	8	3	2	0	312	21	4.04
UNIVERSITY OF WISCONSIN	G.	W.	L.	T.	Min.	Goals	Avg.
Gary Baxter	17	10	6	0	889	55	3.71
Gary Mill	2	0	0	0	59	4	4.07
Terry Kleisinger	24	11	11	1	1406	96	4.10
YALE UNIVERSITY	G.	W.	L.	T.	Min.	Goals	Avg.
Michael Schwalb	11	...	...	...	598	29	2.91
Paul Tortorella	16	...	...	...	907	53	3.51
Scott Relick	2	...	...	...	66	9	8.18

TSN First Team All-Star center Wayne Gretzky of Edmonton

NATIONAL HOCKEY LEAGUE SCHEDULE
1984-85

*Denotes afternoon game.

THURSDAY, OCTOBER 11
Pittsburgh at Boston
Hartford at N.Y. Rangers
Montreal at Buffalo
Quebec at Vancouver
Washington at Philadelphia
Toronto at Minnesota
Detroit at Chicago
St. Louis at Calgary
Edmonton at Los Angeles

FRIDAY, OCTOBER 12
N.Y. Islanders at New Jersey
St. Louis at Edmonton

SATURDAY, OCTOBER 13
Boston at Hartford
Buffalo at Toronto
Pittsburgh at Montreal
Quebec at Calgary
Chicago at N.Y. Islanders
N.Y. Rangers at Minnesota
New Jersey at Detroit
Philadelphia at Washington
Vancouver at Los Angeles

SUNDAY, OCTOBER 14
Hartford at Boston
Detroit at Buffalo
Quebec at Edmonton
Minnesota at N.Y. Rangers
Washington at Chicago
Toronto at Winnipeg
St. Louis at Los Angeles
Calgary at Vancouver

MONDAY, OCTOBER 15
Philadelphia at Montreal

TUESDAY, OCTOBER 16
Boston at Edmonton
New Jersey at N.Y. Islanders
Los Angeles at Washington

WEDNESDAY, OCTOBER 17
Hartford at Toronto
Buffalo at Quebec
N.Y. Islanders at Detroit
Vancouver at Pittsburgh
St. Louis at Chicago
Winnipeg at Calgary

THURSDAY, OCTOBER 18
Detroit at Hartford
Los Angeles at Montreal
Vancouver at Philadelphia
Edmonton at Minnesota

FRIDAY, OCTOBER 19
Boston at Calgary
Quebec at Buffalo
Toronto at New Jersey
Edmonton at Winnipeg

SATURDAY, OCTOBER 20
Vancouver at Hartford
Minnesota at Montreal
Quebec at Toronto
Los Angeles at N.Y. Islanders
N.Y. Rangers at Washington
New Jersey at St. Louis
Philadelphia at Pittsburgh
Chicago at Detroit

SUNDAY, OCTOBER 21
Boston at Winnipeg
Minnesota at Buffalo

N.Y. Islanders at N.Y. Rangers
Pittsburgh at Philadelphia
Los Angeles at Chicago
Calgary at Edmonton

TUESDAY, OCTOBER 23
Hartford at Calgary
Montreal at Quebec
Vancouver at N.Y. Islanders
Philadelphia at Minnesota

WEDNESDAY, OCTOBER 24
Boston St. Louis
Hartford at Winnipeg
New Jersey at Pittsburgh
Washington at Edmonton
Detroit at Toronto
Vancouver at Chicago

THURSDAY, OCTOBER 25
Buffalo at Montreal
N.Y. Rangers at New Jersey
St. Louis at Philadelphia
Washington at Calgary

FRIDAY, OCTOBER 26
Buffalo at Detroit
Toronto at Quebec
Los Angeles at Edmonton

SATURDAY, OCTOBER 27
Boston at N.Y. Islanders
Hartford at Minnesota
Montreal at Pittsburgh
N.Y. Rangers at Quebec
Philadelphia at New Jersey
Calgary at Toronto
Chicago at St. Louis
Los Angeles at Winnipeg

SUNDAY, OCTOBER 28
Boston at N.Y. Rangers
Hartford at Chicago
Calgary at Buffalo
Washington at Vancouver

MONDAY, OCTOBER 29
Quebec at Montreal
Los Angeles at Winnipeg

TUESDAY, OCTOBER 30
N.Y. Rangers at N.Y. Islanders
Detroit at Pittsburgh
Chicago at Minnesota
Vancouver at Edmonton

WEDNESDAY, OCTOBER 31
Quebec at Hartford
Philadelphia at Buffalo
Pittsburgh at New Jersey
Calgary at Washington
Toronto at St. Louis
Los Angeles at Vancouver

THURSDAY, NOVEMBER 1
Quebec at Boston
N.Y. Islanders at Montreal
Winnipeg at Philadelphia
Calgary at Detroit

FRIDAY, NOVEMBER 2
Hartford at Buffalo
Minnesota at New Jersey
Chicago at Edmonton

SATURDAY, NOVEMBER 3
Boston at Montreal
Buffalo at Hartford

N.Y. Islanders at Quebec
N.Y. Rangers at Pittsburgh
New Jersey at Washington
Minnesota at Philadelphia
Toronto at Los Angeles
Winnipeg at Detroit
Chicago at Vancouver
Calgary at St. Louis

SUNDAY, NOVEMBER 4
N.Y. Islanders at Boston
Edmonton at Winnipeg

MONDAY, NOVEMBER 5
Toronto at Minnesota
Chicago at Los Angeles

TUESDAY, NOVEMBER 6
Montreal at Detroit
Winnipeg at Quebec
St. Louis at N.Y. Islanders
Edmonton at Pittsburgh

WEDNESDAY, NOVEMBER 7
Winnipeg at Hartford
Buffalo at Minnesota
Washington at N.Y. Rangers
Vancouver at Toronto
Chicago at Calgary

THURSDAY, NOVEMBER 8
Detroit at Boston
Edmonton at New Jersey
St. Louis at Pittsburgh

FRIDAY, NOVEMBER 9
Buffalo at Los Angeles
N.Y. Islanders at N.Y. Rangers
St. Louis at Philadelphia
Edmonton at Washington
Vancouver at Winnipeg

SATURDAY, NOVEMBER 10
Boston at Detroit
Hartford at Quebec
Montreal at Calgary
Pittsburgh at N.Y. Islanders
Washington at New Jersey
Chicago at Toronto
Vancouver at Minnesota

SUNDAY, NOVEMBER 11
St. Louis at Boston
Buffalo at Winnipeg
Los Angeles at N.Y. Rangers
Edmonton at Philadelphia
Minnesota at Toronto

MONDAY, NOVEMBER 12
Montreal at Vancouver

TUESDAY, NOVEMBER 13
Los Angeles at Quebec
Minnesota at Washington
Detroit at Calgary

WEDNESDAY, NOVEMBER 14
Boston at Buffalo
Montreal at Edmonton
Quebec at St. Louis
N.Y. Rangers at Chicago
Pittsburgh at Winnipeg
Los Angeles at Toronto
Detroit at Vancouver

THURSDAY, NOVEMBER 15
New Jersey at Boston
Hartford at Philadelphia
Minnesota at N.Y. Islanders
Edmonton at Calgary

— 227 —

FRIDAY, NOVEMBER 16
Washington at Buffalo
Quebec at St. Louis
Pittsburgh at Vancouver
Calgary at Winnipeg

SATURDAY, NOVEMBER 17
Philadelphia at Boston
Chicago at Hartford
Buffalo at Washington
New Jersey at Montreal
N.Y. Rangers at N.Y. Islanders
Pittsburgh at Los Angeles
Winnipeg at Toronto
Detroit at Minnesota
Vancouver at Edmonton

SUNDAY, NOVEMBER 18
Quebec at Chicago
N.Y. Islanders at Philadelphia
New Jersey at N.Y. Rangers

MONDAY, NOVEMBER 19
Toronto at Montreal
Calgary at Los Angeles

TUESDAY, NOVEMBER 20
Chicago at Quebec
Washington at N.Y. Islanders
St. Louis at Vancouver

WEDNESDAY, NOVEMBER 21
Boston at Philadelphia
Hartford at Detroit
Buffalo at N.Y. Rangers
New Jersey at Los Angeles
Washington at Pittsburgh
Toronto at Minnesota
Winnipeg at Edmonton
Vancouver at Calgary

THURSDAY, NOVEMBER 22
Pittsburgh at Hartford
Chicago at Montreal

FRIDAY, NOVEMBER 23
Philadelphia at Buffalo
N.Y. Islanders at Washington
New Jersey at Minnesota
Toronto at Detroit
St. Louis at Calgary
Winnipeg at Vancouver

SATURDAY, NOVEMBER 24
*Chicago at Boston
Philadelphia at Hartford
Buffalo at N.Y. Islanders
Detroit at Montreal
N.Y. Rangers at Quebec
New Jersey at Pittsburgh
Minnesota at Toronto
St. Louis at Edmonton
Winnipeg at Los Angeles

SUNDAY, NOVEMBER 25
Montreal at Boston
Quebec at N.Y. Rangers
Chicago at Washington
Calgary at Vancouver

TUESDAY, NOVEMBER 27
Buffalo at Pittsburgh
Washington at Quebec
Minnesota at New Jersey
Chicago at Philadelphia
Edmonton at Toronto
St. Louis at Vancouver
Winnipeg at Los Angeles

WEDNESDAY, NOVEMBER 28
Minnesota at Hartford
Montreal at Detroit
N.Y. Islanders at Calgary
Washington at N.Y. Rangers

THURSDAY, NOVEMBER 29
Edmonton at Boston
New Jersey at Philadelphia
Chicago at Pittsburgh
Vancouver at Los Angeles

FRIDAY, NOVEMBER 30
Edmonton at Hartford
Montreal at Buffalo
N.Y. Islanders at Winnipeg
Toronto at N.Y. Rangers
St. Louis at Detroit

SATURDAY, DECEMBER 1
*Washington at Boston
Hartford at Quebec
Buffalo at Montreal
N.Y. Rangers at Toronto
*Chicago at New Jersey
*Pittsburgh at Philadelphia
Detroit at St. Louis
Calgary at Minnesota
Vancouver at Los Angeles

SUNDAY, DECEMBER 2
Pittsburgh at Washington
Calgary at Winnipeg

MONDAY, DECEMBER 3
Boston at Quebec
Hartford at Montreal
N.Y. Islanders at Vancouver
Philadelphia at N.Y. Rangers

TUESDAY, DECEMBER 4
New Jersey at Washington
Toronto at Detroit
Winnipeg at St. Louis
Los Angeles at Minnesota

WEDNESDAY, DECEMBER 5
Boston at Buffalo
Montreal at Hartford
N.Y. Islanders at Edmonton
Calgary at N.Y. Rangers
St. Louis at Pittsburgh
Detroit at Toronto
Los Angeles at Chicago

THURSDAY, DECEMBER 6
Montreal at Boston
Quebec at Philadelphia

FRIDAY, DECEMBER 7
Pittsburgh at N.Y. Rangers
Calgary at New Jersey
Winnipeg at Washington
Minnesota at Edmonton

SATURDAY, DECEMBER 8
*Buffalo at Boston
Hartford at N.Y. Islanders
Los Angeles at Montreal
New Jersey at Quebec
N.Y. Rangers at Philadelphia
Calgary at Pittsburgh
Toronto at St. Louis
*Chicago at Detroit
Edmonton at Vancouver

SUNDAY, DECEMBER 9
Quebec at Buffalo
*Detroit at Washington
Toronto at Chicago
Minnesota at Winnipeg

MONDAY, DECEMBER 10
Los Angeles at N.Y. Rangers
Detroit at Minnesota

TUESDAY, DECEMBER 11
Vancouver at Quebec
New Jersey at N.Y. Islanders
Philadelphia at Winnipeg
Washington at St. Louis

WEDNESDAY, DECEMBER 12
Boston at N.Y. Rangers
Buffalo at Hartford
N.Y. Islanders at Pittsburgh
Philadelphia at Toronto
Washington at Minnesota
Detroit at Chicago
Winnipeg at Calgary

THURSDAY, DECEMBER 13
Quebec at Boston
Vancouver at Montreal
St. Louis at New Jersey
Edmonton at Los Angeles

FRIDAY, DECEMBER 14
Detroit at Buffalo
Toronto at Winnipeg

SATURDAY, DECEMBER 15
*Vancouver at Boston
Montreal at Hartford
Quebec at New Jersey
Philadelphia at N.Y. Islanders
N.Y. Rangers at Washington
Pittsburgh at Toronto
Chicago at Minnesota
Edmonton at St. Louis
Calgary at Los Angeles

SUNDAY, DECEMBER 16
Vancouver at Buffalo
Montreal at Philadelphia
Washington at N.Y. Rangers
Detroit at Winnipeg
Minnesota at Chicago

MONDAY, DECEMBER 17
Edmonton at New Jersey
St. Louis at Toronto

TUESDAY, DECEMBER 18
Boston at Montreal
Washington at Quebec
Winnipeg at N.Y. Islanders
Los Angeles at Calgary

WEDNESDAY, DECEMBER 19
Boston at Hartford
Buffalo at Chicago
Winnipeg at N.Y. Rangers
New Jersey at Pittsburgh
Minnesota at St. Louis
Los Angeles at Edmonton

THURSDAY, DECEMBER 20
Washington at Montreal
Quebec at Detroit
New Jersey at Philadelphia
Vancouver at Calgary

FRIDAY, DECEMBER 21
N.Y. Islanders at Hartford
Philadelphia at Pittsburgh
Toronto at Chicago
Vancouver at Edmonton

SATURDAY, DECEMBER 22
Boston at Toronto
Hartford at Montreal
Buffalo at Quebec
Pittsburgh at N.Y. Islanders
N.Y. Rangers at New Jersey
St. Louis at Washington
Minnesota at Detroit
Los Angeles at Winnipeg
Calgary at Edmonton

SUNDAY, DECEMBER 23
Minnesota at Boston
St. Louis at Buffalo
Montreal at N.Y. Rangers
Quebec at Chicago
Washington at Philadelphia

TSN First Team All-Star right wing Rick Middleton of Boston

Los Angeles at Winnipeg
Calgary at Vancouver

WEDNESDAY, DECEMBER 26
New Jersey at Hartford
Toronto at Buffalo
N.Y. Islanders at Pittsburgh
N.Y. Rangers at Detroit
Philadelphia at Washington
Chicago at St. Louis
Winnipeg at Minnesota
Edmonton at Calgary
Los Angeles at Vancouver

THURSDAY, DECEMBER 27
Boston at Los Angeles
Montreal at Quebec
Washington at N.Y. Islanders
Toronto at New Jersey

FRIDAY, DECEMBER 28
Hartford at Pittsburgh
Winnipeg at Buffalo
Philadelphia at Vancouver
Detroit at Calgary

SATURDAY, DECEMBER 29
*Boston at Minnesota
Hartford at Washington
Buffalo at New Jersey
N.Y. Rangers at Montreal
Pittsburgh at Quebec
N.Y. Islanders at St. Louis
Chicago at Toronto
Detroit at Edmonton

SUNDAY, DECEMBER 30
Boston at Winnipeg
St. Louis at N.Y. Rangers
Philadelphia at Los Angeles
Calgary at Chicago
Edmonton at Vancouver

MONDAY, DECEMBER 31
New Jersey at Buffalo
Quebec at Montreal
N.Y. Islanders at Minnesota
Pittsburgh at Detroit

TUESDAY, JANUARY 1
*Boston at Washington
*Calgary at Winnipeg

WEDNESDAY, JANUARY 2
Hartford at Quebec
Montreal at Chicago
N.Y. Islanders at Detroit
Vancouver at N.Y. Rangers
Philadelphia at Edmonton
Pittsburgh at Toronto

THURSDAY, JANUARY 3
Detroit at Hartford
Montreal at St. Louis
Vancouver at New Jersey
Philadelphia at Calgary
Minnesota at Los Angeles

FRIDAY, JANUARY 4
Pittsburgh at Buffalo
Quebec at Washington
Winnipeg at Edmonton

SATURDAY, JANUARY 5
*N.Y. Rangers at Boston
Chicago at Hartford
Buffalo at N.Y. Islanders
*Montreal at New Jersey
Quebec at Pittsburgh
Philadelphia at St. Louis
Vancouver at Toronto
Los Angeles at Detroit
Minnesota at Calgary

SUNDAY, JANUARY 6
New Jersey at N.Y. Rangers
St. Louis at Chicago
Edmonton at Winnipeg

MONDAY, JANUARY 7
Los Angeles at Boston
Hartford at Toronto

TUESDAY, JANUARY 8
Hartford at Buffalo
Montreal at N.Y. Islanders
Edmonton at Quebec
Vancouver at Philadelphia
Washington at Detroit

WEDNESDAY, JANUARY 9
Boston at Toronto
N.Y. Rangers at Winnipeg
Vancouver at Pittsburgh
Washington at St. Louis
Minnesota at Chicago
Los Angeles at Calgary

THURSDAY, JANUARY 10
Buffalo at Boston
Edmonton at Montreal
N.Y. Islanders at New Jersey
Chicago at Philadelphia
St. Louis at Minnesota

FRIDAY, JANUARY 11
Calgary at Quebec

SATURDAY, JANUARY 12
*Detroit at Boston
Hartford at Minnesota
Buffalo at Montreal
Philadelphia at N.Y. Islanders
N.Y. Rangers at St. Louis
*Washington at New Jersey
Edmonton at Pittsburgh
Winnipeg at Los Angeles

SUNDAY, JANUARY 13
Edmonton at Buffalo
Detroit at Quebec
N.Y. Islanders at Chicago
*Calgary at Philadelphia
Toronto at Vancouver
Winnipeg at Los Angeles

MONDAY, JANUARY 14
New Jersey at N.Y. Rangers
Minnesota at Washington

TUESDAY, JANUARY 15
Boston at New Jersey
Calgary at Hartford
Montreal at Quebec
N.Y. Islanders at Vancouver

WEDNESDAY, JANUARY 16
Buffalo at N.Y. Rangers
N.Y. Islanders at Edmonton
Philadelphia at Detroit
Washington at Pittsburgh
Toronto at Los Angeles
Winnipeg at Chicago
St. Louis at Minnesota

THURSDAY, JANUARY 17
Calgary at Boston
Hartford at Montreal
Detroit at Philadelphia
Pittsburgh at Washington

FRIDAY, JANUARY 18
Chicago at Buffalo
N.Y. Rangers at New Jersey
St. Louis at Winnipeg
Edmonton at Vancouver

SATURDAY, JANUARY 19
Boston at Quebec
Buffalo at Hartford
New Jersey at Montreal
N.Y. Islanders at Los Angeles
N.Y. Rangers at Washington
Philadelphia at Minnesota
Chicago at Pittsburgh
St. Louis at Toronto
Winnipeg at Detroit
Vancouver at Edmonton

MONDAY, JANUARY 21
Montreal at Boston
Pittsburgh at Winnipeg
St. Louis at Detroit
Minnesota at Chicago
Calgary at Vancouver
Los Angeles at Edmonton

TUESDAY, JANUARY 22
Montreal at Hartford
N.Y. Rangers at Buffalo
Toronto at Quebec
Detroit at N.Y. Islanders

WEDNESDAY, JANUARY 23
New Jersey at Calgary
Philadelphia at Los Angeles
Pittsburgh at Minnesota
Washington at Chicago
Winnipeg at Vancouver

THURSDAY, JANUARY 24
Buffalo at Boston
Quebec at Montreal
Toronto at N.Y. Islanders
Detroit at N.Y. Rangers

FRIDAY, JANUARY 25
Buffalo at Quebec
New Jersey at Edmonton
Pittsburgh at Calgary
Los Angeles at St. Louis
Winnipeg at Vancouver

SATURDAY, JANUARY 26
*Hartford at Boston
N.Y. Rangers at Montreal
Washington at N.Y. Islanders
Pittsburgh at Edmonton
Chicago at Toronto
Detroit at Minnesota
Los Angeles at St. Louis
Vancouver at Calgary

SUNDAY, JANUARY 27
*Boston at Hartford
Quebec at Buffalo
*N.Y. Islanders at Washington
Minnesota at N.Y. Rangers
Philadelphia at Winnipeg
Toronto at Chicago

MONDAY, JANUARY 28
Calgary at Edmonton

TUESDAY, JANUARY 29
Minnesota at N.Y. Islanders
New Jersey at Los Angeles
Washington at Detroit
Winnipeg at St. Louis
Edmonton at Calgary

WEDNESDAY, JANUARY 30
Boston at Buffalo
Montreal at Vancouver
Toronto at Pittsburgh
Winnipeg at Chicago

THURSDAY, JANUARY 31
Quebec at Boston
Hartford at Los Angeles
N.Y. Rangers at Calgary

TSN First Team All-Star left wing Michel Goulet of Quebec

New Jersey at Philadelphia
Detroit at St. Louis

FRIDAY, FEBRUARY 1
Hartford at Vancouver
N.Y. Islanders at New Jersey
Toronto at Washington

SATURDAY, FEBRUARY 2
*Winnipeg at Boston
*Buffalo at Philadelphia
Montreal at Los Angeles
*Quebec at Detroit
N.Y. Islanders at Pittsburgh
N.Y. Rangers at Edmonton
Minnesota at Toronto
Chicago at St. Louis

SUNDAY, FEBRUARY 3
Hartford at Edmonton
Calgary at Buffalo
Minnesota at Quebec
N.Y. Rangers at Vancouver
Detroit at New Jersey
*Winnipeg at Washington
*St. Louis at Chicago

TUESDAY, FEBRUARY 5
Calgary at Montreal
Philadelphia at N.Y. Islanders
N.Y. Rangers at Los Angeles
Washington at Toronto

WEDNESDAY, FEBRUARY 6
Calgary at Hartford
Buffalo at Minnesota
Toronto at Chicago
Vancouver at St. Louis
Edmonton at Winnipeg

THURSDAY, FEBRUARY 7
Hartford at Boston
Montreal at Quebec
N.Y. Rangers at N.Y. Islanders
Pittsburgh at New Jersey
Los Angeles at Philadelphia
St. Louis at Detroit

FRIDAY, FEBRUARY 8
Los Angeles at Washington
Edmonton at Minnesota
Vancouver at Winnipeg

SATURDAY, FEBRUARY 9
Chicago at Boston
N.Y. Rangers at Hartford
Buffalo at Calgary
Toronto at Montreal
*New Jersey at Quebec
Pittsburgh at N.Y. Islanders
Philadelphia at Washington
Edmonton at Detroit
Minnesota at St. Louis

SUNDAY, FEBRUARY 10
*Boston at Chicago
*Quebec at Hartford
Montreal at Toronto
N.Y. Rangers at Philadelphia
Los Angeles at Pittsburgh
*Vancouver at Winnipeg

TUESDAY, FEBRUARY 12
All-Star Game at Calgary

WEDNESDAY, FEBRUARY 13
Washington at Winnipeg

THURSDAY, FEBRUARY 14
Boston at Los Angeles
Hartford at New Jersey
Quebec at Philadelphia
Pittsburgh at Chicago
Washington at Calgary

Toronto at St. Louis
Minnesota at Detroit

FRIDAY, FEBRUARY 15
Montreal at Buffalo
Edmonton at N.Y. Rangers

SATURDAY, FEBRUARY 16
Boston at Vancouver
Hartford at N.Y. Islanders
Buffalo at Montreal
Quebec at Pittsburgh
New Jersey at Toronto
Edmonton at Philadelphia
Washington at Los Angeles
*Chicago at Detroit
Minnesota at St. Louis
Winnipeg at Calgary

SUNDAY, FEBRUARY 17
*Toronto at Hartford
Quebec at Minnesota
N.Y. Islanders at N.Y. Rangers
New Jersey at Winnipeg
*Detroit at Chicago

MONDAY, FEBRUARY 18
Edmonton at Buffalo
*Pittsburgh at Philadelphia

TUESDAY, FEBRUARY 19
Hartford at Winnipeg
Montreal at St. Louis
Los Angeles at Quebec
Calgary at N.Y. Islanders
New Jersey at Vancouver
Edmonton at Toronto

WEDNESDAY, FEBRUARY 20
Boston at Minnesota
Montreal at Chicago
Calgary at Pittsburgh
St. Louis at Detroit

THURSDAY, FEBRUARY 21
Hartford at N.Y. Rangers
Winnipeg at N.Y. Islanders
Los Angeles at New Jersey
Toronto at Philadelphia
Washington at Vancouver

FRIDAY, FEBRUARY 22
St. Louis at Buffalo
Quebec at Edmonton
N.Y. Rangers at Pittsburgh
Chicago at Minnesota

SATURDAY, FEBRUARY 23
Boston at N.Y. Islanders
Los Angeles at Hartford
Winnipeg at Montreal
Quebec at Vancouver
*Calgary at New Jersey
Pittsburgh at Minnesota
Washington at Edmonton
*Toronto at Detroit

SUNDAY, FEBRUARY 24
*St. Louis at Hartford
Los Angeles at Buffalo
N.Y. Islanders at Montreal
Calgary at Philadelphia
*Detroit at Chicago

MONDAY, FEBRUARY 25
Winnipeg at N.Y. Rangers
Minnesota at Pittsburgh
Chicago at Toronto

TUESDAY, FEBRUARY 26
Philadelphia at Hartford
Buffalo at New Jersey
Vancouver at Washington

WEDNESDAY, FEBRUARY 27
Buffalo at St. Louis
Montreal at Edmonton
Quebec at Los Angeles
N.Y. Islanders at Calgary
New Jersey at Chicago
Winnipeg at Pittsburgh
Minnesota at Toronto
Vancouver at Detroit

THURSDAY, FEBRUARY 28
Philadelphia at Boston
Washington at N.Y. Rangers

FRIDAY, MARCH 1
Hartford at New Jersey
Montreal at Calgary
Minnesota at Detroit
Los Angeles at Edmonton

SATURDAY, MARCH 2
*Vancouver at Boston
Buffalo at Washington
Philadelphia at Quebec
N.Y. Islanders at Toronto
N.Y. Rangers at Pittsburgh
Detroit at Minnesota
Chicago at St. Louis

SUNDAY, MARCH 3
*Vancouver at Hartford
N.Y. Islanders at Buffalo
Pittsburgh at N.Y. Rangers
Philadelphia at New Jersey
*St. Louis at Chicago
Winnipeg at Edmonton
Los Angeles at Calgary

MONDAY, MARCH 4
Montreal at Minnesota

TUESDAY, MARCH 5
Boston at Quebec
Hartford at Buffalo
Philadelphia at N.Y. Islanders
New Jersey at Washington
Pittsburgh at Los Angeles
Toronto at St. Louis
Edmonton at Calgary

WEDNESDAY, MARCH 6
Montreal at Winnipeg
N.Y. Rangers at Vancouver
Detroit at Toronto
Chicago at Minnesota

THURSDAY, MARCH 7
Hartford at Boston
N.Y. Islanders at New Jersey
N.Y. Rangers at Calgary
Washington at Philadelphia
Pittsburgh at St. Louis

FRIDAY, MARCH 8
Chicago at Buffalo
Quebec at Winnipeg
Philadelphia at Washington
Los Angeles at Vancouver

SATURDAY, MARCH 9
*Pittsburgh at Boston
Hartford at Montreal
Quebec at Calgary
Toronto at N.Y. Islanders
N.Y. Rangers at Edmonton
*New Jersey at Detroit
*St. Louis at Minnesota

SUNDAY, MARCH 10
*Boston at Washington
Montreal at Hartford
Buffalo at Los Angeles
*New Jersey at Winnipeg
Pittsburgh at Philadelphia

TSN First Team All-Star defenseman Rod Langway of Washington

Detroit at St. Louis
Minnesota at Chicago
Edmonton at Vancouver

MONDAY, MARCH 11
Chicago at N.Y. Rangers

TUESDAY, MARCH 12
N.Y. Islanders at St. Louis
Winnipeg at New Jersey

WEDNESDAY, MARCH 13
Boston at Pittsburgh
Hartford at Los Angeles
Buffalo at Vancouver
Minnesota at Quebec
N.Y. Islanders at Chicago
Philadelphia at N.Y. Rangers
Calgary at Toronto
Detroit at Edmonton

THURSDAY, MARCH 14
Boston at New Jersey
Winnipeg at Montreal
Toronto at Washington

FRIDAY, MARCH 15
Buffalo at Edmonton
Winnipeg at Quebec
Detroit at Vancouver

SATURDAY, MARCH 16
*Calgary at Boston
Hartford at St. Louis
Minnesota at Montreal
Washington at N.Y. Islanders
*N.Y. Rangers at Pittsburgh
Philadelphia at Toronto
Detroit at Los Angeles

SUNDAY, MARCH 17
Pittsburgh at Hartford
*Buffalo at Winnipeg
*N.Y. Islanders at Philadelphia
New Jersey at N.Y. Rangers
Chicago at Vancouver
Edmonton at Los Angeles

MONDAY, MARCH 18
Quebec at Boston
St. Louis at Toronto
Calgary at Minnesota

TUESDAY, MARCH 19
Los Angeles at N.Y. Islanders
New Jersey at Washington
Philadelphia at Pittsburgh

WEDNESDAY, MARCH 20
St. Louis at Hartford
Vancouver at Buffalo
Toronto at Calgary
Los Angeles at Detroit

Chicago at Edmonton
Minnesota at Winnipeg

THURSDAY, MARCH 21
St. Louis at Boston
Washington at Montreal
Quebec at N.Y. Islanders
N.Y. Rangers at Philadelphia
Vancouver at New Jersey

FRIDAY, MARCH 22
Pittsburgh at Buffalo
Montreal at Washington
N.Y. Rangers at Detroit
Toronto at Edmonton
Chicago at Calgary

SATURDAY, MARCH 23
Boston at Hartford
*Philadelphia at New Jersey
Minnesota at St. Louis
Vancouver at Winnipeg
Calgary at Los Angeles

SUNDAY, MARCH 24
Boston at Buffalo
*Quebec at Hartford
Montreal at Philadelphia
N.Y. Islanders at N.Y. Rangers
*Pittsburgh at Washington
Toronto at Detroit

MONDAY, MARCH 25
Vancouver at Minnesota

TUESDAY, MARCH 26
Boston at Montreal
Buffalo at Quebec
Edmonton at N.Y. Islanders
Pittsburgh at N.Y. Rangers
Minnesota at Detroit

WEDNESDAY, MARCH 27
Hartford at Washington
New Jersey at Pittsburgh
Philadelphia at Chicago
St. Louis at Toronto
Winnipeg at Vancouver
Calgary at Los Angeles

THURSDAY, MARCH 28
Edmonton at Boston
St. Louis at Montreal
N.Y. Islanders at Quebec
Washington at New Jersey
Detroit at Philadelphia

FRIDAY, MARCH 29
Edmonton at Hartford
Chicago at Winnipeg
Los Angeles at Calgary

SATURDAY, MARCH 30
*Montreal at Boston
Buffalo at Hartford
St. Louis at Quebec
N.Y. Islanders at Washington
*N.Y. Rangers at Philadelphia
*Pittsburgh at New Jersey
Detroit at Toronto
Minnesota at Los Angeles

SUNDAY, MARCH 31
Quebec at Buffalo
Montreal at Pittsburgh
Toronto at N.Y. Rangers
*Edmonton at Chicago
Minnesota at Vancouver
*Calgary at Winnipeg

TUESDAY, APRIL 2
Boston at Quebec
Hartford at Buffalo
Pittsburgh at N.Y. Islanders
Philadelphia at N.Y. Rangers
New Jersey at St. Louis
Edmonton at Los Angeles

WEDNESDAY, APRIL 3
New Jersey at Chicago
Detroit at Pittsburgh
Toronto at Minnesota
Vancouver at Calgary

THURSDAY, APRIL 4
Buffalo at Boston
Washington at Hartford
Quebec at Montreal
N.Y. Islanders at Philadelphia
N.Y. Rangers at St. Louis

FRIDAY, APRIL 5
Calgary at Edmonton
Los Angeles at Vancouver

SATURDAY, APRIL 6
Boston at Montreal
Quebec at Hartford
Buffalo at Toronto
New Jersey at N.Y. Islanders
Washington at Pittsburgh
*Chicago at Detroit
St. Louis at Minnesota
Winnipeg at Edmonton
Vancouver at Los Angeles

SUNDAY, APRIL 7
Toronto at Boston
Hartford at Quebec
Montreal at Buffalo
*N.Y. Rangers at Chicago
Philadelphia at New Jersey
Pittsburgh at Washington
Detroit at St. Louis
Winnipeg at Calgary

TSN First Team All-Star defenseman Ray Bourque of Boston

TSN First Team All-Star goaltender Pat Riggin of Washington

NOTES

NOTES

NOTES

NOTES